THE YALE EDITIONS OF
The Private Papers of James Boswell

Margaret Montgomerie, who married Boswell in 1769. This undated and unsigned painting is the only portrait of Mrs. Boswell known to exist.

Boswell:
THE ENGLISH EXPERIMENT
1785-1789

EDITED BY IRMA S. LUSTIG

RESEARCH ASSOCIATE IN ENGLISH

UNIVERSITY OF PENNSYLVANIA

AND FREDERICK A. POTTLE

STERLING PROFESSOR OF ENGLISH EMERITUS

YALE UNIVERSITY

McGRAW-HILL BOOK COMPANY

NEW YORK   TORONTO   LONDON

1 2 3 4 5 6 7 8 9 D O C D O C 8 7 6

ISBN 0-07-039116-5

LIBRARY OF CONGRESS CATALOGING-IN-PUBLICATION DATA

Boswell, James, 1740–1795.
  Boswell, the English experiment, 1785–1879.
  (The Yale editions of the private papers of
James Boswell)
  Bibliography: p.
  Includes index.
  1. Boswell, James, 1740–1795—Diaries. 2. Authors, Scottish—18th century—Diaries. 3. London (England) —Intellectual life—18th century—Sources. I. Lustig, Irma S. II. Pottle, Frederick Albert, 1897– III. Title. IV. Series: Boswell, James, 1740–1795. Selections. 1950. McGraw-Hill.
PR3325.A7994 1986   828'.603 [B]   85-24193
ISBN 0-07-039116-5

The preparation of *Boswell: The English Experiment, 1785–1789* was generously supported by the National Endowment for the Humanities. We are also deeply grateful for timely donations of matching funds and other gifts from

The Chrysler Corporation
The James J. Colt Foundation, Inc.
The DeWitt Wallace Fund
The Andrew W. Mellon Foundation
The North American Watch Corporation
The L. J. Skaggs and Mary C. Skaggs Foundation
Barry Diller
Richard Goodyear
Charles W. Loeb
Arthur G. Rippey
An anonymous donor
and
A gift in memory of
Norman Floyd McGowin, Sr.

The Yale Editions of the Private Papers of James Boswell consist of two independent but parallel series. One, the "research" series, gives complete texts of Boswell's journals, diaries, and memoranda, his correspondence, and the *Life of Johnson*. It preserves the spelling and capitalization of the original documents and is provided with extensive scholarly annotation. A large group of editors is engaged in this comprehensive undertaking. The first three volumes of what will be at least thirty appeared in 1966, 1969, and 1976, respectively. The other series, the reading or "trade" edition, selects from the total mass of papers those portions that appear likely to be of general interest and presents them in modern spelling and with appropriate annotation. The publishers have also issued limited de luxe printings of some of the trade volumes, with extra illustrations and special editorial matter, but neither the trade volumes nor the de luxe printings include matter from Boswell's archives that will not appear in the research edition.

The present volume is the twelfth in the trade edition of the journals, the thirteenth in the entire trade series.

CONTENTS

ILLUSTRATIONS

frontispiece

Margaret Boswell, reproduced from the painting in the Hyde Collection, Somerville, New Jersey.

following p. 160

Alexander Macdonald of Sleat, first Baron Macdonald, artist unknown. Reproduced by permission of Lord Macdonald of Sleat.

"Revising for the Second Edition," from Rowlandson's engravings *Picturesque Beauties of Boswell*. Reproduced by permission of the Harvard College Library, Harry Elkins Widener Collection.

"The Biographers," engraving by James Sayers. Courtesy of the Print Collection, Lewis Walpole Library, Yale University.

James Lowther, first Earl of Lonsdale, painting by Thomas Hudson. Reproduced by permission of the Lonsdale Estate Trust, in which copyright resides.

Boswell's journal entries for Thursday 30 November and part of Friday 1 December 1786. From the Yale Collection.

Nos. 55–56, Great Queen Street, watercolour by John W. Archer. Reproduced by permission of the Trustees of the British Library.

Edward Thurlow, first Baron Thurlow, painting by Sir Joshua Reynolds. Reproduced by courtesy of the Marquess of Bath, Longleat House, Warminster, Wiltshire.

Robert Burns's letter to Bruce Campbell, 13 November 1788. From the Yale Collection.

INTRODUCTION

In the unfolding saga of Boswell's life this volume of journals is the most painful. Yet in the insistent immediacy of Boswell's record and the relentless drive of forces, within and without, it can also be the most compelling. Boswell was committing himself in mid-life to the most significant decision of his career: a permanent removal from the Scottish to the English bar. Perpetually in need of what he called "agitation," he was happiest when animated intellectually and elevated by community with men of power and accomplishment. Such happiness, he felt, was possible only in London, where since early manhood he had wished to centre his existence, preferably as a Member of Parliament.

For almost twenty years Boswell had bustled about as an Edinburgh advocate in pursuit of prominence and a seat in the House of Commons, but by 1785 all his manoeuvres to win political patronage at home—appeals to great men, timely pamphlets, patriotic Addresses, and electoral negotiations—had failed him, and panic had set in at the prospect of living out his life in the removes of Scotland. Now he was to try an alternate route to felicity. Since 1775 he had been taking the required meals in the Inner Temple, all that was technically necessary to qualify him for the English bar. The transfer was not so easy, however, for Scots practice is based on Roman (or civil) law and English practice on common law, and Boswell had to imagine that an ability to make friends quickly, a confidence in his courtroom eloquence, and a good deal of luck would compensate for his ignorance of legal forms and lack of background or connections.

Those who know the *Journal of a Tour to the Hebrides* and the *Life of Johnson* to be among the great works of our language are sometimes dismayed to discover that literary immortality was not Boswell's foremost aspiration. In attitude and practice he was a professional writer, but he was not, like Johnson, a writer by profession. He was a landed gentleman, proud, like other Scots, of his ancient lineage. His position counteracted the persistent feelings of low self-esteem with which his father's authoritarian disapproval and caustic tongue had crippled him. At the heart of Boswell's mystery lies an insatiable need for attention and approval. Though he was often bold, original, and uninhibited, his goals conformed to the ideals of his class and time. Centre stage for the aristocracy and gentry that ruled Britain was the floor of the House of Commons. Enjoy a sociable existence and stick to writing the *Life of Johnson*, his friend Edmond Malone urged him, but Boswell continued to struggle for patronage and the recognition of his contemporaries. Though he wanted an immediately visible success, his sense of himself also needed to be validated in writing. In one disillusioned moment he thought "All my English bar scheme was chiefly with a view of how it would *tell* in my *life* in the *Biographia*" (Journal, 23 June 1786).

To transplant the family to London, leave Auchinleck in the hands of an overseer, and, heavily encumbered with debt, begin a totally different kind of legal practice at the age of forty-five was so hazardous an undertaking that Boswell was tormented by indecision both in contemplating the move and after he had made it. Mental and emotional turmoil mark the entire stretch of journal 1785–89. Still, he put a brave face on things: he celebrated his call to the English bar with a memorable dinner for his well-wishers (13 February 1786)—the lustre in the Inner Temple hall being lighted for the first time in thirty years—and attended the courts assiduously. In March he set off for the Northern Circuit, remarking at Lancaster, "Here now did I *perfectly* and *clearly* realize my ideas of being a counsel on the Northern Circuit and being an easy gentleman with Lancashire ladies, with no gloom, no embarrassment" (Journal, 5 April 1786).

The next day Boswell's fellow counsel tricked him with a feigned brief. They were fond of horseplay, and he was an oddity, the Junior on the circuit, charged with mess arrangements, communal bills, and such, an apprentice among youths half his age. When he returned to the Northern Circuit two years later, still without practice, he had to rebuff, with patient dignity, an attempt to reinstate him as Junior. The effort required of this proud man to continue to go the circuit and make a show of fellowship, though he was conspicuous by idleness, reveals the intensity of his desire to succeed in England.

But in London or on circuit, success would only come with some brilliant *coup de main*, and no opportunities presented themselves. A growing sense of failure oppressed him; tears ran down his cheeks one day as he wandered aimlessly through the streets of London, and he imprudently told everyone his troubles, even his own client, because "mental pain could not be endured quietly" (Journal, 5 July 1786). The shadow of his wife Margaret's persistent, losing battle with consumption hung over him. Yet his temper was so volatile that less than ten days later he could write, "My spirits were as good as ever I re-member them" (Journal, 14 July 1786), perhaps because in the interim he had started to draft the *Life of Johnson*.

Suddenly and ambiguously, fortune offered: out of nowhere the celebrated boroughmonger Lord Lonsdale took him up, dangling the position of Recorder (chief legal officer) of Carlisle before him. Lons-dale had a reputation for being eccentric and difficult, but Boswell's stillborn English practice left him no other means of satisfying ambition or even of decently maintaining his family in London. As a promissory move he was glad to accept appointment as counsel to the Mayor of Carlisle (a Lonsdale creature) in a disputed Parliamentary by-election.

Boswell's stay in Carlisle—it is now December 1786—taught him what Lonsdale's veteran dependants already knew: that he had no rule but his own whim. Boswell, ninth Laird of Auchinleck, beleaguered defender of free will against the paralysing onslaught of determinism, glimpses what he can become. Surely, he thinks, he can reconcile the roles of Lonsdale protégé and steadfast "old Tory baron." He performs his duties conscientiously: takes notes on the relevant statutes, worries over the legal technicalities, and ends by doing what he is told to do. On the election's central issue, the right of honorary freemen (Lons-dale's suborned voters) to cast ballots, Boswell delivers an animated, ingenious, and necessarily favourable opinion. In private he listens to Lonsdale recite poetry and harangue his captive audience endlessly. Occasionally Boswell resists his insolence and once even asks for white wine, which Lonsdale had always reserved for himself. Nothing can alter his imperial ways: he is sadistic as well as capricious, and the struggle undoubtedly heightened his pleasure in the conquest. A fa-mous author, the representative of a well-respected family, the good friend of some of the most distinguished men in Great Britain follows in his train.

The second trip north with Lonsdale, in December 1787, reads like a longer, harsher variation on the previous theme. This time there was a definite promise of the Recordership, and beyond it glittered the possibility of a seat in Parliament, to which Lonsdale had promoted the previous Recorder. Unexpectedly Boswell held back. He had had a full taste of Lonsdale's company, and he was "somewhat embarrassed" to be publicly befriended by such a notorious bully. Still, Margaret, always sensitive to his deeper wishes, urged him to go, and his brother T.D. "thought *it could do no harm*" (Journal, 20 December 1787).

Boswell went and was miserable. The start was inauspicious: he cooled his heels while his patron dawdled for hours, and the journey was unpleasant. After five days at Lowther Castle in Westmorland,

numbed with contempt and cold—to save money Lonsdale forbade
fires for his guests—Boswell acknowledged his folly and escaped to
nearby Penrith. But Margaret, he rationalized, would despise him for
his impulsive flight and Lonsdale was likely to resent it. A Lonsdale
toady he met at an inn confirmed this fear, and "better for exercise"
and a warming snack he trudged back, heavy travelling-bag in hand,
through five miles of snow to confront his torturer. Merely to explain
why he no longer wished to be made Recorder, he assured himself,
but we sense that he is lost.

Boswell gives all the particulars of the great scene that followed,
but they must be read in their place. Lonsdale overcame his attempt
to resign with a forceful reminder that Boswell had repeatedly asked
for the position, and a friendly gesture in providing coffee (never seen
before at Lowther) ratified Boswell's submission. Lonsdale paid him
the attention his self-respect demanded, while exerting that sense of
authority which, as with his father and Johnson, tended to awe and
quiet him.

Despite Boswell's social forwardness he was timid in certain ways,
and his wife and five children were hostages to fortune. Lonsdale was
the very symbol of unbridled will. His dark, dramatic presence, his
strength of purpose, even his brutal indifference to the emotional or
practical needs of others clearly fascinated Boswell. No idea and certainly no natural scene could compete with the infinite variety of mankind for his attention. From youth he had preserved specimens in his
journal, fixing philosopher, lady's-maid, cockbreeder, statesman, by
name, date, physiognomy, and characteristic speech. He had invaded
the privacy of such figures as Rousseau, Voltaire, Paoli, and Hume, as
well as Johnson, to discern the individual beneath the façade of reputation. Now James Lowther, first Earl of Lonsdale, took his turn.
Obliged to daily attendance, Boswell observed him closely, and in the
long hours of enforced idleness recorded his impressions in detail.
Like other Boswellian portraits, what began in personal absorption
developed into at least—as Boswell put it—the *disjecta membra* (unconnected parts) of a striking biography. Lonsdale, as subject, met his basic
criterion: he had strong, individual lineaments.

Ruthlessness was Lonsdale's outstanding trait. The concentration
of three inheritances reputedly had made him the richest commoner
in Britain, and by his own aggressive initiative he had increased that
wealth and translated it into rank (an earldom) and power. His nine
M.P.s ("Lowther's ninepins") were forced to recognize that they were
at his absolute command. His aim was domination. Boswell recorded
a long story of Lonsdale's sufferings as a child at the hands of his older

schoolmates, and drew the obvious conclusion: Lonsdale was still exacting repayment. He surrounded himself with inferiors and repressed the slightest tendency towards independence; publicly, he reached out to bring as much of the north of England as possible under his political control. He was mean and stingy but lacked neither courage nor literary taste. Occasional moments of graciousness, in which he seemed to recall the existence of others, kept Boswell off-balance.

Lonsdale was a dangerous, unpredictable man, and it may be that Boswell kept the two stretches of northern journal in a rudimentary Italian constantly breaking down into English in order to assure the privacy of his record. Or he may simply have wanted to renew his Italian: many of the most incriminating passages are written in English, and carried away with his subject as the journal grew, he fell increasingly into his own language. It is seldom clear why Boswell kept certain things secret and not others. His motives may have been obscure even to himself; after all, he once said that he wished everything about himself to be known. What his combination of schoolboy Italian and English does demonstrate unquestionably is the lucid, flowing, confident way in which he always recorded thought and experience.

By nature and behaviour Lonsdale suits the role of Vice in this quasi-allegorical story. For three years his patronage encouraged Boswell to enact the destructive fantasy that he could find a short cut to eminence and prosperity. But despite the lure, Boswell must take responsibility for what happened to him. In the long run he would have to acknowledge that association with Lonsdale involved not only the daily miseries of propinquity but also the loss of the independence he cherished. The short-term effect was virtually to legitimize Boswell's neglect of his family. Despite all the attention recorded in the journal— the anxious negotiations for a house in London, the arrangements to move, the fussing over the children's education—from the time Boswell made up his mind to migrate to England he put his own needs first. The chief victim was Margaret, not only his wife but, as he often called her, his "most valuable friend." As Boswell responded to the calls of pleasure or his patron, she was left to suffer and to die alone.

Though much enduring, Margaret Boswell was neither dull nor passive. She had long since, however, made the basic decision of her life: on becoming engaged, she had written to Boswell that whither he would go, she would follow. She kept her commitment, merging her destiny with his as a wife was expected to do. When his behaviour was intolerable, she continued her duties but separated herself by denying him her bed. Leaving all that was familiar and comfortable for a treacherous experiment in a new country, this acute, level-headed woman

had few illusions about her husband's prospects, but she knew him
thoroughly: at this crisis in his life further vacillation would be unen-
durable, and if she held him to Scotland and the safe but depressing
prospect of a narrow future as a judge in the Court of Session, he
would always reproach her. Competent and determined—"the mind
has much influence over the body," she wrote to a friend (22 November
1788)—as long as her health held out she could make her way to
London. But her adherence to Boswell's decision did not mean she
had abandoned her powers of judgement. She was outspoken, indeed
vigorous-tongued, and delivered her opinions freely. Boswell had great
respect for her honesty and good sense, though only his own wishes
were irresistible.

The outcome of the move justified their worst fears. As Boswell
had already admitted to himself, "*Imaginary* London, gilded with all
the brilliancy of warm fancy as I have viewed it, and London as a scene
of real business, are quite different" (Journal, 27 January 1786). He
was no longer visiting on holiday but pursuing an unprofitable profession in a workaday world and burdened with the presence of his family.
Margaret's health over the months clearly suffered from the smoke
and strangeness of London. When she had been very ill in the summer
of 1782, Boswell had tended her patiently: he had read aloud to her,
taken her on outings, and insisted she go to his cousin's in Fife for a
vacation because he thought the country might do her good; also (a
characteristic recourse) he had kept an almost clinical, separate journal
of her condition. Now her worsening state—coughing, fever, emacia-
tion, spitting of blood—frightened and repelled him, and though a
stay at Auchinleck (August–September 1787) momentarily revived her
strength, on his return from his second trip to Carlisle, now "Mr.
Recorder," Boswell saw from her appearance that "she had been at
the gates of death" (Journal, 14 January 1788).

The support and comfort he could offer her were ineffectual. She
was too rational, Boswell wrote, to respond to religious consolation:
"Oh! I am terrified for the dark passage," she told him (Journal, 19
April 1788). More and more she pressed him to settle at Auchinleck,
to admit that his English experiment was a failure. Swept by feelings
of guilt, he took the family home in May 1788, and he and Margaret
reached an unsatisfactory compromise: he would return to London
that autumn and she would remain behind. The following April he
visited Auchinleck again, apprehensive that her end was near and on
purpose to solace her. But again he escaped the evidence of her ordeal
by a ceaseless round of politics and pleasure. Forced by Lonsdale to
return to London, two months later he received the dreaded message
and posted north night and day, but arrived to find her dead.

Boswell was sorely punished for his treatment of Margaret, and to berate him at length now for what was obvious even at the time will only display the sensibilities of the accuser. Unable to control his behaviour, equally unable to control his anguish over it, he laid out his sins openly and either rationalized or wept over them. He told himself that he felt less tenderly than he had during Margaret's past illnesses because his mind was "so deadened by melancholy." Out all day once though she was feeling worse, he wrote, "I upbraided myself with seeming indifference and thought how very differently she would have behaved had I been ill. But my own wretchedness had engrossed me" (Journal, 17, 16 March 1788).

Ground between the millstones of Lonsdale's tyranny and Margaret's mortality, Boswell led what may seem, in retrospect, an unbearable existence; but he also lived in the present, and on 11 May 1787 he felt able to write to Sir William Forbes that since their parting the previous summer "I have upon the whole had a very good life." This claim may represent a conscious effort to count his blessings, but the journal shows that he also spoke truth. His affair with Margaret Caroline Rudd, to take an outstanding instance, gave him the keenest sexual pleasure he was ever to know. Even during the bleak winter and spring of 1788–89 he had intervals of enjoyment. Though he constantly lamented his separation from his wife, he assured her (was she comforted?) in a letter of 8 February 1789, "Yet I am upon the whole wonderfully well, owing, I do believe (though perhaps I should be sorry for it), to my having lived very *heartily* [that is, having drunk a good deal] and being in much variety."

Credit for such intervals belongs mainly to the mode of living Boswell had evolved for himself. Dinner, we recall, was the pivot of London recreation. Some years earlier Boswell had remarked in an *Hypochondriack* essay that it is "the mark of a brutish disposition to feed alone, or even to eat perpetually with one's family, which is comparatively unsocial and makes one figure a group of beasts in the same den day after day" (No. 58, July 1782). The statement, though extreme, expressed a prevailing attitude. To be unsocial was to be not quite human. Dinner, beginning at four or five o'clock, and sometimes prolonged through tea, supper, and the circulation of the bottle, could occupy the entire latter part of the day and go well into the night. To leave one's family and dine abroad was a recurring temptation for a man like Boswell, of convivial temperament and no pressing duties, especially since Margaret's presence was a standing reproach at home.

Dinner had other, more positive, appeals as well. It gave the day stretching before Boswell a structure, and London conversation provided necessary intellectual stimulus he found nowhere else. Though occasionally he claimed otherwise, Boswell had a wide circle of friends and acquaintances who made him welcome. Most important, his association with Malone, Sir Joshua Reynolds, and John Courtenay ("the Gang," as they were called) became the settled core of his existence. They were very partial to Boswell (Malone especially): encouraged him to migrate to London, revived his enthusiasm for his English scheme when it flagged, and provided a warm intimacy that kept him alive and writing. Malone and Reynolds were bachelors with flexible evening hours; Reynolds also kept a very hospitable table, noted for its heterogeneous company. Courtenay seems to have taken the cares of a wife and seven children lightly. Domesticity did not intrude on this society.

Boswell himself, with economy as his excuse, seldom entertained, though he noticed when Malone and another friend came to supper that "it was wonderful what a change for the better their agreeable society made on my wife and daughters, who had been long shut up in almost constant dull solitude" (Journal, 17 February 1788). Elsewhere, however, he could forget his troubles. He was also cushioning himself against the inevitable, as he was sometimes aware. Time and circumstances had modified his feeling for Margaret; he wrote; "I . . . could look with my mind's eye upon the event of her being removed by death with more composure than formerly. This I considered as humanely ordained by Providence; yet I was not without some upbraidings, as if I were too selfish from leading what may be called a life of pleasure" (Journal, 28 March 1788).

The cool appraisal is honest but inadequate. Time, routine, and familiarity may dampen passion; they also forge an intimacy which can never be reproduced. Boswell knew that as well as he knew he would soon be alone, alone not merely with the burden of home and children, responsibilities that Margaret had always assumed, but alone emotionally. No number of friends would ever stand as close as she did. He could not have observed her deterioration without recalling the Peggie who bloomed even in her late pregnancies and caught at his heart as she did when they were young. No opportunities remained now to make amends for his infidelities except by attending her faithfully to the end, and of that he was incapable. Without immediate promise of parliamentary seat or judge's robes, he could no longer hope to confer on her the status he believed she merited as his wife. Even his satisfaction in the publication of the *Life of Johnson* would be diminished if she did not share it. Oscillating between guilty resentment of her illness and regret, he fled home to escape both the present and the future.

One task Boswell never abandoned, the task he had set himself as a young man not quite twenty-four. Writing to Johnson literally on the gravestone of the great German reformer Melanchthon, he vowed not only "eternal attachment" but also, "to do honour" to his memory if Johnson should die before him (30 September 1764). The letter Boswell kept back "as too superstitious and too enthusiastic"—he sent it years later—but his vow led directly to the huge biography he was now struggling with. Caught up in the turmoil of Boswell's story, the colour, vividness, and pace of his journal, the reader can glide over Boswell's notations of work on his Magnum Opus. He began collecting materials in 1785, started to write in July 1786, and completed a draft in January 1789. The *Life* was published on 16 May 1791, the twenty-eighth anniversary of his first meeting with Johnson.

During this long process of gestation, Malone, though deep in his remarkable edition of Shakespeare, prodded, cajoled, fed, and amused Boswell, helped him to organize his massive collection of documents and later to revise copy for the printer. While indulging Boswell's dreams, Malone supported him firmly as he fulfilled his genius. Few persons have contributed so selflessly and significantly to the work of another. Even among literary wives, Margaret Boswell's generosity was also unusual, and this volume of journals makes plain the honour and gratitude we owe to her.

But the aesthetic vision and the accomplishment were Boswell's. He commended himself, and properly, for his assiduity in collecting and verifying the vast accumulation of materials on which the *Life of Johnson*'s notable authenticity rests. He has never been praised sufficiently as an artist, however, for creating a biography of such sweep and brilliance amidst prolonged distraction and sorrow. Out of much pain a great work was born. It proved Boswell's tenacity and seriousness of purpose, and gave his life focus and meaning.

I. S. L.

Broomall, Pennsylvania
19 December 1985

STATEMENT OF EDITORIAL PRACTICES

Spelling, capitalization, and punctuation of text and notes (including quotations in the notes from all sources) have been brought close to modern norms, Boswell being allowed to retain a few idiosyncrasies.

The standard of spelling for all but proper names is *The Concise Oxford Dictionary*, 6th ed., 1976. For place names, F. H. Groome's *Ordnance Gazetteer of Scotland*, J. G. Bartholomew's *Survey Gazetteer of the British Isles*, and *London Past and Present* by Peter Cunningham and H. B. Wheatley have been followed. Family names have been conformed to the usage of the *Dictionary of National Biography*, Mrs. Margaret Stuart's *Scottish Family History*, George F. Black's *Surnames of Scotland*, G. E. Cokayne's *Complete Baronetage and Complete Peerage*, Sir James Balfour Paul's *Scots Peerage*, and various other special books of reference.

Abbreviations and contractions have been silently expanded at will. Names of speakers in conversations cast dramatically are set in small capitals. Names of speakers which Boswell failed to provide in conversations cast dramatically are supplied silently when there is no doubt as to who is speaking. A few clear inadvertencies of various sorts have been put right without notice. Otherwise, all words whatever added by the editors where the documents show no defects are enclosed in square brackets. Words or parts of words missing from the manuscripts through crumbling are restored silently when the sense (not necessarily the exact words or order of words) seems certain; restorations involving any considerable degree of conjecture are enclosed in angular brackets. Omissions are indicated by ellipses. References to the *Life of Johnson* are made by date so that the reader can use any edition at hand. A text complete in one volume and the scholar's edition are listed in the selected bibliography under Documentation, section C.

ACKNOWLEDGEMENTS

The preparation of text and annotation for this volume of the trade edition owes much to earlier studies in Boswell and Johnson, most of which are described in the Bibliography at pp. 293–96. A great deal of unpublished research is available in the Boswell Office, which was established at Yale University in 1931. Marion S. Pottle's forthcoming *Catalogue* of Boswell's Papers at Yale, a multi-volume work incorporating bibliographical descriptions and minutes of content of the many papers of the entire collection, served us for many years in typescript and recently in galley proofs. The late Charles H. Bennett's exceptionally accurate annotations of the text were a valuable resource for all the journal in the present volume except for the sections reported as previously unpublished in Documentation, sections A and B. Between 1937 and 1945 Professor Pottle drew on Bennett's collection of notes and his own researches for a trade or reading edition of all the fully written journal, to be published as a set in several volumes. Lt.-Colonel Isham's acquisition in 1948, by judicial award and by purchase, of the Fettercairn and further Malahide papers, and the sale of his collection to Yale University the next year led to a radical reorganization and change of editorial policy. In 1950 the Yale Editions of the Private Papers of James Boswell and the McGraw-Hill Book Company began serial publication of a trade edition of the journal. *Boswell: The English Experiment*, like the eleven volumes which have preceded it, was raised on a foundation of Pottle's unpublished manuscript and Bennett's findings, revised extensively to incorporate the "newer" Boswell papers, and more fully annotated, not merely to take recent scholarship into account but also to fit each volume to appear as a separate, self-contained work.

The preparation of a book in the trade series of the Yale Boswell Editions is in many ways a collective enterprise. The office staff, as well as Frank Brady, Herman W. Liebert, and Marshall Waingrow of the Editorial Committee read galley proofs. Of the Advisory Committee, Thomas G. Bergin, Bertrand Bronson, Marion S. Pottle, Gordon P. Hoyle, Roger Lonsdale, and Warren H. Smith all kindly read the book in galley proof and returned valuable suggestions. We are grateful to Viscountess Eccles for her continued expert assistance and for providing us access to, and permission to quote from, documents in the Hyde Collection. For permission to quote from other documents in private collections and libraries, we thank Janet Dick-Cunyngham; the Pierpont Morgan Library; the Rosenbach Museum & Library; the Crown Court, Liverpool; and the Scottish Public Record Office.

We welcome the opportunity to acknowledge publicly the versatile staff, past and present, of the Boswell Editions, and the extraordinary range and quality of its assistance. Our sincere thanks to Irene Adams, Harriet Chidester, Tulin Duda, Niki Gekas, Barbara Hurwitz, Caterina Kazemzadeh, Roger Kohn, Rachel McClellan, Carolyn Cott McPhail, Maura Shaw Tantillo, and Nancy Wright. Barbara Hurwitz prepared a preliminary index of names for the comprehensive index, which was compiled mainly by Ms. Duda.

We also acknowledge various kinds of expert assistance from A. H. Aldous, G. H. Ballantyne, Roger Billcliffe, John Brooke, A. E. Brown, T. W. Copeland, Mrs. M. I. Cottom, J. K. Dudley, Barrows Dunham, C. N. Fifer, Joseph Foladare, P. D. R. Gardiner, Paul Goldman, C. J. Herington, James Holloway, Maynard Mack, Georges May, R. A. C. Meredith, Jean Munro, D. F. Musto, K. C. Newton, H. J. Pettit, Nicholas

Phillipson, F. C. Robinson, J. H. Salmon, Peter Smith, D. L. Thomas, Roland Thorne, G. M. C. Thornley, G. B. Watts, Elizabeth Welles, James William, and G. W. Williams.

For his kindness and continued support, we thank our publisher, Thomas H. Quinn, representative of McGraw-Hill on the Editorial Committee.

Mrs. Lustig acknowledges with special gratitude an individual research grant from the National Endowment for the Humanities, a grant-in-aid from the American Council for Learned Societies, and two grants from the Penrose Fund of the American Philosophical Society. Whatever understanding and compassion she has contributed to this volume she owes to the example over many years of her late husband, Morton Lustig. No one would have rejoiced more at the publication of this volume.

I. S. L.
F. A. P.

Boswell:

THE ENGLISH
EXPERIMENT

1785-1789

BOSWELL:
THE ENGLISH EXPERIMENT
1785–1789

I got to town in time enough to go with Sir Joshua Reynolds in his coach to Mr. Wilkes's at Kensington Gore, where we had an excellent entertainment: turtle, venison, ices, fruits, burgundy, champagne, cyprus, claret, etc., coffee, tea, and liqueur. Miss Arnold [Wilkes's mistress] was at table. Courtenay and Malone and no more made our party. Malone and I eat lobster and drank wine and water at Courtenay's after returning to London. This was a day.

[28 JULY 1786]

Whelpdale said nobody submitted to keep company with him [Lonsdale] but needy people for the good of their families, or people who had some view of self-interest. . . . I felt myself very awkward amidst such people. But I thought, "What does the world imagine *as to the* consequence *of living intimately with the* GREAT LOWTHER, *the powerful proprietor of £50,000 a year?" And in the world's estimation one wishes to exist high.*

[30 DECEMBER 1787]

My wife, who had been free of fever all night and part of the day, had a severe return, which depressed me sadly. I called Sir George Baker again at night, and he ordered a blister on her breast and that she should be blooded again next day. Poor woman, she had said to me mournfully this afternoon, "Oh, Mr. Boswell, I fear I'm dying."

[17 MARCH 1788]

Boswell: The English Experiment

1785-1789

SKETCH OF BOSWELL'S LIFE TO 12 NOVEMBER 1785. James Boswell was born in Edinburgh, 29 October 1740, eldest son of Alexander Boswell of Auchinleck, an extensive property in Ayrshire. James IV had conferred it in 1504 on Thomas Boswell, who in 1513 fell with him at the battle of Flodden Field. Through both his father and his mother James Boswell could claim connection with the royal line of Scotland and with several noble Scottish families. As judge in the Court of Session and the High Court of Justiciary (respectively the supreme courts in Scotland for civil and criminal cases), Alexander Boswell bore the judicial style of Lord Auchinleck. Shrewd, hard-working, and disciplined, he sought, above all, to enlarge and improve his landed estate and, as his eldest son was to inherit it all, he not unreasonably expected Boswell to display the qualities of thrift, regularity, and prudence which Lord Auchinleck and his father (James Boswell, a highly successful advocate) had so conspicuously displayed. If Lord Auchinleck had been capable of unearned affection, both he and his son would have been spared much suffering.

Boswell was educated at a private school for boys and girls, by domestic tutors, and in the Universities of Edinburgh and Glasgow. Timid as a child, and thought by his mother to be delicate, he emerged from a severe mental depression at the age of seventeen robust and gregarious, the associate of players and scribbler of theatrical criticism. He became infatuated with a married actress, was whisked away to Glasgow by his father, converted himself by reading to Roman Catholicism, and in his twentieth year ran away to London, intending to become a monk or a priest. His intention was subverted, at Lord Auchinleck's request (he could not have approved of all the means employed), by the tenth Earl of Eglinton, an Ayrshire neighbour residing in London, who brought Boswell into the circles of the great, the gay, and the ingenious (Boswell's own words), and introduced him to the pleasures of life, both high and low, in the metropolis. Boswell went back to Edinburgh convinced that what he *really* wanted was a commission in the Royal Foot Guards, not because he yearned for service in the field but because such a profession was gentlemanly and would keep him permanently in London. In 1762 he and his father struck a bargain: if Boswell would pass the examination in Civil Law of the Faculty of Advocates, he might go up to London with an assured income of £200 a year and try to persuade someone in power there to obtain a commission for him by interest. After months in London, he awoke to the futility of a pursuit known to be contrary to his father's wishes, but meantime he had thoroughly savoured the delights of the theatre and of good conversation, had explored the many amusements of the city, had conducted with a pretty actress an intrigue with a surprise ending, and by resilience and likeability had extended a bruising introduction to Samuel Johnson into a close and enduring friendship. The continuous journal he kept from 15 November 1762 to 4 August 1763 is in some respects the finest of his entire career.

In August 1763 Johnson made a two-day trip to Harwich to see Boswell off in the Dutch packet. For ten months, by agreement with his father, he studied civil law in Utrecht, his reward to be a tour of the German courts. During the whole period he was chaste, and for most of it gloomy. His most memorable acquaintance, the Dutch bluestocking, Belle de Zuylen (he called her by her pen-name, Zélide), fascinated and repelled him; she remained for some time on his list of possible wives. The elegant variety of the German courts pleased him but paled in interest beside the meetings he achieved later with Rousseau and Voltaire. Assuming a greater indulgence than Lord Auchinleck had ever intended, he went on for a year in Italy, culminating (October and November 1765) in an excursion into the mountain fastnesses of Corsica to interview General Pasquale Paoli, leader of the resistance against the Genoese and later the French. The meeting led to a lifelong friendship.

At Paris on his return home Boswell read in a newspaper of his mother's death. He passed advocate (26 July 1766) in Edinburgh and settled down to a practice of more than average competence and promise. Had he given undivided attention to his profession, he might ultimately have worn the robe of a Lord of Session. But that ambition was second to his heart's desire, a seat in Parliament or other high office that would assure him residence in London as well as in Scotland.

In 1768 he published his *Account of Corsica, the Journal of a Tour to That Island, and Memoirs of Pascal Paoli*, a very successful work (three editions in England, three in Ireland, translations into Dutch, French, German, and Italian). His total minor publication was considerable: songs, verses, broadsides, pamphlets, contributions signed, unsigned, and pseudonymous to magazines and newspapers. His essay series *The Hypochondriack* (seventy monthly essays) appeared in the *London Magazine* (October 1777–August 1783).

After half-hearted pursuit of a succession of heiresses, Boswell yielded to a deep affection for an almost penniless first cousin, Margaret Montgomerie, a handsome woman of quick intelligence and great strength of character. They were married 25 November 1769 at Lainshaw, Ayrshire. Lord Auchinleck, who did not approve of the match, married his own first cousin, Elizabeth Boswell, on the same day at Edinburgh. Boswell, whose sexual behaviour since 1765 had been profusely irregular, remained a contented and proper husband for three years, but the urge for wine and sexual adventure grew compulsive and he returned to his old ways. Margaret knew and forgave him; he was remorseful but not effectively so, and her generosity was sorely tried. In 1785, when the present volume opens, they were the devoted parents of five children: Veronica ("Ve," aged thirteen), Euphemia ("Phemie," eleven), Alexander ("Sandy," ten), James ("Jamie," seven), and Elizabeth ("Betsy," five).

Boswell's programme often included a long spring vacation in London. He was admitted to The Club on Johnson's nomination, 30 April 1773, and made excursions with Johnson to Oxford, Lichfield, Ashbourne, and, most notably, to the Hebrides (1773).

On 30 August 1782 Lord Auchinleck died after prolonged illness, and Boswell at the age of forty-one assumed responsibility for the family estate. Some idyllic months as Laird ensued, but before the year was out he longed for London again. After much badgering, Johnson gave reluctant approval to his ambitious scheme of being called to the English bar. The dramatic political reversals of the time fired his hopes of getting into Parliament. In 1783 he published a *Letter to the People of Scotland* supporting the King and Pitt in their opposition to the Fox-Burke East India Bill; the next year he declared (in vain) his availability as a candidate for Ayrshire in the election that followed the fall of the Fox-North Coalition. In May 1785 he challenged Henry Dundas, political manager for Scotland, with an effective but intemperate *Letter to the People of Scotland* opposing a bill to reduce the number of the Lords of Session from fifteen to ten and to increase the salaries of the remaining judges.

Boswell learned of Johnson's death on 17 December 1784, and almost simultaneously received a letter from the publisher Charles Dilly requesting copy for his biography of Johnson. He resolved to proceed deliberately with the *Life* but meanwhile to bring out the independently publishable journal of the Hebridean tour. He returned to London in the spring of 1785 and stayed on nearly to the end of September, selflessly encouraged and assisted by Edmond Malone in revising the manuscript of the *Journal of a Tour to the Hebrides* and seeing it through the press. He arrived back at Auchinleck on 3 October 1785 after his longest sojourn in London since 1762–1763.

The Journal of a Tour to the Hebrides was published on 1 October 1785 and the whole impression of 1,500 copies was sold out by the 17th. Boswell and Malone through the post began revising for a second edition.

There is no journal for 28 September–12 November 1785. Boswell remained at Auchinleck for a month after his return, collecting rents, entertaining company, and paying visits—the usual autumn pattern. On 4 November he started for London, via Edinburgh, to complete the set number of meals at the Inner Temple necessary for his admission to the English bar. He remained at Edinburgh only a week, during which time he was too involved in other matters to record the death on 10 November of his beloved old friend, Sir Alexander Dick.

Boswell was deeply concerned, for one thing, with the extent to which he would have to emend the *Tour*. He and Johnson had gone to the Hebrides not so much to look at scenery as to examine the clan system as it actually stood, hoping to find still there significant remains of a social state in which (they liked to believe) the chieftains maintained arms, roasted oxen whole, and hung out flags to invite the clansmen to beef and whisky. The first chieftain they had visited was Sir Alexander Macdonald of Sleat (later Lord Macdonald), and he proved most unsatisfactory. As Boswell reported in the *Tour*, he was a stingy host, and his rapacious policy as a landlord forced his tenants to emigrate.

Before his departure from Auchinleck Boswell had learned from Malone that a pamphlet attacking the *Tour* was being published in London, which he feared, incorrectly, had been written by Lord Macdonald. Boswell had already softened some references to him, but Mrs. Boswell reproved Boswell for printing what remained and was fearful that Lord Macdonald would challenge him to a duel. It was better, Boswell thought, to make further changes on his own account—if he had to. He therefore revised a passage when he reached Edinburgh and sent it to Malone for approval. "I have the milk of human kindness in abundance," Boswell told him; on the other hand, "much changing may have the appearance of wavering," and Malone was not to cancel the leaf if he knew "for *certain* that Lord M——d does not take it *hot*" (To Malone, 11 November 1785).

Boswell was also shocked to find awaiting him at Edinburgh an angry letter from his fellow advocate Alexander Fraser Tytler, who he had said in the *Tour* was sharply corrected by Johnson in an encounter over the authenticity of *Fingal*. Boswell returned a conciliatory reply, protesting that he had discussed the matter with Tytler himself the previous winter and had understood Tytler to say that he might reprint the anecdote with Tytler's name if he also printed with his own name a ridiculous anecdote of his having once entertained the audience at Drury Lane Theatre by lowing like a cow. He offered to rewrite the passage in the second edition to suit Tytler and, having made this concession, he thought it fair to request an explicit apology for the language of Tytler's letter. No reply had arrived when he left for London, agitated by this quarrel and his inner conflict over his proposed transfer to the English bar.

It will be convenient for the reader if we identify here a handful of close friends who surround Boswell in the first few entries of the journal. Like him, most were well known in their time, all except his brother finding a place in the *Dictionary of National Biography*.

THOMAS DAVID BOSWELL (1748–1826), called T.D., Boswell's youngest brother, conventional, reliable, and punctilious. For many years a merchant in Spain, he had been forced by the recent war to leave that country and was now a commission agent in London. Christened David, he had prefixed the Thomas because of the Spanish prejudice against Old Testament names.

JOHN COURTENAY (1738–1816), Irish-born M.P., personally genial but one of the most withering debaters in the House of Commons. A follower of Fox, he later advocated the abolition of the slave trade and supported the French Revolution along with the maintenance of constitutional rights in Great Britain and Ireland when they were threatened during that period. Versifier, essayist. A recent friend.

GEORGE DEMPSTER (1732–1818), M.P. for the Perth Burghs since 1761; an independent Whig, active in the Commons. One of the oldest of Boswell's friends.

CHARLES DILLY (1739–1807), bookseller and publisher; with his older brother Edward he had published Boswell's *Account of Corsica*. For years his hospitable house in the Poultry had been Boswell's point of arrival in, and departure from, London.

BENNET LANGTON (1737–1801), representative of an ancient Lincolnshire family, Greek scholar, military engineer, intimate friend of Johnson, and an original member of The Club. Boswell admired him for his learning and piety. They had been friends since at least 1768.

JOHN LEE (?1733–1793), barrister and M.P. for Clitheroe, a forthright and coarse-tongued politician known at the bar as "honest Jack

Lee." Avowed enemy to the influence of the Crown, he had been Solicitor-General in the second Rockingham administration, and was promoted to Attorney-General under the Fox-North Coalition. Unitarian and associate of Joseph Priestley and Richard Price. A recently made friend whom Boswell much admired, "though I believe there are not any two specific propositions of any sort in which we exactly agree" (*Letter to the People of Scotland*, 1785, p. 75).

EDMOND MALONE (1741–1812), Irishman, non-practising barrister, literary scholar and critic, recent member of The Club. Boswell first met him in 1781 at the home of their common friend, Sir Joshua Reynolds. "Kind and elegant," he had sat day after day with Boswell assisting him in the preparation of printer's copy for the *Tour* despite his own commitment to a monumental edition of Shakespeare's plays (ten volumes in eleven, 1790).

PASQUALE PAOLI (1725–1807), politician and legislator, General of the Corsicans in the heroic struggle for independence, first from Genoa and then from France. Since the defeat of the rebellion by France (1769), he, with some followers, had lived in England on a generous pension from the British Crown. An intimate friend and counsellor of Boswell's since 1765. His residence, now 1, Upper Seymour Street, Portman Square, was Boswell's usual home during his visits to London.

SIR JOSHUA REYNOLDS (1723–1792), renowned artist, President of the Royal Academy, one of Johnson's most intimate friends and, with him, founder of The Club. Oliver Goldsmith had introduced Boswell to him in 1769. An equable and generous man, Reynolds over the years had become a good friend of Boswell's, whose affection and admiration for him never wavered.

Journal in England and Scotland
12 November 1785 to 24 May 1789

LEFT EDINBURGH, 12 NOVEMBER (Saturday), in a chaise with Lady Betty Hope[1] and her governess, Mrs. Dawkins. Had but a dull journey, being in very bad spirits. Arrived in London, Thursday the 17; dined with Mr. Malone; came to Mr. Dilly's at night.

FRIDAY 18 NOVEMBER. Consulted Mr. Malone and Mr. Courtenay as to Mr. Tytler. They both agreed it was absolutely necessary to have an apology. So I wrote.[2] Dined Temple. Mr. Dilly's, night.

SATURDAY 19 NOVEMBER. Dined Mr. Langton's (having broke bread in Temple). T.D. breakfasted. Not well. Night Dilly's.

SUNDAY 20 NOVEMBER. Heard Dr. Mayo preach.[3] Was as ill as ever in a Scotch kirk. Dined Temple; coffee and tea T.D.'s. Night Dilly's. Quite dreary.

MONDAY 21 NOVEMBER. Went to General Paoli's.[4] All seemed confused. Dined, tea, and supped Courtenay's with Malone and Palmer. A little better. General's, night.

TUESDAY 22 NOVEMBER. Breakfast Malone's. Wrote distracted letter to M.M.[5] Dined General's. Home all evening. Whist.

WEDNESDAY 23 NOVEMBER. Sauntered; Westminster Hall.[6] Mr. Lee took me home to dinner. Was somewhat comfortable. But could not fix plan of settling here. Home.

THURSDAY 24 NOVEMBER. Not at all right. Breakfasted Sir J.

---

[1] Daughter of John Hope, the late Earl of Hopetoun. She was in her seventeenth year.

[2] Boswell insisted again that Tytler retract an injurious expression, "absolutely false," in his initial letter to Boswell.

[3] Minister of the Independent Congregation in Nightingale Lane, Wapping; known as the "Literary Anvil" because he remained steadfast under Johnson's blows in a famous argument on liberty of conscience.

[4] That is, moved to Paoli's ("home" from now on) from Dilly's.

[5] Margaret Montgomerie Boswell, his wife.

[6] Each of the three Common Law courts (King's Bench, Common Pleas, and Exchequer) sat *in banc* at Westminster four times a year for periods of about three weeks each. Hilary Term was 27 January to 12 February; Michaelmas 6 to 28 November. Easter and Trinity terms varied according to the date of Easter.

Dick.[7] Had cravings. Visited Mrs. R. Indifferent. Then gross folly.[8] Then Chapter Coffee-house. Then Dilly's, and was introduced to Cumberland.[9] Dined General's. To bed between six and seven.

FRIDAY 25 NOVEMBER. Not well. General for my consulting physicians, and clear for my not becoming an English barrister, as it would involve me in expense and in dependence on attorneys. Dined Temple commons. Dilly's, night. Quite sunk. Had visited Mrs. Bosville in the morning, who told me she was sorry Lord Macdonald was much offended at my treatment of him in my book and was going to write something in the newspapers against me. I met my Chief Bosville in Cranbourne Alley, who told me the same, but that he had persuaded him against it. He said he would call on Lord M. next day and meet me at night at the Mount and tell me the result.[1] I this forenoon visited also Dempster out at Brompton Row, and told him how ill I was, and how I was wavering and wretched.

SATURDAY 26 NOVEMBER. Visited T.D., and was fully resolved to return to Scotland, which pleased him. Visited Courtenay a little. Called on Sir Joshua Reynolds and was asked to his family dinner, to which I went (only he, his niece, and Dick Burke, Senior,[2] whose energy roused me somewhat), and the whole scene revived my wish for a London settlement. Yet I soon wearied. At the Mount, Colonel Johnston of the Guards told me how angry Lord M. was. In a little after came Bosville and told me Lord M. was to do nothing, only he desired not to be acquainted with me. When I came home, found a sensible, cheerful letter from my dear wife. I adored her. Yet I was vexed to be away from her. She was settled as to coming to London, but bid

[7]Distant cousin of the late Sir Alexander Dick; Comptroller of Accounts in the War Office. Boswell had met him in 1765 at Leghorn, where he was then British consul, and he had been most helpful in gathering materials for *An Account of Corsica*. Boswell had repaid his help by being instrumental in getting Dick his baronetcy.

[8]Boswell later deleted "had cravings" and "gross." Margaret Caroline Rudd ("Mrs. R.") is the notorious enchantress he had sought out in 1776 after she had been acquitted of a charge of forgery when she turned King's evidence. Her accomplices, the Perreau brothers, had been hanged. She had initiated a renewal of intimacy with Boswell in August, after he had lost sight of her for nine years.

[9]Richard Cumberland, the dramatist.

[1]Mrs. Bosville, widow of Godfrey Bosville of Gunthwaite, Yorkshire, was the mother of Lady Macdonald and of William Bosville, late lieutenant in the Coldstream Guards and now head of the family. Boswell calls William Bosville "Chief" because of a mistaken belief that the Boswells of Auchinleck were ultimately cadets of the Bosvilles of Gunthwaite. The Mount was a well-known coffee-house.

[2]Sir Joshua's niece, Mary Palmer (later Countess of Inchiquin), made her home with him and served as his hostess. Richard Burke, Senior, was Edmund's brother; Richard, Junior, was Edmund's son.

me not be uneasy as to returning with a good grace, for I had a true Montgomerie,[3] who would find out many and various excuses.

SUNDAY 27 NOVEMBER. Was somewhat better. Met T.D. by appointment at the Chapelle Helvétique and heard M. Roustan, a distinguished orator. Felt a renewal of my father's Dutch ideas.[4] Home and read the Ely Cause, which fixed my attention a little.[5] Dined Malone's with Courtenay and Reed,[6] and stayed coffee and tea. Was not *qualis eram.*[7] On my return home, found a most shocking, abusive letter from Lord M. which I thought made it indispensable for me to fight him.[8] Was quite dismal. Such a dreary force upon me in my gloomy state was terrible. I thought of my dear wife and children with anxious affection. Could not rest. Had a thousand thoughts.

MONDAY 28 NOVEMBER. Rose agitated. Went to the worthy General. Read him Lord M.'s letter. He was clear I should not resent, and said he would go to him along with Mr. Bosville. I found Bosville in bed, and he agreed I should not resent, and he would go to Lord M. with the General at eleven. He told me Lord M. was not willing to meet me, but said to him he wished I could be frightened for some days that he was looking for me; and he said if he could get me to contradict anything in my book, he would publish it—ungenerous, ungentlemanly thought! I then instead of returning to the General went to Malone's. We sent for Courtenay, and all agreed that an *unsigned* letter should not be noticed, and besides it said no apology could be received, and yet it did not *challenge* me. Courtenay said it was a womanish, a poltroonish, letter. I however wrote a letter to Mr. Bosville (not at all

[3]So Boswell had called her in *Letter to the People of Scotland,* 1785.
[4]Presumably Boswell means that the chapel and sermon remind him of a Calvinist church in Holland, but it is not clear why he refers to his father.
[5]A complicated, interfamilial Irish lawsuit which dragged on for almost thirty years. Thomas Barnard, Bishop of Killaloe, had sent Boswell a parcel of papers in the case.
[6]Isaac Reed, the Shakespearian editor.
[7]As I used to be.
[8]Over four large quarto pages, unsigned, in a very small hand. The carefully docketed Macdonald dossier in the Boswell Papers is voluminous, but the fact that the journal is fully written makes it unnecessary to present the Macdonald documents in systematic detail. This is no loss to the reader, for Macdonald wrote in an atrocious style: arch, pretentious, obscure, and pedantic. (He is likely at any moment to burst into original Latin verse.) The reader may take the following as a fair specimen of his abuse: "Your violation of the acknowledged laws of hospitality by the wanton *affront* put upon me [in the *Journal of a Tour to the Hebrides*] after such a lapse of time is without a parallel in the annals of civilized nations, and could only have proceeded from a mind tainted with prejudices of the most dark and malignant kind, unsusceptible of the least spark of generosity and refinement and accustomed to arrogate to itself a licence to treat mankind in general with indignity and insolence."

referring to *it*) begging of him as a common friend to tell Lord Macdonald that I had some weeks before entirely of my own accord left out some passages which might be disagreeable to him. I went to Bosville's and stayed at his lodgings till he went to Lord M.'s and returned and told me there would be no more of it. Dined comfortably with the General.

TUESDAY 29 NOVEMBER. Attended Courts of Exchequer and King's Bench. Had a good deal of conversation with Mr. Macdonald, Solicitor-General, who was not at all displeased with my book.[9] Walked home with him. Envied the comfort of being with one's family. Was to have dined at Courtenay's but, business having called him away, Malone had dinner for me. We had a good tête-à-tête. I grew somewhat better.

WEDNESDAY 30 NOVEMBER. Malone and I dined at Courtenay's. I had walked to the City and met T.D., who was vexed at my being in London. Met also Preston,[1] and felt myself confused and uneasy. The dinner at Courtenay's with his wife and two daughters, Malone and myself, was truly good. A letter of apology came from Tytler, which made me quite easy. We stayed till near one in the morning.

THURSDAY 1 DECEMBER. Was uneasy from having been kept up till near one, and drank[2] a little punch, and the weather being cold. Rose, however, and sallied forth to get the reviews of my *Tour*, and carried them to Malone's and read them at breakfast. The *Monthly* had not yet noticed me. The *Critical* and *English* were unfavourable; the *Gentleman's Magazine* very favourable.[3] I was in dejected perplexity still what to do about settling in London. The idea of making my children *aliens* from Scotland was dismal. How strangely can imagination operate! My dear wife's cough, which she had when I left her, alarmed me.[4] I came home and found two most consolatory letters from her. I worshipped her. The General being to dine abroad, I was unsettled and uneasy where to dine. I called again on Malone, who luckily was to dine at home by himself and kindly asked me to dine with him. We were cordial. But I shrunk from the English bar, as he suggested how

[9]Archibald Macdonald, a younger brother of Lord Macdonald.
[1]Capt. Robert Preston, Boswell's first cousin once removed, M.P. for Dover, successful owner-manager of various East Indiamen.
[2]That is, having drunk.
[3]*The Monthly Review* did not notice the *Tour* till the issue of April 1786. The review in the *Critical* is on the whole not unfavourable, but treats Boswell without dignity, saying that his "good-humoured vanity generally pleases." Substantial extracts from all the reviews Boswell mentions appear in *Boswell: The Applause of the Jury, 1782–1785*, ed. I. S. Lustig and F. A. Pottle, 1981, pp. 347–50. The review in the *Gentleman's Magazine* was by John Nichols.
[4]Margaret Boswell had long been consumptive, with remissions.

I should study. Came home about ten and read some English law. Was very sad.

FRIDAY 2 DECEMBER. Dined at home and played whist.

SATURDAY 3 DECEMBER. Attended Lord Mansfield's sittings in Westminster Hall,[5] and was pretty well for the moment. Dined at home. Then Mr. Malone's (tea and a little supper and good conversation), and was *quite well* for an interval.

SUNDAY 4 DECEMBER. A disagreeable day. Ill again. Went in stage to Putney. Walked from thence to Richmond Lodge.[6] Colonel St. Paul[7] and lady there. It was observed I was quite dull. Mrs. S. was against my going home now. At night the Colonel was strong against my coming to the English bar, and thought I should be called and perhaps go a circuit,[8] but not bring my family to London.

MONDAY 5 DECEMBER. Very ill. Walked as far as Dempster's (Knightsbridge);[9] found him and complained sadly. He treated my anxieties lightly, and said I need be under no concern as to *appearances*, but just follow my *inclination*. He was for my going home as a jaunt. He drove me in his chariot to town. I was excessively ill. The General and Mr. Gentili[10] were very kind. Even the two Corsican valets were much concerned for me, for I was indeed very ill. Thought I was engaged to dine at Sir Joshua's. Went there. But the day was Wednesday. Dined disagreeably at a coffee-house. Drank tea with Malone and grew a little better. Came home and went to bed early. Was weak and gloomy.

TUESDAY 6 DECEMBER. The Hon. Mr. Ward had written very kindly to me and relieved me from any suspicion that he was offended on account of Lord Macdonald.[1] He had invited me twice to dinner

[5] William Murray, first Earl of Mansfield, Lord Chief Justice of the Court of King's Bench; the greatest British judge of the century.

[6] The residence in Richmond Park of Lt.-Col. the Hon. James Archibald Stuart, the Deputy Ranger and second son of the Earl of Bute. Boswell claimed friendship with him and with his wife, in whom he confided freely. She was also an intimate friend of Mrs. Boswell's.

[7] Former Secretary of the British Embassy in Paris.

[8] It was common practice among London barristers to attach themselves to one or other of the seven circuits of England and Wales, divided by district, for the purpose of attending the assizes, or courts, normally held four times a year in the major towns of each circuit. Civil actions and criminal cases were tried, priority being given to the latter.

[9] About nine miles from Richmond.

[10] Paoli's trusted friend and secretary, a gallant fighter in the Corsican revolt against the Genoese when he was barely sixteen.

[1] William Ward, M.P. for Worcester, later Viscount Dudley and Ward of Dudley. His wife, Julia Bosville, was Lady Macdonald's sister.

when I was engaged. I sat with him awhile this forenoon, and felt myself much better. He owned he was always against my engaging in the laborious law in London. The General was very good today in counselling me freely to prudence and not to yield to melancholy. I visited Lady Betty Hope at Mrs. Beaver's. I dined at the Prince of Orange Coffee-house with the two Bosvilles,[2] etc. Then met Malone and Courtenay at Drury Lane playhouse. We went home to Malone's and talked seriously of Lord Macdonald's letter to me, of which they had advised me to take no notice. But it had occurred to worthy Courtenay that Lord M. might show it about or even publish it, and *then* I would be *obliged* to call him out. Therefore, as I was going to Scotland, it was proper to fix him down *now* not to do so. Or if he refused, it was better to call on him for satisfaction before I should appear *forced* to it. We concerted what I should write down as my sentiments. Mr. Courtenay undertook to go to Lord M. next morning and read the paper and get his answer, to be also put in writing. In short, he was to manage the whole affair in the best manner. I got into good spirits and felt myself firm enough. But we sat till two, and I was vexed at disturbing the General's quiet house. Lord M.'s affair had been still hanging upon my mind, and it was very kind in Courtenay to think of relieving me. Malone told me it had kept Courtenay two hours awake the night before. What mischief may imprudent publications bring upon even a good man!

WEDNESDAY 7 DECEMBER. Mr. Courtenay having sent a note the night before to Lord M. that at *my* request he begged to wait on him, Lord M. came to him and had a long conversation, which, although a paper written by me insisting that no use public or private should be made of his letter was read to him,[3] came to no conclusion but that he desired till tomorrow to consider of it. I dined at Mr. Courtenay's with Lord Townshend, his nephew Mr. Orme, a clergyman, and Mr. Malone.[4] I was very dreary.

THURSDAY 8 DECEMBER. I waited several hours at Mr. Malone's

[2] William and Thomas, his younger brother, lieutenant in the Coldstream Guards and captain in the army.

[3] "However harsh and unmerited (and on any other occasion inexcusable) the terms of Lord Macdonald's letter are, Mr. Boswell, as he had previously shown himself sensible that the passages expunged were in some sort exceptionable, is therefore willing to overlook Lord Macdonald's letter and to consider it as not existing. At the same time, Mr. Boswell trusts and expects that no use, public or private, is to be made of that letter."

[4] Apparently in his distress of mind he forgot that he was engaged for dinner to Sir Joshua Reynolds. See above, 5 December 1785.

while Mr. Courtenay was with Lord Macdonald at his house. My anxiety was most distressing. Still there was no conclusion, but Lord M. appeared obstinate.[5] By the advice of Messrs. Courtenay and Malone, I wrote another paper which Mr. Courtenay undertook to show to Lord M. next day.[6] I dined at the General's, my brother David there. But I was in sad agitation, and mentioned the cause. The General thought I was ill-advised in taking notice of Lord M.'s letter. I went at night to Mr. Dilly's; Braithwaite and Bezley there.[7] Drank too much calcavella,[8] and half confused, half asleep, talked of Lord M.'s affair, which was wrong. But I found his attacking me was known.

FRIDAY 9 DECEMBER. Awaked very ill both in body and mind. I thought of my wife and children with tender pain, and had death before my eyes. Hastened to Courtenay's. Lord M. came to him and then I went to Malone's, where I waited till Courtenay sent a note that Lord M. would not yet comply.[9] I went to Courtenay and wrote a note to Lord M. requesting to know if his objection was that my letter

[5]Courtenay brought back a paper reportedly dictated to him by Lord Macdonald: "That Mr. Boswell had allowed himself twelve years to reflect and to be informed concerning every allegation inserted in his *Tour*, which during the aforesaid period ought to have been explained to Mr. Boswell's own satisfaction, without challenging an answer by publishing them according to his own conceptions. That Lord Macdonald's ideas of an author are these: that he gives to the world observations by which he is willing to abide, and exposes himself to recrimination (if the subject is personal) and animadversion equally poignant and reciprocal. . . . That Lord Macdonald holds himself not to be in the predicament to make a concession to Mr. Boswell which a renunciation of his letter or a declaration of its non-existence would imply, and saves to himself the full exercise of his judgement in as ample a manner as the author of a *Tour to the Hebrides* has possessed it."

[6]Boswell sent Macdonald a copy of his letter to Bosville, 28 November 1785 (see above), which contained an admission that he had overstepped the bounds of propriety in printing certain reflections on Macdonald, that he had deleted those passages in his second edition, and was "very sorry they ever should have appeared." Macdonald, he said, might publish *that* letter, so long as he made no use of the long unsigned letter of 26 November. Boswell also on this day formally appointed Courtenay his second, sending him the whole correspondence. "Having done all I possibly could as a gentleman to conciliate, I beg you may at once bring the business to a crisis, for I am resolved it shall not hang on."

[7]Daniel Braithwaite, an amiable, highly trusted official in the Postmaster's Office, was an old friend of Dilly's and of many of the *literati*'s. Bezley is not certainly identified. A John Beazley was surveyor of the City of London.

[8]A sweet white wine, so called from Carcavelhos, Portugal.

[9]Courtenay brought back a one-sentence reply: "Lord Macdonald does not choose to publish Mr. Boswell's letter to Mr. Bosville, not being at liberty to put to the press abstract correspondence." Courtenay did not know what Macdonald meant, nor did Boswell and Malone.

(mentioning my having expunged passages that might hurt him and that I was sorry they had appeared) was addressed to Mr. Bosville and not to Lord M., and begged an explicit answer might be sent to Berners Street, No. 7,[1] by five o'clock. I was prevailed on to dine at Malone's with Lord Townshend, old Macklin,[2] and Courtenay. I was in a dreary state. I wrote to my wife before dinner, under an apprehension it might be the last letter. Courtenay, on my asking him, directed me how to stand and fire a pistol. My heart failed me, but I found myself under an absolute necessity to go on. Courtenay said he thought Lord M. a mean poltroon, who, conscious that he was not to proceed to the last extremity, as he could at any time put an end to the matter, wished to appear bold and work my feelings; for it seems he had proposed to refer the affair to a committee of the gentlemen who attend the Mount Coffee-house. I grew somewhat better in the evening, though no answer came from Lord M.; and then I with the help of Courtenay and Malone wrote a paper shortly stating the case and showing that Lord M. forced me in vindication of my honour to challenge him.[3] This paper Mr. C. was to read to Lord M. next day. And if he still stood out, was to have a note in my handwriting and also read that to him, desiring a personal meeting at the Ring in Hyde Park the same day at three o'clock, for C. said it was better to have the matter ended speedily and not suffer it to hang on. I was pretty calm, but when I came home and found a letter from my wife and one from my daughter Veronica, I was much affected. What misery, real and imaginary, do I endure!

SATURDAY 10 DECEMBER. Had slept not five minutes all night. The alternative of killing or being killed distracted me. I breakfasted at Mr. Malone's and waited till Mr. Courtenay returned from Lord M.'s, whom he found very obstinate after the first paper was read, and would give no answer; till Mr. C. having said he must then read him another paper, he wrote a note that he would deliberate and take advice of his confidential friends. Mr. C. returned to Mr. M.'s and said "it would now be settled"; but the misery was, I was still to be kept in

[1]Courtenay's house.

[2]Charles Macklin, playwright and actor. He was probably at this time in his eighty-ninth year, and was to live till 1797.

[3]A five-paragraph summary of the interchange to date, ending as follows: "Such being the state of the case between Lord Macdonald and Mr. Boswell, it is for his Lordship to consider that if he refuses to comply with the reasonable condition of making no use, public or private, of his letter to Mr. Boswell, Mr. Boswell must understand that his Lordship means to asperse him by showing it, and therefore Lord Macdonald lays him under the absolute necessity of asserting his honour in the only way which his Lordship has left him."

suspense. I met Sir John Dick, went home with him, and dined tête-à-tête; drank tea and supped cordially at Mr. Ward's. He was sorry I had said anything to give pain to Lord M., but thought him *now* in the wrong.

SUNDAY 11 DECEMBER. After another night of torment, breakfasted with Mr. C. No answer yet. My mind was weakened by such a continuation of uneasiness. I called on Bosville, who told me Lord M. had been with him, and was to expunge all the injurious passages in his letter. He and I were quite well together. It was a dreary day. I was part of the forenoon at Malone's. I dined and drank tea at Mr. Ward's, and was well for the moment. Then went to Courtenay's, who showed me a letter to him from Lord M., which he called ridiculous and puzzling. It yielded parts of his letter and explained away parts and had veins of nonsense in it. In short, Malone having been sent for, we were satisfied the creature meant just to play with my feelings, conscious that he could at any time get off. We concerted a final letter from me to Mr. C., to be read to Lord M. next day, insisting on an explicit answer.[4] Or——.

MONDAY 12 DECEMBER. The night was passed somewhat more easily, but I was still in feverish agitation. Breakfasted with Malone. Called on C., who went to Lord M. with my letter and then came to Malone's, having taken down an agreement that all the passages in his letter *scored* by Mr. C. should be expunged; therefore Mr. C. and all of us were satisfied *that* letter was now done away; and he promised upon his honour that the agreement should be sent by him in a letter under his hand to Mr. C. Mr. M. and I dined most agreeably at Mr. C.'s. In the evening I was tolerably serene at the General's, but wavered a little as to going *home*, having found a letter from my wife advising me against coming down. Yet I thought I could not be at rest till I had seen her and my children again after this horrible agitation. It was terrible to think that *death* is *certain* at *some* period. But a *violent* death, especially when a man by his fault occasions it, is shocking. I endeavoured to cherish pious hope.

TUESDAY 13 DECEMBER. Malone and I dined at Dilly's with a Counsellor Bond[5] and a Mr. Tew, student of law. A day not bright.

---

[4]Boswell pointed out that occasional and haphazard deletions and explanations would not do. Macdonald is "at liberty in any letter of *a new date* addressed to me or any other person, or in any other mode that he shall think proper, to avail himself of any observations in his letter of the 26th of November on me or my journal, provided they are expressed in terms not personally injurious to the feelings of a man of honour."
[5]Bond, a coarse-mannered but successful barrister (Middle Temple), was made serjeant-at-law (the highest rank among barristers) in the summer of 1786.

But Malone did very well. Home with Malone. Courtenay came to us and brought a very satisfactory paper sent to him by Lord Macdonald.[6] So we were cordial and joyous. Courtenay thought I should not go to Scotland *now*, as they were prejudiced against me there.[7] Saw Robert Preston.

WEDNESDAY 14 DECEMBER. Dined at Mrs. Bosville's, and was a little at her rout. Then Malone's, wonderfully well.

THURSDAY 15 DECEMBER. Visited Langton. Was undecided. Dined evening and supper Mr. Ward's and was rational and quiet. Mrs. Abington there.[8]

FRIDAY 16 DECEMBER. Awaked gloomily ill. Sallied forth in a kind of despair. Breakfasted with Seward, and was a little relieved by talking of melancholy and hearing how he often was afflicted with it.[9] I was sensible it was wrong to speak of it. But the torment was such that I could not conceal it. Was at the Mount Coffee-house with Mr. Bosville, who consulted me on his affairs confidentially (he being greatly in debt), and amidst my hypochondria I gave him judicious advice. At Malone's awhile assisting in making a table of contents of my *Tour*. Courtenay came. I was now resolved to set out for Scotland on Sunday evening in the stage. This was a comfortable thought. Yet I was quite undecided as to trying the English bar, and this made me wretched. I dined at worthy Langton's; by agreement nobody there. We talked of my indecision. He was for a trial. I was all restlessness and vexation. He started a doubt as to my leaving London without waiting on the King, who had behaved so handsomely as to the grandson of King James II, who had appeared pleased with my *Tour*, and who had been

[6]Macdonald returned his letter of 26 November, accepting all of Courtenay's scorings, which Courtenay had made with a fine pen. Much still remained unscored that Boswell would have found unpleasant, but nothing that he could have considered "personally injurious to the feelings of a man of honour." Macdonald wrote: "Mr. Boswell has discovered some expressions in that letter which he did not relish; there are also some in his *Journal* which Mr. Boswell has acknowledged with much truth to have struck him as likely to give offence. . . . Lord Macdonald has of himself obliterated certain passages which he apprehends might be misconstrued, and from motives of reciprocal courtesy agrees to leave out in his second edition some few passages which come scratched to hand." Very neat. One would not have thought him capable of it.
[7]Because of his qualified defence in the *Tour to the Hebrides* of Johnson's strictures on Scotland in his *Journey to the Western Islands* and in the *Tour* itself.
[8]The former flower-girl who had been Queen of Comedy with Garrick at Drury Lane and now reigned at Covent Garden.
[9]William Seward, man of letters and a pronounced hypochondriac. It is reported that when he made the "western tour" of England in 1781 he called about his health on a doctor or an apothecary in every town.

told by Langton that I was come.[1] I ran home and found an admirable letter from my wife and a very friendly one from Lord Rockville.[2] I grew better. Passed the evening at Malone's (Courtenay there); felt myself quite well, though undecided even as to my going on Sunday.

SATURDAY 17 DECEMBER. Not so well, but pretty easy. General Paoli was for my staying for the King. Went and called on Mr. James Chalmers about Mr. Bruce Campbell.[3] Found him civil. He was against my coming to Westminster Hall, as a desertion of Auchinleck. Went to my tailor's to order a suit of Court mourning.[4] Dilly's a little. Tried to fast today, but being faint breakfasted at a coffee-house. Called on Mr. Atkins;[5] was pleased with his steady sense and engaged to dine with him on Monday. Called at Malone's and found a note from Courtenay pressing me to meet him at dinner at Lord Lucan's, though I had refused. Went home, dressed, and went. Grew much better. Lady Lucan exceedingly entertaining.[6] His Lordship hospitable. No company there, only his son and Miss Molesworth, his niece. Was pleased to see an Irish family that goes home every year, yet comfortable in London.[7] Courtenay and I passed the evening at Malone's. Home before twelve and had a pleasing chat with the General.

SUNDAY 18 DECEMBER. At home all day calm. The General talked steadily of his faith in revelation. My brother T.D. sat with me some time; complained of my never almost seeing him, and pressed upon

[1] In a letter to the King (6 June 1785) Boswell had requested permission to style the Stuart leader of the uprising of 1745 "Prince Charles" rather than "the Pretender" when referring to him in the *Tour to the Hebrides*. When Boswell pressed the question at the levee on 15 June, the King appeared to demur at "Prince Charles" but explicitly approved "the grandson of King James the Second." Boswell used the latter style in introducing Charles Edward in the *Tour* but thereafter called him "Prince" because (he said) his mother was a daughter of the King of Poland and he was therefore a prince by courtesy.

[2] The Hon. Alexander ("Sandy") Gordon, an intimate Scotch friend only one year older than Boswell who had been raised to the bench of the Court of Session, 1 July 1784, as Lord Rockville.

[3] Bruce Campbell, Boswell's second cousin and supervisor of Auchinleck, was trying to hold Sir George Colebrooke, owner of Grongar in Ayrshire, to a lease on that property which Campbell had negotiated with the former owner. James Chalmers, Writer to the Signet (a superior class of solicitor), acted for Colebrooke.

[4] The Court was in mourning for Prince George of Mecklenburg-Strelitz, youngest brother of the Queen.

[5] See below, 19 December 1785.

[6] A clever copyist in water-colours much admired by Horace Walpole, she later devoted sixteen years, 1790–1806, to illustrating Shakespeare's history plays, published in five volumes.

[7] They were from Castlebar, Co. Mayo.

me my duty as the head of our Family, entreating me to reside at Auchinleck. I was moved, and regretted much my feverish fancy for London. There was a numerous company at the General's. In the evening I went early to bed. A poor existence. Giacomo Pietro and Giuseppe, the General's servants, were attentive.

MONDAY 19 DECEMBER. Not so well as yesterday. Breakfasted Malone's; called on Courtenay and found him. Dined with Mr. Atkins, Russia merchant in Austin Friars, formerly proprietor of *Hern*, who showed me all respect as Laird of Auchinleck.[8] Evening Malone's.

TUESDAY 20 DECEMBER. Awaked *quite well.* Strange. Went to Seward and showed myself recovered. Breakfasted with Malone and revised the last sheets of the second edition of my *Tour*. Wrote to my dear wife that I was *now* coming home, not for *relief* but for the *pleasure* of being with her and the children. Malone and I dined at Courtenay's. I was quite happy. My mind saw rest and comfort whether I should resolve to take a house in London or not. *My wife's inclination shall determine.* Let me remember this.

WEDNESDAY 21 DECEMBER. Went to the levee at St. James's. The foreign ambassadors and many more were there, so the King had not much time for me. He asked me when I came from the north. I said, "About a month ago." And (as an apology for not having waited on His Majesty sooner) added, "I have not been well." The King said, "You have been confined." This was all that passed, and I was a little disappointed that my book was not mentioned. I, however, made allowance on account of what I have marked, and I considered that as a report had circulated that the King was not pleased with me, it was of consequence for me to be seen well received at Court.[9] I then hurried home, changed my clothes, and got my portmanteau and all my things ready, and drove in a hackney-coach with them to Mr. Malone's, where I dined; nobody there but Mr. Courtenay and his son. I was wonderfully well, and went at night to Dilly's.

THURSDAY 22 DECEMBER. Rose wonderfully well. Secured my place in the stage-coach to York, to set out at night. Breakfasted with my brother. Met Dr. Johnson's Frank in the street, and he promised to search for every scrap of his

[8] Hern was now a part of the estate of Auchinleck.
[9] Langton later told Boswell that the King had been displeased by his inquiries concerning the style of Charles Edward, though Boswell had not thought so at the time. See below, 23 April 1788.

master's handwriting and give all to me.[1] It vexed me to be told that he had burnt some letters from Dr. Johnson to Mrs. Johnson. I called once more on my amiable Malone, and he and I paid a visit to Sir Joshua. I was in a sort of dissipation of mind from my late gloom and the prospect of a winter journey to Scotland and seeing my family. Dined and drank tea at Dilly's with Mr. and Mrs. Knox, Braithwaite, Sharp, Rev. Mr. Fell (whom I was glad to meet, though we had little conversation: he appeared very modest),[2] and the Rev. Mr. Fullarton from Jamaica. Set out about nine. Left London quite easily, as one at home in it and soon to return. Had hard travelling with various company without going to bed till I reached York on Saturday night. I was comfortable at

24 DEC. the Black Swan Inn, and next day (Christmas and Sunday)
25 DEC. I worshipped and received the Holy Sacrament in the Cathedral. Mr. Mason was the prebendary in residence. He officiated with great propriety, and I received from his hand the consecrated bread. I had many thoughts passing in my mind while I beheld him as the author of *Elfrida*, etc., and the friend of Gray.[3] He courteously asked me to dine with him. I went home for a while with Dr. Burgh.[4] He and I and Mr. Croft, another prebendary, dined with Mr. Mason. We had a good dinner and good wine, and he did the honours of his table very well, without any affectation. He, however, attacked my great friend Dr. Johnson; said he was not great in any one branch—he had only arrogance and an odd manner of expression, and was flattered by people about him who were his superiors in parts. Dr. Burgh joined. Mason said he wondered a man of my spirit could submit to him. That long before he had heard my father's epithet of *Ursa Major*, he

[1] Frank Barber, Johnson's black servant and residuary legatee, made good his promise. He seems also to have been the agent through whom Boswell's sealed letters to Johnson were returned (as Johnson had directed) within a few weeks of his death.
[2] Vicesimus Knox, D.D., author of the popular *Essays Moral and Literary*, 1778–79, which Boswell had thought superior to his own *Hypochondriack* essays; Richard Sharp, a hat manufacturer, generally styled "Conversation Sharp" because of his outstanding talent for social talk; and the Rev. John Fell, a dissenting clergyman and essayist.
[3] William Mason, minor poet and dramatist, whom Gray liked to call "Scroddles."
[4] William Burgh, D.C.L., Mason's close friend. He had recently brought out an edition of Mason's poem *The English Garden*.

had called him a *bear on stilts*.[5] He said Johnson had applied
to him to write in the *Rambler*. (I doubt some mistake.) He
refused, and ever after Johnson was violent against him.[6] He
said he was very angry that he was not attacked by Johnson
in my *Tour*. "It looks," said he, "as if one was nobody." I told
him truly that he was not mentioned during that period, but
he should appear in the *Life*. He said one such Christian as
Johnson did more hurt to religion than many Humes. I expressed my wonder at his differing so much from me. He
said Mr. Gray had read my *Account of Corsica* with great pleasure. This flattered me highly.[7] He said except myself and a
very few more (about six) he never had known Scotchmen
have the sense of ridicule—*humour* I understood he meant.
He called for gingerbread nuts after dinner and eat[8] some,
saying this was his dessert; it was good for digestion. Said I,
"This will be told." He and I attended evening prayers, and
he invited me back to coffee and tea. I went accordingly, and
was very well. He repeated an epigram which he had made
on Johnson's *Irene* when it first appeared: how it agreed with
the rule that terror and pity should be mixed in tragedy, for
the story was horrid, the diction pitiful. He, however, would
not give me it. I said I would show him what Dr. Johnson
said against him before printing it. He seemed not to desire
this, but I shall do it.[9] He took me by the hand as I was going
away and politely hoped I did not take amiss his talking so

---

[5]Boswell reported in the *Tour* (6 November 1773) that Lord Auchinleck had imparted
this "sly abrupt expression" to another judge in the Court of Session while Johnson
stood out of hearing. It was common to compare Johnson with a bear. Mason had
called Johnson "a bear upon stilts" in a letter dated 26 June 1782 (Hyde Collection).
[6]Boswell was probably justified in his scepticism as to Mason's having been asked to
write for the *Rambler*. Johnson thought little of Mason's poetry and called him a prig
and a Whig; Mason disliked Johnson in part because of his low esteem of Gray's poetry.
In general, the Walpole-Gray-Mason faction disliked Johnson and vice versa.
[7]Mason kindly suppressed the less flattering portion of Gray's criticism. Referring
especially to the "Memoirs of Pascal Paoli," the last section of *An Account of Corsica*,
Gray told Horace Walpole, "The pamphlet proves what I have always maintained,
that any fool may write a most valuable book by chance, if he will only tell us what he
heard and saw with veracity. Of Mr. Boswell's truth I have not the least suspicion,
because I am sure he could invent nothing of this kind. The true title of this part of
his work is 'A Dialogue between a Green-goose and a Hero' " (*Horace Walpole's Correspondence with Thomas Gray*, ed. W. S. Lewis, et al., 1948, xiv. 174–75).
[8]Ate, pronounced "et."
[9]There is no record of his having done so.

freely of Dr. Johnson. "By no means," said I. "As he never altered me as to you, so you never alter me as to him." I had much speculation in my own mind on my being thus entertained on Christmas Day by Mr. Mason, of whom Temple and I used long ago to talk with such admiration.[1] But I find nothing in life is equal in *reality* to *previous imagination*; at least it is very seldom so. But I was not a fair judge in the present state of my spirits. I went to my inn and took a little burnt port and went to bed.

MONDAY 26 DECEMBER. Set out early in the diligence; nobody with me but Mr. Somerville, (I believe) partner with Allan and Steuart.[2] We had a safe journey and arrived at
28 DEC. Edinburgh about four o'clock on Wednesday the 28. I felt a little strange but not so much so as I expected. Had the highest consolation in seeing my dear wife and children, and the cloud of melancholy was quite dissipated by *experiencing* that I could so soon be at home from London.

THURSDAY 29 DECEMBER. Cold weather. At home all day except seeing Grange, who had been very gloomy, but was better.[3]

FRIDAY 30 DECEMBER. Had visits of Sir W. Forbes, Captain A. Cochrane, Balmuto, and Mr. Stobie.[4] At home all day. Enjoyed my tranquillity, but dreaded a relapse.

SATURDAY 31 DECEMBER. Mr. John Dundas and Mr. Neilson were with me on Dr. Webster's trust.[5] Walked out with Captain A. Cochrane and dined with Commissioner Cochrane, who was very glad to see me. Mr. Stobie there. It was a great comfort to me after my dreary suffering to find old ideas of Sir John Cochrane of Ochiltree, and of Culross,

---

[1]The Rev. William Johnson Temple, whom Boswell often identifies as his "old and most intimate friend," had shared Boswell's literary enthusiasms when they were students at the University of Edinburgh.

[2]Allan and Steuart were bankers in Edinburgh; Somerville is not further identified.

[3]John Johnston, of Grange, a farm in Dumfriesshire; "writer" (solicitor) and another close friend of Boswell's since their student days at the University of Edinburgh. Like Boswell, he was a hypochondriac and a Tory with a romantic attachment to the Stuarts.

[4]Sir William Forbes of Pitsligo, Bt., head of Forbes, Hunter, and Company, the most distinguished private banking-house in Edinburgh, and Boswell's banker and confidant; Andrew Cochrane, captain in the Royal Navy, a cousin of Boswell's mother; Claude Irvine Boswell of Balmuto (raised to the Court of Session in 1799 as Lord Balmuto), Lady Auchinleck's brother, and also Boswell's cousin once removed; and John Stobie, formerly Lord Auchinleck's law clerk, now agent for his widow.

[5]Dr. Alexander Webster, minister of the Tolbooth Church, Boswell's uncle by marriage and one of his convivial older friends, had died in January 1784.

etc., revived.[6] I just enjoyed the *present*, seeing the Commissioner easy and cheerful. Heated myself somewhat with wine, which made me a little violent in my temper when I came home. Visited my brother John. ——.[7]

[6]Basil Cochrane, Commissioner of Customs in Scotland, lived at Pinkie, about six miles from Edinburgh. He was uncle to Capt. Andrew Cochrane and to Boswell's mother, Euphemia Erskine. Sir John Cochrane, second son of the first Earl of Dundonald, had founded the line at Ochiltree. Commissioner Cochrane and his sister, Euphemia Cochrane, Boswell's grandmother, had grown up in Culross Abbey House, about twenty miles from Edinburgh. Cochrane had been sympathetic to Boswell in the years when he was quarrelling with his father.
[7]Boswell was attentive all his adult life to his morose younger brother, a lieutenant in the army retired on half-pay and periodically confined to private asylums for the insane. The dash is one of Boswell's symbols for conjugal intercourse.

1786

SUNDAY 1 JANUARY. Heard Dr. Blair preach an admirable sermon on "Peace be with thee, peace be with thy household," etc.[8] Visited him between sermons and found him wonderfully pleased with my *Tour* and Court of Session letter.[9] Heard a Mr. Finlayson preach in the afternoon. My brother John drank tea with us. In the evening, heard my children say divine lessons. Grange supped with us. The result of being abroad this day convinced me that my *imaginations* as to *conjectures* about my settling in London, and *difficulties* of various sorts, were only in my own mind. Grange supped with us, and grew quite comfortable. ——.

MONDAY 2 JANUARY. Lady Auchinleck paid us a visit. Grange and his nephew Brown dined. I had read in Blackstone for some days. I was pretty well, but had no vivid views of life. Sir William and Lady Forbes and Mr. Nairne supped with us.[1] I was glad to feel that the return to domestic and friendly intercourse was simple and might be at any time——.[2]

TUESDAY 3 JANUARY. Having drank wine the day before both at dinner and supper, and the frost being intense, I had a headache, and breakfasted calmly in bed. I had done some good since I came home in assisting Sandy in Latin and Veronica and Phemie in French. Mr. G. Wallace paid me a visit. His intelligent and firm conversation and his opinion that I should make a fair trial of the English bar (though he did not imagine I could have great success); and he suggested that there are a great many places in the gift of the Lord Chancellor, who might give me one.[3] He was clear that if the trial should not succeed,

[8] I Samuel 25:6. Dr. Hugh Blair, Regius Professor of Rhetoric and Belles-Lettres in the University of Edinburgh, was one of the two ministers of the New (or High) Church, which occupied the east end of St. Giles's Church. Blair's sermons, which he published, were celebrated throughout Great Britain and in America.
[9] *Letter to the People of Scotland*, 1785.
[1] William Nairne (later Bt.), a close friend in the Faculty of Advocates. He was appointed to the Court of Session in March of this year as Lord Dunsinnan.
[2] The dash here may indicate only an unfinished sentence.
[3] Boswell forgot the beginning of this sentence, which may have been written at two different times, as a new page begins with "and he suggested." George Wallace was an advocate for whom Boswell expressed admiration as early as 1767. The Lord Chancellor was Edward Thurlow.

I need be under no difficulty of returning to the Court of Session. In short, I was much the better for hearing his thoughts. Lunardi (at the earnest desire of my children I invited him) and Corri and Miss Mary Grant supped with us.[4] We had a cheerful gay evening, and I thought with pleasure of having a house in London. ——.

WEDNESDAY 4 JANUARY. Dr. Gillespie sat a long time with me, and his active mind cheered me. Mr. James Donaldson was also with me.[5] Grange and his nephew Brown paid me a forenoon visit. I had been visited before this by Sir William Dick and Mr. and Mrs. Mingay.[6] I went and sat an hour with Mr. George Wallace, who read me part of a curious essay he had written on the east wind. George Campbell dined with us.[7] He and I drank tea with Lady Auchinleck, nobody with her but her old mother. I was quieted and had my loose fancy consolidated by her steady sense and firmness of spirit, and by the recollection of my worthy respectable father. What a blessing it is to have a strong mind! In the evening helped my children with their lessons, but still I was so sickly in mind that I could not *feel* the advantage of good education. Mr. Wood had been with me one morning. He was of opinion that if I had not come down to see my family, my disease might have pressed upon me to such a degree that I might not have recovered for some time.[8] The frost was intense. ——.

THURSDAY 5 JANUARY. Very bad weather. At home all day. Helped my children with their lessons. Played at whist with my wife and some of them. Sir Archibald Grant visited us in the forenoon, Robert Boswell in the evening.[9]

FRIDAY 6 JANUARY. Went with my wife and two eldest daughters

---

[4]Vincenzo Lunardi, a celebrated balloonist, had made his most recent ascent in Edinburgh on 20 December 1785, when he fell into the sea and narrowly escaped drowning. Domenico Corri, a native of Rome, conducted the concerts of the Musical Society in Edinburgh.

[5]Dr. Gillespie had been Lord Auchinleck's physician by retainer in his last years; he also attended Mrs. Boswell. Donaldson, printer and bookseller, was editor of the *Edinburgh Advertiser*.

[6]Sir William was the eldest son and heir of the late Sir Alexander Dick, and Ann Mingay the only daughter and heiress of the late Dr. Alexander Webster.

[7]George James Campbell, the orphaned son of James Campbell of Treesbank and Mrs. Boswell's sister Mary; he was now almost eighteen years old. Boswell, one of his legal guardians, and particularly attentive to his interests, was trying to place him in life.

[8]"Lang Sandy" Wood, a skilful and popular surgeon, was Boswell's friend as well as the family physician.

[9]Grant was an advocate, and Robert Boswell, W.S., was a first cousin. He was Boswell's business agent in Scotland.

to see the model of a balloon in the Outer Parliament House. Walked in it and in the Inner House with curious sensations. Went a little into the Advocates' Library. Felt how easily I could return to my place as an advocate. But it seemed a narrow sphere. Sat some time with Sir William Forbes. Called on Lord President; was told he was very busy with his papers. Left a message that I had called but would not disturb him. Called on Harry Erskine; not at home.[1] Sat a good while with Maclaurin, who was of opinion I would succeed in Westminster Hall, and if not, that there was not the least objection to my returning to the Court of Session.[2] It relieved me to find that what I had dreaded as alarming, dangerous, and ruinous was a simple and easy experiment. After dinner even three glasses of port heated me and made me restless and weary and fretful. Tea did me good. Knockroon, who had come to town today, was with us and did me good.[3] My wife was not well tonight.

SATURDAY 7 JANUARY. Visited Grange, as I have done many times which are not mentioned. Bad day. Life was passed much in the same way as it has been on several days since I came last down. My brother John and Mr. Lawrie[4] dined with us. ——.

SUNDAY 8 JANUARY. I set out, intending to walk to Prestonfield,[5] being uneasy that I had delayed so long to pay my respects to the family of my valuable departed friend. But as I passed by Mr. Gib's seceding meeting-house, I asked if he was to preach, and being informed he was, I thought I would gratify my curiosity in experiencing in some degree the vulgar and dreary fanaticism of the last century in Scotland. So in I went and heard him preach with great fluency, in their way, though now very old.[6] A probationer also preached, so I was too late for Prestonfield. They did not preach long, and there was nothing wild, but just the common old-fashioned Presbyterian way of haranguing. I sat with Mr. G. Wallace an hour, and then heard Dr.

[1] The Lord President, Robert Dundas, was Henry Dundas's elder half-brother. Henry Erskine, a popular and respected advocate, was a leader of the Opposition in Scotland. He was a remote relation.
[2] John Maclaurin, one of Boswell's closer friends among the Faculty of Advocates, shared his interest in writing essays and verse.
[3] John Boswell of Knockroon, "writer" and clerk to the Commissioners of Supply in Ayr; a collateral descendant of the Auchinleck line and a friend.
[4] Boswell's clerk for almost fifteen years.
[5] Sir William Dick's handsome estate, located below Arthur's Seat. It was very often the goal of Boswell's Sunday walks during Sir Alexander's time.
[6] The Rev. Adam Gib ("Pope Gib"), the dogmatic but courageous advocate of a strict Presbyterianism, now in his seventy-second year, still commanded a large following at the meeting-house at No. 169, Nicholson Street.

Robertson preach in his own church. He seemed to be quite sound and entire. But his doctrine as to prayer was the *imperfect* system which Ogden has so ably refuted.[7] In the evening heard the children say divine lessons. ——.

MONDAY 9 JANUARY. My wife and I went in a coach and paid a visit at Prestonfield. I was much affected to think that Sir Alexander was gone. Grange dined with us. In the afternoon I received a long letter from the Lord Chancellor which I thought seemed to decide against my venturing in Westminster Hall. It sunk me a good deal. But my excellent wife suggested that I could not take it as a *decision*, but only as an able evasion of taking any charge of me.[8] I was somewhat vexed by a letter from Colonel Craufurd complaining as if I had abandoned the cause of juries in civil causes because I had owned I was now convinced it was unreasonable to oppose an augmentation of the judges' salaries.[9] I saw it was very wrong to *own any change of opinion* unless when it is absolutely necessary to do it.

TUESDAY 10 JANUARY. Sir Charles and Colonel George Preston visited us.[1] It pleased me that I was every day of *some* use to my children in assisting them in their lessons. Mr. George Wallace came and stayed dinner. I had a bowel complaint from cold, and drank rather too much warm punch. He made my staying here, going and returning—in short, doing as I should find agreeable—to be not at all embarrassing. But I had no keen and high impulses. Dr. Grant came in the evening for some time.

WEDNESDAY 11 JANUARY. Very bad weather. I was somewhat uneasy from having taken punch yesterday. It always disagrees with me. My wife talked to me most rationally of taking care of my estate and living within my income, and thus (whatever trials I should make) being independent.

[7]Samuel Ogden, Boswell's favourite sermon writer, maintained that intercessory prayer is doubly efficacious: it improves him who prays, and may be of advantage to him who is prayed for. Boswell detects in Dr. William Robertson, historian, Principal of the University of Edinburgh, and minister of the Old Greyfriars, a tendency to limit the benefits of prayer to the intercessor.

[8]Boswell had high hopes that his career at the English bar would be aided by Lord Thurlow. He wrote to Thurlow an extraordinary letter outlining these hopes, which with Thurlow's reply is printed below, in the Appendix.

[9]In recent letters to the newspapers, Boswell had favoured augmenting the salaries of the judges of the Court of Session, which he had opposed in his *Letter to the People of Scotland*, 1785, so long as the number of judges was not diminished. This point had nothing to do with his demand for the introduction of juries in civil causes. Lt.-Col. John Walkinshaw Craufurd was a friend and vocal supporter on public issues.

[1]Both Boswell's first cousins once removed: Sir Charles Preston of Valleyfield, Bt., Fife, and his younger brother, lieutenant-colonel in the Marines.

THURSDAY 12 JANUARY. Was at a meeting of the curators of the Advocates' Library.[2] Felt myself very easy. Lord Monboddo came into the Library. I bowed to him, but he did not speak to me. I understood afterwards that he was violent against me.[3] I did not care. I considered that it would make him *fair game* in Dr. Johnson's *Life*. I sat some time in the room behind Creech's shop, and had an impression of Edinburgh being a very good place.[4] In the evening attended a meeting of Dr. Webster's trustees. So I was quite Scottish today. The sight of the old house affected me.[5]

FRIDAY 13 JANUARY. Breakfasted at Lady Colville's; was very well received and asked to dine. Walked into town with the Hon. A. E., and compared notes on hypochondria.[6] He had felt its making one imagine oneself inferior to every mortal. I went out and dined. He and the ladies all thought that my making a trial of the English bar was rational, since I had such a desire for it, and I might afterwards be quiet. He and I drank claret cordially till near ten at night and had a great deal of good conversation. But I did not see the ladies again.

SATURDAY 14 JANUARY. Not being in the habit of drinking much wine, I awaked uneasy. I walked out to Lady Colville's and made my apology to the ladies, who told me they were happy I had done so well. My spirits, however, were a good deal sunk. The Hon. A. E. and I walked into town, and for a large portion of the way had the company of Sir John Whitefoord,[7] who met us. He wished I were returned from my trial of London, for that "our lots were not cast there."[8] I had at dinner Mr. French, Mr. Cauvin, Mr. Stalker, my children's masters,

[2] He had been appointed a curator on 24 December 1784.

[3] And with some cause. Monboddo (James Burnett), judge in the Court of Session and a prolific writer on philosophy, anthropology, and linguistics, was ahead of his time in studying man as one of the animals. Boswell had referred to him in the *Letter* as a "grotesque philosopher, whom ludicrous *fable* represents as going about avowing his hunger, and wagging his tail, fain to become cannibal, and eat his deceased brethren." Monboddo and his beliefs provide a running joke in the first half of the *Tour*.

[4] The bookshop of William Creech (Burns's first Edinburgh publisher), just north of St. Giles's, was a literary meeting place.

[5] Dr. Webster's house on Castle Hill.

[6] Elizabeth Erskine, Lady Colville, a childless widow, her unmarried sister, Lady Anne Erskine, and her brother, the Hon. Andrew Erskine, former army officer, poet, and hypochondriac, lived at Drumsheugh House, just north-west of the New Town of Edinburgh. They were very old friends of Boswell's.

[7] Of Ballochmyle, Boswell's near neighbour and Erskine's intimate friend. Whitefoord frequently joined Erskine on his long walks, and Erskine being tall and shy and his companion short, they were called the "gowk and the titling": the cuckoo and the meadow pipit (John Kay, *Original Portraits*, 1877, iii. 59).

[8] A generalized reference to the choosing of land by lot in the Bible, as in Joshua, chs. 13–23.

and Mr. Legat, who engraved the print from my picture of Mary, Queen of Scots. I had one of these days walked with Principal Robertson, who was much pleased with the print, and in good humour with my *Tour*.[9]

SUNDAY 15 JANUARY. Went to the New Church in the forenoon. Lord Rockville paid me a visit, and was clear that I should appear in court in my wig and gown as usual. The children said divine lessons. Went with Sir Charles and Colonel George Preston and dined soberly at Commissioner Cochrane's, supposing that we should not all meet again.[1] Sir Charles drank tea at our house, and he and George and Grange supped. It was comfortable to feel myself as much *at home* as ever.

MONDAY 16 JANUARY. [*Nil.*]

TUESDAY 17 JANUARY. Went to the Court of Session, and first walked in with my hat and stick as a gentleman. My spirits were good, so that though I felt a little awkwardly, I was not uneasy. My brethren stared a good deal at me in the Inner House. Upon which I said, "I must go and put on my wig and gown, not to be particular." Having done so, I walked about and shook hands with numbers, and talked quite easily of having two strings to my bow, and not ceasing to be an *advocate* by taking my degree as a *barrister*; and I was most agreeably surprised to find that I might go and come as [I] found most agreeable. I then went with my wife and two eldest daughters and called on Lady Auchinleck; not in. Sat some time with Mr. Robert Boswell and his family, and with Mr. Baron Gordon.[2] Drank tea with Sir Archibald Grant very cordially.

WEDNESDAY 18 JANUARY. Again attended the Court of Session, and had this day a Petition for Fairlie, which I had drawn with great care, put in as a proof that I might practise when I chose to do it. I drank tea with Mr. George Wallace.

THURSDAY 19 JANUARY. This morning my Petition for Fairlie was moved in court, and I took care to support it by a few words from the bar, that my voice might again be heard. I was listened to with attention, and my Petition had the effect of showing the judges that

[9]The print of Mary, Queen of Scots, being forced to resign her crown, dated 2 January 1786, was published in London by John Boydell. Boswell had taken the theme from Principal Robertson's *History of Scotland* and commissioned the picture by Gavin Hamilton, a fellow Scot with a considerable reputation as a portrait painter, when they were both in Rome in 1765.

[1]The Prestons' late mother was the Commissioner's sister. He was about eighty-five.

[2]Cosmo Gordon, one of the four Barons of the Court of Exchequer, the superior court with jurisdiction over customs, excise, and all other revenue matters.

their former interlocutor, which had been pronounced in my absence, *nem. con.*, was not just; so it was ordered to be answered.[3] The Lord President then said, "My Lords, I yesterday found fault with papers I have much more pleasure in commending. And I must say that this petition by my friend Mr. Boswell (whom I am happy to see here) is very well drawn, both as to matter and manner. And let me tell him, as we know he can do so well, we will not take worse off his hand." I bowed respectfully and said, "I am always happy when I am honoured with the approbation of your Lordships."[4] He then sent one of the clerks of court to invite me to dine with him next day. I went round to the back of his chair and told him I was very sorry I was engaged next day to the christening of Balmuto's son. "But," said I, "I won't be without my dinner with your Lordship. I'll wait upon you any day you please." "Come today at four," said he. This public praise and this invitation (which I took care to make known) had a wonderful effect. The narrow-minded and timid were confounded at my being so received after my *Letter* upon diminishing the number of the judges, etc. I had a very hearty day with the President, and it would have been more so had not Balmuto been there, for he was a check on my gaiety. There was nobody else but Mr. Liston, minister of Aberdour, Newbigging his clerk, and a young man who seemed to be a reader to him or one in some such capacity. We drank till near nine. His Lordship and I took a better share than the rest. He was now almost deprived of sight, but his animal spirits were as good as ever. His coarseness was not pleasing. But upon the whole we did admirably.

FRIDAY 20 JANUARY. Appeared in the Court of Session, and talked of my jovial interview of yesterday. I felt with disgust the vulgar familiarity of some of my brethren, and contrasted it with the manners of my London friends. It provoked me a little that my literary superiority seemed to have no effect here. I went to Prestonfield and attended a meeting of the guardians of Sir Alexander Dick's younger children. I then was present at the baptism of Balmuto's son and heir, and dined with Balmuto; Dr. Blair, etc., there. Not London, yet I *judged* it *unreasonable* to be dissatisfied in Edinburgh.

SATURDAY 21 JANUARY. One evening of this week Grange supped with us. I appeared today in the Court of Session and attended a meeting of the Faculty of Advocates, where the Judges' Bill was *certainly* to be considered. But upon Lord Advocate's saying that he *believed* it

[3] Alexander Fairlie, a noted agricultural improver, was being sued for non-payment by Thomas Clayton, a plasterer, who had worked on Fairlie's new house. Boswell, a good friend of Fairlie's, having offered to submit a petition on his behalf, drew one up on very short notice.

[4] The Court nevertheless upheld its earlier decision in favour of Clayton by one vote.

would be given up so far as concerned diminishing the number, they agreed to *adjourn* the consideration of it, and though I moved that as our opinion might have some influence we should now consider it, not one would second me. I heartily despised their servility.[5] I dined at the annual meeting of Mundell's scholars.[6] Did not get drunk.

SUNDAY 22 JANUARY. New Church forenoon; sat awhile with Lord Rockville, also with Grange, who dined with us after sermons and drank tea, as did Mr. Nairne. I stayed at home all the afternoon and evening, read the Bible, and heard the children say divine lessons. Was not by any means well as I could wish to be, nor have I been so for some days. Veronica alarmed us by spitting a little blood; we hoped it was a stress in throwing up from a disordered stomach.[7]

MONDAY 23 JANUARY. The forenoon was wasted at home in idleness. I walked in the street a little before dinner. I was melancholy from thinking that I was so soon to leave my wife and children, and was uncertain what plan of life to pursue; sat awhile with Grange, who was himself much hipped. Lady Colville and Lady Anne Erskine drank tea with us and played whist. My views were dim and dreary. Yet I thought I might yet enjoy existence.

TUESDAY 24 JANUARY. Little done. My brother John drank a glass with me after dinner. I drank tea at Dr. Grant's.

WEDNESDAY 25 JANUARY. Miss Preston dined with us. I heated myself a little with wine. Drank tea at old Mr. Spence's, then visited Lord Eskgrove, who was very kind.

THURSDAY 26 JANUARY. Having resolved to set out for London next day, I put some books, etc., in order. Went and heard Mr. French's class. Visited Lord Dumfries and Lady Dundonald[8] (if not a day before), and saw no difficulty in trying London. Visited M. Dupont in

[5] Ilay Campbell, the Lord Advocate, had presented the Diminishing Bill in the House of Commons and published a pamphlet in its defence. The Faculty of Advocates depended for preferment on Henry Dundas, who was the basic sponsor of the Bill. In June 1786 the Commons approved an increase in the judges' salaries; the rest of the Bill was dropped.

[6] An association which included many notable men begun after the death of the schoolmaster James Mundell in 1762. Boswell had missed few of the annual dinners since 1772, although he had hated Mundell's academy and left it at the age of eight.

[7] She had previously spat blood in August 1781, but the journal records no further symptoms. She died of consumption, however, in September 1795, only four months after her father.

[8] Patrick Macdowall-Crichton, fifth Earl of Dumfries, whose estate adjoined Auchinleck, and Jean (Stuart) Cochrane, Countess of Dundonald, widow (thirty years younger) of Boswell's maternal granduncle, the eighth Earl of Dundonald. Lady Dundonald lived at Belleville in Edinburgh.

the evening.[9] Grange supped with us. It was animating to find my children desirous of going to London.[1] I thought they would be improved by it.

FRIDAY 27 JANUARY. My son Alexander kindly accompanied me to the inn from whence the Newcastle fly set out at six in the morning. Mr. John Wilson, son of my old friend Mr. William Wilson who gave me my first fee, went with me, and as he had been for some years in the profession of an attorney and solicitor in London, he entertained me usefully with information upon points of practice, and made me feel solidly as to London. The truth is that *imaginary* London, gilded with all the brilliancy of warm fancy as I have viewed it, and London as a scene of real business, are quite different; and as the *changes* of fanciful sensation are very painful, it is more comfortable to have the duller sensation of reality. We

28, stayed on Saturday night and Sunday all day at Newcastle.

29 JAN. Mr. Leighton, the surgeon, supped with us on Saturday, and on Sunday we dined and drank tea at Dr. Hall's, where was Mr. Warrilow, an English Jesuit.[2] I attended part of the service in two different churches. The weather was uncommonly mild.[3] We had a good journey to London, where we arrived

1 FEB. on Wednesday 1 February, about five in the afternoon. Mr.

---

[9]So far as we know, his last visit to the Rev. Pierre Loumeau Dupont, minister of the French church in Edinburgh, to whom he had been attached for many years. M. Dupont died that March, at the age of eighty-seven.

[1]Veronica, at least, appears to have been motivated by *his* desires. She wrote to him the day after he left home, "My dear Papa, I hope by the time you receive this you will have arrived safe at London and have got the house. We were all very sorry to part with you, but hope you will be happier in London than here."

[2]Boswell became a familiar visitor at Dr. Hall's when his brother John was resident there during periods of insanity. The Jesuit order was suppressed in England from 1773 to 1814.

[3]Among the Boswell Papers there is also a leaf, torn from a small pocket notebook, bearing the following memorandum: "Newcastle, 28 January 1786. You felt *serenely* that there is nothing wild or even difficult in making a trial of your abilities as an English barrister, and that the transition from London to Auchinleck, and connection between them, may appear quite easy and plain. All depends upon the state of the mind, and *that* probably on the state of the blood and other corporeal circumstances. Many Scotch people are not strange in London. Was not Lady Betty Bruce [Boswell's grandmother] much there with her father, Lord Kincardine? Was not Sir William Gordon's family there? Are not numberless worthy, quiet families there? The very *hopes* there are better than *realities* in a narrow sphere to a man of *fancy* who is not without a *moderate fortune*. Occasional clouds pass away as if they never had been, and then all the train of events and variety of ideas are valuable and pleasing."

Wilson and I and the Rev. Mr. Cooper, another passenger, dined at our inn; and then I went to Dilly's, where we had a cheerful supper with Reed, Braithwaite, Sharp, etc.

THURSDAY 2 FEBRUARY. Up clear and well. Strange how different from myself when last in town. Met Sir Charles Preston. Visited Captain Preston. Went to the treasurer's office, Inner Temple, and learned from Mr. Spinks all the forms of being called to the bar. Met Courtenay. Home with him, and was in perfect spirits. He and I dined with Malone. Before this had visited Mrs. Strange and heard all about Hoole's house, which I inspected; and though I found it old-fashioned and part of it dark, resolved to fix it. Rev. Mr. Hoole went with me to Mr. Bang's in Lyon's Inn, the attorney who was to let it.[4] He promised to get his client's answer next week. Dilly's, evening.

FRIDAY 3 FEBRUARY. Visited my brother T.D., and perceived that my determined confidence in coming to London overpowered opposition. With Malone a little. Also with Sir Joshua. Dined Inner Temple very comfortably. Tea T.D., quite well. In the forenoon had visited Mr. Rudd, Mr. Dilly's attorney, and talked of Mr. Dilly's cause.[5] Evening Rudd, Braithwaite, etc., supped with us at Dilly's jovially. Either yesterday or today visited M.C.,[6] who was delighted to see me so well, and fixed meeting Saturday.

SATURDAY 4 FEBRUARY. Breakfasted with Mr. Lee, whom I found easy and cordial. I said, "I do not want you to take me upon your back, but you must give me instruction from time to time." "I will," said he. I went with him in his coach to Westminster Hall. He advised me to go the very first Northern Circuit[7] after being called. I *felt* that I should imperceptibly acquire the skill and address of practice. I had a good deal of conversation with young Strange, who contributed to remove apprehensions of difficulty, and also showed me that I might have

[4]The house, No. 56, Great Queen Street, attributed to Inigo Jones or to his pupil, John Webb, was once owned and occupied by Sir Godfrey Kneller. The previous tenant had been the Rev. Samuel Hoole's father, John Hoole, translator of Ariosto and Tasso and recorder of Johnson's last days. A plaque on the house now commemorates Boswell's residence. His old friend, Isabella Strange, was the wife of the noted engraver, Robert Strange; they lived at No. 52.

[5]Dilly was suing his landlords in the Poultry, Samuel and William Salte, linen-drapers, for violating his lease by erecting another structure on the same property. The case was finally tried a year later, and Dilly won damages and costs. Boswell, who wrote the brief, was paid a fee of five guineas.

[6]Margaret Caroline Rudd.

[7]The assizes held in Yorkshire, Durham, Northumberland, Westmorland, Cumberland, and Lancashire.

Sandy *comfortably* at Westminster School and at home at night.[8] At twelve, M.C.[9] Wonderful. Dined Temple; heated myself a little with wine and had almost lost my great coat. Evening, Squire Dilly had arrived.[1] He and I were too jovial at supper, and I foolishly mentioned M.C.

SUNDAY 5 FEBRUARY. Awaked ill and vexed. Took hackney-coach; called M.C. gratefully. Then to General Paoli's. Well received. Vespers in Portuguese Chapel, calm. Dined tête-à-tête with Malone.

MONDAY 6 FEBRUARY. Breakfasted at home. Visited Langton and Wilkes, and *Jack* insisted I should dine with him.[2] As I walked up the Strand near the Adelphi, Mr. Crickitt, Member for Ipswich, who was driving home with Alderman Hammett in his coach, called to me that he saw a boy (whom he pointed out) pick my pocket of my handkerchief. I missed it and seized the boy, who said another boy had it. A man brought him to me, and he *had* the handkerchief. I seized him too. I was confused and awkward; but Mr. Crickitt insisted I should carry them before the Justice in Bow Street.[3] "Will you then, Sir, be so good as go along with me?" "I will be ready at a call." "Pray then, let me have your name?" Having got his *card*, I marched up the Strand and Southampton Street and across Covent Garden to Bow Street, and delivered the rogues to some of the office people, and promised to come next forenoon and bring Mr. Crickitt. The boy who took the handkerchief muttered and complained and pleaded to get away and he would not do so any more. I told him, "This will save you from the gallows." A detachment of the mob accompanied me while I led them by the collar, one in each hand. I dined with Wilkes and his daughter very pleasantly, only their imperfect articulation made them not easily understood.[4] Alderman Kitchin, to whom Wilkes was *next*, was just

[8]Thomas Andrew Lumisden Strange, son of the engraver, later knighted and distinguished as president of the court of Madras. Since he had recently been called to the bar, he could be especially useful to Boswell. He was an Old Westminster.

[9]After "M.C." both here and at the end of the entry Boswell has blotted out another initial, presumably "S," for Stewart, the name Mrs. Rudd was using. Her mother was the natural daughter of a Major W. Stewart of the Irish Dragoons.

[1]Charles Dilly's elder brother John, proprietor of the family home at Southill, Bedfordshire.

[2]The once notorious radical, John Wilkes, M.P. for Middlesex, now an adherent of law and order but still vivacious. He and Boswell were old friends.

[3]Sir Sampson Wright, who succeeded Sir John Fielding in 1780.

[4]"When Mr. Boswell related to Mr. Wilkes his late adventure of having his pocket picked of his handkerchief, that never-failing wit hinted that there might be some *ostentation* in a Scotchman to have it *known* he *had* a handkerchief." Obviously a self-advertising item published by Boswell in the *Public Advertiser* for 14 February 1786 and in two other newspapers the next day.

dead. I tried to give this a *serious* turn to him. He was still the old man. He answered, "Proximus *ardet* (for you know he is in *hell*)."[5] We drank good port without excess till near ten. I then sat awhile with Malone.

TUESDAY 7 FEBRUARY. Found Mr. Burke at his lodgings, No. 45, Pall Mall, and sat about half an hour with him. Talking of my journal, he said, "Vita senis—votiva pateat veluti descripta tabella."[6] I imprudently touched on a calumny against Mr. Burke, in order to be enabled to refute it. We parted on sad terms. I was very uneasy. Dined Temple. Drank coffee with Mr. Eliot. Then by appointment, M.C. Coffee. Malone's. Wrote to Burke. This affair was happily settled in letters between us. I need not give the detail.[7]

WEDNESDAY 8 FEBRUARY. Awaked in distress, having cried in my sleep from an alarm in dreaming about my dear wife, and that Dr. Monro told me her cough was dangerous. Walked about in the forenoon. Called M.C. Told of my distress, and was answered that such a dream imported all was well at home. Was engaged to dine at Courtenay's. But he put it off on account of a debate in the House. Went to Malone's. His dinner over. So ran to a pastry cook's and had excellent collared beef, and returned and drank my wine and tea with Malone. Then Essex Head Club.[8] A good rational evening.

THURSDAY 9 FEBRUARY. Breakfasted with Malone. Sat awhile with Courtenay. Attended Common Pleas awhile. Repaired to Temple. Settled all dues; dined at the students' table for the last time. Had a full feeling of all the ideas of Inns of Court, Westminster Hall, etc., etc. Gave a bottle of port to the mess (two before being drank). Some time

[5] Horace, *Epistles* I. xviii. 84, trans. H. R. Fairclough, Loeb ed.: "['Tis your own safety that's at stake, when] your neighbour's [wall] is in flames." Kitchin was alderman of Farringdon Within, Wilkes of Farringdon Without.
[6] Horace, *Satires* II. i. 32–34, trans. H. R. Fairclough, Loeb ed.:

Quo fit, ut omnis
votiva pateat veluti descripta tabella
vita senis:

"[Lucilius . . . in olden days would trust his secrets to his books, as if to faithful friends . . . whether things went well with him or ill.] So it comes that the old poet's whole life is open to view, as if painted on a votive tablet." Boswell used this passage as the epigraph to the *Life of Johnson*.
[7] The three letters (two by Boswell and one by Burke) leave utterly unidentified the calumny which Boswell asked Burke to explain. He told Boswell for his "private satisfaction, and for that only," that the report was "absolutely false; and this is all I shall ever say to calumnies" (9 February 1786). A great many were being circulated; indeed, it is said that Burke's East-India opponents spent £20,000 at about this time to discredit him.
[8] Founded by Johnson a year before he died to relieve his solitude by meetings three nights a week at the Essex Head, an inn in the Strand near his home.

after dinner, the head porter announced a *call*. Then I, the Hon. John Eliot, and Mr. William Dowdeswell, nephew of the Chancellor of the Exchequer, were introduced (with each a band, and holding a *pileus* or black cap) into the chamber where the benchers were sitting at table, and were told of our being called to the rank of barristers-at-law.[9] I said, "We return you ten thousand thanks for the honour that has been done us," and then retreated. I *added* this ceremony to the Laird of Auchinleck, in my own consciousness. Mr. Salt, the treasurer, followed me to the door, took me by the hand, and said, "I wish you all the honours of your profession."[1] Dowdeswell insisted that he and I, who alone were left in the Hall, should drink a glass of wine together. We had an *old* bottle and were very hearty. But I was too much intoxicated. Wandered idly in the streets (but *innocuously*) and went to Dilly's and dozed in company after supper.

FRIDAY 10 FEBRUARY. Rose not at all well, but walked to Westminster Hall and grew better. Found at the General's that an elegant company of ladies and foreign noblemen was to dine with him. Shrunk at first, but altered my mind and enjoyed the scene. Evening had the chariot and visited M.C. for a few minutes. Home quiet.

SATURDAY 11 FEBRUARY. Sat quiet in the forenoon. Malone walked with me to the Temple and subscribed my bond as my surety. My two brethren and I took the Oaths of Allegiance and Supremacy before the benchers.[2] I dined most comfortably and drank coffee tête-à-tête with Malone. Courtenay joined us at night, and we had stewed oysters and a little wine and enjoyed life.

SUNDAY 12 FEBRUARY. After breakfasting at home, walked about a great deal. Called Macbride's; not at home. Sat awhile with old John Ross.[3] Was uncertain where to dine. Called at Sir Joshua's. Old Mr. Ralph Kirkley, who has been with him five-and-twenty years, said "Not at home"; but he afterwards was sent after me, and found me in Sidney's Alley and told me his master was at home and wished I would dine with him. "Just what I wanted," said I. "He has asked me two or

[9]Eliot, M.P. for Liskeard, later first Earl of St. Germans, was twenty-five years old, as was Dowdeswell, whose uncle, also named William Dowdeswell, was Burke's friend and Chancellor of the Exchequer in the first Rockingham Administration.

[1]This was the formal conclusion of the ceremony. The treasurer was the head of the Inn.

[2]The taker of the Oath of Supremacy swore to abjure papal or any other foreign supremacy over Great Britain.

[3]Captain (later Admiral) John Macbride, M.P. for Plymouth, an Irish cousin of Mrs. Boswell's; and Lord Auchinleck's friend, the advocate and politician John Ross Mackye, now almost seventy-nine years of age.

three times of late, when I was engaged, and I thought I would take my chance today." There were no strangers, only Mr. ———, his first scholar, who sat quiet and soon disappeared, his nieces, Mrs. Gwatkin and Miss Palmer, and his nephew, the Rev. Mr. ——— Palmer.[4] We were quite easy and happy and temperate, and then had tea. When I came home early in the evening I found my brother T.D., whom I quieted as to my trying the English bar. This comforted me, and I went early to bed. I was sorry I had been at no church today.

MONDAY 13 FEBRUARY. Hastened to Westminster. Breakfasted at Alice's Coffee-house.[5] Young Willes sat by me and was pleasingly civil. Invited me to his father's that evening, and when I told him I should dine so as probably not to be quite fit to come, he said his father would be glad to see me any other evening.[6] He being now the Junior on the Northern Circuit and I being to succeed to him, he said he should have the pleasure to deliver to me the record and the circuit purse, and he promised to give me all my instructions. Young Strange then came and accompanied me to a barber's shop in one of the passages from the Hall (Mr. Parrat), where he and I put on our gowns, wigs, and bands, and then he showed me the way into the Court of King's Bench, where I took the oaths, along with a number of other people. It was agreeable to experience that no notice was taken of it. I then took my seat at the bar, and felt myself a member of the ancient Court of King's Bench, and did not despair of yet being a judge in it. My mind was firm and serene and my imagination bright. It was the last day of term,[7] and I was amused with the various judicial acts. I was in the Inner Temple Hall before four o'clock and wrote letters, waiting till the company invited to the inauguration dinner of myself and my two brethren, called at the same time, should come. I was quite the *Laird of Auchinleck in the Inner Temple,* free from any *imaginary distance.* My guests were the Hon. Daines Barrington, Sir Joshua Reynolds, Mr. Wilkes, Mr. Malone, Mr. Courtenay, young Mr. Strange, Dr. Brocklesby, Mr. Dilly my bookseller, Mr. Baldwin my printer, and my brother

---

[4]Giuseppe Marchi, whom Reynolds brought back from Rome, his assistant painter and restorer until Reynolds's death; Theophila ("Offy") Gwatkin, wife of Robert Lovell Gwatkin, who was later High Sheriff of Cornwall; and either John or Joseph Palmer, both clergymen.

[5]Restricted to Lords, Members of the House of Commons, and barristers.

[6]Edward Willes, judge in the King's Bench, was a man of easy humour as well as sound law. He and Boswell had taken to each other quickly when they met at the Carlisle Assizes in 1778. "Young Willes" had been called to the bar at Lincoln's Inn in 1785.

[7]Because 12 February was a Sunday. See above, 23 November 1785, n. 6.

T.D.[8] Mr. Eliot's guest was the Hon. Counsellor Perceval.[9] Mr. Dow-deswell's guests were Mr. Hay, nephew of Lord Kinnoul, and Mr. James Martin, M.P. We were in all sixteen. I sat at the head of the table and Mr. Dowdeswell at the foot, and a more jovial, pleasant day never was passed. I had fixed a dinner by myself. My two brethren joined me. I ordered everything. We had a course of fish, a course of ham, fowls, and greens, a course of roast beef and apple pies, a dessert of cheese and fruit, madeira, port, and as good claret as ever was drank. The officers of the Society attended us. And the lustre was lighted, which had not been the case for thirty years, as I was told.[1] The company dropped off gradually. Malone and Courtenay and I walked home, in excellent spirits and not drunk, towards eleven. It shall ever be in my mind *dies memorabilis*.

TUESDAY 14 FEBRUARY. Attended Lord Mansfield's sittings at *nisi prius* in Westminster Hall,[2] and was both entertained and instructed. Dined at the Literary Club. Present: Bishop of St. Asaph, Sir Joseph Banks, Mr. Windham, young Mr. Burke, Dr. Burney, and myself.[3] The want of Johnson was much felt. There was no vigorous exertion of intellect. Found M.C. a little. Sat an hour with Malone and settled

[8]Barrington, Master of the Bench in the Inner Temple, a naturalist and antiquarian of wide scope, was the first person to propose a voyage to the North Pole. A friend of Johnson's, he had proposed Boswell for membership in the Essex Head Club. Dr. Richard Brocklesby, Johnson's physician and friend, had attended him on his death-bed.

[9]Spencer Perceval (at this time aged twenty-three) became Prime Minister late in 1809 and was assassinated in the House of Commons by a lunatic on 11 May 1812.

[1]An example of Boswell's flair but also of the decline of feasts and revels in the Inns of Court since the collegiate educational system disappeared at the end of the sev-enteenth century. The inns were now simply professional associations. Boswell's bill for the dinner amounted to £7. 13s. 7d.; the liquors consumed, twenty-six bottles of claret, eight of port, and four of madeira, cost £8. 17s. 8d., exclusive of service. Candles: 4s.

[2]Trials of issues of fact before a jury and one presiding judge conducted after term, generally at Guildhall. So called because formerly such trials were to be held at the superior courts at Westminster *nisi prius* ("unless before") that day they had taken place before justices of the assizes in the counties where the causes arose.

[3]Jonathan Shipley, Bishop of St. Asaph, friend of Benjamin Franklin and the American colonies, and the only Bishop to speak out in 1779 for the repeal of all laws against Protestant dissenters; Banks, the naturalist who accompanied Captain Cook in the voyage of the *Endeavour* around the world and served as President of the Royal Society from 1778 until his death in 1820; William Windham, M.P. for Norwich, noted for talent, charm, and indecision, a member of the Foxite Opposition, who vacillated between politics and scholarship; Edmund Burke's beloved son, Richard, known at The Club as "the Whelp"; and Charles Burney, composer, author of a four-volume *History of Music* (1776–89), and father of Fanny Burney.

an affidavit to file a bill in Chancery against Robinson in Paternoster Row, for publishing a great part of my *Tour* as *Johnson's Table Talk.*

WEDNESDAY 15 FEBRUARY. Lord Mansfield sat in Guildhall, and I did not go. I went to Mr. Irving in the Temple to have a bill filed against Robinson. He exerted himself by going to Strahan and Cadell and getting information how to proceed.[4] Cadell advised that I should first speak to Robinson. I accordingly did so; and he assured me he did not know of the invasion of my property. But in the hurry of business he purchased the *Table Talk* from a young man, McDonnell from Cork, and gave him ten guineas, for which he showed me his receipt. He said he would either account to me for all the impression, or burn it, or do what I pleased. I met Dilly and returned to Robinson with him, and took Robinson's word of honour that no more of the impression should be sold in Britain. He behaved, I thought, honestly and frankly.[5] I then called M.C. and took a walk. Dined at Mrs. and Captain Bosville's (my Chief); Mr. and Mrs. Ward, Miss Mellish, Mr. and Miss Wilkes, the Rev. Mr. Mackreth of Wakefield and his wife there. A good hearty day. Evening M.C. Malone's a little.

THURSDAY 16 FEBRUARY. Attended Lord Mansfield's sittings with great relish. Dined at home, General Rainsford with us, hearty and animated.[6] Drank tea with Malone. Then to Mrs. Strange, and consulted fully as to my house, bringing up furniture, engaging servants, etc. Was wonderfully pleased to find there was no mystery or difficulty in what my creative gloom had represented in such monstrous shapes. How humiliating is it that I am so much under the dominion of fancy!

FRIDAY 17 FEBRUARY. Attended the sittings with great relish. Called on Courtenay in my way home. He carried me to the House of Commons to hear Burke arraign Hastings. He did it with extraordinary ability, but now and then lessened the solemn effect by oratorical sallies. Before he began, I heard Jenkinson speak upon another motion, and thought him the most manly, dignified speaker of them all.[7] Dundas

---

[4]John Irving, a Scots solicitor long established in London; George Robinson, "king of booksellers," proprietor of an extensive wholesale trade; and Andrew Strahan and Thomas Cadell, publishers and booksellers.

[5]*Dr. Johnson's Table Talk* is found in few copies. The compiler, hitherto unidentified, was David Evans Macdonnel, who in 1797 brought out a very popular *Dictionary of Quotations* translated from five languages and published by Robinson. The receipt for ten guineas, signed "D. E. McDonnell" and dated 24 December 1785, is in the Hyde Collection.

[6]At his death in 1809 he left nearly forty volumes of autobiographical papers relating to duty in Portugal, Germany, and Gibraltar.

[7]Charles Jenkinson (the King's confidant and later first Earl of Liverpool) as a member of the Board of Trade moved successfully that a bill regulating commerce between Britain and the United States be continued for another year.

spoke with amazing effrontery, and (as I thought) with only a coarse bellowing. It provoked me that he was so high, as I knew him all along to be my inferior in learning and talents, and as he was a downright Swiss of every Ministry. Pitt defended him with much appearance of zeal, which hurt me much, and so *young* was I that this night, for the *first* time, I was *convinced* that there is no public virtue in actual politicians, but that all of them merely act a part as may best serve their interest and ambition. I heard many speakers; stayed till eleven, was tired, and came home and had parmesan and bread and port and water.[8]

SATURDAY 18 FEBRUARY. Attended the sittings with relish. Dined at Malone's with Courtenay and Devaynes.[9] Evening M.C., Charles Street.

SUNDAY 19 FEBRUARY. Breakfast home. Neapolitan Chapel. Visited young Willes and received instructions as Junior on the Northern Circuit. Visited M.C. Sat awhile with Mrs. Kennedy, wife of heir of Cassillis.[1] Dined Captain Macbride's: Colonel Strickland and lady, etc. Evening Miss Monckton's.[2] Quite easy.

MONDAY 20 FEBRUARY. Attended the sittings. Dined Sir Joshua's to meet Mr. Gwatkin, a most amiable man. After dinner wrote some anecdotes of Dr. Johnson dictated by Sir Joshua. Visited M.C.

TUESDAY 21 FEBRUARY. Attended the sittings. Visited M.C. Malone and I went by appointment to dine with Courtenay, who *sicut mos*

[8]These speeches were the opening guns in the *cause célèbre* of the period, the trial of Warren Hastings. Though now coming under closer supervision by the Government, British India was still ruled by the East India Company. Hastings, its Governor-General, had been accused of participating in widespread corruption and of extending British control unjustifiably over Indian territories, and had returned home the previous June. In May 1782 the House of Commons, on the basis of reports from a Secret Committee headed by Dundas, had passed a resolution demanding Hastings's recall. Burke now reminded the Commons of that resolution, suggested that Hastings be impeached before the bar of the House of Lords, and moved that certain of Hastings's papers be laid before the House. Dundas, whom Boswell criticizes for his skill in shifting from one Administration to the next, responded that he thought Hastings's actions culpable but not criminal, and praised his abilities and public service. Though Pitt took the high ground of principle, his argument defending Dundas's change of mind was casuistical, and it was widely believed that he acted from political expediency.
[9]Apothecary (general medical practitioner) to George III. He attended Johnson in his last illness.
[1]Mrs. Kennedy was an American descended from the oldest families in New York State; Archibald Kennedy, a New Yorker who sat out the American Revolution, later succeeded as eleventh Earl of Cassillis. His town house, No. 1 Broadway, at the Battery, was appropriated for George Washington.
[2]A charming bluestocking, daughter of the first Viscount Galway. She conducted celebrated conversaziones at her mother's house in Berkeley Square, where she was married in June to the Earl of Cork and Orrery.

est[3] had forgot it. So we went and dined at the Piazza Coffee-house. The scene of beings eating *isolés*, which I once thought London independence, seemed dreary. The frost was intense. Went home with Malone and had coffee and tea comfortably.

WEDNESDAY 22 FEBRUARY. Attended sittings.[4] Took an impatient fit to see M.C. Visited there. Not well. No meeting for some time. Called Sir Joshua. Asked to family dinner. Returned to sittings. Dined agreeably at Sir Joshua's. This day in the Court of King's Bench Mr. McDougal, clerk to Mr. Irving of the Inner Temple and connected with Mr. Currie, an attorney, handed me my first brief, with two guineas. Captain Gregor Farquharson and others were prosecutors of an indictment for perjury against Thomas Jackson; and Farquharson, who when a *writer* at Edinburgh had employed me, I suppose suggested me on this occasion. I was very happy to get business the second week I was at the bar, when many able men stand for years unemployed. I had a boyish fondness for my first brief and fee, and put up the guineas as *medals*.[5] I came home to tea, and the pannier-man[6] and cook of the Inner Temple came by appointment and received payment for the entertainment on occasion of my being called. I shook hands with both of them, wishing them success in the fullness of my heart, and feeling myself consequential. Went to the Essex Head Club, where were Barrington, Devaynes, Brocklesby, Poore, Jodrell, Sastres. I eat and drank heartily, and there was good talk, which I enjoyed but do not recollect. Sastres walked home with me.[7] I was now quite tranquillized as to London.

THURSDAY 23 FEBRUARY. Attended the sittings. Mr. Justice Buller presided.[8] The cold was excessive. Called on Malone between four and

[3] As his habit is.
[4] Boswell kept a clasped leather-bound notebook, interleaved with blotting-paper and sewn at the top, in which he made notes of cases heard in the King's Bench and on the assizes he attended from 1786 until 20 July 1787. The earliest dated entry is for this day and records a prosecution for assaulting a boy. The style throughout the notebook is like that of the condensed journal, long speeches having been reduced to their essence in a few sentences. The notebook was Boswell's pathetic substitute for methodical study of English law. He also attended cases in Chancery.
[5] They were doubtless "put up" in a descriptive wrapper (whereabouts now unknown) and preserved among the other coins and medals in the black ebony cabinet now in the Donald F. Hyde Room at Houghton Library, Harvard University.
[6] Table waiter.
[7] Francesco Sastres, Italian teacher and translator, seems to have sent Boswell some interesting Johnsoniana shortly after this meeting.
[8] Because of Lord Mansfield's failing health. He was in his thirtieth year as Lord Chief Justice of the King's Bench, the last he actually presided over his court.

five, and (as the General dined abroad) most luckily found roast beef
and hearty welcome. Conversation never fails between him and me.
FRIDAY 24 FEBRUARY. Breakfasted with Mr. Crickitt and went
with him in his coach to the sessions on Clerkenwell Green, where we
were examined before the grand jury, and a bill was found against the
two pickpockets seized by me. I was uneasy lest my cause in the K.B.
should come on before I got down. Mr. Mainwaring, the chairman,
obligingly fixed the trial next day at ten. Hastened to Westminster.
Read in the hackney-coach as I drove along a scurrilous attack in verse
upon me under the name of Peter Pindar.[9] Was in good time for my
cause. Old Baldwin[1] had told me just to state that it was indictment
for perjury, to which the defendant had pleaded not guilty. But Erskine, who was leading counsel along with me, said, "You must *open*
it"; and he obligingly wrote on the margin of the brief all that I should
do. I felt a *little* trepidation when I first heard my voice *in banco*.[2] But
I was not uneasy and did very properly what I had to do, and no more.
I resolved to have no exordium, no any one flourish, as to my first
appearance, that I might not be charged with ostentation. We lost the
cause instantly by the ignorance of the attorney in not having the *record*
of the trial, in which the perjury was charged to be committed, sufficiently authenticated. Erskine said to me, "To know the forms is the
difficulty of our profession.[3] In reasoning, a man should take his own
way, but where a thing must be done in one particular way, I took the
liberty to direct you, that no puppy might have it to say you did not

[9]*A Poetical and Congratulatory Epistle to James Boswell, Esq., on His Journal of a Tour to the
Hebrides with the Celebrated Doctor Johnson*, by John Wolcot ("Peter Pindar"), followed
in the same year by *Bozzy and Piozzi, or, the British Biographers*, which ran to ten editions
within three years. Boswell would have been especially angered by Wolcot's clear charge
that Lord Macdonald had forced him to modify the text of the *Tour*:

> Let Lord Macdonald threat thy breech to kick
> And o'er thy shrinking shoulders shake his stick:
> Treat with contempt the menace of this Lord;
> 'Tis History's province, Bozzy, to *record*.

A paragraph in the *St. James's Chronicle* for 2–4 March 1786 is almost certainly by
Boswell: "It having been asserted in a scurrilous pamphlet that some alterations were
made in the second edition of a late work in consequence of a letter from a noble lord
to the author, we have authority to say that the assertion is false." Wolcot's two poems
and the Collings-Rowlandson caricatures of Johnson and Boswell on their Hebridean
tour did more harm to Boswell's reputation than all other contemporary attacks on
him taken together.
[1]Presumably Boswell is distinguishing William Baldwin from his son, also a lawyer.
[2]In the King's Bench.
[3]The technicalities of English law were intricately minute, and a case could easily be
lost, as here, if some form was violated.

do it as it ought to be done." This was very friendly.[4] Sat awhile with Malone. I dined very comfortably at the General's, who was much pleased with Erskine's behaviour to me, and said he had always a good opinion of him. I drank tea with Mrs. and Captain Bosville, and he set me down in his chariot at M.C.'s, where I sat two hours, and was assured that this was a very flattering attention, when, on account of "certain reasons best known to ourselves,"[5] there could be no gratification of one kind.

SATURDAY 25 FEBRUARY. Breakfasted again with Mr. Crickitt, and again went with him in his coach to the Middlesex Sessions, where upon our evidence my two pickpockets were convicted and sentenced to a month's imprisonment and to be whipped. The actual thief, Daniel Merchant, confessed and cried bitterly, and said he was turned out to the streets by his mother. Though he was an ill-looking young dog, I considered that this might be true, and meditated doing something to put him into a better situation.[6] Mr. Crickitt and I congratulated ourselves on thus becoming accidentally acquainted. I called on M.C.; not up. Waited and then had a short agreeable interview. Called on T.D., dry as usual. Knew not where to dine. Thought of going to the play, but was not easy enough with T.D. to propose sharing his family dinner, and he did not say anything as to where I was to dine. Went to Dilly's, who had dined, as he was going early to Mrs. Henderson's benefit;[7] but he hospitably ordered pork steaks and greens for me, and eat a little with me; and as it snowed much, I resolved to sit by his fire and write letters, and look into a MS. treatise on Justices of Peace by Capell Lofft, to judge if it should be published by Mr. Dilly.[8] I did both, but

[4]Thomas Erskine has been called the greatest advocate ever to practice at the English bar. A remote cousin of Boswell and ten years his junior, Erskine had been an officer in the navy and then in the army before he was called to the bar, 3 July 1778, where he almost immediately made an overwhelming impression as a trial lawyer. By 1783 he was supposed to be earning more than £3,000 a year in practice. A good friend of Fox's, he later defended Thomas Paine and other supporters of the French Revolution. As first Baron Erskine he briefly became Lord Chancellor in 1806.
[5]If Boswell is quoting something, his source has not been identified.
[6]Boswell undertook shortly afterwards to get him a berth at sea, but Merchant, who tearfully accepted the offer, disappeared a month later when discharged from prison. He was fourteen years old. While in prison he had admitted under close questioning by T. D. Boswell, Boswell's emissary, that he had left both his home and his employer of his own accord. Boswell continued his interest in Merchant, but we do not know if anything came of it.
[7]Otway's *Venice Preserved*, at Covent Garden. John Henderson, "the Roscius of Bath," had recently died. The performance was reported to have made nearly £600 for his widow and infant child.
[8]The book appears not to have been published. Lofft, a barrister, wrote numerous works on legal matters.

felt myself grow dull; and the snow having ceased, I after some comfortable tea walked home.

SUNDAY 26 FEBRUARY. I recollect imperfectly how I passed the forenoon. I was part of it at Malone's and part with M.C., who was serious and pleasing and friendly. Dined at Lord Falmouth's. Found his lady a plain, cheerful Cheshire woman, and had much conversation with her about my Chester acquaintances.[9] Mr. and Mrs. Gwatkin there. I drank rather too liberally and sat too late, as I was to go to the Lord Chancellor's levee. I did not get to his house till half an hour past nine. I was shown up to the drawing-room. Everybody was gone, and my Lord had left the room. But the servant said he would let his Lordship know. In a little he came, took me by the hand courteously, and as soon as we were seated (as I had written to him that I was called to the bar and was resolved to try my fortune some time in Westminster Hall), he said, "You are come to settle here." BOSWELL. "Yes, my Lord." CHANCELLOR. "I am glad of it." BOSWELL. "It makes me very happy to hear your Lordship say so. For I was afraid you might be offended, as your Lordship's letter seemed to be against it.[1] But I could not help it. I had so strong an impulse." CHANCELLOR. "A strong impulse should decide. If you had told me you had a strong impulse, I should have advised you to come. You are going to publish something more about Dr. Johnson?" BOSWELL. "Yes, my Lord. I am going to give *tota vita senis*.[2] Your Lordship did me the honour to read my *Tour*?" CHANCELLOR. "Yes, every word of it; and yet one cannot tell how. Why should one wish to go on and read how Dr. Johnson went from one place to another? Can you give a rule for writing in that manner? Longinus could not. But indeed I always thought rules absurd." BOSWELL. "Your Lordship's getting through the book is as extraordinary as Dr. Johnson's getting through the tour. He was a most extraordinary man; and, my Lord, as life is uncertain, and it is possible I may die or your Lordship may die before my *Life of Dr. Johnson* is published, let me now have the pleasure of telling you a very high compliment which he paid your Lordship. He said, 'I would prepare myself for no man in England except Lord Thurlow. But when I am to meet Lord Thurlow, I should wish to know a day before.' " The Chancellor smiled complacent at this. I proceeded: "It would be curious to conjecture *how* he would prepare himself."

I then, I know not how, introduced the King's having refused an

---

[9]Boswell had spent two animated weeks at Chester in October 1779, in company with Col. James Archibald Stuart at the headquarters of the 92nd Regiment.

[1]See above, 9 January 1786 and n. 8.

[2]See above, 7 February 1786, n. 6.

addition to Dr. Johnson's pension, and I said, "My Lord, I am a very forward man. Your Lordship will check me, or you may knock me down if I say what is improper. But I put it fairly to your Lordship: was not the King made to understand that Dr. Johnson wished to have an addition to his pension to enable him to go abroad, and yet His Majesty did not grant it?" The Chancellor admitted it was so.[3] "But," said he, "will you make no allowance for an east wind, or any other circumstance? A philosophical mind will do the same justice to a king as to a beggar. In the multiplicity of applications which press upon the King, that may not have been attended to." In short, the Sovereign was much obliged to his Chancellor, who shielded him very ably. I was, however, very sorry, and mentioned Sir Joshua's saying that he did not expect generosity from the King. But that merely as a good economist he wondered that the application was not successful, for how could he lay out his money so well in purchasing fame? "Then," said Lord Chancellor, "Sir Joshua is angry that the King is not so vain as he would have him" (smiling). "*That* is a good answer to *Sir Joshua's* argument."

Talking of the diminution of the number of the Lords of Session, which he introduced by saying he wished to have two of them to sit in the House of Lords, his Lordship said he had read my book (pamphlet he should have said); that he thought the only question was whether the business of the Outer House could be done by fewer judges. He did not seem to perceive the importance of having a large number in the Inner House. He said he never could get any of our Lords of Session to talk like men upon it. I suppose I was somewhat elevated by Lord Falmouth's champagne and claret. I was, however, vastly well in my own feelings. When I went away his Lordship said, "I am obliged to you, Mr. Boswell." I hastened in fine spirits to communicate this good reception to M.C. I was first told not at home. "Not at home!" said I. "Gone to bed." "Gone to bed!" said I. "At this time of night?" "Has on night clothes, but I dare say will see you," says John. In I went. But was reproved and hastened away. Supped on cold meat at Malone's with Courtenay most agreeably.

MONDAY 27 FEBRUARY. Note from M.C. to come. Went and found my last night's visit a dreadful offence. Was shocked to find even in enchantress such serious anger. Was long fine and easy; then vexed; then angry partly and partly sorry. Went off abruptly. Snow deep.

---

[3] Johnson in 1784 thought his life might be extended if he could winter in Italy. Boswell, after consulting with Reynolds, had applied to Thurlow for an addition to Johnson's pension.

Resolutions wild. Dined at Langton's most cordially with his lady and nine children. Taylor the Grecian joined us after dinner. Mrs. Langton appeared at tea.[4] I was mild good company, but troubled about M.C. and resolving to break off. Home at night.

TUESDAY 28 FEBRUARY. Breakfasted with Mrs. Bosville, and felt settling in London quite easy. Could not stay from M.C. Found a gentler reception, and after some conversation, was forgiven and told this would do me good by teaching me prudence.[5] I got into delightful spirits. Called on Mrs. Strange and talked about arranging my house. Home; dressed. Dined Club. Very well, but no animated exertion. Malone, Windham, and I went home with Sir Joshua and drank tea. I stayed the evening, played cards and supped, and calmly amused the hours.

WEDNESDAY 1 MARCH. This being Ash Wednesday, went to the Neapolitan Chapel early in the morning, and kneeling before the altar, had my forehead crossed by a holy priest's finger dipped in ashes, who solemnly pronounced to each of us, "Memento, homo, quod pulvis es, et in pulverem reverteris."[6] I then breakfasted with Malone. Then waited on Sir Francis Lumm, who had obligingly procured me from Sir John Caldwell a minute of the conversation between the King and Dr. Johnson which was in the late Sir James Caldwell's repositories. Sir Francis was a very polite man and had an elegant house. He gave me Lord Carmarthen's letter to him containing His Majesty's permission that the minute should be delivered to me to make what use of it I should think proper in my *Life of Dr. Johnson.*[7] Sat a little with Mr. MacLeod of Colbecks and had Highland and Ayrshire ideas revived.

---

[4]Thomas Taylor, later known for his translations of Plato, Plotinus, and other classical authors. Mrs. Langton is Langton's mother. Boswell would have styled Langton's wife, who was the widow of the Earl of Rothes, Lady Rothes.

[5]On the back of a letter which Boswell had received this or the previous day he drafted a note almost surely addressed to Mrs. Rudd but perhaps never sent: "To affect anger or indifference *now* would be *falsehood.* Take then my genuine sentiments. With the warmest gratitude for your generous goodness, with the deepest concern for an inconsiderate offence, I will endeavour resolutely to submit to the severest punishment, which is never again to run the risk of giving so much pain to one for whom I shall ever retain an affectionate admiration."

[6]"Remember, man, that thou art dust, and unto dust shalt thou return."

[7]One of the two great showpieces of the *Life of Johnson,* the other being Johnson's letter to Lord Chesterfield, February 1755. Boswell caused both to be printed as pamphlets and registered apart from the *Life* in order to secure his exclusive right to use the material. The conversation (a long tête-à-tête) occurred in the library of Buckingham House, February 1767. Johnson had given a minute of it to Sir James Caldwell. Lord Carmarthen, later Duke of Leeds, was one of the principal Secretaries of State.

Dined at home meagre[8] and did not go out after dinner.

THURSDAY 2 MARCH. Went to the drawing-room at St. James's. Was perfectly independent and easy. A great many people there. The King only asked me about the weather, and if I walked or moved about, or some such nothing. I wished to have had some conversation with the Queen. But I did not get near her. As Dempster (from a lady about Court) and Mr. Cooper, who teaches Her Majesty to draw, had assured me she liked my *Hebrides* much, it would have been very pleasing to me to hear it from herself. I resolved to go some day with Langton, a well-known favourite, and stand close to him, by which means I could not fail to be talked to by Her Majesty.[9] I had been informed that DOUGLAS was weak enough to be angry at my mentioning in my *Hebrides* Dr. Johnson's witty attack on his *filiation*, though I, his zealous supporter, repelled it.[1] He was formally cold today. I never minded it; nor did I mind Lord Graham, who was flippant.[2] I found Lord Townshend and several more quite easy with me. Seeing people at Court is a trial of their disposition. If they appear differently from their usual way, they are either feebly timid or foolishly vain. I dined at home. Then visited M.C. Fixed to meet Saturday and stay to dine. "Well, I will stay and eat a boiled chicken with you." Malone's agreeably, as at all times. Home.

FRIDAY 3 MARCH. I did not attend the sittings at Guildhall after this Hilary term. I am sorry I did not, as I should have learned a good deal, and as I should have had at least one brief, as Mr. McDougal, clerk to Mr. Irving, informed me; for an acquaintance of his wanted to employ me and did not know where I was to be found. The truth is there is very little room for counsel at Guildhall and, besides, I was as yet at a very great distance while in Portman Square. But I might have taken my quarters at Dilly's. I shall henceforth attend at Guildhall. I this morning called on Malone and also on Dilly, with whom I stayed

[8]That is, he kept Ash Wednesday without eating meat.
[9]According to Fanny Burney, the Queen said that Boswell "is so extraordinary a man that perhaps he will devise something extraordinary" in the *Life of Johnson*—an ambiguous remark (Burney's journal, 20 Dec. 1785).
[1]"Sir, Sir, don't be too severe upon the gentleman; don't accuse him of want of filial piety [in not roofing the chapel of Holyroodhouse where she lay buried]! Lady Jane Douglas was not *his* mother" (Journal, 26 October 1773). The Hamilton party in the great Douglas Cause maintained that Archibald Douglas was a French child, bought in Paris to impose upon the rightful heir. Boswell had written songs, pamphlets, and newspaper items on behalf of Douglas and was made one of his counsel later in the action. In his journal Boswell typically wrote Douglas's name in capital letters.
[2]James Graham, Marquess of Graham (later third Duke of Montrose), was brother to Douglas's first wife.

a short time. The streets were choked with snow. Mrs. Bosville and her two sons and Mr. and Mrs. Ward and Baron Wessenberg, a rich German canon of Worms, etc., who will probably be an Elector and speaks English wonderfully well, and is quite gay, quite *du monde*, a little man, somewhat crooked.[3] This dinner was proposed by Mr. Gentili and most kindly given by the excellent General, who thus entertained my English connections. We had an admirable dinner and were very cheerful. In the evening I sat some time with Malone.

SATURDAY 4 MARCH. Stayed at home quietly writing till *one*.[4] Then met M.C. in Charles Street. A pretty little dinner; much agreeable conversation (Rousseau's creed; Lord Mountstuart should have stood by the Crown like ——— in de Retz),[5] while I was quite at my ease. Coffee too. I sung "Is there a charm, ye powers above"[6] and some other songs, and was pleasant upon inadvertently hitting on,

> O what pain it is to part,
> But if fate my love should thwart,
> And bring thee to the fatal cart.[7]

Accompanied in coach to near home at nine o'clock. Then happy at Malone's.

SUNDAY 5 MARCH. After my comfortable breakfast at home, took

---

[3]Boswell forgot the beginning of his sentence, which he may have written at two different times, for a fresh page begins with "and is quite gay." Baron von Wessenberg's hopes of becoming an Elector by becoming Archbishop of Mainz, Trier, or Cologne were never realized.

[4]He wrote to Veronica, Euphemia, and Sandy, but only the letter to Euphemia has been recovered. He counselled her to be attentive to her mother and to her studies, assuring her that he was striving to reunite the family in London within a month or two.

[5]The cues for this conversation are a crowded interlinear addition. "Rousseau's Creed" is presumably the "Profession of Faith of the Savoyard Vicar" in *Emile*: a Lenten discussion of the topic by Boswell and Mrs. Rudd would not be without interest. The other cue has not been read confidently. It is clear, however, that Boswell alludes to Mountstuart's adherence to the Foxite Opposition. The eldest son of the third Earl of Bute, Mountstuart had been a friend and potential patron of Boswell's since 1765, when they had travelled together in Italy. They were now estranged by political differences.

[6]"The Power of Beauty," music attributed to Henry Carey, lyricist unknown:
> Is there a charm, ye powers above,
>   To ease a wounded breast;
> Through reason's glass to look at love,
>   To wish and yet to rest?

[7]Polly's song in *The Beggar's Opera* (air 17). Mrs. Rudd narrowly escaped hanging when she was tried with the Perreau brothers.

a second at Spottiswoode's, from whom had received a note yesterday wishing that I would not delay to draw the respondent's case in the Appeal, Cuninghame against Cuninghame, etc.[8] I settled with him to come to his office next day, and he would have a clerk ready, to whom I would dictate it. I found Lord Advocate at home, and talked with him of the tax on attorneys being very hard on the procurators in Scotland, as to which I had a letter from the procurators at Ayr. He gave me reason to hope that relief would be given without their petitioning Parliament.[9] We then were pleasant as to the Lords of Session not being to be diminished. He said, "You may be a Lord of Session now if you like it." He allowed he had given up the scheme of diminishing, and I said, "Well, you have sheathed your dirk." It was very agreeable to be so easy with him. I then went and worshipped in the Bavarian Chapel, then made several calls, then went home and brought forward my journal, then dined very happily at the General's with a select company of foreigners. Eat and drank rather too much. Went in the evening to Miss Monckton's. Had a little conversation with Madame d'Eon, who had heard my *Hebrides* praised. I was shocked somewhat to think of her as a kind of monster by metamorphosis. She appeared to me a man in woman's clothes, like Hecate on the stage.[1] Miss Monckton at my request presented me to Lord Rawdon. I told her I was not so greedy of great people as I used to be. But there were *some* whom I had a great desire to be acquainted with, and Lord Rawdon was one. "Ay," said she, "He's a hero."[2] (This passed after I was introduced to his Lordship.) When Miss Monckton presented me, Lord Rawdon said, "It is what I have" (either *much* or *long*) "wished." I told him that Dr. Johnson and I had a letter of introduction to him from Dr. Scott when we were on our tour,[3] the regiment to which he belonged being then in Scotland, but we found his Lordship had gone

[8]Cuninghame *v.* Cuninghame is explained below, 24 April 1786, n. 5. John Spottiswoode, an English solicitor of Scottish origin, had engaged Boswell previously in various cases before the House of Lords.
[9]An annual tax of £5 on solicitors and attorneys in London and Edinburgh and £3 elsewhere had gone into effect on 1 November 1785. Increased later at various times, it was not dropped until 1949.
[1]Charles-Geneviève de Beaumont, Chevalier d'Eon, the most famous transvestite in history, was revealed as a man after his death in 1810. He had held various posts in London for the French government, the last as Minister Plenipotentiary.
[2]Rawdon, later Earl of Moira and Marquess of Hastings, had served with distinction in the American war, notably at Bunker Hill, where he received two bullets through his cap, and in South Carolina, where he commanded the left wing of the British forces at the battle of Camden.
[3]Their tour of the Highlands and Hebrides in 1773.

to Ireland. I was very desirous to hear from himself something about Mrs. Rudd, who told me they were third cousins, and that the Moira family had it now under consideration to do something handsome for her. I with great address introduced her name by saying that I did not know his Lordship's connection with Scotland till lately, when talking with Mr. Cummyng of our Herald's Office about a celebrated but unfortunate lady, Mrs. Rudd, he assured me of her being related to Lord Rawdon, both being descended of a Scotch family. His Lordship bowed, and mentioned the family, and that he thought he had a right to the title of Menteith; but finding that another had it, he had given all the aid in his power to forward the claim. I then purposely went wrong in mentioning Mrs. Rudd's maiden name, calling it *Young*. His Lordship corrected this and mentioned *Youngson*. The fact however is, as Mrs. Rudd told me, that *Youngson*, like a patronymic formed with "O' " or "Mac," has been a change from Young, she being by the father's side of the family of Young of Auldbar. It pleased me that I could now tell her how Lord Rawdon admitted her relationship to him in my presence.[4] I said to him it was nine years since I first was acquainted with her; that I thought she had been dead but the acquaintance was lately renewed, and that she was a very sensible, agreeable woman. I went quietly home.

MONDAY 6 MARCH. Dictated Case at Spottiswoode's all the forenoon; dined and drank tea at Mr. Ward's; rather too much wine. Hastened to M.C. and charmed her with an account of what had passed with Lord Rawdon. This had a fine effect. Returned to Spottiswoode's, and with my own hand, partly before, partly after supper, wrote the *reasons* to the Case. Mr. Haggart, advocate, just come from Edinburgh, revived Scottish ideas. Got home about one in the morning. Found a romantic letter from M.C.

TUESDAY 7 MARCH. An additional reason to the Case having occurred, I hastened to Spottiswoode's and inserted it. Was pleased to be thus active. Set out for Richmond Lodge. Stopped a little at Dempster's and was quite cheerful. Got into Fulham coach. Walked over Ham Common. The road was good, though snow lay deep all around. But as I approached the park it was difficult to walk. Luckily I met Mrs. Stuart in her chariot. She took me up, and I went with her and sat in it till she paid a visit, and then she drove me to the Lodge. No

---

[4]Rawdon had been assisting Mrs. Rudd financially, but two years later she published a pamphlet declaring that she was impoverished, and that he had not only stopped providing help but had discouraged others from doing so.

company there. The Colonel and I drank till within five minutes of twelve, and then supped, and he drank punch and I negus. I perceived him to be too much tinctured with Scottish sentiments, and that many envious malevolent reports against me were made to him. I had raved to Mrs. Stuart of M.C., who with great propriety said that a woman who thought as she did might retire with a lover to a desert island without remorse, but was culpable in offending against the laws of society. Yet she could not but in some measure be pleased with her extraordinary talents. The Colonel swore at all this and said he would think of her only as a w—re. I was shocked by his hardness.

WEDNESDAY 8 MARCH. Awaked excessively ill, but was obliged to get up as Mrs. Stuart was to take me to town in her chariot with her two eldest daughters. I was vexed that *still* I was not safe from such an *excess* as that of yesterday. I looked miserably, and she pleasantly said, "I wish Margaret Caroline saw you now." She said her husband was now perpetually devoted to his bottle. What would he be at three-score? Within this fortnight she had beseeched him on her knees to live differently. I had sufficient reason now for resolving to keep myself civilly abstracted from this family, seeing them only seldom, but in good humour, for they saw my faults with too sharp an eye as I was too open and did not at all check my vivacity and humour. A man *exists* just as he chooses his *atmosphere*. I am quite another man with M.C., Malone, Courtenay. So let me be civil to all, even the rankest Scots, but let my free intimacies be select. Mrs. Stuart carried me to London in her coach with her two eldest daughters. I visited my Chief Bosville at the Royal Hotel, Pall Mall, and was able to take tea and bread and butter. Was *nervous*. His quiet sense soothed me. Called on Courtenay, and found I was to dine at his house with Malone, which I did most cordially, and in the evening repaired to Dilly's to be in readiness to set out on the Northern Circuit.

THURSDAY 9 MARCH. Awaked well. After breakfast, walked to the west end of the town. Called in my way on Jack Lee and had a good second breakfast. He said (laughingly), "Now that I am not able to attend the Circuit from age and infirmity, I think myself entitled to give you advice like a Nestor.[5] Attend regularly the courts, take notes, think nothing beneath you, and have as much conference with your brethren upon law as you can." He added, "I take it for granted you'll be very rich." "Why so?" said I. "Because I take you to be a prudent man." I *am* so, as to money and expense. I then found M.C. dressing,

---

[5] Lee was only six or seven years older than Boswell, but he had been called to the English bar thirty years earlier.

and was told she had sent me a note. She would meet me at one. Never shall I forget the scene. So good, so generous, was she. Elegantly dressed: satin *couleur de rose*; her hair in perfect taste—not to be discomposed. A kind wish to give me felicity before a separation.[6]

Called T.D. Was glad he was not at home, he is such a restraint on me. Met him as I walked on, and was pretty easy.[7] Malone, Braithwaite, and Sharp dined with me at Dilly's. Courtenay and Wilkes, who should have been there, could not come. Sat till near nine. Then Malone accompanied me in a hackney-coach to the George and Blue Boar, Holborn, where I was to get into the Newcastle coach to carry me in the best manner to Ferrybridge, from whence I could get in another machine to York.

11 MARCH
10 MARCH
12 MARCH

I had a very safe journey, and took the York coach at Ferrybridge to Tadcaster, where I arrived on Saturday night. On Friday I supped with the Reverend Dr. Palmer at Grantham.[8] On Sunday I went to church in the forenoon at Tadcaster. I was in great spirits all the journey, and wrote well to Malone. Mr. Sigston, one of the jury at York, a schoolfellow of Jack Lee's, was my companion in a post-chaise to that city.

[EDITORIAL NOTE. If Boswell kept a journal during the assizes at York, it is now missing. A selection of minutes from his Register of Letters furnishes excellent material, however, for filling the gap in the

[6]In two undated memoranda Boswell tried to catch some of his feelings about Mrs. Rudd. The first reads: "Tasting wondrous tree of old made us know the difference between good and evil. Tasting thee, my Margaret, the reverse, for it confounds it, and all thy arts and all thy evil is lost in the blaze of thy charms. Thus I at first exclaimed—till through time and on a calm and steady view I found that it was true. My eyes were opened and that all the bad imputed to thee was false, and I now saw thee good, generous, etc., etc." The second reads: "If the Roman Emperor who had exhausted delight offered a reward for the inventor of a new pleasure, how much do I owe to thee, who hast made the greatest pleasure of human life new to me. I used to look on love with feverish joy or childish fondness. All madness or folly, though delight. Thou hast shown me it rational, pure from evil. How keen the fire that thus clears the dross from the most precious ore!"

[7]T.D. was not. He complained in a letter of 24 March 1786 that he had seen very little of Boswell during his last three visits to London. He would, however, always show Boswell firm attachment, as representative of the Family, and the affection of a brother, "however unsteady and guided by caprice you may be."

[8]Boswell had stopped at Grantham to visit him since 1769. In a letter to Malone written this day he described Palmer as "an old clergyman, a very reading man who knew Warburton at an early period."

journal to 27 March 1786 and for annotating some of the entries when it is resumed the next day.]

Sent, 10 March. Edmond Malone, Esq., from Grantham, about my fortification ballad,[9] and as to contradicting a report as to alterations in the second edition of my *Hebrides.*[1]

Sent, 12 March. Edmond Malone, Esq., from Tadcaster, more as to the above. Also as to Courtenay's verses on Dr. Johnson.[2] That whatever good may come of the English bar trial, I shall owe it to him, he having *held* me to it—in great spirits.

Sent, 16 March. [York.] Mr. Dilly, begging he may put off the dinner at his house till after the 22 April with Rudd, etc., etc. How would it do to print a third edition of my *Hebrides* at Edinburgh?

Sent, 16 March. York. Robert Preston, Esq., that I do not despair of yet being counsel for his India Company, in support of which I volunteered so zealously. That though he did not approve of my coming to the English bar, I am sure he wishes me well. I should be happy to have a line from him to tell me how he is.

Sent, 16 March. York. T. D. Boswell, Esq., a kind letter to inquire for a manservant.

Sent, 18 March. York. James Cummyng, Esq., for the pedigree of Menteith,[3] etc. (Copy).

[9]One of Boswell's efforts at topical verse. It concerned a bill in the House of Commons about the fortification of the dockyards at Plymouth and Portsmouth. Having judged his effort to be "one of the best political ballads of this reign," Boswell asked Malone to arrange for its printing, but if he did no copies have been recovered. Some scraps survive in manuscript.

[1]Boswell wrote a signed letter to the press admitting that he had left out twenty-six lines "relative to a noble lord" from the second edition of his *Tour* but further denying the reports given currency by Peter Pindar (above, 24 February 1786) that he had made the changes because of Lord Macdonald's threats. Malone had the letter printed in at least four London newspapers.

[2]*A Poetical Review of the Literary and Moral Character of the Late Dr. Samuel Johnson*, which was still undergoing revision. The poem contained some flattering verses on Boswell:
> Amid these names can BOSWELL be forgot,
> Scarce by North Britons now esteemed a Scot?
> Who to the Sage devoted from his youth,
> Imbibed from him the sacred love of truth;
> The keen research, the exercise of mind,
> And that best art, the art to know mankind.

Boswell was especially concerned that "keen research" should be retained. The poem, published on 6 April, ran through three editions by 20 May 1786.

[3]In order to investigate Mrs. Rudd's claim; perhaps to show it to Lord Rawdon. Cummyng was employed in the Herald's Office in Edinburgh.

Sent, 19 March. [York.] T.D. Boswell, Esq., to inquire about Daniel Merchant, my pickpocket.[4]

Sent, 20 March. [York.] Edmond Malone, Esq., that I am *learning* wonderfully, and am assured that my assiduous attention will procure me business—his letters make me *carior mihi*.[5] A few remarks on Courtenay's verses. Proposing to prosecute the publisher of Peter Pindar for the *false* dialogue to injure my life of Dr. Johnson, the *éclat* of which might be raised by the action—by Erskine expatiating, etc.[6] (A confidential note within.)

Sent, 23 March. [York.] Edmond Malone, Esq., all confidential, for advice concerning an unfortunate matter.[7]

Sent, 26 March. [York.] Edmond Malone, Esq., to send me Signora Piozzi's book in franks, etc.[8]

Sent, 28 March. York. M.C.S., a confession.[9]

Received, 29 March. [Lancaster.] Edmond Malone, Esq., friendly as to my confidential affair; concerning Signora Piozzi's *Anecdotes of Dr. Johnson.*

Received. [Same date. Lancaster.] Edmond Malone, Esq., supposing me much more indisposed than I proved to be, advising me to leave the Circuit directly and return to London to take care of my health. More concerning Signora Piozzi's *Anecdotes.* A good trimming of that lady.[1]

[4]See above, 25 February 1786 and n. 6.

[5]"Dearer to myself." The letter itself adds "as poor Sam wrote to Lord Thurlow." Johnson used the phrase in a letter of September 1784 declining the Chancellor's personal offer to advance enough money on his pension so that he could spend the winter in Italy.

[6]In an invented dialogue which Wolcot appended to his *Epistle*, Johnson, on being told that Boswell means to write his life, is made to say, "Were I sure that James Boswell would write *my* life, I do not know whether I would not anticipate the measure by taking *his*." Boswell did not really think the dialogue would hurt the sale of his *Life of Johnson*, but he thought an action for libel, whatever the verdict, might be useful publicity.

[7]A venereal infection apparently picked up after he left London.

[8]*Anecdotes of the Late Samuel Johnson*, by Hester Thrale Piozzi, Johnson's beloved friend and hostess, had been published the previous day. Boswell calls her "Signora" because of her marriage, commonly considered a *mésalliance*, to Gabriel Piozzi, an Italian singer, in July 1784. They were now on a protracted honeymoon in Italy. Mrs. Piozzi's marriage had caused a permanent breach with Johnson, and many of his friends felt that she had deserted him in his final days.

[9]Margaret Caroline Stewart [Rudd], a confession that he had a venereal disease.

[1]In Malone's first letter, dated 25 March, he described the *Anecdotes* as "very entertaining," though he thought the separate little stories not sufficiently dramatized. He precipitated a bitter literary controversy, moreover, by reporting the postscript in which Mrs. Piozzi attempted to deny Johnson's statement in the *Tour* that she, as well

Received, 30 March. [Lancaster.] Mr. Dilly, with Signora Piozzi's *Anecdotes* by the stage-coach; insisting that I shall dine at his house on the 20 April, as he has engaged Mr. Rudd his attorney and many more to meet me.

Sent, 31 March. York. Edmond Malone, Esq., that I am much better and shall stay out the Circuit. Obviating Signora Piozzi's insinuation that it is *not true* she ever disapproved of Mrs. Montagu's book.

Received, 1 April. [York.] M.C.S., spirited, romantic, and kind.

Sent, 3 April. York. Edmond Malone, Esq., enclosing a refutation of Signora Piozzi, upon recollecting that she had read my *Tour* in manuscript and had not denied what is reported of her slighting Mrs. Montagu's book—leaving to him to publish or not in the newspapers with my name and, more or less, as he might think best.[2]

[EDITORIAL NOTE. We return to the journal, with Boswell on the road from York to Lancaster.]

TUESDAY 28 MARCH. Bolton[3] and I set out in a post-chaise, and were rationally hearty. Came to Skipton to dinner. Found six of the Circuit sitting. Let them go on, and we resolved to stay that night. Walked out after dinner and saw vast lime rock. Tea, after which came another division of our brethren, and we supped together. I had quite English circuit ideas realized. Heard of Norton's death.[4] Was like one in a regiment.

WEDNESDAY 29 MARCH. I had been much pleased with the wild moors. Dined at Hornby. A number of us there. I went with Wood and John Heywood and saw the Castle.[5] Judge Willes was gone to Durham. Serjeant Walker went on to open the commission. Burke's lodgings, which I was to have had, were engaged by poor Norton, whose corpse was there.[6] Reaston not being to come tonight, I got his

as he, could not get through Elizabeth Montagu's *Essay on Shakespeare*. The second letter, dated 27 March, analyses other misrepresentations in the *Anecdotes* and indicates that Malone was more violent against Mrs. Piozzi than Boswell was and encouraged him in asperities.

[2]See below, 15 April 1786 and n. 4.

[3]James Clayton Bolton, serjeant-at-law.

[4]Edward Norton, M.P. for Carlisle, 1784–86, one of the nine seats controlled by the Earl of Lonsdale, a Cumberland and Westmorland magnate of immense wealth and political power (his Members were known as Lonsdale's "ninepins"). Norton had died earlier this month, according to rumour because of fatigue following his service as Lonsdale's chief agent in the Lancaster by-election.

[5]An ancient keep in a commanding situation, "modernized" by Francis Charteris, M.P. and heir to vast estates in Lancashire.

[6]Boswell is now at Lancaster. Richard Burke, formerly Junior on the Circuit, had

room in the house with Bolton, who had given me much instruction upon the road, and had recommended to me to go to a special pleader, both to learn the necessary legal forms and to hang out a sign of being in earnest to take business.[7] Had the comfort to find at Norton's a good letter from *home*.

THURSDAY 30 MARCH. Went to court a little to show myself. Dined at our mess. Evening got into small lodgings. Was quiet.

FRIDAY 31 MARCH. Had a *motion* handed to me in court with *half a guinea* by Mr. Cross of Preston, protonotary of the Court of Lancaster. Bolton had made me acquainted with him, and I suppose I owed my being thus launched on the *Circuit* to *him*. Attended forenoon and afternoon. Dined at our mess. Quiet at night.

SATURDAY 1 APRIL. Johnson breakfasted with me. Dined at the Judge's with all the counsel. Court forenoon and afternoon.[8] Grand Night.[9] We had resolved to be grave on account of Norton. But animal spirits broke loose. Fine letter from M.C.

SUNDAY 2 APRIL. Breakfasted with Johnson. Went to church. Sat just behind the Judge, who pronounced the service admirably well. It was truly edifying. The High Sheriff's chaplain in his prayer before the sermon mentioned the churches of England, *Scotland*, and Ireland, of which the Judge took notice to me.[1] The Rev. Dr. Marton, who has the living here in his own right, had sent to our inn to know if I was the Mr. Boswell who travelled with Dr. Johnson and, if I was, he was coming to wait on me. Mr. Serjeant Walker introduced me to him in church, and he engaged me to dine with him. Young Willes obligingly offered to walk with me, which he did, and showed me a good part of the environs. We met his father and mother airing in their carriage. The Judge asked me to dinner today. I was engaged. Then asked for tomorrow. I was very well at the Rev. Dr. Oliver Marton's, who had lost his teeth and spoke inarticulately, but had the manners of a gentle-

transferred to the milder climate of the Oxford Circuit for reasons of health.

[7] Most new lawyers put in several years' work in the office of a special pleader, an expert in legal technicalities and the drawing of pleadings, before even appearing in the courts.

[8] On this day a woman named Margaret Hamilton, alias Margaret Montgomery, was tried for housebreaking, "upon which Mr. Boswell was instantly called on by his brethren at the bar to be counsel for the prisoner" (as we learn from a paragraph in the *London Chronicle* for 6–9 May obviously composed by Boswell himself). "He readily undertook the office; but his client, instead of a *true Montgomery*, turned out to be a *false thief*, and was convicted of felony." She was sentenced to be hanged, but was reprieved and finally pardoned on condition of imprisonment for two years in the House of Correction.

[9] On "Grand Night" the Grand Court of the Circuit was held (see below, p. 232).

[1] The point is that the established Church of Scotland is Presbyterian, not Anglican.

man, was a scholar, and had seen much good company. Mrs. Marton and I *took much to one another*, as this was a keen Lowther family.[2] Serjeant Walker and Reaston were here. I drank rather too liberally. In the evening went to our inn, and (what was not decent) played at whist. I supped at the mess, and was in too high spirits.

MONDAY 3 APRIL. At court forenoon and afternoon, which is to be understood constantly unless I mention *not*. Dined with the Judge, a private party: Dr. and Mrs. Marton, etc. Eat and drank rather too well. After court returned to tea and played whist. Then assembly. Danced a minuet with Miss Nelly Welsh, an elegant, pleasing girl very like Mrs. Rudd. She and I also *took* to one another from *Lowther* agreement. I danced three country dances with Mrs. Marton; foolishly, for it heated me too much. I liked the ease of the Lancaster assembly much, and was pleased with the sweet *tone* of the ladies.

TUESDAY 4 APRIL. A little feverish; dined very moderately at the mess; drank tea at Dr. Marton's with young Willes and Chambré,[3] etc., and played at *vingt-et-un*.

WEDNESDAY 5 APRIL. Dined at the mess moderately. Evening went to the assembly, but wisely did not dance. Played at whist and drank tea with the ladies, and was quite gay. Here now did I *perfectly* and *clearly* realize my *ideas* of being a counsel on the Northern Circuit, and being an easy gentleman with Lancashire ladies, with no gloom, no embarrassment. *How* I was so well I know not. A constancy of this *may* be the existence of some.

THURSDAY 6 APRIL. Last night a feigned brief had been left at my lodgings.

[EDITORIAL NOTE. The journal breaks off here in the middle of a page, perhaps because Boswell was ashamed at having taken up the feigned brief. It was customary on Grand Night and at other times for Circuit members to play jokes on new barristers, but Boswell, a seasoned advocate at least twenty years older than the other juniors, would have felt keenly the loss of dignity resulting from such a public exposure of his ignorance. He preserved the brief, however, which was discovered in a wrapper labelled "Lancaster, March Assizes, 1786. A circuit joke by which I was for some time deceived." We now print the brief for the first time.]

[2]Boswell had become an enthusiastic partisan of Lord Lonsdale, formerly Sir James Lowther (see above, 28 March 1786, n. 4), whom he had praised effusively in his *Letter to the People of Scotland*, 1785, and in the *Tour*.
[3]Alan Chambré, a bencher of Gray's Inn and a leader on the Northern Circuit.

Brief for Defendant.   The King on the Prosecution of
                                         David Duffus *v.* John Timperley

Indictment
> Preferred at the Liverpool Borough Sessions, found at the Preston
> General Quarter Sessions, removed afterwards by "Accedas ad
> Curiam"[4] hither, and states that, etc. (*vide* Indictment on the Pro-
> tonotary's file)
>   Plea: Not Guilty

Case
> Prosecutor is a man of a very indifferent character and lives by
> gaming and swindling and is also a noted smuggler. Defendant is
> a poor, industrious man and (unfortunately for him) hath been
> very active in detecting the wiles of the prosecutor, which hath
> excited his resentment against him. And upon the 14th of April
> last, as the defendant was attending the Custom House upon the
> quay of Liverpool, the prosecutor called him a *ragged-arse dog* and
> told him he would give him a douse on the chops, upon which the
> defendant, irritated by this foul language, threw a dead cat in pros-
> ecutor's face, which is the whole foundation of the present malicious
> prosecution.

Proofs
> To prove that the facts are as above stated, be pleased to call John
> Anderson, Thomas Timperley (who is brother to the defendant).

Observation
> Jonathan Duffus, the prosecutor's son, was also present and, if
> pressed, must relate as above, but it is submitted that it may be
> dangerous to call him, as he certainly is not a willing witness.

Request
> If there should not appear a full traverse jury, be pleased to pray
> a *tales*,[5] and do not forget to plead hard for costs.

[EDITORIAL NOTE. Absurd and trivial as the action of the fraudulent
brief may appear, it is not so far removed in substance from actual
suits of personal abuse reported in contemporary newspapers and in
Boswell's own legal papers. At least two accounts of this incident survive, the better-known one appearing in a book of anecdotes compiled
long afterwards by John Scott (later Lord Chancellor and first Earl of
Eldon), for the amusement of his grandson. Scott was a leading bar-

---

[4]That you go to court. A writ directing the sheriff to go to a lower court, enrol the
proceedings, and set up the record.
[5]A traverse jury is a trial or petty jury. A *tales* is a writ for summoning persons to fill
out a jury.

rister on the Northern Circuit at the time. Readers may find it interesting to compare the actual document, found in Boswell's papers, with
a legend which helped to shape a stubborn popular image:

"At an assizes at Lancaster, we found Dr. Johnson's friend, Jemmy
Boswell, lying upon the pavement—inebriated. We subscribed at supper a guinea for him and half a crown for his clerk, and sent him,
when he waked next morning, a brief with instructions to move for
what we denominated the writ of 'Quare adhaesit pavimento,' with
observations duly calculated to induce him to think that it required
great learning to explain the necessity of granting it to the judge before
he was to move. Boswell sent all round the town to attorneys for books
that might enable him to distinguish himself, but in vain. He moved,
however, for the writ, making the best use he could of the observations
in the brief. The judge was perfectly astonished, and the audience
amazed. The judge said, 'I never heard of such a writ; what can it be
that adheres *pavimento*? Are any of you gentlement of the bar able to
explain this?' The bar laughed. At last one of them said, 'My Lord,
Mr. Boswell last night *adhaesit pavimento*. There was no moving him
for some time. At last he was carried to bed, and he has been dreaming
about himself and the pavement.' "

Boswell could have been found in the condition alleged, but his
journal shows that he was not drunk on the night of 5 April. Further,
the accuracy of Eldon's anecdote has long been questioned on other
grounds. For one, though Boswell's ignorance of English law was virtually complete, it is at least doubtful that he could have been tricked
into moving a writ with the title Eldon gave it, because the ignorance
assumed is of a different sort: *Adhaesit pavimento* is the title given to
verses 25–32 of Psalm 119 ("My soul cleaveth unto the dust") in the
Book of Common Prayer, with which Boswell's journals and other
writings show him to have been familiar.

Boswell left the Circuit at Lancaster in order to attend the House
of Lords for an appeal in which he was counsel, Cuninghame *v.* Cuninghame. He had written to John Spottiswoode on 16 and 25 March
begging him to secure a postponement to 12 April; Spottiswoode expected him for a consultation on the 10th.]

MONDAY 10 APRIL.   Arrived early in town. Breakfasted Dilly. Malone. General's. Dined Courtenay with Malone and Erskine.

TUESDAY 11 APRIL. Walked about. House of Lords. Dined home
comfortably. In all afternoon and night.

WEDNESDAY 12 APRIL[6]. Wrote letters. Matra and Charles Medows

[6]Cuninghame *v.* Cuninghame was after all postponed to the 24th (see below).

visited.[7] Saw Mrs. Strange and concerted about house. Dined Malone's with Courtenay.

THURSDAY 13 APRIL. Walked a little. Dined home, and in all night.

FRIDAY 14 APRIL. Had resisted seeing M.C.[8] Winter called and gave advice as to his *medicines*.[9] Was comforted. Fulfilled a romantic design to have M.C.'s religious system. Wrote with sincerity as an ancient chivalry Baron: love and piety. Too late for forenoon either Catholic chapel or Church of England. Went to Westminster Abbey a little. Then St. Margaret's Church; in Sir J. Hawkins's seat by chance. Then (strange prescription for illness) Polly Wilson.[1] Then Langton's with design to drink tea and not dine.[2] But he had salt fish, potatoes, and tart. I partook. Then tea, most comfortable. Young Rev. Mr. Cambridge[3] came and praised Courtenay's poem.

SATURDAY 15 APRIL. Breakfasted Malone. Courtenay came. Concerted my answer to Mrs. Piozzi.[4] Had just time before dining with him to take a short walk. Was quite placid, and did not feel the *agitation* of London.

SUNDAY 16 APRIL. (Easter Day.) After rich breakfast at home, also Chapter,[5] St. Paul's. Holy Sacrament; bread from Bishop of Lincoln. Dilly's. Then M.C., most amiable. Dined home; T.D. by invitation. No crowd; a good company.

MONDAY 17 APRIL. Walked in Bedford Square, etc., with M.C. Dined at Mr. Ward's with Mr. Carver. Played whist. Had a headache from a cold, and did not stay supper.

TUESDAY 18 APRIL. Dined at Courtenay's with Malone and old

---

[7]James Maria Matra, British consul to the Canaries, whose *Proposal for Establishing a Settlement in New South Wales* (1784) was the first step in the establishment of the penal colony in Australia; Medows, later first Earl Manvers, was M.P. for Nottinghamshire.
[8]Presumably because he feared he was still ill.
[9]Possibly George Winter, a surgeon.
[1]A prostitute Boswell had met a year earlier.
[2]Because it was Good Friday.
[3]Son of Richard Owen Cambridge, author and wit.
[4]In his reply to Mrs. Piozzi, printed in the newspapers a few days later, Boswell pointed out that it was Johnson, not he, who had said that Mrs. Piozzi could not get through Mrs. Montagu's *Essay on Shakespeare*, that the postscript to Mrs. Piozzi's *Anecdotes* never actually asserted that she had, and that Mrs. Piozzi (then Mrs. Thrale) herself had read Johnson's remark in Boswell's journal without objecting to it. At one point, Boswell also wrote, he had struck her name from his account, but a friend (Courtenay) had persuaded him he had no right to deprive Mrs. Piozzi of the honour Johnson had done her by linking her opinion with his and Beauclerk's, and Boswell had therefore restored it.
[5]The Chapter Coffee-house.

Macklin and his wife and Devaynes. Had been with M.C., who fixed I should drink coffee with her on Sunday and go to Magdalen.[6]

WEDNESDAY 19 APRIL. Dined Sir John Dick's with Sir William and Lady Dick, Mr. and Mrs. Strange, etc., General, and Mr. Gentili. Evening, club: Brocklesby, Sastres, Wyatt, only.[7] Very well. At night Dilly's.

THURSDAY 20 APRIL. My good Piozzian verses made me hasten to Malone's (after writing letters). Neither he nor Courtenay could find me out. Both liked them.[8] Quiet dinner with Dilly. Read John Hunter on venereal disorder.[9] Made one at tea and supper with Mr. Rudd, the attorney, and wife, etc., etc. Had seen M.C. in the morning. She asked me to dine on Sunday, etc.

FRIDAY 21 APRIL. Home a little. Dined Mr. Strange's with Sir William and Lady Dick, Sir John Dick, etc. Was disgusted with Mrs. Strange's Scotch.[1] Wondered how I should be able to do my *duty* as a *laird*. Malone's for relief; he not at home. Found Seward and got well.

SATURDAY 22 APRIL. Called at Ward's to know if he dined at home; not in. The moment he came, a kind invitation. Just he, she, and I. She spoke most kindly as to being well with my family when they came.

SUNDAY 23 APRIL. Comfortable breakfast as usual. Called on Lord Advocate; not in. Found Lord Justice Clerk there, an awkward meeting.[2] Then Bavarian Chapel and revived my first London ideas. Found Lord Eglinton, and was easy but distant.[3] Malone's. Dined with

---

[6]The Magdalen Hospital, an institution for penitent prostitutes, then in St. George's Fields. It was a common practice to make up fashionable parties to visit it.

[7]A meeting of the Essex Head Club. James Wyatt, R.A. (dubbed "the Destroyer" by contemporary archaeologists) restored Salisbury, Lincoln, Hereford, and Lichfield cathedrals and stimulated the great revival of interest in the Gothic arch.

[8]The "Piozzian Rhymes," eighteen rhymed couplets signed "Old Salusbury Briar" accusing Mrs. Piozzi of marketing Johnson for her own profit (a charge to which Boswell himself was vulnerable, of course), were published in the newspapers this day on the same pages as Boswell's signed letter replying to Mrs. Piozzi's postscript to the *Anecdotes*. Her maiden name was Salusbury.

[9]This medical classic had been published on 3 April.

[1]Her accent.

[2]Boswell was involved in a dispute with his neighbour, Sir Thomas Miller, Lord Glenlee, Lord Justice Clerk (presiding judge) in the Scottish High Court of Justiciary, over the stool (new growth from old stumps) of Turnerhill wood, which Miller's uncle, then the owner, had exchanged with Lord Auchinleck for other land about forty years earlier. See below, 20 February 1788.

[3]Boswell had been one of Eglinton's counsel in the Court of Session and had considered him his political "chief" in Ayrshire. Eglinton was also the head of the Montgomeries, his wife's family. But they were fundamentally unlike, and Boswell felt that Eglinton had acted badly by entering into an Ayrshire election arrangement in 1784 with their former opponents, Henry Dundas and Sir Adam Fergusson.

M.C.; boiled fowl and oyster sauce, cold roast mutton and salad of her dressing. Dumb waiter. (Damascene tart by her maid.) Porter, white wine, port. Felt strangely. Then coffee. By and by came Mrs. Ewen of Argyll Buildings and her husband's nephew, an officer of marines from the north of Scotland. We all went in a hackney-coach to the *Magdalen.* (Courtenay had pleasantly said, "To *leave* her there?") Was in quiet frame and pleased with the music. Dr. Harrison preached. She told me she used to hear him in St. Martin's. "But I don't go now. You know who is buried there." (Viz., D. Perreau.) I was struck, but said, "You are an affectionate creature." We walked to her lodgings. I disliked this *low* association.[4] Home.

MONDAY 24 APRIL. Went to the House of Lords on the appeal, Cuninghame against Cuninghame.[5] The Lord Chancellor started a crotchet which Lord Advocate was afraid might be fatal to us, though quite wrong. I was in sad fear. Dined at home. The French Commissary in Corsica was there. The General's *address* was wonderful. The Commissary said, "Je ne parlerai pas ici comme dans le cabinet de Versailles," and owned that "nos bourreaux et nos lois" only had subdued for a time the Corsican spirit,[6] but it would break out whenever there was an opportunity. Malone's some time.

TUESDAY 25 APRIL. Breakfasted at Lord Advocate's by appointment, along with Mr. Taylor, Writer to the Signet, and had a serious consultation on Cuninghame's appeal. His. . . .[7] Appeal ended. Dilly's and brother's, tea. Home; cold meat.

WEDNESDAY 26 APRIL. Dined home.

THURSDAY 27 APRIL. To Oxford.[8]

FRIDAY 28 APRIL. Dined Adams's and supped.

[4]This appears to have been the last time that Boswell ever saw Mrs. Rudd, though he attempted to call upon her in the next year (see below, 29 May 1787).
[5]Boswell and the Lord Advocate (Ilay Campbell) were counsel for Henry Drumlanrig Cuninghame, Mrs. Boswell's nephew, and other creditors on the estate of Lainshaw against the appellant, William Cuninghame, its purchaser, who complained of two decisions of the Court of Session concerning the profits from a lease. The case was continued on 25 April, the appeal dismissed, and the former judgements affirmed.
[6]"I shall not talk here as I would in the Cabinet at Versailles"; he admitted that France had subdued Corsica only by hangmen and the law.
[7]Boswell broke off here at the foot of a page with a blank reverse. The record is continued by very brief notes to the end of May.
[8]With Malone, to collect more materials for the *Life of Johnson* from Johnson's old friend, Dr. William Adams, Master of Pembroke College, and from the poet and scholar, Thomas Warton, who had recently sent Boswell transcripts of nineteen early letters from Johnson.

SATURDAY 29 APRIL. Breakfasted inn. Laureate dined with us.[9] Supped Adams.

SUNDAY 30 APRIL. Felt dreary. With Malone to St. Mary's. Dr. Wetherell's, etc. Dined Adams; tea Wall's. Visit Adee.[1] Sup Adams.

MONDAY 1 MAY. To London.

TUESDAY 2 MAY. Courtenay's with Malone.

WEDNESDAY 3 MAY. Dined Malone's with Courtenay and Kemble.[2]

THURSDAY 4 MAY. Madam's letter.[3] Dined home.

FRIDAY 5 MAY. [*Nil.*]

SATURDAY 6 MAY. Dined home.

SUNDAY 7 MAY. Langton's, calm.

MONDAY 8 MAY. Dined home.

TUESDAY 9 MAY. Dined home.

WEDNESDAY 10 MAY. Breakfasted Earl Fife's. Dined Dilly's.

THURSDAY 11 MAY. All forenoon for poem.[4] Courtenay's with Malone. Not Westminster Hall.

FRIDAY 12 MAY. Tea Owen's. *Beggar's Opera.*[5]

SATURDAY 13 MAY. Malone's with Courtenay. Breakfasted Sir J. Dick. No Westminster Hall. Miss Monckton's. Lord Eglinton's.

SUNDAY 14 MAY. Lay till half past three. Ill and sunk. T.D. dined. Tea Malone.

[9]Thomas Warton.
[1]The Rev. Dr. Nathan Wetherell, Master of University College, Oxford; Dr. Martin Wall, Lichfield Professor of Clinical Medicine; and Dr. Swithin Adee, a distinguished physician who died later this year, aged 81.
[2]Boswell's first recorded meeting with the great actor, John Philip Kemble, with whom he later became good friends.
[3]Probably Mrs. Piozzi, possibly a letter published in the newspapers over her name, though we have failed to find any such. If "Madam's letter" could be stretched to mean "newspaper paragraph attacking Mrs. Piozzi," a plausible identification would be a paragraph in the *General Evening Post* for this day, almost certainly written by Boswell: "We hear that Madam Piozzi, with her *cara sposa* [dear spouse], will soon return to England—when she intends to have him naturalized, and take the name of her ancestors; how far the name and family of Salusbury may be enriched or ennobled by such an alliance and union, she certainly can best explain to the public."
[4]Almost certainly "Lines Supposed to be Written by Mrs. Piozzi in Italy," eight four-line stanzas that play coarsely on Mrs. Piozzi's "fleshly fun," confess her longing for England, and explain the *Anecdotes* as a test of public reaction to her proposed return under the protection of Mrs. Montagu. The manuscript is unfinished, and the piece seems never to have been published.
[5]A benefit at the Haymarket for a retired actress, Mrs. Pinto, formerly Miss Brent. "Owen's" is probably Owen's and Seagoe's Coffee-house, No. 20, Holborn, much frequented by lawyers.

MONDAY 15 MAY. Dined home, Colonel Erskine there. Chapter, Scots newspapers.

TUESDAY 16 MAY. Dined home. Entered my house.[6]

WEDNESDAY 17 MAY. Breakfasted Langton. Dined Malone's.

THURSDAY 18 MAY. Breakfasted Sir Joshua with Bishop of Killaloe. Kensington with Malone. Dined Courtenay.

[Boswell to Margaret Boswell]

London, 18 May 1786

MY DEAREST LIFE,—You are too good to me. I had your letter of the 11th yesterday, and today I have that of the 13th. I am afraid you hurt yourself by writing to me oftener than you should do, that I may not be too much alarmed. I have been two nights in the Queen Street house, the solitude of which is very dreary and gives room for very uneasy thought. Your illness distresses me deeply;[7] and the situation of my affairs is really wretched. I begin to apprehend that it was very ill-judged in me to venture to come to the English bar at my time of life. I see numbers of barristers who I really believe are much better qualified for the profession than I am languishing from want of employment. How then can I reasonably hope to be more successful than they? The encouraging speeches made me by many people I suspect

[6] He has left Paoli's and is entering his own (as yet unfurnished) house in Great Queen Street. Mrs. Boswell, who had moved with the children to Auchinleck, shipped him twenty-one parcels of furnishings from the house in Edinburgh. They included, she wrote, "twelve hair-bottomed chairs, in six parcels, two dining-tables with four blankets, the curtains of the tent-bed, two mattresses, two carpets, a bolster and three pillows all packed in them, a breakfast table, a large box with three mirrors and several prints, a hair trunk with sheets, table-cloths, top sheets, bolster slips, pillowslips, six teaspoons, your glasses of your inkstand, some shirts of yours and eight of mine, a box with my laces and a piece of silk for a gown, towels and kitchen cloths and three window curtains and four pair of coarse sheets for servants. There is also two grates, one for a dining-room and one for a bedroom, with two pairs of tongs and one poker and one shovel and two fenders; a large packing box full of law books excepting a few English ones, your inkstand and two packs of cards at the top to fill it up and which I thought would be necessary to have. The key of the trunk is marked as one of the parcels. There is also a cask with six dozen of Hall's port. . . . There is a small box containing marmalade and honey and one with a silver sugar dish, six silver table-spoons, two sauce-spoons, some knives and forks, a teapot, milk-pot, and six breakfast basins, and four coffee or chocolate cups which will serve you in the afternoon."

[7] On 9 May Boswell wrote a letter to Alexander Wood which he registered as follows: "Anxious as to my wife's return of spitting of blood; begging to have his sincere opinion; suggesting that moderate journeys and change of air may be of service to her, and that she would not be hurt by living in my house in London, which is in a wide, well-aired street."

were made merely to please me, or without any serious consideration. I indeed see the necessary application to be much more difficult than I imagined. Yet, on the other hand, my long-indulged notion that I might rise to wealth and honour at the *English bar* is not yet quite subdued; and it may be advisable to make a farther trial to get myself thoroughly satisfied, so as never again to be disturbed by it should I not succeed. In this wavering state I go on attending Westminster Hall, where, however, I own I am entertained, as business is done with so much accuracy and in so agreeable a manner. If I do not hear soon that you are better I will hasten down to you, for all considerations on earth are nothing compared with your comfort. If you should by GOD's blessing have a speedy recovery, I should wish that you would come up by slow journeys; because if I do continue making the trial of the bar here it would be proper to attend till this and the next term are over, and to go the Home Circuit,[8] by which means I could not get home till the middle of August, and that is a long, long time from this date. The distance at which we are is terrible. May GOD in His infinite mercy grant us a more pleasing prospect. I am quite cast down.

The difficulty of determining what to do with my sons here is another uneasy consideration. Worthy Langton is so afraid of public schools that he teaches his himself. Both of mine have such constitutions that I should think it too great a risk to board them with strangers amongst many boys, and yet I could not well have them at home. At this moment it seems to me a curse that I ever saw London, since it has occasioned so much vexation to my family and may estrange us from our own fine Place. I am not *now* much disturbed by apprehensions of being ashamed to return to Scotland, for during my last visit I was convinced that I can put a good face on it. But perhaps it would be better to let our children have a year or two of this place and then quietly retreat. I am pretty sure that London will not be the same to me as a settled man that it was to me as an occasional man. O! my dearest, most valuable friend, counsel me! The great consolation is that we can stop when we please.

I cannot think but what there will be money for you to receive at Auchinleck. I wish things there may be properly managed. I spoke to Mr. Strange about Lady Colville's painter. He had already recommended a Mr. Allan. Lady Dick and Sir William are foolishly afraid. I will publish nothing about Sir Alexander that will not do him credit.[9] The worthy General at whose house I am now writing is sin-

---

[8] The assizes in Hertfordshire, Essex, Surrey, Sussex, and Kent.
[9] Boswell intended to write a biography of Sir Alexander Dick.

cerely concerned about you. He imagines you are very unwilling to come to London, and he does not wonder at it. But if it shall please heaven to allow you to come, you will find him truly kind, as also Mr. Gentili, the amiable Corsican gentleman who lives with him. Should you be able to come soon, we may perhaps contrive together to do pretty well in all respects, and I will not go to Scotland this year except perhaps for a forthnight to look after the estate.

This is a woeful day with me. I have not been at Westminster Hall but with Mr. Malone at Kensington, hearing speeches delivered by young gentlemen at the academy kept by Dr. Thomson, whom you have seen at Mr. Kincaid's. It is a very good academy. Mr. Courtenay has two sons at it. Mr. Malone and I are to dine with Mr. Courtenay today. The expense of the academy is great, £70 or £80 a boy; at least Courtenay's eldest son says *his* comes to that.

I hope James has not been at a play, as I am very desirous that he should go first [with] myself. Yet I do not deserve that pleasure, for leaving my family so much. The thought of it shocks me. Yet it was meant for their advantage, upon the whole.

This letter will be directed to Edinburgh, in case you should not have left it. My next will be directed to Auchinleck. I have no expectation now of any continued happiness in this life, as it appears to me I shall only suffer disappointments. Let me be thankful for such a blessing as my dear, dear M.M. and such fine children. I am ever most affectionately yours,

J.B.

How will you do for a manservant at Auchinleck? I insist on your having a chaise often for an airing.

FRIDAY 19 MAY. Dined Ward's with Colonel Sutton, etc. Alarmed about wife.

SATURDAY 20 MAY. Very uneasy about wife. Desponding; sinking into melancholy. Roused. Dined Malone's with Courtenay, Sir Joshua, etc. Sat till twelve.

SUNDAY 21 MAY. Breakfasted Malone. Much cast down about wife. Dilly's a little, which consoled me. Dined General's.

MONDAY 22 MAY. Still uneasy. Dined Wilkes', most friendly.

TUESDAY 23 MAY. *Club.*[1]

WEDNESDAY 24 MAY. Carlisle Committee.[2] Dined General's: Ma-

[1] The Literary Club, now called simply The Club.
[2] The Select Committee of the House of Commons concerning the disputed Carlisle election.

lone, Seward, Ross Mackye, Sir George Collier. In great anxiety about wife.

THURSDAY 25 MAY. Carlisle Committee. Dined Malone's tête-à-tête. In great anxiety. Dilly's, night. Wavering as to schemes. Thought of quitting here at once.

FRIDAY 26 MAY. Carlisle Committee. Dined Dilly's with Counsellor Bond, etc. Letter from wife; better. Relieved as if from rack. Dilly's. He and I met Jerry Palmer. Supped Queen's Head, Holborn. Home, twelve. Rats; shocking.

SATURDAY 27 MAY. Dined Windham's with Malone, Courtenay, etc.

SUNDAY 28 MAY. Breakfasted Martin and went with him and Chenery to Woodford.[3] Excellent, without excess. Night Dilly's.

MONDAY 29 MAY. Carlisle Committee. Dined General's.

TUESDAY 30 MAY. Report of Carlisle Committee. Was really sorry.[4]

After a dissipated interval, I shall endeavour to resume my journal with some distinctness.

THURSDAY 1 JUNE. The morning was passed away doing little. I dined at Sir Joshua Reynolds's with the Bishops of Killaloe and Down,[5] Mr. Malone, etc.

FRIDAY 2 JUNE. Attended the sittings in K.B.: *Buller, J.*[6] Was well entertained. Dined at Mr. Ward's.

SATURDAY 3 JUNE. Went to T.D. in the morning, much cast down as to my settling in London. He pressed me strongly not to bring up my family, as it would involve me in difficulties and estrange me from Auchinleck. I saw all this strongly, and half resolved to go down without delay. Called on Lord Advocate, just setting out. He was for my making a fair trial. I dined at Malone's, and at first was in a very gloomy frame. But good eating and wine and conversation revived me. Byng's family[7] was there, and Courtenay. After supper Malone, Courtenay,

---

[3] Robert Preston's country place. Martin was his clerk.
[4] The Committee had unseated John Lowther, Lonsdale's cousin and henchman, for blatant vote-making in the special election held on 10 April to fill the vacancy caused by Norton's death. Boswell made no entry in the journal for the 31st.
[5] William Dickson, a close friend of Fox, to whom he was indebted for a rapid promotion to the bishopric of Down.
[6] He was sitting justice (see above, 23 February 1786 and n. 8). A provocative item appeared in the *Public Advertiser* for this date: "Mr. Boswell is said to have had the offer of the first vacancy as a Lord of Session."
[7] John Byng (later fifth Viscount Torrington), a Commissioner of Stamps, whose family finally consisted of five sons and seven daughters.

and I got into good conversation upon human life, and Malone with ability showed me that I had no reason to be discontented, and that making a trial in London was right. He raised my spirits to a manly pitch, and I came home at three in the morning quite resolved to stay in London at least a term or two more.

SUNDAY 4 JUNE. Rose heated but not ill; breakfasted with Jack Lee, who had come to town two days ago; found him pretty well, but not disposed to attend Westminster Hall. His solid talk did me good. I satisfied him that it would be best for me to go the Home Circuit. I told him I had as yet no practice, and that I would not hang on long. He said I should not much derange my affairs (or some such phrase) in trying. He appeared very indifferent. I went a little into Long Acre Chapel, occupied by Methodists, and felt piously. I had received a day or two ago a very severe remonstrance from the Hon. Mrs. Stuart, supposing my conduct worse than it was, by ill-natured information. It was in such terms that I resolved neither to answer it nor go to her till I should hear from her again.[8] I called on Courtenay and introduced him to Miss Seward, now in town.[9] Then he and I went to Malone's. Both of them were ill from yesterday's excess. I then introduced him to the Bishop of Killaloe, with whom we sat some time. I felt uneasy that I could not entertain at my house as I wished to do. We walked in St. James's Park. I dined at General Paoli's. The foreign company, good dishes, and good wine raised my spirits. I talked cordially with worthy Gentili, who was clear for my giving Westminster Hall a fair trial, and said, "Would you go down, just to come up again?" I was impatient to see my dear wife, and wished much she would come up soon. I visited Mrs. Love.[1] Went home and to bed in good time.

MONDAY 5 JUNE. At home all forenoon sorting materials for Dr. Johnson's *Life*.[2] Dined at Mr. Taylor's, Old Burlington Street, with Seward, the Rev. Dr. Maxwell of Ireland, who had lived twenty-five

[8] Boswell had never kept his infidelities secret from Mrs. Stuart (see above, 7–8 March 1786, p. 50), but she may well have thought his affair with Mrs. Rudd particularly unfeeling in view of Mrs. Boswell's illness and the burden of responsibility she was being made to bear because of the imminent removal to London. Mrs. Stuart had written to her on 31 May 1786 that "when I consider what an effort it is, how uncertain whither [a Scotticism] you will be able to reconcile yourself to London and its ways, I pity you with all my heart."

[9] The poet Anna Seward, the "Swan of Lichfield," with whom he had been attempting to revive a flirtation she had cooled the previous year.

[1] Actress, widow of James Dance, alias Love, actor, manager, and author. Boswell had had an affair with her in Edinburgh when he was twenty-one and she perhaps forty. He seems to have renewed it in London in 1776 and 1778.

[2] The first mention in the journal that Boswell was actually starting to put the *Life of Johnson* together.

years in London and been much with Dr. Johnson, and Captain Cord-
well, with whom I had not been in company since (I think) the year
1758, when he lived in Mrs. Rainie's (same house with me),
Edinburgh.[3] Curious thought. Mr. Taylor had through Seward asked
me to meet Dr. Maxwell, and had called on me in the forenoon. He
was a gentleman of the law and had a place in Exchequer. His lady
was a beautiful young creature. Maxwell had a good deal of
Johnson.[4] Home evening.

TUESDAY 6 JUNE. Dined at Courtenay's with Malone. Was mod-
erate, and went home quietly. Had met Mr. Matra by appointment at
Sir Joseph Banks's at breakfast, and then been introduced by him to
Mr. Hargrave. Shrunk from his law learning.[5]

WEDNESDAY 7 JUNE. Breakfasted with the Bishop of Killaloe. Was
in sad despondency as to my London plan. Had wavered lately so
wretchedly that I had talked both to Murphy[5a] and Lord Advocate of
going back to the Scotch bar directly. Strange how hypochondria per-
verts the judgement! The Bishop, as both Murphy and Lord Advocate,
was for a fair trial being made. He went with me to Westminster Hall,
and walked about with me in my *bar dress*. He said we had had a
comfortable morning. I saw and heard Buller, J., decide admirably *nisi
prius* cases. But I was languid. Dined General Paoli's very dreary. Tea
Malone's. Home; "gloomy solitude."[6]

THURSDAY 8 JUNE. Rose sadly irresolute. Almost cried. Was weak
enough to try to get comfort from Mrs. Strange. Her vulgar Scotch
disgusted me. Left her and called on Jack Lee, but he did not rouse
me sufficiently. Went again to Mrs. Strange and fairly complained to
her of her speaking so broad, and got her a little refined. She was very
sensible, and thought that my making my trial here would really be
an economical plan for some time. I grew somewhat better. Went home
and did a little in sorting Johnsonian materials. Was visited by Mr.

[3] Boswell went into lodgings in the spring of that year to complete the term at Edinburgh
University after the Court of Session rose and his family left its town house for
Auchinleck.

[4] He later sent Boswell the very valuable *collectanea* which appear in the *Life of Johnson*
at the end of the year 1770.

[5] Francis Hargrave was approximately Boswell's age, but he had already published
various legal treatises and collections including his well-known *Argument in the Case of
James Sommersett, a Negro*, 1772, which demonstrated the illegality of domestic slavery
in England.

[5a] Arthur Murphy, actor, barrister, dramatist, and author of *An Essay on the Life and
Genius of Samuel Johnson, LL.D.*, 1792.

[6] Johnson used the phrase "this gloom of solitude" in the last paragraph of his Preface
to the *Dictionary*.

Malon and Mr. Kemble, the actor. Also by Mr. Hargrave, who sat a long time with me, and I did not shrink so much from his law learning as on Tuesday, being firmer. I dined by appointment with my brother T.D. He was quite eager against my continuing here, or bringing up my family. I said I *must* make the experiment. He and I walked in the Temple. Then returned to his house to tea. Then was restless, and thought of supping somewhere. Sir Joshua not at home, nor Seward. Wisely came home.

FRIDAY 9 JUNE. Was in a very irresolute frame. Thought of trying to get a loan of a hundred or two from some friend. Breakfasted at General Paoli's and grew better. Found Mr. Ward, but checked myself in the wish to borrow of him, as it might occasion a coldness, when we were, and might ever be, well together, and he perhaps of essential service to me one day. Out to Dempster's. Not at home. Malone's a little, and got advice as to my *Life of Dr. Johnson*: to make a skeleton with references to the materials, in order of time. Called at the *academy* in Soho Square. Talked with the Rev. Dr. Barrow, the Master. Found that Colonel Drummond of the Artillery had two sons there, and I really thought it would do well for my sons. This was comfortable. Ten prints in burlesque of my *Tour to the Hebrides* were published this morning.[7] This enlivened the demand for the book. It was now out of print. I went to Baldwin's to hasten the third edition, and intended to dine with him. Found him just sitting down with his family, and was made heartily welcome. Drank rather too much mountain,[8] but was in excellent sound spirits, and wrote to my dear wife, *cheerfully resolved* that she and the children should come to me as soon as she was able to travel. Was too late for the post, though I ran to Dilly's. Found him, and was cordial with him, as indeed he is my steady friend as far as it is in his power to be. Home quiet. Was stunned by finding a letter from Captain Robert Preston asking me to *settle my note*, i.e., to pay him £500 with two years' interest, within a month. I trusted I should persuade

[7]The first volume of the famous series of caricatures, *Picturesque Beauties of Boswell*, drawn by Samuel Collings and engraved by Thomas Rowlandson. The second volume containing ten additional caricatures was advertised for publication on 29 June 1786: this includes the one print in the whole series which Boswell would seem likely to have deeply resented. It is entitled "Revising for the Second Edition" (see illustration, following p. 160). Lord Macdonald holds Boswell by the throat and points sternly at an open copy of the *Tour*. Two leaves, on which the page numbers 165 and 167 appear, have been torn out and lie on the ground, and Boswell, in an agony of terror, is begging for mercy.
[8]A variety of malaga, made from grapes grown on the mountains.

him to give me a delay till next spring.[9] But the feeling of being in debt and liable to such alarms was very painful. But there was now no help for it. I flattered myself that in a few years, by strict economy, I should be clear. It was now *plain* to my *undisturbed reason* that it would be absurd not to remain for some time at the English bar; for I should ever fret were I to return to Scotland as unsatisfied as formerly. And I really thought that, upon the whole, I could live at less expense than in Scotland.

SATURDAY 10 JUNE. I dined at Malone's with Dr. Kearney, late of Trinity College, Dublin. Malone and Courtenay and the Bishop of Killaloe breakfasted with me. The Bishop was the first person whom I entertained in my London house. Dilly also was with me.

SUNDAY 11 JUNE. Was agreeably surprised in the morning by a visit of Sir William Forbes. He *comforted* me and made me sensible that my being some time in Westminster Hall would not be against my getting a judge's place in Scotland. I went with him to Lothian's Hotel and waited on Lady Forbes. Then was in sundry churches. Called Malone's a little. Dined at General Paoli's with Matra, etc. T.D. there. Walked out to Kensington Gore to insist on Wilkes's dining at Dilly's next Saturday. He was denied. Left a note for him. Visited Dempster in my way home. Found an old Mr. Brice, etc., etc., with him. Saw him in as dull a state as if at Edinburgh. But Matra's remark is just: that by having a house in London, one can be in London in a minute. Came to Malone, and had something cold and some wine.

MONDAY 12 JUNE. Sir William and Lady Forbes, Langton and his son, breakfasted with me. This was truly cheering, and I saw no distance between London and Edinburgh. I cannot put upon paper the various agreeable sensations. Robert Boswell called and was some time with me. I went with Langton and was introduced by him to Judge Gould, whose placid manners did me good.[1] He said, "Mr. Langton, I am much obliged to you for introducing me to Mr. Boswell." I sat at home all day, sorting materials for Johnson's *Life,* and took neither dinner nor tea. This was wrong. I was faint and uneasy. At half past ten went out, not knowing well whither I should go. Called at Lord Eglinton's;

[9]Preston granted the postponement (see below, 18 May and 26 October 1787). Boswell had borrowed the money to cover an earlier loan to Margaret's nephew Alexander ("Sandy") Cuninghame, who died of consumption in 1784. In 1790 Boswell was still trying to collect on extensive loans he had made to the Cuninghame brothers to get them started in life.

[1]Sir Henry Gould, Senior Judge of the Court of Common Pleas.

gone to Ranelagh. Found Seward, and had cold roast beef and wine, and grew better, but sat too late and did not get home till half past one.

TUESDAY 13 JUNE. Awaked with a headache, and could not do anything. Went to Courtenay's and had some tea. Went to Malone's, and in a little Courtenay followed me. Was quite relaxed[2] and quite helpless, as I knew not where to dine. Happily Malone asked me. I walked out with Courtenay. We overtook Burke in Pall Mall, going to the House. He talked of secret influence and bad government, and I felt awkwardly as being so conspicuously on the other side. It was unpleasant. I parted from them as soon as I decently could. I lamented that politics made a cold separation between us which never could be got over.[3] I dined most comfortably and soberly with Malone, and went home in good time.

WEDNESDAY 14 JUNE. Was now very well reconciled to the solitude of my present state. Sorted Johnsonian materials a little. Went with Sastres and was introduced to Mrs. ———,[4] widow of an Irish dean, who with her sister Miss Cotterell (who lives with her but who was not at home) were old acquaintances of Dr. Johnson, and made him and Sir Joshua Reynolds acquainted. She could give me no materials for his *Life*.[5] I dressed at General Paoli's, and dined at Mr. Ward's; my Chief and his mother and the Rev. Mr. Carver there. Drank tea at Malone's. Mr. Reed there. Then was at the Essex Head Club (last night this year). Royal Ross was there as Mr. Barrington's guest.[6] I was in excellent spirits. Murphy walked near home with me, and I told him I now had nerves to persist patiently in Westminster Hall. Indeed my dear wife's recovery consoled me into excellent spirits. I thought I would make a steady trial of the English bar; and if I could but get business, would certainly distinguish myself, notwithstanding the ill-natured observations of too many enemies. I had left a card at Dundas's

---

[2]Enfeebled.

[3]Burke was a prominent member of the Foxite Opposition, while Boswell supported Pitt, the Prime Minister.

[4]Lewis.

[5]That is, she *would* give him nothing. But she later complained to Mrs. Piozzi that Boswell's account of the meeting of Johnson and Reynolds (which he had from Reynolds) was inaccurate.

[6]David Ross, actor, dubbed "Royal" because he was the initial patentee and manager of the Theatre Royal, the first legal theatre in Edinburgh. (Boswell wrote the Prologue for the opening performance in 1767.) Now lame and very poor, Ross survived on an anonymous annual gift from Admiral Samuel Barrington, his host's brother.

door a week ago.[7] I this day left a *second* at DOUGLAS's, that he might be fully in the wrong should he neglect one to whom he was very much obliged.

THURSDAY 15 JUNE. Stayed at home all forenoon sorting Johnsonian materials. But there was something in the weather which relaxed me so that I was quite inactive. However, I kept at it. I dined (for the first time) with the Right Hon. William Gerard Hamilton, with Courtenay and Malone, to whom were added Lord Lucan and General Dalrymple, just returned from Italy. I was pleased to think that so able and so elegant a man as Hamilton was my second cousin.[8] The occasion of my being at length invited to his house was my being engaged in writing Dr. Johnson's *Life.* He promised to give me two letters of the Doctor's to him and some anecdotes. The elegance of Hamilton's house, table, and manners, and particularly his beautiful language and pronunciation, pleased me very much. I was glad that I had removed to London. Thus comfortably did I feel being in the best company, and having possibilities of promotion. I flattered myself that I might have one of my sons such a man as Hamilton. It is impossible to register the various workings of my mind, while there was a *background*, however, of *thoughtfulness.* Yet I experienced how happy one may be after having almost despaired. We did not drink long. But had tea and coffee, and sat a long time in the twilight chatting. We parted between ten and eleven, and I went quietly home.

FRIDAY 16 JUNE. Trinity term began, and I felt myself animated by seeing Westminster Hall crowded with lawyers. Lord Mansfield's taking his seat again upon the bench was a striking sight. Yet one could not help perceiving that all was vanity. I breakfasted at Langton's with Sir William and Lady Forbes and the Bishop of Killaloe, and I dined at Sir Joshua Reynolds's with the Bishop, Burke, Sir William Forbes, Langton, Malone, Courtenay; an excellent day.

SATURDAY 17 JUNE. Was at Westminster Hall in good time. Then stole away and went with Sir William Forbes to Malone's. Then returned with Sir William to his hotel. Lady Forbes charged me with a dangerous connection. I assured her *it did not exist.* I satisfied Sir William, and he promised to contradict the ill-natured report. He also in

---

[7] For Boswell's hope that Dundas, an old schoolfellow and family friend, would help him, see below, 8 July 1786 and n. 4.

[8] Through his mother, both men being great-grandsons of Sir Charles Erskine of Alva. Hamilton, nicknamed "Single Speech," sat in the House of Commons from 1754 until his death in 1796, but he seldom spoke after his celebrated maiden speech. Johnson's friend and Burke's first patron, he enjoyed a reputation for wit and fastidiousness.

a very friendly manner engaged to talk of my returning to the Court
of Session as a thing that I intended in case either of want of success
in Westminster Hall or of my wife's health not agreeing with London;
and thus there would be no appearance of fickleness. I dined at Dilly's
with the Bishop of Killaloe, Malone, Courtenay, Wilkes. The Rev. Mr.
Fullarton from Jamaica and Mr. Sharp were also there. We had an
excellent day. But I drank rather too much wine. The Bishop walked
home with me to my house and left me to go to bed, it being between
ten and eleven. But I was restless. So supped at Lord Eglinton's; Lord
Elphinstone and Major Mackay there. I was prudently *retenu*[9] and
drank port negus, but came home at two in the morning much heated.

SUNDAY 18 JUNE. Was feverish. Breakfasted at the Chapter
Coffee-house. Sat awhile with Dilly; grew calm. Went to Temple Church
and heard part of the evening service and a sermon, and was devout.
Went to dine at General Paoli's, but a number being there, went to
Mr. Ward's, where I was invited. Found Carver, Topham, and
Andrews.[10] Was in good spirits. Drank rather too much. Called a little
at General Paoli's. Home in good time.

MONDAY 19 JUNE. Was feverish. Did not get a seat in the King's
Bench, and standing and the heat hurt me. So I left it soon. Dined at
Mr. Devaynes's, the King's Apothecary, with Seward. Drank again rather
too much. In the evening went to Malone's, where I had been asked
to dine; found Farmer, Lort,[1] Reed, Courtenay; supped and was jovial.
Home late.

TUESDAY 20 JUNE. Was again not easy in the King's Bench. Went
to Woodfall's to see a letter mentioned in his paper as sent to him with
my name forged to it.[2] He was not at home. Met the Bishop of Killaloe
in St. Paul's Churchyard. Walked with him to some shops, looking at
cheap watches. He came home to my house and sat a little while with
me. Dined at the Literary Club: present, the Bishop of Killaloe, Lord

[9]Reserved, restrained.
[10]Edward Topham, journalist and playwright (chiefly farces), founder the next year
of *The World*, a daily newspaper notorious for gossip and character assassination; and
Miles Peter Andrews, author of many farces, comedies, and light musical plays, and
co-director of *The World*.
[1]Richard Farmer, D.D., Master of Emmanuel College, Principal Librarian of Cambridge University, and a member of The Club, said to have loved three things above
all others: "old port, old clothes, and old books"; and Michael Lort, D.D., distinguished
antiquary, from 1759 to 1777 Regius Professor of Greek at Cambridge.
[2]The *Public Advertiser* for this date announced that it would not print the letter because
the signature was forged.

Spencer, Dr. Burney, Mr. Malone, Mr. Windham, Mr. Steevens,[3] and myself. Social enough, but not conversation for the money. Walked quietly home and went early to bed.

WEDNESDAY 21 JUNE. Dined at Mr. Ward's with the celebrated Captain Morris, who sung one of his political songs.[4]

THURSDAY 22 JUNE. Was at home soon from Westminster Hall. Resolved to sit all day sorting Johnsonian materials. Bishop of Chester paid me a visit. Hon. Mrs. Stuart called, and I went into the coach with her and her daughter. She told me she had had a letter from my wife, begging she would let her know *upon honour* how I was; for if I was dreary in solitude, she would come to me directly at all risks. How kind was this. Mrs. Stuart and I agreed to let her determine to come now or afterwards as she should think most agreeable. Returned home and sorted till I was stupefied. Drank tea at Anderton's Coffee-house. Supped at Mr. Strange's. It was quite *Edinburgh*.

FRIDAY 23 JUNE. This was a curious day. I had resolved to attend strictly in the King's Bench. But I met Strange at Charing Cross, who told me all the places were taken, so I need not hurry down. I therefore went to make some calls. Sat awhile with Sir W. Forbes, and with the Bishop of Killaloe. Met Bosville in Pall Mall, who asked me to breakfast with him, which I did. His brother joined us, and I sat so long that when I got to Westminster, court was up. Visited Dr. Kippis,[5] as also Mr. Ross Mackye, who had been ill. Felt the misery of having no settled place to dine at. Went to General Paoli's. Tenducci there.[6] Evening Malone's, Courtenay there. They were entertained with my dissipated day, so different from what I had planned. They gave me a strong impression of the error of my fancy in wishing to live so as that it may *tell*. I ought to do what I found most agreeable. I came home inclined to go to Auchinleck, as all my English bar scheme was chiefly with a view to how it would *tell* in my *life* in the *Biographia*.

[3]George John Spencer, second Earl Spencer, later First Lord of the Admiralty and Home Secretary, said to have collected the finest private library in Europe; and George Steevens, editor of Shakespeare (a rival of Malone) and intimate of Johnson, known as "the asp" for his anonymous slander of his literary friends in print.

[4]Charles Morris. A Foxite and intimate friend (later pensioner) of the Prince of Wales, he wrote very popular songs for the Whigs, among them "Billy's Too Young to Drive Us."

[5]Presbyterian minister, editor of the *Biographia Britannica*, and author of a life of Sir John Pringle, close friend of both Boswell and his father. Kippis was now tutor at the new dissenting college at Hackney, where Price and Priestley were his colleagues and William Godwin one of his pupils.

[6]A castrato of Sienese origin prominent at Covent Garden and Drury Lane.

SATURDAY 24 JUNE. Was sadly dispirited. The court did not meet. Went to Richmond Lodge. Colonel Stuart not well. Dined tête-à-tête with him on cold meat and drank only cider. He was still against my English bar scheme. Sir William and Lady Cunyngham were here. I walked with Mrs. Stuart and them in the evening. The fine scene had no good effect on me.

SUNDAY 25 JUNE. Came to town early in Sir W. Cunyngham's chaise. Was disgusted by his bringing Scottish ideas full upon me. Was in wretched spirits. Went to Seward's and had some tea, and was relieved by him. Then some chocolade with Malone. Then Temple Church and commons at barristers' table. Then Dilly's and supped with Tunbridge Knox and his wife.[7]

MONDAY 26 JUNE. Attended Westminster Hall pretty well. Had resolved to take one week of the barristers' table, Inner Temple Hall, and refused every invitation to any other place. But Wilkes insisted I should dine with him and meet Counsellor Jekyll. I could not resist, and I was well entertained. Home in good time.

TUESDAY 27 JUNE. Attended K.B. very strictly.[8] Having broke the Temple week's dining yesterday, Malone prevailed with me to dine at Dr. Brocklesby's, where I had made my excuse. It was very comfortable. Nobody there but he and I, Murphy, and Counsellor Cooke.[9] We were sober and calm. Malone and I walked in the Temple garden. He then went home with me and had some bread and wine and water, and heard me read some Johnsoniana. He argued clearly with me not to be uneasy, for that I might be at the English bar, or the Scotch bar, or no bar at all, and nobody would trouble their heads about what I

[7]Vicesimus Knox, Headmaster of Tunbridge School (see above, 22 December 1785, n. 2).

[8]The Legal Notebook bears witness to his strictness on this day. He took down nine pages of highly condensed notes on two cases and began to take notes on another, concerning a will; but after a few lines he found it too much for him and wrote, "Saw I could not understand this. So went away."

[9]William Cooke of the Middle Temple, miscellaneous writer and constant member of the Essex Head Club; later called "Conversation Cooke" on account of his poem *Conversation* (1796). He added to the fourth edition (1815) "poetical portraits" of some members of The Club and of the Essex Head Club, among them Boswell,

> whose roving fancy sought
> By turns—the charms of pleasantry and thought;
> Whatever subject met his mental view,
> He added something pertinent or new;
> For such the fullness of his jocund mind,
> He needed no preparatives to find.
> His humour, like the beauties of a face,
> Cost him no trouble—it was nature's grace.

did. And I might make a trial at Westminster Hall at little expense, and have my children improved by being in London.[1]

WEDNESDAY 28 JUNE. Attended K.B. strictly; always taking notes is understood. Dined Inner Temple. Drank tea at my brother's, he not at home. Just as I left his house, met Captain Bruce Boswell, returned from India.[2] Sat some time with Malone. Home in good time. But nothing yet done to Johnson's *Life*.

THURSDAY 29 JUNE. Westminster Hall. Resolved to fast and try to write. Could do little. Dr. Hall of Newcastle's two sons drank tea with me. I felt myself not a bit better than long ago at Edinburgh College when students visited me. They sat on, and I got cold beef and wine for them.

FRIDAY 30 JUNE. Not at all well.[3] I dined at Wilkes's with Mr. Robert Mackintosh,[4] etc. Mackintosh and I drank five bottles of mountain. Sat till near one. A curious scene.

SATURDAY 1 JULY. Walked about in the City after having been at Westminster Hall a short time, my yesterday's intemperance making me restless. Dined in the Inner Temple Hall comfortably. Had breakfasted with Sir W. Forbes and settled that I should quit English bar, either directly or after a winter's trial. My valuable spouse's health was one great objection.

SUNDAY 2 JULY. Worthy Langton came and breakfasted with me, and I took him to the Moravian Chapel in Fetter Lane. We were too late, so heard no prayers; but we had a sermon from Mr. La Trobe,[5] who delivered himself with a manly and pleasing propriety. Walked in the park and was very gloomy. Felt London quite ineffectual. Imag-

---

[1]He further fortified his resolution by the following memorandum, written on a separate piece of paper: "Tuesday 27 June 1786. Remember how well Mr. Malone made you. You saw that London and Auchinleck may be *united*. If you go there every year, the distance will be nothing. Your *records* and *memorandums* of the Inner Temple will be in the family archives, and you *may* have a fortunate display and get a brilliant fortune. Be firm, then, and see what time will produce. If you sink, you will be in worse misery. But be habitually sober and *retenu*."

[2]Boswell's first cousin. He had brought back the *Earl of Chesterfield*, which he commanded, from an ill-managed and luckless trading venture and was shortly afterwards removed from his post and the East India Company on charges of private trading and failure to obey orders. Boswell was concerned with his cousin's career because he had borrowed £500 to help him undertake this venture.

[3]He attended court, however, and took down four and a half pages of notes. They were the last he recorded this term, which ended on Wednesday 5 July.

[4]An able but unpopular advocate, who after having left the Scottish bar more than twenty-five years earlier had had a varied career in politics and business. He had recently failed to re-establish a legal practice in Edinburgh.

[5]Benjamin La Trobe, a leader of the Moravian sect in England.

ined I should be well if I were at Auchinleck. Dined General Paoli's. Had no comfort in existing.

[EDITORIAL NOTE. Some time the next day Boswell wrote the following letter to Margaret Boswell.]

[Boswell to Margaret Boswell]

London, 3 July 1786

MY DEAREST LIFE,—That I am very selfish you have told me, and I have acknowledged it. But I am not so *excessively* selfish as to resist your very strong and persuasive letter of the 23 June, in which you describe the uneasiness it would give you should our family be removed to London and the desolation of Auchinleck so feelingly, that I yield to you. Enclosed is a note which I wrote to my brother next morning after receiving your letter, as also a very earnest one from him to me on the 9th of February.

For some time past, my constitutional melancholy has been grievous. The solitude of this house has frightened me into constant dissipation. I do not mean vice but a perpetual succession of company; and my mind has been quite unhinged. My anxiety about you and the children has been dreary, and I have upbraided myself for neglecting you.

I am now *convinced* that there is no *probability* of my getting great practice at the English bar; and therefore there is not an *adequate reason* for putting you and my children into a state of *inferiority* and running the risk of their being estranged from Auchinleck.

The difficult question then is, what should be done? Lady Forbes says that if you are assured that I will return with you to Scotland in the spring you will have no objection to come to London and bring Veronica and Phemie and pass the winter; and your mind being relieved from the imagination of being banished forever from your country and friends, *that much* of London would do you no harm, and then I shall have made a fair trial of my chance in Westminster Hall. But, in truth, I already see clearly that I have so poor a chance that it is not advisable to persist. Mr. Malone thinks otherwise, and I am loath to contradict his opinion. Yet it is shocking to me, who have been used to have a competent share of practice, to be altogether without it, and I am impatient and fretful. Lady Forbes and Sir William are full of your kind attention to them last winter, and have proposed that as it may be better for Sandy to be at the High School while we are in London, he shall be at their house as one of their own sons. How agreeable is it to be so well with them!

My next consideration is Dr. Johnson's *Life*, which it is necessary I should get ready for the press soon, that the public attention may not be diverted to some other object; and as I have collected a great variety of materials, it will probably be a work of considerable value. Mr. Malone thinks I can write it nowhere but in London. But I *feel* that it is almost impossible for me to settle to it here on account of the agitation to which I have been used; and, especially in the present state of my mind, how can I settle to it, when I am in a kind of fever to think of my absence from *her I love*, and who is *my own*, and with whose illness I was lately so deeply alarmed? My intention therefore is, that as the term . . . .[6]

MONDAY 3 JULY. One of the days of last week, when very dejected, I visited Mr. Paradise,[7] with whom I talked freely; and I found that though then pretty well, he suffered severely from hypochondria, and used to take to his bed. We consoled one another. This day I attended in K.B. some time, and was in sad spirits. But Courtenay and Malone having often talked of my giving them a bit of mutton in my house, I had settled to have a good company today "in a half-furnished house to take plain fare."[8] They were Courtenay and Malone, with the Hon. Mr. Ward, Sir Joshua Reynolds, Mr. Wilkes, and Sir William Forbes, who was truly happy to be one of such a party. My drawing-room was as yet a lumber-room, but it was a kind of pleasantry to have them in it thus. And Wilkes joked on my old chairs from Scotland. Courtenay asked if they had been brought by *habeas corpus*. I gave a good plain dinner: a turbot, roast beef, beans and bacon and other vegetables, and a cherry and currant tart; claret, port, sherry, cider, porter, small beer. I worked myself into tolerable spirits. But there was an inward gloom from the thought that I was to give up London. But, alas! is not my *station* at Auchinleck? We had an excellent day. Courtenay, Malone, and Sir W. Forbes stayed till past twelve.

TUESDAY 4 JULY. Was very ill in K.B. and so restless that I could not stay. I walked into the City and wandered among its streets, which I have found a kind of relief. I was *distracted* between making a farther trial of the English bar and quitting it at once. I sat awhile with Royal Ross, who was for my quitting. Neither Mr. Dilly nor Mr. Preston, with either of whom I thought of dining, were at home. I sauntered into various coffee-houses "seeking rest and finding none."[9] The Virginia,

[6]The rest of the letter is lost.
[7]Linguist (Oxford honoured him with the D.C.L.), close friend of Johnson, and member of the Essex Head Club.
[8]Boswell seems to be quoting from his own letter inviting the guests.
[9]Luke 11:24.

Maryland, and *Greenland* Coffee-house attracted my curiosity, but I found nothing particular in it. I walked on beyond Cornhill to see if there were any coffee-houses so far east. I grew somewhat weary. I perceived *Aldgate Coffee-house*. Went into it and had tea and dry toast and butter. This was a poor relief. When I got into the streets again I was so depressed that the tears run down my cheeks. I thought of my dear wife and children with tender affection. I upbraided myself for being so long absent from them. I upbraided myself for neglecting Auchinleck. I found young Mr. Atkins, the Russia merchant, at home, and had some conversation with him upon the money left by one Aitken in Russia, as to which I took some concern for Ayrshire people.[1] I was so uneasy that I could not help talking to *him* of my not continuing at the English bar. I then found Dr. Scott of the Commons. Dr. Calvert, Dean of the Arches, was with him.[2] I felt a sad distance between myself and them, whom I saw steady in business. When Scott and I were alone, we talked seriously of my attempt in Westminster Hall. He thought I might now judge, for if I was to succeed at all it must be by a *coup de main*; and he was for my quietly returning to the Scotch bar. This I at *that time* in my woeful dejection resolved I would do. I then found Dilly, to whom I groaned, and also declared my resolution of going off to Scotland. I came to my solitary house drearily, as to a prison. What a poor, wretched day!

WEDNESDAY 5 JULY. Was still dreary. Breakfasted with Sir William Forbes. Breakfasted also with my Chief Bosville, who owned he was quite melancholy. He was worse than I was. Matra, who was now appointed to go King's Agent or Envoy to the Emperor of Morocco, also breakfasted. I grew a little better. It was the last day of term, so I showed myself in Westminster Hall. Was weary and fretted, and talked to many of the counsel that I intended to return to the Scotch bar. This was imprudent. But mental pain could not be endured quietly. I had talked in the same way to Mrs. Strange. I called on Malone. Courtenay came, and Malone insisted that we should dine with him. We did

[1]Atkins's father (like the son, named Hugh), founder of the business in Austin Friars, had recovered the few hundred pounds left on the death of Aitken (or Atkin), a bankrupt Scottish schoolmaster whom he had helped to migrate to Russia. Boswell, working without fee, was attempting to arrange out of court a division of the money between Aitken's sisters and the four needy children of his deceased brother.

[2]William Scott (later first Baron Stowell), five years younger than Boswell, was a distinguished historian and His Majesty's Advocate in the Admiralty Office. Doctors' Commons housed the Admiralty and Ecclesiastical Courts and the Doctors of Civil Law of Oxford and Cambridge who practised there. "Dean of the Arches" was the lay judge of the Court of Arches, the court of appeal in the Church of England for the province of Canterbury.

so. My spirit revived, and I had as full enjoyment of life as at any time. We had coffee and tea, then pickled salmon, and sat till one, full of excellent conversation. Good madeira and port warmed and elevated me.

THURSDAY 6 JULY. Assisted at the annual breakfast at my brother David's with General Paoli, Gentili, and Masseria. I was again depressed a little, but became insensibly cheerful. Called on Mr. Bosville to console him. Found he was much better. Went a little into Westminster Hall and was present at Judge Buller's sittings, but without my dress. Walked in the Hall awhile with young Strange, who thought it madness for one who had such an estate and so fine a Place as I had to come to be dependent on business; that he had said to his mother he never expected I would get into great practice; and therefore I should take the bar only as a mode of passing time agreeably, unless I would set myself with serious diligence to it. I quite desponded, and saw all the technical difficulties terribly magnified. I dined at General Paoli's, and was much cast down when he said, "You are past the age of ambition. You should determine to be happy with your wife and children." The solitude of my house in London I thought sunk my spirits. Good Gentili proposed that I should resume my bed at the General's. This, though I felt it weak, I resolved to do. I was gloomily restless. Went to Dilly's, thinking to sleep there. But he had a Kentish clergyman and his wife in the house. I supped with him and them and grew a little better. About eleven I went to the "Friends round the Globe," finding Akerman was there,[3] and though all was sickly in my mind, contrived to do very well. Gave a *star* (i.e., three bottles) on my being called to the bar, and stayed till about one.

FRIDAY 7 JULY. Rose sadly ill. By Matra's recommendation took an emetic. Brother T.D. called and was for my going to Scotland directly. I put it off. Dined at Mr. Ward's, faint and dreary. Was comforted somewhat by excellent cheer, and took very little wine. Drank tea at General Paoli's. Sat awhile with Malone, who thought my not going next circuit looked like quitting the English bar and thought I did not give it a fair trial. He talked of the success I *perhaps* might have in such spirited terms that, though I timidly shrunk and was ashamed, I had yet some stirrings of ambition, which distracted me. Courtenay came. I stayed a little, but not being well, went home before twelve. Had today an enchanting letter from my wife.

SATURDAY 8 JULY. Sat at home all forenoon, partly talking with Langton, who called on me, partly drawing up a state of my claim for

---

[3]Richard Akerman, Keeper of Newgate, had introduced Boswell to the club the previous July. It met nightly at the Globe Tavern in Fleet Street.

a Lord of Session's place to be sent to Mr. Dundas, to whom I had applied for a meeting to point out what would make me and my family comfortable, and he had wished I would rather write to him. I considered that he probably had old hereditary friendship to a certain degree, and that as a politician he might think it judicious to oblige me and be unwilling to offend me, so as to afford solid cause for complaint; and that at any rate my trying him could do no harm, as it was in *confidence*.[4] I dined at General Paoli's and had resolved to return at night. Drank tea at Langton's and had a conference with him and Sir John Hawkins upon a delicate question, which Langton assured me I weighed and decided upon as well as he could suppose it to be done.[5] Yet I *imagined* myself a poor, weak, miserable wretch. Talking seriously with Langton on the deceitfulness of all our hopes of enjoyment on earth, while I at this moment languished for the comfort of being at home with my wife and children, the worthy man, from whom one would not expect it, suggested how domestic happiness was deceitful and how often we feel disgusted and weary when with our family. This calmed me—gave me pause. I returned to the General's. Luckily my room was not properly prepared, which prevented me from feebly and foolishly quitting my house and creeping into my old quarters as a sickly minded being. I went home determined to confine myself for some time.

SUNDAY 9, MONDAY 10, TUESDAY 11 JULY. These three days I confined myself to the house and took only tea and dry toast to breakfast and boiled milk and dry toast at night, and this discipline made me quiet, and I did the first part of Dr. Johnson's *Life* and made

---

[4]Boswell's long "confidential case," sent two days later, was a desperate move, since he had attacked Dundas vigorously and effectively in his *Letter to the People of Scotland*, 1785, the year before. After a frank statement of his professional and financial embarrassment, he asks Dundas to procure him also a post of two or three hundred pounds a year to keep him afloat at the English bar until there should be a vacancy in the Court of Session. When Dundas responded six months later, he pointed out that appointment for "political merit" was one of the reasons he believed the judges in Scotland too numerous, and Boswell's application was well-grounded only if his promotion would "give satisfaction to the bench, the bar, and the country." He returned the confidential paper, which he had shown only to Pitt, since he understood it to be meant for him also.

[5]Boswell, in a "grave and earnest" conversation with Hawkins, 7 May 1785, also at Langton's, had learned that Hawkins had read something in a diary of Johnson's no longer extant that convinced him that Johnson's fear of death resulted from remorse for sexual irregularities. On the present occasion Boswell appears to have worked out an agreement with Hawkins, who was also writing a life of Johnson, that they would both report these lapses, placing them at the time when Johnson first came to London and was under the influence of Richard Savage, but giving no details and citing no source.

arrangements for more of it. My resolution now was to put it in such a way that I could carry it on at Auchinleck, and as soon as I had it so, I was to set out, and wrote so to my wife. My brother T.D. called and was earnest for my doing this; and as I was to return in November to polish and complete the *Life*, he was for my instantly letting my house, so as to have no kind of *settlement* in London, and not to bring up my wife to be in an *inferior* state. I was sadly dejected and very impatient to be gone. Fortunately Malone called on me on Tuesday, and with his judicious and elegant spirit roused me from despair. He urged that I must act rationally; that I must not appear so ridiculous as to fly off from Westminster Hall before there was time for its being well known that I was in it; that I must fulfil what I had proposed, and must certainly be at least one winter at the bar; that going no circuit was a kind of declaration that I did not mean to continue in the profession, therefore I must go the Home Circuit. He did not insist upon my going to every one of the towns, but I must go to one or two of them, so as that it might be said I went the Home Circuit. That I might then go to Scotland and bring up my wife and two eldest daughters for the winter and live upon a very moderate scale; and that all my notions about *inferiority* were *pride*, which ought to be repressed. He thus saved me from acting in a way of which I must have repented grievously. When the fit of melancholy was off I should have seen the despicable fickleness of my conduct and been vexed by the ridicule with which I should have perceived myself looked upon.

WEDNESDAY 12 JULY. My intention was to persevere in confinement and fasting for a week. But about four o'clock, in came Malone and Courtenay in good spirits and told me I must go with them and have a ramble into the country and dine at Dulwich. I was feeble in body and dim in mind. But I was complaisant to my two excellent friends, dressed quickly, and away we walked beyond Westminster Bridge, while London and all its animated objects only oppressed my sensorium. We took a hackney-coach at length, and the motion did me good. Courtenay, who while in the Ordnance made many friends, called at a Captain Dickinson's at Camberwell and got a couple of bottles of madeira for us. I had never been this way before, and I imperceptibly got some relish of the beautiful scenes around. The old College at Dulwich pleased me much.[6] We found at this place the Greyhound, the best inn, just as ill-provided as one in the remote parts of Scotland

[6]Malone had become interested in Dulwich College because it possessed the library and manuscripts of its founder, the Elizabethan actor Edward Alleyn, and of his father-in-law, Philip Henslowe, the theatrical manager. Malone, whose own collection of Elizabethan texts was extensive, is said to have persuaded the Master to exchange the College's remarkable collection of quartos for an equal number of printed sermons.

or Ireland. However, we got bacon and eggs and mutton chops. It was curious to me after my three milk diet days to have for the first time in my mouth bacon and eggs. I eat hearty. We had a bottle of port, but it was such stuff we did not drink it. Small beer, good ale, and our admirable madeira warmed me and raised me again into temporary felicity while in such company. We walked pleasantly to London and had some cold beef and wine and water at my house. The gallant Captain Dickinson had waited for us as we returned, and wished much that we should stop at his house, but it would have made us too late.

THURSDAY 13 JULY. Could not rest at home, but did not lose the day, for I went to Malone's and with his assistance traced Dr. Johnson's publications chronologically through the *Gentleman's Magazine*, and wrote their titles down under each year. I dined at General Paoli's and returned to Malone's, and thus pursued my task, which entertained me.

FRIDAY 14 JULY. My spirits were as good as ever I remember them. I had now balm-tea for breakfast. Covent Garden is the best garden in the world.[7] I stayed in till between three and four doing something to Dr. Johnson's *Life*. I wrote in a sound and gay frame to my dear wife, informing her how well I now was and how *fixed* by my friend Malone. I had a consultation with Mrs. Strange, to whom I talked too freely of my waverings; for she said I had need of a good nurse, and by all accounts I had an excellent one. She was clear for my not going to Scotland this year, but that my wife and two eldest daughters should come to me as soon as they conveniently could, and the other three children should stay all winter at Auchinleck. I wrote a note to this purpose and sealed it in the cover of my letter to my wife and felt myself easy. I then set out on a brisk walk to Richmond Lodge, where I intended to be all night; but when I came to the gate of the Park I was informed of the death of Miss Charlotte, the second daughter of my friends at the Lodge.[8] I however walked on to the house and inquired particularly about them, and having rested a few minutes, I resolutely walked home, stopping only a little while at Putney to take some gin with milk and sugar and a biscuit. I was very hot and very wearied when I got to my door. But having told my man that I was not to be back that night, he and his wife had gone out somewhere, and I had to walk like a sentry for almost three quarters of an hour. When I got in I shifted myself and had some ham and bread, a bottle of cider and a glass of port, and was very comfortable.

SATURDAY 15 JULY. My spirits were delightfully good. But the impression of the uncertainty of life made upon me by the death of

[7]A reference to Covent Garden market, notable for its fruit, vegetables, and herbs.
[8]She was fifteen years old.

Colonel Stuart's daughter changed my yesterday's purpose of not going to Scotland, for I was tenderly anxious to see my three youngest children, whether I should bring them to London or not; and being in a sound and vigorous frame, I thought I might be of essential service to the business of my estate. I therefore wrote to my wife trusting that she would not be set out before my letter would reach her, and telling her that I intended to come home whenever I had finished my appearance on the Home Circuit. I dined most agreeably at Malone's with Courtenay.

SUNDAY 16 JULY. Breakfasted at Mr. Strange's. Went into the Sardinian Chapel, but found it too crowded. Then went to prayers in Great Queen Street Chapel, which I found thinly attended but very comfortable. Was glad to think it was within a few doors of my house. Malone and Courtenay and young Courtenay came about one in a hackney-coach and I joined them to go, as we had fixed on Wednesday, to see Norwood and dine in the open air.[9] We clubbed our dinner. Courtenay furnished two bottles of madeira, Malone, a couple of roasted chickens. I furnished cold roast beef, some slices of ham, a loaf, two bottles of port, a bottle of cider, salt, table-cloth, plates, glasses, knives, and forks. My servant went on the back of the coach. It was a delightful day. We did not find the gipsies; indeed we did not look much for them, but dined under a tree. I wished for a room and table and chairs. We were troubled by ants. However, it was very well. We walked to the top of the hill above Dulwich, from whence we saw all London before us on one side and on the other an extensive rich country. I wished to have a house here. It was as wild as Arthur's Seat.[1] We walked home, drank tea at Camberwell like sober citizens, and had some pickled salmon, etc., at my house.

MONDAY 17 JULY. Mr. Andrew Lumisden breakfasted with me, and I read an article on Scotch music and one on pastes in imitation of precious stones and intaglios and cameos, both which articles he had furnished to the new *Encyclopédie* at Paris.[2] Lord Kirkcudbright and my very old acquaintance Dr. Wright[3] sat with us some time. My spirits were calm and pure and gay. I then visited young Willes, who was ill

[9]This village south of London scattered around a large wild common was a favourite haunt of gipsies, who were sought out for fortune-telling (Pepys reports his wife going there for that purpose). They were also hunted down and prosecuted for vagrancy.
[1]The eminence overlooking Edinburgh on the east where Boswell had walked and which he had romanticized since his youth.
[2]These articles have not been located in the revised (but confused and incomplete) edition of the famous *Encyclopédie*.
[3]William Wright and Boswell had been at the University of Edinburgh thirty years before. Most of Wright's life since had been spent in Jamaica, as physician, botanist, and slave-trader.

and confined at his father's house in town. I delivered him the records and purse of the Northern Circuit.[4] I dined at General Paoli's. Met there Mr. Matra and his brother the Major, whom I had not seen before.[5] He owned hypochondria, of which we talked freely. I drank tea at Malone's, and had really a good day of it.

TUESDAY 18 JULY. I did something to Dr. Johnson's *Life*. Langton sat awhile with me. I dined at General Paoli's, where was Abate Andrei.[6] I drank tea at Langton's. Was wonderfully well. Home quietly.

WEDNESDAY 19 JULY. Was a little restless. Called on Sir James Erskine in Cavendish Square and left a note that, as I was going the Home Circuit, I would be obliged to him if he would present me to Lord Loughborough, if upon inquiry he found it would be agreeable to his Lordship, and left my address that he might send and let me know.[7] I had called on Courtenay and promised to go with him to call on Wilkes. Went to Malone's for a little while. Then went with Courtenay and called on Wilkes and Langton. Neither at home. Then went to call on old Macklin. Courtenay had ordered in some mutton for chops. But both he and I were ready for any social party. Luckily we met Wilkes in a hackney-coach in the Strand, who asked us to dine with him. We sat awhile with Macklin, and then had a pleasant trio at Wilkes's. I was obliged to be home at nine to receive Mr. Irving, the solicitor, whom I had asked to eat a bit of pickled salmon and drink a glass of port with me. Mr. Spottiswoode was to have been with us had he come to town, but he did not. Between nine and ten, while Mr. Irving was with me, I was surprised by a visit of Langton, his mother, and son, who sat some time. Irving and I then had our cold repast and drank three bottles of port. I mentioned how I had been going to quit the English bar in despair, but that I had been advised to continue for some time. He said, "We must see what can be done." My having him with me was right. But as before I was called to the bar, he had spontaneously said he should be glad to be of any service to

[4] As Junior on the Circuit in Boswell's absence. See above, 13 February 1786, p. 36.
[5] The Major had retained the surname "Magra," which the family had adopted when it migrated from Corsica, probably because two relatives named "Matra" were defeated rivals of General Paoli.
[6] Paoli's secretary; poet and parodist.
[7] Erskine, Boswell's remote relation, was nephew and heir to Alexander Wedderburn, first Baron Loughborough, Chief Justice of the Court of Common Pleas. A Scottish advocate who had transplanted himself to the English bar at an early age, Loughborough had risen to his present office by proving his usefulness to a series of politicians, and Boswell must have taken his career as a model to some extent for the one he hoped to pursue. He had struck up a conversation with Loughborough at Court several years earlier, but Loughborough's "cold stiffness" had kept him at a distance (Journal, 16 May 1781). Now Boswell is trying to arrange a formal introduction.

me yet had not given me a brief, I could not depend much on what he threw out.

THURSDAY 20 JULY. I was not the worse for my last night's port. I was at home, arranging the order of Dr. Johnson's *Life*, part of the morning—I believe indeed the whole. Dined at Ward's with a Mr. and Mrs. Hesse. Stayed the evening; played whist and lost and was vexed somewhat; supped. Did not get home till two in the morning.

FRIDAY 21 JULY. Either yesterday or this day went to Nichols, the editor of the *Gentleman's Magazine*, who pointed out to me some particulars concerning Dr. Johnson. Dined at Courtenay's with Wilkes and Malone, a very pleasant day. When I got home, found a charming letter from my dear wife, clear for not deciding hastily as to my London scheme. I found to my no small surprise a card from Lord Lonsdale asking me to dinner next Monday to a turtle. This was truly a stirring of my blood. I strutted and said to myself, "Well, it is right to be in this metropolis. Things at last come forward unexpectedly. The great LOWTHER himself has now taken me up. I may be raised to eminence in the state." Yet as I was not at all acquainted with him, had never called on him, and he had not left a card for me, I resolved to be at the bottom of the affair next morning.

SATURDAY 22 JULY. Went to Malone and consulted him. He thought my suspicion was probably well founded. But I urged that poor Norton, who was his confidential counsel, told me he was a man *sui generis*, and therefore, though his inviting me to dine with him without having called on me was not *comme il faut*, it might be in character for such a potentate. I went and called on Mr. Garforth, his capital manager and one of his Members of Parliament, with whom I had got acquainted while the Carlisle election was before the Committee. He could have ascertained the fact for me, but was not in town. Malone's servant, who is a sensible, clever fellow, was then sent to Lord Lonsdale's house with the card, to inquire if it had been sent to me—to speak to the butler or *valet de chambre*, but to send no message upstairs. He returned with information that it *was* sent; that he had been shown the list of company for Monday and read my name in it; and had been told that a gentleman who dined lately with Lord Lonsdale had informed him where I lived. This was all well. But the question was what I should do. I was engaged to dine at Malone's on Monday with Wilkes, whom I had introduced to him, Sir Joshua Reynolds, etc. And although I might *perhaps* have gone to the great LOWTHER's dinner without having had the honour of a previous visit had I not been engaged, it was as well that I could excuse myself by mentioning a respectable engagement. I hesitated much, as this approach to him might be a great crisis in my fortune. But Malone thought that my calling on him on Tuesday would give me a better opportunity of having particular conversation with him, and that it was best to act with some dignity. I thought so too, and said I would not meet him but as an ancient Baron. So I wrote the following card:

"Mr. Boswell presents his compliments to Lord Lonsdale, and is exceedingly sorry that it is not in his power to accept his Lordship's obliging invitation, having been for some time engaged to dine on Monday next at Mr. Malone's with Sir Joshua Reynolds, Mr. Wilkes, and some other friends.

Saturday 22 July."

I walked about in the forenoon and dined at General Paoli's with only himself and Gentili. Was in fine spirits. Found Miss W———n at home, pleasing as ever, but kept my resolution of fidelity.[8] Supped at Mr. Strange's. It was London Scottified. But I was well enough not to be fretted.

SUNDAY 23 JULY. Rose a little uneasy, I believe from having drunk some strong beer last night. Went a little while to the Sardinian Chapel, and a little while to the Methodists' Chapel in Long Acre. Between one and two Malone called by appointment and we went to visit Murphy, that he might be asked to be one of our party at dinner next day. But he was gone upon the Circuit. We then proceeded to Wilkes's, where Malone left a card. I next persuaded him to walk with me in the Mall. Lord Eglinton was walking there with Bosville and came up to me with a speech inquiring how I had been. Now he had never once called on me since I went into my house, nor asked me to dine in a proper manner, but only once casually in the street; and I had asked him to introduce me to Lord Lonsdale, at least I think I had hinted it, and he had evaded it, having no wish to do an obliging thing to me and being pleased that I wanted something which it was in his power to procure me. I told him with an air of triumph, "I have been vastly well." "I have heard of you," said he. "You may have heard of me, my Lord. But you have not seen me, though I have had the honour of leaving a card at your Lordship's several times."[9] He seemed a little out. I followed my blow: "Pray, my Lord, do you by chance dine with Lord Lonsdale tomorrow? I have got a card to a turtle." "No," said he, drily. And then said, "I think Lord Lonsdale a great bore. He'll

[8]Possibly Polly Wilson.
[9]Boswell had, in fact, supped at Eglinton's on 17 June (see above), without invitation, it appears; presumably this did not count as a formal visit.

tell you a long story of—" I broke in: "What, the great Lowther himself! the potentate!"—looking elated and keeping aloof, and then, not to be questioned, broke off—"But I must follow my friend" (Malone, who had walked on). So I flew off, and left him to meditate and chew. This was all fair. I said to Malone it was not *tantal*izing but *turtle*izing him.

I was quite fatigued and faint and would have given half a guinea to annihilate the hour between four and five, that I might get dinner at General Paoli's. I met Courtenay in Portman Square and sauntered a little while with him. Then dined at the General's with two Poles, Matra, my brother T.D., etc. I grew much better. My brother got into an expostulation with me on my saying that I might find it advisable to reside some years in London, and became really upbraidingly warm. He had the old-fashioned principle as to *residence* as a *Baron* as strong as ever and a great deal of that *pride* which cannot brook that a *respectable* gentleman should be of no *consequence* by being in a metropolis, though he may be *happier*. Poor man! I felt for him, as he really suffered. But I saw that there was no *mystery* in having my family for some time in London and that I might keep a constant intercourse with Auchinleck, be at it every autumn myself, and return with my family to it whenever I pleased. I went to Malone's and sat some time.

MONDAY 24 JULY. Either yesterday or today I visited young Willes. Saw the Judge and Mrs. Willes also. I dined at Malone's with Wilkes, Sir Joshua Reynolds, and Courtenay and had an excellent day. Courtenay and I stayed till about one in the morning. Ward had called on me in the forenoon by appointment and we had gone to old Macklin's, Courtenay's, and Malone's, that he might visit them. None of them at home.

TUESDAY 25 JULY. Did a little to Johnson's *Life*. Malone asked me to eat the debris of yesterday's dinner with him. I could not refuse, and we were vastly well. I had been in the City in the forenoon; visited my brother and Mr. Forbes, who was rationally pleasing as to my trying my fortune in Westminster Hall and as to the propriety of using the ordinary means of getting business, by cultivating attorneys and their connections. I felt London quite easy, not at all as a strange land; not as *totally* different from Scotland in producing feelings but only as better. I called on Mr. A. Anderson; did not find him, but met him on 'Change. Was quite calm. Was comfortable in the thought of being to set out the next day on the *Home Circuit*.[1]

WEDNESDAY 26 JULY. My brother T.D. called and saw me into a post-chaise between seven and eight, my servant William Gardiner with

[1] It is odd that the journal makes no reference to the proposed call on Lonsdale on which Boswell had set so much store. He may have called and found him out.

me. It was a delightful day. I was sorry that I could not find a companion to divide the expense of posting with me. At Ingatestone I found Counsellor Park in a post-chaise alone. I joined him, and he engaged to return with me on Friday, as I had engaged to come if I could and dine that day at Wilkes's with the party at Malone's. I was much pleased with Chelmsford (which I had only passed through in my way to Harwich, without observing it)—the neat, clean, new appearance of the houses, excellent well-furnished shops, and a stream running down the middle of the High Street. I was recommended by Mr. Strange, who was gone to the Northern Circuit, to Mr. Stanes, bookseller and stationer, in whose house I had a large, cheerful, well-furnished room and accommodation for my servant. I knew by this time most of the counsel upon this Circuit, and soon got acquainted with more. I found myself the *Junior* here as upon the Northern, but the office was not near so burthensome, there being no *courts* nor no *record*. I had only to take care of dinner and supper and the bills. Indeed, I was considered as in the *chair*, and every speech made in the way of general communication was addressed to me. I resolved to be upon my guard and to establish a character for sobriety and prudence. There was no excess here, and I liked their style much. They were all from London, with the *temper* of the capital unblunted by long absence from it, as on other circuits, and the mind was not oppressed by the weight of a tedious continuance in one place. Some of us had tea at a coffee-house newly set up and walked in the cool of the evening. Lord Loughborough arrived in the afternoon but did nothing tonight. I had been offended at Sir James Erskine for taking no notice of my note wishing to be presented to his uncle if agreeable to him. I suspected my having mentioned in my printed letter to the Bishop of Derry that Sir George Savile, on Wedderburn's boasting what he had *gained* by going over to the Court, had said, "This House *knows* what he has *lost*," might have offended him, so that he might not choose to see me;[2] but civility required *some* answer from Sir James. This night I received a very polite letter from him: that he had been out of town (no matter whether true or not), so that it was too late to go with me; but Lord Loughborough would receive me with pleasure. We had today after

[2]In 1784–85, Boswell had published in the newspapers an exchange of letters, dated some years earlier, between himself and Frederick Augustus Hervey, Bishop of Derry (also fourth Earl of Bristol), on what the Union of 1707 between England and Scotland presaged for a proposed union between Great Britain and Ireland. Loughborough, after opposing Lord North violently, had accepted the post of Solicitor-General and become North's devoted follower. Savile had made his statement in the House of Commons.

dinner a treat of good claret from Mr. George Bond on his being raised to the dignity of serjeant; and though I was not of the Circuit at *the time*, he obligingly presented me with one of his gold rings, so that I was by *retrospect* made quite like the rest. I felt this attention very warmly. It was a proof to me that my *character* attended me. Supped at the *mess*.

THURSDAY 27 JULY. Attended the court; dined and supped at the *mess*. I was much upon my guard to acquire a character of prudent reserve, though pleasant. The counsel upon this Circuit were very moderate in drinking. I once thought of going to wait on Lord Lough-borough. But I resolved that he should make the first advance, as became his high station; for the truth was, I had no desire to press for his acquaintance as I thought him a cold, artificial man. I meant merely to have the *formal* advantage, such as it was, of being known to him as a judge, if it came easily.

FRIDAY 28 JULY. Counsellor Park joined in post-chaising it with me, and my servant was left to come by the stage-coach. I got to town in time enough to go with Sir Joshua Reynolds in his coach to Mr. Wilkes's at Kensington Gore, where we had an excellent entertainment: turtle, venison, ices, fruits, burgundy, champagne, cyprus, claret, etc., coffee, tea, and liqueur. Miss Arnold was at table.[3] Courtenay and Malone and no more made our party. Malone and I eat lobster and drank wine and water at Courtenay's after returning to London. This was a day.

SATURDAY 29 JULY. At home in the forenoon, doing something to Dr. Johnson's *Life*. Put off time till it was too late to walk to Richmond Lodge before dinner. Called on Malone for a little. Walked to Richmond Lodge, without dining. Mrs. Stuart was in great distress for the death of her daughter Charlotte. The Colonel felt it more tenderly than I could have supposed. He had written me a kind letter, which I found yesterday. I supped well on cold meat, and had cider, etc.

SUNDAY 30 JULY. Mrs. Stuart and I walked in the garden, and she cried much but expressed her firm trust in GOD. I stayed as a comforter to this family till between one and two, when I walked to Richmond, where the party of Friday was to dine at Sir Joshua Reynolds's country-house. I met Dr. Scott and Dr. Calvert. How different was I now from what I was when I saw them last! I told Scott I *could* not quit the English bar yet and was now of the Home Circuit. He acquiesced. We had Wilkes for the first time at Sir Joshua's (though

[3]"Milly," Wilkes's mistress for the past nine years and the mother of his daughter Harriet.

old acquaintances), Courtenay, Malone, Lord Wentworth,[4] Richard Owen Cambridge, Mr. Metcalfe,[5] Mr. Hodgkinson (uncle to Sir Joseph Banks); turtle, venison, etc. I recollect none of the conversation except Wilkes's maintaining that matter of fact was of little consequence, even in history. He wished to have entertaining accounts—a sad, shallow taste. We were very pleasant. Courtenay and Malone and I walked till we were past Turnham Green. I went home and slept well. I should have mentioned that I attended a part of the evening service in Richmond Church. I love the saying of Judge Gould to Langton: "Friend Langton, I don't feel myself easy if I have not been at church upon Sunday."

MONDAY 31 JULY. Hesitated some time whether to take a stage-coach part of the way to Maidstone, as the expense of a post-chaise was very heavy; but I considered that the appearance of a lawyer during the circuit is open to observation, and the rule being that it is *infra dignitatem* for counsel to go in public vehicles, I thought it much better to save at any other time. So drove with my servant in a post-chaise through Dartford and Rochester to Maidstone. It rained a good deal as I travelled. I liked to catch the smart pronunciation *Medstone*, and was in good spirits. Dinner at the mess was almost over when I arrived. But Venner and Marsh, two Kentish counsel, and I dined in another room, and joined the corps afterwards. I was amused with seeing new provincial additions such as the gentlemen I have named, and Mr. Robinson, Recorder of Canterbury, a stately, lawyer-like man. I got small, quiet lodgings at Mr. ———— the organist's,[6] who had a noble harpsichord which cost him £70, the last which Kircher made with his own hands.[7] He told me he *allowed his housekeeper* to let a part of his house at the assize time. Mr. Serjeant Bond went to church as judge. I was much pleased with its spaciousness, and with a good sermon on the immortality of the soul by the Rev. ————. I then drank tea at the coffee-house, and spent the evening at Parkington's lodgings, playing whist with some more of the counsel.

TUESDAY 1 AUGUST. I attended the *nisi prius* court held by Lord Loughborough all day and took notes; dined and supped at the mess.

WEDNESDAY 2 AUGUST. I attended some capital trials, in which

---

[4]Thomas Noel. His niece, Anne Isabella Milbanke, who succeeded to the barony of Wentworth in 1856, was the wife of Lord Byron.
[5]Wealthy brewer and M.P. for Horsham, Reynolds's intimate friend (later one of his executors), and trustee of Johnson's annuity to Francis Barber.
[6]Probably Matthew Davis, so identified in a contemporary directory for Maidstone.
[7]An unusual instance of Boswell's mistaking a name. The harpsichord-maker was Jakob Kirchmann or Kirkman, a German who came to England about 1740.

Lord Loughborough appeared to great advantage. For though his utterance was entirely artificial, his manner was dignified and elegant and calm, and he showed an uniform leaning to the merciful side. I was so much pleased today, feeling myself quite at home in *Kent*, that I secretly regretted that I had signified to Mr. Dundas in my last fit of despondency my wish to be a Lord of Session; for I thought that I might raise myself in the wide sphere of Great Britain, and that if I were a Lord of Session all my former dreary sensations would recur. I however thought that *probably* Dundas would not apply to have me made a Lord of Session, it being now a great political bribe; so that by signifying to him my wish to accept of what ambition had made me consider as beneath me I had put him in a situation either to get £1,000 a year for me, which would be a. . . .

[EDITORIAL NOTE. The entry breaks off here at the foot of a full leaf and was probably never completed. Boswell was back in London the next day and seems to have remained there at least two weeks longer. The following letter is one of the few that survive from this period.]

[Boswell to Alexander Boswell]

London, 4 August 1786

MY DEAR SANDY,—I had letters some time ago from your sisters Veronica and Phemie, which I answered. I should be happy to have also a letter from you, which I hope this will procure me.

It gives me great satisfaction to hear from Mr. Millar that you are behaving well and making progress in your education. You may be assured that the more you learn when you are young, the better it will be for you when you grow up. I flatter myself that you will ever retain the good principles which you now have, and will indeed *live a worthy gentleman*.

The death of my oldest friend Grange, who was steady to me upon all occasions, is a melancholy event. I was much shocked last night when I came home from the Circuit at Maidstone and found a letter from Mr. Lawrie with this sad intelligence. It is a loss that never can be made up to me. My comfort is that he was a benevolent and pious man; so that I trust he is gone to a better place, where it may please GOD that we may meet, never to undergo the distress of being separated.

I am uneasy to hear that your health has not been quite good of late. You must do everything that your dear mother desires you to do for your recovery. Probably a journey to London and change of air will be of service to you; and you may depend upon it, my dear Sandy, that I will take care that you shall be in an agreeable way while you are here. I love you most sincerely, and as I wish that we should live like friends, you shall be consulted with as to the particulars of your education. Mr. Millar, to whom you are all much obliged, tells me that your brother James reads admirably. He will, I should think, be much improved by being some time in England.

Let me know what you would choose to have from London. Give my best compliments to Mr. Millar and my love to your brother and sisters. I ever am, my dear Sandy, your affectionate father,

JAMES BOSWELL.

[EDITORIAL NOTE. Boswell arrived at Auchinleck on 21 August and stayed there quietly until 20 September, when he and his entire family set out for London. The journal which begins with this day is headed "Full Trial of My Fortune at the English Bar." Underneath Boswell has added, "View of My Life till 1 November 1786 When No Diary."]

20 SEPT. LEFT Auchinleck on Wednesday the 20 September 1786 with my wife and five children and Mrs. Bruce, the housekeeper, in two post-chaises. Had a very good journey and arrived in
25 SEPT. London on Monday the 25th, about two o'clock, at my house in Great Queen Street, Lincoln's Inn Fields. Treesbank arrived in a day or two after us.[8] I wondered and was dissatisfied that none of them were struck with London in a warm degree, as I was. I soon fell into a sad state of spirits. The death of worthy Grange came upon me from time to time with a melancholy weight. I shrunk from the practice of the law of England; I read almost nothing and went on very slowly with Dr. Johnson's *Life*. I was quite unhappy about my sons, not being able to determine where to send them and being vexed to see them miserably idle. At last I sent James to Dr. Barrow's academy in Soho Square, which so far[9] relieved me. I still hesitated as to the eldest between Westminster School and the Charterhouse. But after talking with Mr. Malone, Mr. Byng, Sir John Hawkins, and several more, I resolved to

[8]Boswell notes in his Book of Company that when he arrived at Auchinleck he "found Treesbank [George James Campbell] and sister [Jean Campbell] as part of the family."
[9]An expression used elsewhere by Boswell, generally meaning "a considerable distance" but in this instance something like "a good deal."

prefer the Charterhouse, as by much the safest for his morals. But upon waiting on Dr. Berdmore, the Master, whom I found to be a most excellent man, I was told there would be no room in his house for some time; and it was too far off for my son to be a day-scholar. Dr. Berdmore thought he might do well enough at Soho Square in the mean time, so I put him there. The Master being a Doctor of Oxford, a Yorkshireman, and appearing to be judicious and conscientious, I hoped my sons might get a very decent education there.

My wife and some of our children and I dined once at Mr. Strange's and once at Mr. Dilly's, where I played cards and stayed supper, and my wife and I dined at my brother David's. We had at dinner with us one day Colonel Craufurd of Craufurdland, alone; another day the Colonel, Mr. Malone, and Mr. Dilly; another, General Paoli, Mr. Gentili, Captain Imperiani (a Corsican gentleman), and my brother David; another, Sir Joshua Reynolds, Mr. Malone, Mr. Courtenay, Dr. Brocklesby, Mr. Devaynes (the King's Apothecary); the three first stayed to supper; another, my brother David, his wife and her mother; another, them also with Squire Bosville, Mr. Matra, Mr. Masseria. I dined often at Mr. Malone's, and

18 OCT. once at Sir Joshua Reynolds's; and on St. Luke's Day he carried me to dine with the Painter-Stainers in their hall.[1] A City feast pleased me, and I think I relished it almost as well as if I had been free of bad spirits. Mrs. Stuart, her eldest daughter, and two eldest sons were with us from Richmond Lodge one Sunday morning a little after ten, and breakfasted with us. It was almost sixteen years since my wife and she had met. I felt London little different from Edinburgh, such was my state of insensibility. My wife and I and our children, all but Betty, breakfasted one morning at General Paoli's. He paid us three visits, and he and Mr. Gentili went to Bath, but I dined with him twice before he went. Mrs. Bosville and Mrs. Ward called on my wife. Mrs. Bosville asked us to dinner and Mrs. Ward to tea and cards. Mr. and Miss Wilkes called and asked us to dinner. My wife and I found Mrs. Bosville at home and called on Mrs. Ward and Mr. and Miss Wilkes.

[1]St. Luke was tutelary patron of the Painter-Stainers, which presented Reynolds with the freedom of the Company in 1784. He invited Boswell to accompany him to the fête "as you love to see life in all its modes" (*Letters of Sir Joshua Reynolds*, ed. F. W. Hilles, 1929, p. 168).

I dined one day with Colonel Craufurd, who lived at Mr. Coutts's house in his absence, as well as when he was in London.[2] He said to my wife that he thought I should persist for some time at the English bar, as there had been many instances of great practice coming all of a sudden. But so ill was I, partly from a disorder in my stomach, partly from scurvy in my blood, and partly from some inexplicable cause, that I was wretchedly despondent; nay, my mind could not perceive the distinction between what was excellent and what not, at least with any clearness; and what is most strange, I again felt what repeated experience of recovery has not been able to correct: a dismal apprehension that I should never again be well or have any relish of anything. So weak was I that my best relief was playing at draughts for hours with Treesbank, who lived in our house till he should go abroad or join his regiment, he having now a cornetcy in the 7 Dragoons.[3] I played for a hundred apples a game and felt in a degree all the uneasiness of gaming, for I lost a great many games, he having somehow got the knack of it. There was a craving at my stomach which made eating a satisfaction, and I had some enjoyment when warm in bed. The weather was excessively cold. My wife found herself quite easy in London, going about to markets and all manner of shops with perfect freedom. She had catched cold upon the journey up and had a severe cough, but she stirred so briskly that she kept herself up admirably. And now again let me try to keep a diary shortly.

WEDNESDAY 1 NOVEMBER. My wife had found out a very good boarding-school for our daughters, to which they began this day to go as day-scholars: Miss Roubell's in Lincoln's Inn Fields. We thought it might do very well for them for some time, and afterwards they might go to one of higher fashion. I went to the Sardinian Chapel, and wrote some of Johnson's *Life*.

THURSDAY 2 NOVEMBER. I was very ill with a nervous headache.

FRIDAY 3 NOVEMBER. My nervous headache was so bad that I lay till near four; but being engaged to dine at Malone's with Courtenay, I could not resist trying to have that happiness. So I rose, took a hackney-coach and, while I went along in the dusky cold, was very ill,

[2]Thomas Coutts, Craufurd's devoted cousin, was the founder, with his brother, of the great banking-house. His splendid residence was above the bank in the Strand.
[3]Boswell had spent a good deal of time, as the Register of Letters shows, in securing this cornetcy for his ward. It cost £1,350, paid for from Treesbank's estate.

but after I was fairly set down grew better. Sir J. Reynolds came to us in the evening, and we supped. I was glad I had gone.

SATURDAY 4 NOVEMBER. Wrote some of Johnson's *Life*. Mr. and Mrs. Strange, their son and daughter and Mr. Seward dined with us. My headache still troubled me. My spirits were not good.

SUNDAY 5 NOVEMBER. My headache was worse. I tried twice to get up and was obliged to lie down again. I read Dr. Beattie's *Evidences of the Christian Religion* and was much dissatisfied that the book was so superficial and so dear; and it struck me as a servile compliment to Mrs. Montagu that among the great names of whom he boasts as believers he did not mention Johnson.[4] I rose by my wife's entreaty and came down to dinner, but was sick and peevish, and so gloomy that I would not sit at table, but went into the drawing-room and shut out the light and brooded over my supposed wretchedness. My valuable spouse came and comforted me; showed me that I might remain in London as long as I found it proper, and had always an excellent retreat. And she directed my mind to piety, telling me that she checked discontent by repeating from the eighth Psalm,

> Then, say I, what is man, that he
> Remembered is by Thee?
> Or what the son of man, that Thou
> So kind to him shouldst be?

This had a benignant effect upon me.

MONDAY 6 NOVEMBER. I was pleased showing my wife and children the procession of the Lord Chancellor, etc., on the first day of term. I then went to Westminster Hall and was curiously contemplative on seeing Lord Mansfield sit at his great age; but the near prospect of his dissolution damped one's ardour.[5]

TUESDAY 7 NOVEMBER. Was down in time to have a seat in the King's Bench, which was over a little after ten, so I had leisure to see Malone, with whom I drank some chocolade. His conversation never fails to console and cheer me. He encourages me to go on with Johnson's *Life*. One morning we revised a part of it, which he thought well

---

[4]The price of the *Evidences* was not high (5*s.* for two volumes), but it had been "driven out" to occupy considerably more space than was necessary. Johnson had quarrelled with Mrs. Montagu (Beattie's patroness) in 1781 over disparaging remarks about her friend, the first Baron Lyttelton, in his *Lives of the Poets*. This quarrel had been papered over, but Mrs. Montagu must have been angered by the publicity given Johnson's statement, in Boswell's *Tour* and Mrs. Piozzi's *Anecdotes*, that he could not get through her *Essay on Shakespeare*.

[5]He was in his eighty-second year.

of, and dispelled my vaporish diffidence; and he surprised me another day with a page of it on two different types, that we might settle how it was to be printed.

WEDNESDAY 8 NOVEMBER. I attended all the morning in the King's Bench, without a seat, and afterwards some time in Chancery. I visited Lord Sunderlin, whose arrival on Monday I had heard of from his brother.[6] I was very relaxed. When at dinner with my family, there came a card from Malone begging I would come and dine with him and meet Lord Sunderlin. I said I would come in the evening, but went directly and took the second half of dinner with them very agreeably. Mr. Burch, Seal Engraver to the King, came after dinner to receive instructions to cut Lord Sunderlin's arms. He knew me by Sir Joshua's picture of me,[7] and asked me to come and see his things. Malone insisted that I should dine again with him next day with Lord Sunderlin and Courtenay. I said, "I cannot dine with you for ever. I had better board with you." However, I agreed. I then went to the Essex Head Club, first meeting for the winter. Present: Barrington, Brocklesby, Cooke, Sastres, Murphy, Wyatt, and myself. I had tolerable enjoyment of the conversation and came home soon after eleven, like a decent housekeeper.

THURSDAY 9 NOVEMBER. Attended all the morning in Chancery. Dined at Malone's with Lord Sunderlin, Courtenay, and Dr. Brocklesby. Sir Joshua Reynolds came to us in the evening. I walked away in good time with Brocklesby and came home.

FRIDAY 10 NOVEMBER. Partly in K.B., partly in Chancery. At Mrs. Ward's in the evening; played whist and won a trifle.

SATURDAY 11 NOVEMBER. Sat in K.B. and heard Erskine make a long speech for Mellish *v.* Rankin. It seemed dull. Langton, who had come to town last night, his lady, son, and two daughters drank tea and supped with us comfortably. He gave me Johnsoniana.

SUNDAY 12 NOVEMBER. Slept so long as to be too late for public worship in the forenoon. In the afternoon my wife and I went to St. Martin's. The children said divine lessons in the evening.

MONDAY 13 NOVEMBER. Was some time in K.B. My brother David, whom I had talked with on Saturday and who comes frequently to us and has our children with him frequently, had cautiously advised me

[6]Richard Malone, formerly M.P. in the Irish House of Commons, was raised to the Irish peerage on 30 June 1785.

[7]It had been engraved by John Jones and published 17 January 1786. According to the *Morning Herald* of 18 February, "Mr. Editor Boswell" had contrived to get it exhibited like a mezzotint of Fanny Kemble's portrait, which "stares us in the face from every printseller's window in the metropolis."

to look after a bond granted to me by Captain Bruce Boswell five years ago for £500, which I had borrowed and lent to him.[8] It is hardly credible that I should for no less than five years have allowed the bond to remain in Mr. Anderson of Lothbury's hands, without once desiring to have it or taking any document that he had it. I called on Captain Boswell and talked to him of indemnifying my brother David of any loss he might suffer by being one of his owners from friendship. He told me earnestly that he did not incline to admit any obligation, but upon his honour it was his wish to make up the loss when he was able.[9] I then went to Mr. Anderson and got up Captain Boswell's bond to me. I visited Mr. Atkins of Austin Friars and condoled with him on his father's death. I read in the Chapter Coffee-house the *Mercury* and *Courant* for some weeks and drank a little brandy and water, the cold being intense. I am ashamed to say that dining at home seemed dull to me. I drank tea with Mr. Malone, with whom I am always happy.

TUESDAY 14 NOVEMBER. Was in K.B. Did a little of Johnson's *Life*.

WEDNESDAY 15 NOVEMBER. Was in K.B. Visited Mr. and Mrs. Cosway;[1] dined at Dr. Brocklesby's with Sir J. R., Courtenay, Lord Sunderlin, Malone, Murphy, Devaynes. Keen frost. At Essex Head Club with Barrington, Brocklesby, Wyatt, Devaynes, Sastres.[2]

THURSDAY 16 NOVEMBER. In K.B. Dined at Sir J. R.'s with Brocklesby, Murphy, Devaynes, Sir W. Chambers, Metcalfe, Kemble, Courtenay, Edmund Burke, and his son. Burke was full of Ireland, having just returned from a visit to it after an absence of twenty years. The earnest animation with which he talked of trade and architecture and improvements of all sorts made me wonder and feel my own languor. He was violent against Dr. Johnson's political writings. He said that he[3] ascribed to Opposition an endeavour to involve the nation in a war

---

[8]See above, 28 June 1786, n. 2.

[9]We do not know whether T. D. Boswell was compensated for his losses as a backer of Bruce Boswell's venture. James Boswell's loan was not repaid until after his death. In 1787 he forwarded Bruce's account of the voyage of the *Chesterfield* to Henry Dundas and appealed for his help. Bruce was restored to the East India Company late the next year, but he was not relieved financially until 1792, when he was appointed to the lucrative office of Marine Paymaster and Naval Storekeeper in the Bengal Establishment.

[1]Richard Cosway, the miniaturist, and Maria, also a painter and a close friend of General Paoli's. They had only recently returned from a sojourn in France, where Maria and Thomas Jefferson had met and immediately fallen in love.

[2]In the manuscript this entry concludes with a long undulating dash, possibly a private symbol.

[3]Johnson.

on account of Falkland's Islands, which he[4] *knew* was a false charge.[5] He[6] imputed to them the wickedness of his own opposition to Walpole. He[7] was intemperately abusive to a departed great man. Sir Joshua and I defended him and said we did not believe he *knew* that it was a false charge against Opposition, for he did not trouble himself to acquire an accurate knowledge of the politics of the day. He took the state of facts as given to him. Murphy flattered Burke much, and in particular said he was the best *punster* of the age; and, after censuring Shakespeare, said, "*You* never pun out of place." Said Burke: "I pun *now—out of place*." Said Courtenay: "I believe you would like better to pun *in* place." "Ay," said Burke. "*Dulce est desipere* in loco"; then played himself as if *sipp*ing wine, saying, "*Desipp*ere, or rather, in place *decipe*re, with a *c*."[8] The only thing at all lively that I said was that Margaret Nicholson's *Petition* to the King with a *knife* in her hand was a *Petition* and *Remonstrance*.[9] Lord Sunderlin and Malone came to us after Brocklesby and Kemble were gone.[1]

FRIDAY 17 NOVEMBER. Breakfasted with Langton. Was in K.B. Captain Bruce Boswell, his wife and sister-in-law,[2] Squire Bosville, and Colonel Craufurd dined and drank tea with us. I was comfortably well. The weather was milder. I had visited Malone in the forenoon.

SATURDAY 18 NOVEMBER. Continued to be much better. Was in K.B. but did not relish it much; was impatient of idleness. Had a conversation walking in the Hall with Bearcroft, who said, "Ours is a

---

[4]Johnson.

[5]*Thoughts on the Late Transactions Respecting Falkland's Islands*, first published 16 March 1771, is, in fact, a shrewd historical analysis of the dispute with Spain, which the young North Ministry had settled honourably and without bloodshed.

[6]Johnson.

[7]Burke.

[8]Horace, *Odes*, IV. xii. 28: "It is pleasant to play the fool on the proper occasion" (literally, "in place"). "Decipere" would mean "deceive" or "cheat." Burke had to specify the spelling because he used the English pronunciation of Latin, in which the two words were sounded alike.

[9]On 2 August of this year Margaret Nicholson, formerly a housemaid, waited for the arrival of the King at the entrance to St. James's Palace, and, as he alighted from his carriage, handed him a paper and at the same moment attempted to stab him. The weapon was an old dessert-knife, so thin that it bent against his waistcoat. At her lodgings were found letters directed to Lord Mansfield and Lord Loughborough in which she maintained her right to the throne. She was committed to Bedlam as insane and died there in 1828. *Petition* and *Remonstrance* may refer to specific documents presented by Parliament to Charles I and to Cromwell.

[1]At the end of the entry is a character which can be roughly described as a small ellipse surmounted by a dot; probably a private symbol.

[2]Bruce Boswell was newly married to Mary Lindsay of Edinburgh.

Negro life. I can labour willingly all the morning, but it is hard that the moment a man's meat is over his throat he should be obliged to set his head to work, ay, and sometimes to work very seriously too."[3] I had thus a kind of consolation under my want of business. Talking of Buller's saying that a popular judge was a pernicious character, Bearcroft said it was a saying of Lord Bacon's, in some quaint expression such as that "a popular judge was an ill-tuned cymbal."[4] "But," said Bearcroft, "a popular judge is bad, and a regal judge is bad, or any judge who has any other motive than fairly pronouncing what is the law; and it is the same thing in private life. It is too much for man to conjecture the consequences of his actions. He is to do what is right." I visited Squire Bosville and drank chocolade with him, of which I felt immediate good effects. He showed me Arnold *On Insanity*,[5] which he advised me to read. He said it was far before Locke *On the Human Understanding*, for he examined not only mind but body; he observed all the symptoms of insanity while those afflicted with it were alive and dissected them after they were dead. Bosville said that after reading Arnold he should never again be low-spirited, for he saw that melancholy was no dark mysterious thing but a bodily disorder. I visited Seward and was introduced to Counsellor Bicknell. I was wonderfully firm and placid.

Had at dinner with us Lord Sunderlin, Mr. Malone, Mr. Courtenay, Mr. Langton, and old Mr. Macklin. Treesbank had gone to Gravesend for two days. I was in perfect serenity and good humour and fully enjoyed the company. Macklin was as usual strongly declamatory. My little son James listened to him with great attention. I was pleased with his perceiving my wife's merit, whom he praised highly as wife, mother, and hostess. We sat at table till half past nine, then went to the drawing-room and had tea and coffee and Macklin had a quart of milk, made very hot. Langton went away. The rest of us had some cold meat and a glass of wine and sat till about one. I thought to myself, "Now here I am in London, living in the best society, and not at an improper expense, so that supposing I should not get practice at the English bar, I am enriching my mind and can retire to my estate when I please."

[3]Edward Bearcroft, M.P. for Hindon, as a result of diligence and hard work was one of the leading barristers in the country.

[4]Bearcroft seems to have yoked two quotations: "A popular judge is a deformed thing, and *plaudites* are fitter for players than for magistrates" ("Speech . . . Before the Summer Circuits, 1617") and "Patience and gravity of hearing is an essential part of justice; and an over-speaking judge is no well-tuned cymbal" ("Of Judicature").

[5]Thomas Arnold, *Observations on the Nature, Kinds, Causes, and Preventions of Insanity, Lunacy, or Madness*, 2 vols., 1782–86.

My debts, however, disconcerted me somewhat, as did letters from Mr. Bruce Campbell which I received today, giving me notice of bad management at Auchinleck.[6]

      I have no particulars marked of my life the following week. I am pretty sure I dined once at General Paoli's and once at Malone's. I attended Westminster Hall with despondency. But (as a proof of unexpected good fortune, which I have always fancied might happen to me in London) upon Thursday the 23, when I had sauntered into the City to drink tea with Dilly, my servant came to me there and told me there was a message that Mr. Garforth from Lord Lonsdale wanted to call on me and was in a great hurry.[7] I hastened home in a flutter of spirits, conjecturing that LOWTHER might want me to go down as counsel at the Carlisle election, which was to come on the next week.[8] I was right. For when Mr. Garforth came, he asked me how my engagements were in town and if it would be convenient for me to take a jaunt into the north to attend the Carlisle election; that if it was, he could only assure me that it would be obliging to Lord Lonsdale, saying something at the same time formally as to peers not interfering in elections.[9] I answered with unreserved frankness that I had been called to the bar in February last and had never yet had but one brief; that it was quite convenient for me to go; and that I was very proud to have it in my power to do anything agreeable to Lord Lonsdale. "When can you set out?" "Tonight if you please." "Very well; you shall know tomorrow." He then said that upon all such occasions he wished to be open and to leave no room for reflections; and therefore he wished to know what I would consider as a sufficient gratuity. I protested (very sincerely) that money was not my object, and I would by no means mention any sum. He begged I would call at his house next morning. After drinking tea with my family in admirable

23 NOV.

---

[6]Campbell, as Boswell's agent, wrote to him at least twice a month for several years after he moved to London.

[7]On 10 November (as the Register of Letters shows) Boswell had sent a letter to Lonsdale saying that he would like to be made Recorder (chief legal officer) of Carlisle.

[8]Because the seat, which Lonsdale had been trying to acquire for many years, had been vacated by the accession of his bitter rival, the Earl of Surrey, as Duke of Norfolk.

[9]It was illegal but exceedingly common for peers to interfere in elections of Members of the House of Commons. Boswell had published his doubts about this practice in the *Tour*. See below, 17 and 22 March 1788.

humour, I hastened to Malone's to communicate to him an incident of felicity in the course to which he had steadily encouraged me, but he was not at home. I felt myself quite a *braced being*. Next. . . .

[EDITORIAL NOTE. The journal breaks off here at the foot of a full page with a catchword, but nothing appears to be lost. Beginning with 25 November we recover a journal recording Boswell's activities at Carlisle. Like a later journal in this volume mainly devoted to recording Lonsdale's traits, it is a headlong medley of English and Italian, the Italian being in the highest degree macaronic (*una perruqua scratcha nera*: a black scratch-wig), unidiomatic, and incorrect. The device may have been adopted in the first place as a cipher (Boswell on this tour had no privacy for papers he did not carry on his person), but cannot wholly be so explained, for some of the most risky reports and judgements of Lonsdale are entirely in English. For a sample of this journal, see the illustration section following p. 160. We have reduced the text wholly to idiomatic English and print it here for the first time.]

SATURDAY 25 NOVEMBER. Left London at twenty minutes after eight in the evening from the Swan with Two Necks. Every member of the company of the mail-coach was called forth as if for *death*. Hard journey, but I was firm. Arrived in Carlisle Tuesday the 28th, between four and five in the morning. Inn confused. To bed a little in my clothes. Then breakfast. Then studied brief. Candidate Knubley sent word that he would dine with me.[1] He came. Pleasant young man but rustic. Captain of militia. We dined tête-à-tête. Then came Captain Satterthwaite, Member for Cockermouth, and Rev. Mr. Grisdale, schoolmaster here. We four supped. No excess in drinking. The Great Man was expected. The candidate spoke of him tête-à-tête with respectful fervour. But in a little saw that Satterthwaite, captain of the 30th Regiment, better informed and more spirited, spoke in a veiled manner against the Potentate's infallibility: "*We* travel by night; we like to do things in our own way." Sir Joseph Senhouse, the mayor, was introduced to me this evening.[2] I did not yet know whether I should be *his* counsel.

SUNDAY 26 NOVEMBER-TUESDAY 28 NOVEMBER. [*Nil.*]

WEDNESDAY 29 NOVEMBER. Mr. Garforth had arrived during the night. He informed me that I should be the *mayor's* counsel. Lonsdale

---

[1]Edward Knubley, Sheriff of Cumberland; the Duke of Norfolk's candidate was Rowland Stephenson, a London banker.

[2]The mayor was returning officer; the sheriff or undersheriff and the clerks they deputized took the poll.

arrived. He received me courteously. Went to the Town Hall. The court was opened. Admitted forty.[3] Dined with Lonsdale, seven or eight in all. He did all the talking. Three Members, Satterthwaite, Garforth, Colonel Lowther, were utterly quiet. "Like Cato, gives his little senate laws."[4] "Yes," might say wit, "gives, etc. But *not* like *Cato.*" The force of his physiognomy, utterance, memory—all taken together struck me. But I was too easily impressed. Old blind Harrison came.[5] Loved to be sensible of the technicalities of English law. To bed in good time.

THURSDAY 30 NOVEMBER. All morning and until about five in Town Hall. Took great pleasure in recalling vividly the time that I was first at *Carlisle in Cumberland,* low-spirited and marvelling at everything English.[6] Now was counsellor-at-law on bench with mayor, deciding on English election law. Dined with mayor. The deaf brother and two nieces, *gentle gales.*[7] Evening, tea Lord Lonsdale.

FRIDAY 1 DECEMBER. Had dreamed of M.M. Was in love with her, and felt tenderly *the want.* But business animated me. Thought how curious it was that the *Laird of Auchinleck* was at Carlisle *directing English proceedings.* There was a real elevation in being a kind of ally of the great Lowther of Westmorland. In court, shocking Border barbarity upon Harrison's blindness. "Let him *look* at Act, etc., etc." *He* to Wybergh,[8] "An insult upon an infirmity. I hope, Sir, *you* shall not be deprived of your eyesight." Tedious poll by protracting purposely, putting *the long oaths.* I read in Douglas's *Elections.*[9] Dined with Lonsdale, Colonel, Whelpdale,[1] etc. HE *harangued,* and when anyone began

[3]Boswell wrote simply "A. 40." The actual poll did not begin until 30 November, but the registration of voters involved a tedious routine of examining credentials and administering an oath. By recent national regulation the poll had to be held at a public place at least seven hours daily, between 8 a.m. and 8 p.m., for no more than fifteen days. It is likely that the court began this preliminary business a day early.
[4]Pope, *Epistle to Dr. Arbuthnot,* l. 209 (from the characterization of Addison): "Like Cato, give his little Senate laws." Col. James Lowther had been Lonsdale's faithful Member for Westmorland since 1775.
[5]Knubley's counsel, "generally employed in contested elections where delay is the object of his employer" (note printed on the poll sheet for days one to four).
[6]In the summer of 1757, when he made a side-trip from Moffat, the watering-place to which he had been sent for a second time to recover from an acute depression.
[7]"Deaf brother" is probably an elder brother, in contrast to the eldest, Humphrey Senhouse (see 21 December 1787, n. 3). The nieces are unidentified. "Gentle gales" occurs as a repeated phrase in Pope's "Autumn" (*Pastorals*). But it may well refer to a song.
[8]Stephenson's counsel, from an ancient family in Westmorland.
[9]Sylvester Douglas, *The History of the Cases of Controverted Elections. . . . XV [and XVI] George III,* 1775–77.
[1]Thomas Whelpdale, another of Lonsdale's hangers-on.

to speak, even to express agreement, he said, "You shall hear." A certain Saul in a black scratch-wig, when Lonsdale treated with contempt an argument which he had advanced, whistled like a bird.[2] I was very prudent. Night, brandy and water and pipe with Colonel Lowther and Rev. Mr. Church in bar. Church had been officer in the army and had observed my father as judge at Aberdeen with much respect. Had been able to recognize me by my resemblance to him.

SATURDAY 2 DECEMBER. In Town Hall again. Dined with Lonsdale near six o'clock. He talked incessantly, and when there was the slightest private conversation he *named* him who spoke, so that *attentique ora tenebant*,[3] at least in appearance. Yesterday I saw some of them asleep. Sometimes Lonsdale appeared to lose himself in the plenitude of circumstances, but always recovered himself. Wonderful how he told everyone's particular history: for example, Hudson, who, for advising how to cheat commoners, was called "Pasture Priest." Assiduous in serving Duke of Portland.[4] Got meat and drink with servants. When offered money: *"No, you shall do something for me."* N.B. See how he detects any such device. Then you must take *gold* in common legal form, and over and above with proper address you can persuade him to give you assistance.

It was marvellous to me to *think to myself* how my existence was now wholly engaged with things that philosophically considered would have appeared of no avail. It is very true what Dr. Johnson says, that a melancholy man likes to be with those of whom he stands in awe.[5] I thought I now saw an example of an aggregate of greatness: ancient family, immense estates, a created peerage, force of intellect, fierceness, Parliamentary interest; and yet he said that he saw no reason to wish life longer than GOD is pleased to grant it. Said that he did not have a single lease because if tenant prospers, he gains. If not, you suffer. *And* there is much trouble in getting the lands again. Qu: But how improve an estate unless landlord does it himself? I am resolved to try this with *one*—Woodside, for instance, after liming it all. Then it is as

[2]George Saul, merchant, member of the Carlisle Common Council.

[3]Virgil, *Aeneid*, ii. 1, trans. H. R. Fairclough, Loeb ed.: "Conticuere omnes intentique ora tenebant: All were hushed, and held their gaze bent upon him."

[4]The Rev. Joseph Hudson had earned the sobriquet in 1768 by effecting the enclosure of extensive common land in the parish of Castle Sowerby. (Boswell's "commoners" means joint holders of rights to common land.) Hudson's skill in deciphering some ancient writings had in the same year settled a suit between Lonsdale and the Duke of Portland over the lordship of Inglewood Forest in favour of Portland, who in gratitude obtained for Hudson a D.D., a prebendaryship, and two vicarages.

[5]"A madman loves to be with people whom he fears; not as a dog fears the lash, but of whom he stands in awe" (Journal, 20 September 1777).

good one year as another, both for ploughing and pasture. Lonsdale
told me in west of England they have seven-years' fines,[6] so that an
estate which without these may be only £1,000, by the occasional course
of their falling in,[7] some one year, some another, may be £6– or £7,000.

Lonsdale was quite serious, joked only very slightly and very seldom,
and then his face relaxed pleasingly from its sternness. I recall a little
bon mot which [he] told of a gentleman who got up early from his wife
to course *hares*, that it was to ——[8] of other *hairs*. His conversation was
chiefly accounts of election contests ably told—histories of particular
men. Perceived he could not bear any obstruction or opposition. The
servant walked heavy. Called: "Don't make such a noise. It makes me
strain my voice." I observed that he was never unwilling[8a] to be interrupted if any incidental business came to be whispered, and that he
immediately resumed his discourse. He was angry because one of the
clergymen he had presented was rejected by the Bishop of Chester,
whom he called "a pert, prim fellow" (or some such word). He also
fulminated about religion—that no one could instruct him by a sermon,
because he already knew it all.

Night, Colonel Lowther, Knubley, Church, and I took a bottle of
claret in the bar. I had observed that Lonsdale had madeira for himself.
He drank almost none. The others took bad port. The Colonel and
candidate both confessed *confidentially* that claret was not given to the
company because it cost six shillings and, in short, that he liked to save.
I had observed a stonemason admitted to his presence who resolutely
charged him with a promise before his own house to pay him for six
days in his service, which Lonsdale evaded, saying he had so many
things in his head that he could not remember this, but that tomorrow
such a man (who was named) would confirm it. Colonel Lowther told
me that at Lowther many times he had only port, not even white wine.
But if I were there he would give me good wine (the miser's feast).

SUNDAY 3 DECEMBER. Got up in good time and took breakfast of
coffee and then second breakfast with the mayor. Went to the Cathedral. Was calm but not animated with devotion. The day was very
damp. Felt a little hypochondria. Harrison came into the parlour to
sit with me. Was a little humiliated by the consciousness of ignorance.
He and I were removed into Lonsdale's dining-room. Lonsdale's force
revived me and we had some hours of the same conversation, so that
I felt that *solidity of life* as many years ago when with father, old Lord

[6]A lump sum seven times the annual rent, paid by a tenant to the landlord upon
obtaining a lease.
[7]Returned to the owner's possession after the termination of a lease.
[8]One or more words omitted in the manuscript.
[8a]Possibly "willing." The manuscript is unclear.

Galloway, etc., etc.[9] Wrote letters. Evening a little weary and restless. Went to bed. A sure relief.

MONDAY 4 DECEMBER. Had dreamed of my honoured father and Lord Justice Clerk restraining me from going to England, and felt that desperate melancholy which afflicted me in my twentieth and twenty-first years. In Town Hall eight hours. Wybergh's violence disgusted me. At dinner the same *harangue*. I felt myself firm in the highest degree. The port was bitter. When I went down to the bar I asked if there were not two kinds. Took a pint of the other kind and drank with Mr. Church. He said to me, "You see who we are that he has about him." He told me that Lonsdale was anxious to save sixpence yet at once would throw away thousands.

TUESDAY 5 DECEMBER. In Town Hall. Wybergh still more violent. Doubted if I ought not to take it personally. Sir William Maxwell, Shaw-Stewart, Enterkine came.[1] I felt a certain curious secret pleasure in being seen by them in my present situation. At dinner, for the first time Lonsdale was silent a little while and drank a glass of port and declared that it was bad. I marvelled that he did not say that he would take care to have better. He showed today another kind of memory. Speaking of an ecclesiastical document called a *si quis* because it begins with these words,[2] he said he remembered a passage in Ovid's *De Arte Amandi* which began thus.[3]

The wind was blowing. He said, "I love to hear that," and repeated

> to hear
> The wind roll o'er the steady battlements
> Exceeds the common luxury of sleep.

He knew not *where* this passage was.[4] He said the most perfect feeling of it was in the house of Dunskey, situated on a rock near a recess into

---

[9]"My father and I dined at Lord Galloway's. Old ideas of true people of quality revived" (Journal, 23 January 1768). Alexander Stewart, sixth Earl of Galloway, was Lord Auchinleck's friend and patron.

[1]Sir William Maxwell of Springkell, Dumfriesshire (Boswell's relation); John Shaw-Stewart, Maxwell's wealthy brother-in-law, the Foxite M.P. for Renfrewshire; and William Cuninghame of Enterkine, Ayrshire.

[2]A notice posted in a candidate's parish church intimating that he intends to present himself for ordination and asking *if any one* knows of an impediment to it.

[3]*The Art of Love*, i. 1–2, trans. J. H. Mozley, Loeb ed.:

> Siquis in hoc artem populo non novit amandi,
> Hoc legat et lecto carmine doctus amet:

"If anyone among this people knows not the art of loving, let him read my poem, and having read, be skilled in love."

[4]Nor do we, despite a conscientious search.

which the sea which rolls between Ireland and Scotland is driven by the storm.[5] He quoted what he thought a fine passage in one of John Home's tragedies:

> A Spaniard's temper,
> A lover's passion, and a husband's honour
> Require no less.[6]

He said that he discovered Home imitated Ovid often but said nothing. "They all imitate," said he. "Now Milton imitates Ovid: 'Ante mare et tellus,' " etc. Repeated down to "semina rerum."[7] Then Milton: "Of man's first," etc., down to ——.[8] (Honest Saul said, "Many forget their Latin." Lonsdale laughed and said, "This is English, Mr. Saul." "Your Lordship," said he, "has repeated both Latin and English.") We all wondered how much poetry he could repeat. "Though," said he, "I am not very fond of poetry, I love elevated thoughts, but I'd like 'em as well when plainly expressed. Now I don't like your singsong poetry. There is Gray's *Elegy in a Country Churchyard*, which was his first and best thing, though he himself did not think so. He liked his *Old Story* best, a parcel of stuff about Lady —— and Miss Speed and I don't know what all.[9] His *Cat Drowned in a Tub of Gold Fishes* has a fine moral." (He repeated it from beginning to end.)[1] Told us that Gray lived over him at Cambridge,[2] and abused him for effeminate priggery and bringing a dirty napkin to commons. "I hate Mason. I never could think him a poet. There is a poet who will have much more fame. That is Armstrong. His *Art of Preserving Health* is a very fine poem, and so is his *Economy of Love*." He then repeated from "When fifteen years," etc.

[5]Dunskey Glen, in Wigtownshire. The house was long a seat of the Hunter Blair family.
[6]Altered from *Alonzo*, Act V.
[7]*Metamorphoses*, i. 5–9. trans. F. J. Miller, Loeb ed.: "Before the sea was, and the lands, and the sky that hangs over all, the face of Nature showed alike in her whole round, which state have men called chaos: a rough, unordered mass of things, nothing at all save lifeless bulk and warring seeds of ill-matched elements heaped in one."
[8]*Paradise Lost*, the opening lines (Boswell did not record Lonsdale's last line). It is actually Milton's description of Chaos (ii. 890–906) that imitates the *Metamorphoses*, i. 5–20.
[9]*A Long Story*, a whimsical ballad, which describes the development of Gray's friendship with the Dowager Viscountess Cobham, his neighbour at Stoke Poges, and her niece, Henrietta Jane Speed.
[1]*Ode on the Death of a Favourite Cat*, ll. 37–38, 42:
> From hence, ye Beauties, undeceived,
> Know, one false step is ne'er retrieved,
> . . . . .
> Nor all, that glisters, gold.

[2]At Peterhouse College in 1752.

down to ——. Also "the stately novelty," etc. for several lines. Also "But O my son."[3]

Today for the first time saw him laugh a little heartily. Satterthwaite used the expression "never darkened his door." Lonsdale said he had never heard it before, and he durst say it was not in print. I said, "It is in an Irish song." (See it also in Shadwell's *Hasty Wedding*, Act III.) Whether the Potentate thought more meant than met the ear, or how it struck him, I know not, but he seemed to be much diverted. Talking of his family, he said, "I'll show you my pedigree at once." Then, throwing a parcel of silver upon the table, he marked each generation by a shilling, but when one had died before his father, he put a sixpence for him. He showed all the branches and each link of the chain most accurately. Mentioned that he had a charter five hundred years old. Seemed to be pleased that he had an ancestor who lived to be above eighty, and said, "I may have children yet. I shall certainly do my endeavour." (So Lady Mary must go.)[4]

He gave us a full account of his quarrel with Serjeant Bolton and said justly that there is no merit in not being afraid. It depended on the nerves. And told us how on the way to Garstang[5] he had held out

---

[3]*The Economy of Love: A Poetical Essay*, 1747, ll. 12–18, 101–6, 191–6:
> Ye youths and virgins, when your generous blood
> Has drunk the warmth of fifteen summers, now
> The loves invite; now to new rapture wakes
> The finished sense: While stung with keen desire
> The maddening boy his bashful fetters bursts;
> And, urged with secret flames, the riper maid,
> Conscious and shy, betrays her smarting breast.

> But O my Son, whether the generous care
> Of propagation, and domestic charge,
> Or soft encounter more attract, renounce
> The vice of monks recluse, the early bane
> Of rising manhood. Banish from thy shades
> Th'ungenerous, selfish, solitary joy.

> Then when her lovely limbs,
> Oft lovely deemed, far lovelier now beheld,
> Through all your trembling joints increase the flame;
> Forthwith discover to her dazzled sight
> The stately novelty, and to her hand
> Usher the new acquaintance.

John Armstrong was both physician and poet.

[4]Lonsdale, now fifty and married for twenty-five years to Mary, the eldest daughter of the third Earl of Bute, died without issue in 1802, his marriage intact.

[5]A market town about ten miles south of Lancaster. We have been able to learn nothing about Lonsdale's quarrel with Bolton.

his arm and said to Colonel Lowther, "Is not that a steady hand?" He told us also the duel of Lord George Sackville and Governor Johnstone,[6] and his calling Wallace a liar and a scoundrel and challenging him, and Wallace's acknowledgement in the Speaker's chamber.[7] He spoke seriously, as I thought, of having time to prepare a man's self to appear before his GOD, and talking of his own situation said that comparing it with that of many others, he should be very ungrateful if he complained. At the same time he considered himself as but a steward, and that of those to whom much was given much would be required.[8] I am *sure* he returned thanks after dinner.

On a question started by me if the law had made stamps *necessary* to an *admission* of freemen or only the sole *written evidence* of it that could be received, he and Harrison were *positive* as to the *first alternative*, and Garforth acquiesced. They still went on this, that if *admission* could be without a stamp there was no penalty on *freemen* to enforce it. I said I wished there *were*, but I had not seen law for it.[9] I soon perceived that *it was better* not to argue with him.

He told us he had been first when about five year old at Marybone School, and about ten went to a school in Hertfordshire, where were Lord North, Lord Dartmouth, Lord Weymouth, etc., etc.[1] He was some time youngest boy and *fag* in a room of about twenty. That they used to be in school summer and winter by six. So about half past five he was ordered out slipshod to the pump to bring in water to them or be

[6]According to Horace Walpole, Lonsdale, Johnstone's second, may have instigated this duel, fought in Hyde Park in 1770, between his protégé, George Johnstone, and Sackville (by this time, Lord George Germain), because Germain had abandoned Lonsdale at an election where he was unseated. Germain had been cashiered after the Battle of Minden in 1759 for disobedience to orders and was widely, if unfairly, suspected of cowardice. Johnstone, notoriously violent, had forced the duel by calling his honour into question in the House of Commons. Neither was hurt.

[7]James Wallace, M.P. for Horsham from 1770 to his death in 1783 and Attorney-General under North, was an ally of the Duke of Portland in Cumberland affairs, but we have learned nothing about this dispute with Lonsdale.

[8]Luke 12:48: "For unto whomsoever much is given, of him shall be much required."

[9]As counsel to the returning officer (the mayor), Boswell had to pass on the technical qualifications of voters. Contemporary statutes imposed duties upon legal documents such as certificates of admission to a company or corporation (governing body). The "freemen" of Carlisle (the legal voters), members of the eight ancient city guilds or sons of freemen, were also members of the Corporation. Lonsdale had insisted successfully in the past that freemen present stamped certificates at an election.

[1]Lord North had been Prime Minister during the war with America; Dartmouth, his elder stepbrother, for whom Dartmouth College is named, and Weymouth had both served in his Cabinet. Except for Weymouth, they could not have been at the Hertfordshire school at the same time as Lonsdale.

heartily licked. That he has pumped till his fingers were quite benumbed. That there was a fire at the end of the room which the big boys had to themselves and would not let the little boys come near it. That they used to take the blankets off the little boys' beds. That the p—ssing place was at the further end of the room from the fire, and the big boys would not take the trouble to go to it, but would p—ss by the little boys' beds. What shocking tyranny! I could not help thinking it curious that HE had once been thus kept in subjection. He approved of the system, *me admodum renitente*.[2] It makes a very pernicious succession of slavery and tyranny. The big boys, recollecting what they have suffered, are barbarously severe upon the little boys; and perhaps his own *domination* has been inflamed by that education. Potter, the Welsh judge, came to be the younger boy to him, and he used to make him fag away. He was his bedfellow, and when he rose in the morning was obliged timidly to creep out of bed without disturbing the clothes so that Lonsdale might not have the cold let in upon him. At this school Lonsdale continued till he was sent to the University of Cambridge.

WEDNESDAY 6 DECEMBER. In Town Hall. Matters went on a little more quietly. Found the Ovid cited by Lonsdale, where there was indeed "*Siquis*," etc. He repeated a great part of *Consedere duces*.[3] Today for the first time I drank rather too much port and port and water. He gave some of us one glass apiece of his madeira. Conversation was chiefly historical, as to his various political contests. Saul, Church, and I sat with him till half past twelve. He said *by way of conversation* that if he had nothing to do, but might just follow his own inclination, he would go to live at Cambridge with the old dons and would pass perhaps two months in London in order to be at the British Museum, and that he would take lodgings near it. Saul and Church, like the philosopher and Alexander the Great, quietly suggested, "Why not do so now?"[4] He seriously (seemingly) answered, "Because he had other duties incumbent upon him" (or some such expression). Colonel Lowther told me afterwards that this was a way of talking he had; that it was just to make people wonder, and he has heard him say, for instance, "If I were a rich man, I would have a bit of fish every day." The Colonel said of him that he had no pleasure in anything in this life, so that he might as well be in one place as another. Church and I went to the bar and had each a cheerer of brandy and water to quiet the cold and

[2]I strongly disagreeing.
[3]"The leaders took their seats," the phrase which prefaces Ajax's speech at the beginning of Book 13 of Ovid's *Metamorphoses*.
[4]This allusion has not been located.

bad port. My head ached a little and I was a little *rampant*, but went to bed and slept.

THURSDAY 7 DECEMBER. Was a little indisposed. In Town Hall. Soon grew well. The Great Question concerning honorary freemen came on.[5] I delivered my opinion with animation and force, so as to prevent tumultous reflections.[6]

I rose and said that I never was clearer in any opinion in law than that the Corporation of Carlisle has a right to make honorary freemen; that I attended the Committee upon the last election for this city and heard the matter argued with very great ability. Being thus clear in my own opinion, I was not a little curious to see if the Committee would come to a different resolution. They did not come to a different resolution, but merely that Mr. Lowther was not duly elected and that Mr. Christian was duly elected.[7] Suppose they had come to a resolution that there was no right in this Corporation to make honorary freemen, it would have had no effect unless reported to the House and approved of. I have no right to divine what were the grounds of the decision of the Committee, since they have not been pleased to tell us. And though I differ in my political notions from every one member of that Committee—not excepting the nominee for the sitting Member[8]—I have so much respect for them as gentlemen, as men of the characters which they bear, that I will not impute to them a ground of decision which in my opinion is absurd and unjust. I hope gentlemen will have equal charity with me and not let a difference in opinion make any difference as to good humour.

My opinion as to the right of this ancient Corporation to make honorary freemen unrestrained and unlimited, as the learned counsel for Mr. Stephenson would persuade you that it is, has been formed, not upon a cursory view of the question, but upon an attentive and

[5]In 1785 Lonsdale had directed the mayor and his other adherents on the Corporation to admit as honorary freemen over 1,440 non-resident colliers and farmers from his widely extended territories, the honorary freemen ("mushrooms") to have votes no less than the "old" freemen. The "mushrooms" were begun to be brought in this day, the seventh day of the poll, because the tally, which had been neck-and-neck, was moving decisively towards Stephenson.

[6]We insert Boswell's speech (as he remembered it) from "Carlisle Election 1786," a series of notes parallel to the present journal but restricted to the legal issues that came before the court. His spelling of *tumultuous* and other words with the same ending must reflect a contemporary pronunciation.

[7]Boswell is referring to the decision of the Select Committee of the House of Commons that John Christian rather than John Lowther had been elected at the by-election of April 1786.

[8]Alderman Townsend. The sitting Member was Lowther.

careful consideration of your charter, of the records of your Corporation, and of your proceedings from time to time. Had the Committee been of a different opinion, considering the characters of the gentlemen who composed it, and particularly considering the character of the Right Honourable gentleman (Mr. Fox) who was nominee for the petitioner, I cannot doubt that they would have boldly and openly declared it. He who framed his renowned India Bill, by which an attack was made on the chartered rights of a great company, would he have shrunk with timidity from the charter of Carlisle?

Besides, Sir,[9] there was before the Committee a petition from certain freemen of Carlisle complaining that they were injured and praying that measures might be taken to secure their just rights in time to come. Had the Committee been of opinion that the Corporation could not make honorary freemen to have a title to vote, would they not in justice to the petitioning freemen and from a due regard to this ancient city, which has been so often shaken by political contests, and which till this question is settled must be kept for ever in hot water, would they not have fairly declared their opinion, for though fifty committees one after another should give such a judgement as in the case of the last election for this city, the returning officer would still be obliged to receive the votes of these honorary freemen. Nay, Sir, a resolution of a committee would have no effect unless confirmed by the House. Should such a resolution be confirmed by the House, I should still retain my own opinion. I should not indeed act against such a resolution of that House, and GOD forbid that I should advise a gentleman in your situation, at whose right I might have the honour to be placed, to proceed in disregard of it.

But, Sir, I say that these honorary freemen who appear upon your books regularly entered upon stamps, whom the Corporation received and in the admission of whom I believe you yourself concurred, have a good right to vote, unless something to the contrary has passed since their admission which has not been pointed out as yet. A clause in the late Act of Parliament has been read to you, Sir, to warn you of your danger. But the learned gentleman must consider that if a complaint may be made by one set of freemen against your receiving the votes of honorary freemen, there would be equal right, and it would seem a stronger one, in the honorary freemen whose votes you should reject to make a complaint that you had done them injustice. And how could you defend yourself, Sir? I shall suppose that you are called to the bar of the House of Commons to answer for your conduct, and that you

[9]Boswell is addressing the mayor.

should say, "I supposed that the Committee had virtually decided that the Corporation of Carlisle had no right to make honorary freemen." Might not the gentlemen of that Committee with some warmth demand of you how you could presume by implication that they had decided so? Might not the Right Honourable nominee for the petitioner rise in his place and tell you, "Mr. Mayor, how could you suppose that I would give a decision against your charter? I have had too much of that kind of proceeding. Burnt children dread the fire, Mr. Mayor. My attempt against chartered rights threw me into the situation in which you now see me and in which I am afraid I shall for ever remain. No, Sir, you shall not catch me again attacking chartered rights. Sir Joseph Senhouse, read your charter, and you will see that you have full power to make honorary freemen."

I think, Sir, you would be a good deal confounded at receiving such a lecture, and would look very foolish on your return to your Corporation. You have declared that you have no doubt as to this question; and if your opinion can be confirmed by mine, you have it in the clearest terms. Indeed, I cannot understand why there has been all this noise against honorary freemen. Some of the old freemen and some of them[1] now stand together in the tally-box like brethren in the most friendly manner, and I cannot perceive any difference between them. In short, Sir, as you were satisfied that these honorary freemen were properly admitted, there has nothing happened since that can make any alteration.[2]

My speech seemed to stun them into quietness. I had much pleasure in the time of it. Afterwards, felt a *little* apprehension that what I had said of Fox might be exaggerated and that he might make it a cause of challenge. So unlucky is it, with boldness of *speech* to have *personal* timidity. When I returned from the court as usual and waited on Lonsdale, I heard as I entered the room somebody talking how well I had spoke. Lonsdale said to me something which implied that he had been informed as to my speech. I left the room that more might be said of it and enjoyed a warm fire in another dining-room. Garforth joined me and told me how he had heard of my giving great satisfaction by my speech. We concerted to go to London together as soon as we could, it being very inconvenient for both of us to be kept away so long; and he told me Mackreth generally dined with him on Sunday; that he was a man of the best education, character, and independent

[1] The honorary freemen.
[2] The text now returns to the journal.

fortune, and I should meet him.[3] Lonsdale today slept a good deal after dinner. I do not have particulars to mark different from that style of behaviour which I have before marked. One trait I omitted, that he hummed "Lillibullero" [and] "The modes of the Court so common are grown." No more of it.[4] I now began to feel a load of weariness and to be surfeited of that greatness which was much enforced by my own imagining. But it was necessary to persevere.

FRIDAY 8 DECEMBER. In Town Hall. At dinner the wine was better and we drank more freely. Lonsdale called for pipes. Sir Michael le Fleming came after dinner.[5] Lonsdale, he, Mr. Knubley, and I smoked. I began to be a little uneasy with tobacco and cold port. Went to the bar and took a little warm brandy and water and had some *unrestrained* talk with Foster, Clerk Barnes, etc.[6] Returned to Lonsdale. Afterwards to bar again. Sir Michael joined me; Howe[7] sat awhile with us. Then Sir Michael and I smoked, and he told me of being at Groningen and harangued on the ancient connection of his family with that of Lonsdale, that all particular friendships should *droop* before this. He pleased me—talked of Johnson, said he spoke with *awe* to me. His antiquity of blood and genteel, fashionable character pleased my fancy, and by his entreaty I sat on with him till ten minutes from four.

SATURDAY 9 DECEMBER. Was so strong that I was not ill but in Town Hall at nine. We were nine hours and a half in court. (I, however, went out for something to eat for about a half hour.) Lonsdale had dined. I did not like this. The two counsel and Garforth were to dine below stairs in a parlour. But Lonsdale insisted we should sit in a corner of *his* dining-room. I was very well. Old Wherlings came and was examined and detained from his post office arbitrarily.[8] I had today

[3]Only a henchman of Lonsdale's would have said so. A waiter at White's (the celebrated gaming club) who became its owner, the usurer and bookmaker Robert Mackreth (M.P. for Ashburton) had just this year lost a notorious and costly suit for fraud to an aristocratic member of his club. Lonsdale was a partner in some of his deals.
[4]*The Beggar's Opera* (one of Boswell's literary favourites), air 44:
> The modes of the Court so common are grown
>> That a true friend can hardly be met;
> Friendship for interest is but a loan
>> Which they let out for what they can get.

"Lillibullero" was a seventeenth-century nonsense song ridiculing Irish Catholics which, according to Bishop Percy, had a significant role in bringing about the Glorious Revolution of 1688.
[5]Le Fleming had been Lonsdale's ward; he had been M.P. for Westmorland since 1774.
[6]Probably Thomas Forster, later Justice of the Peace at Carlisle, and John Barnes, a solicitor.
[7]The landlord of the Bush.
[8]Jeremiah Wherlings ("Red-nosed Jerry"), postmaster, alderman, and mayor of Carlisle, in Lonsdale's service at various times since 1770.

in court taken notes out of one volume of what are called the Orderly
Books of the Corporation, which I perused. It contained twenty years,
from 1733 to 1753. It entertained me. Lonsdale slept again, and I think
really did, although Colonel Lowther told me that generally he pre-
tended to. He and I smoked. *Traits*: He was disconcerted once by my
taking half a sheet of his paper. Colonel Lowther stole away sometimes.
He rated him. He fell asleep. He shouted to him and made him listen.
He by mistake called, "Bring a bottle of *claret*," but *corrected* to *port*.
Would not let Satterthwaite read one of his newspapers. Had some
very bad wine of his own brought from his garrison. I *frankly* preferred
Howe's. Seemed uneasy when by inadvertence he had left his own
bottle on the table, standing by those of the *house*. I unfortunately
asked, "What is the price of a bottle?" He took me up (but not angrily):
"I don't mind the value of the bottle, but that they may not charge it."
The port was squeezed out very slowly. He spoke strongly against Court
of King's Bench. Said it was made neither law nor equity. Arbitrary.
I could hardly stand the repetitions of strong dissertation. He and I
smoked. He said (when I was going), "We know you can sit up. Won't
you sit till I smoke another?" I did. Harrison and I and Colonel Lowther
sat. I was disgusted by Harrison's servility. My bed not being made,
and I having no place to go to but the kitchen, I returned, and Lonsdale, Colonel Lowther, and I kept together a good time.

　　SUNDAY 10 DECEMBER. I was well enough. Alderman Wherlings
came and accompanied me to St. Cuthbert's Church, similar to one of
the London chapels.[9] I sat (he with me) in the Corporation seat. I was
pleased to have the mayor's crimson velvet cushion before me. Dr.
Carlyle's son preached. I was wonderfully content. I sat some time
comfortably by Wherlings's fire, who seemed much pleased with his
house, which was his own property. I had a great deal of conversation
with him about the city constitution. Was long with Lonsdale, with
Harrison, Garforth, etc. looking at Carlisle papers and haranguing.
Satterthwaite and I sat some time by ourselves. He admitted to me that
Lonsdale exerted no interest with Government for his friends; that he
ought to have a Lord of the Treasury, a Lord of the Admiralty, a
Commissioner of Excise, and a Commissioner of the Customs. Colonel
Lowther said he wished to keep none about him but who were de-
pendent, and therefore would ask nothing for them.

　　Some of his new freemen, Dr. Lowther, and Dr. Dun arrived and

---

[9]The modest simplicity of the commodious structure erected in 1778 on the site of
ancient churches reminded him of a Nonconformist chapel in London.

dined with us.¹ He asked, "What will you drink, Dr. Dun?" He answered, "Some white wine and water—if there's white wine." (Now the port was very bad and there was good sherry in the house which had never appeared at Lonsdale's table.) Lonsdale answered, "No. That has never been called for here." I was amazed. I saw him a *forcible* Lord Macdonald. He eat (all but four that Dr. Dun inadvertently took) a whole plate of fresh oysters, without offering anybody one. Colonel Lowther and Saul had stolen away and dined at another public house comfortably and had some good wine. They were frightened to have it discovered, but it came out. Lonsdale scolded the Colonel: "I should not have gone somewhere else and paid for my dinner when I could have dined here." *This* was a striking refutation of "Whose soul is all great."² Yet perhaps his exorbitant tyranny and extreme narrowness may be reckoned great in a bad sense.

He was much in his usual style tonight. I was much fatigued and got early to bed. All these traits I mark as *disjecta membra*³ out of which I may afterwards compile the *real* character of one of whom I *imagined* so highly. I was kept in a kind of fever of agitation, and also in that kind of awe which I had not experienced but in my father's company—seeing all round *kept down*. My absence from home was very hard upon me. I had several times a distressing fancy pressing upon my mind of the state I should be in if actually deprived of M.M.

MONDAY 11 DECEMBER. In Town Hall at eleven as a court of the City of Carlisle had met in the morning. I had written two ballads in the morning concerning this election and had seen Braithwaite, the saddler at Penrith, who had just come from Ayrshire. I felt firm and was pleased that my being here was talked of in my own county. Dinner and declamation as usual.

Evening had a most earnest consultation with Lonsdale and Garforth as to hastening the poll next day. I *doubted* if the oaths could be administered unless by a poll-clerk or poll-clerks who could be sure they were taken. It was proposed to swear five persons only to take the oaths. I could not see authority for swearing any persons but poll-clerks who were to take the poll; and *how* could a poll-clerk be *sure* the oaths were taken if he did not *hear* them?⁴ I talked privately both with

¹William Lowther, D.D., Col. James Lowther's brother, rector of Lowther, Westmorland, and of Aikton, Cumberland, both in Lonsdale's patronage. We have not been able to identify Dr. Dun.
²Boswell's own praise of Lonsdale in the *Letter to the People of Scotland,* 1785.
³Scattered parts.
⁴By law the clerk was required to swear to the returning officer that he would take the poll "truly and indifferently" and poll only those who had sworn the oath.

Garforth and Clerk Barnes. Garforth thought that *five* persons, *each* to take the oaths from one person at *once* but *not to be sworn*, should be chosen, and Lonsdale thought this quite regular. I *doubted* if the poll-clerk could be *safe* to receive them so. Barnes thought it best to swear only three at a time by three different persons. Harrison and Garforth agreed simply with Lonsdale that there was no difficulty. But *I* persisted in having some difficulty. Lonsdale could not bear it. At last I was persuaded that if the poll-clerk was satisfied the oaths were taken it was enough; and if the contrary was asserted, the persons who heard them swear could *prove* it.

Thus we ended, and I went to bed, heated both with anxiety as to this point, sitting up late, and considering that one of my ballads which Knubley had taken to be printed, having been read to a good many people after dinner, would be known to be mine and might expose me to a quarrel for *going out* of the line of my *duty* and, besides, might give occasions to reflections against me of partiality and being ballad-maker for a party, which would sully my professional reputation, which I had maintained with such decorum here.

TUESDAY 12 DECEMBER. I had been very restless all night on account of what is last mentioned. I rose early, went into Knubley's room and told him that I disapproved of printing my ballad, as I was the mayor's counsel. He said he had thought so himself and assured me it should not appear. But in order to be sure, I with true activity hastened to Jollie's, who was printing it, had him called up, and told him that the ballad must not be printed. Very little of it was set, and I not only got up the manuscript, which Mr. Saul had written from the original, but saw all the types taken down. Thus I was made easy.[5] The mayor and I had resolved to sit till eight at night, but Stephenson's people said it would be taking advantage of them, after having gone on so slowly, for that their people were not come to town. The mayor yielded. Lonsdale was very much displeased. But he was

[5]Boswell, however, may have preserved the copy that Knubley had taken to be printed. At least, a broadside headed *Two New Songs*, both of them mocking the opposing candidate Rowland Stephenson, was found among his papers. One called "Rowland Deceived" is to the tune of "Lillibullero" and its lyrics imitate closely, even to the rhymes, the air in *The Beggar's Opera* (see above, 7 December 1786, p. 114 and n. 4):

> The tricks of a faction so shameless are grown,
>   Good Rowland with sad imposition has met;
> The dogs who keep gnawing contention's vile bone,
>   Have hunted all round till a dupe they could get.

And so forth.

pacified by an assurance that we should poll one hundred next day.[6]

At dinner, as I had a cold, I resolved to ask for white wine. Satterthwaite told me Lonsdale and he had taken a bottle of it the day before and it was pretty good, and he promised to second me; but his heart failed him, and Lonsdale said he had been the worse for taking it the day before and that white wine in public houses was often fined with arsenic.[7] I acquiesced, but in a little while he said, "If you choose it, I'll take a glass of white wine with you." BOSWELL. "If your Lordship pleases" (smiling), "I'll be *poisoned* with you." When it came we took it heartily, he calling out, "Mister Boswell of Auchinleck, shall you and I drink a glass of wine together?" We took several, and he was now for the first time that I have seen him *really* pleasant, with an agreeable smile upon his black countenance, and all of us talking a little in our turns.

Mr. Harrison told me he believed he was a happier man for being blind (which he meant, I thought, as having thereby been more religious), though it had prevented him from rising in his profession as he might have done. I was pleased with his calm resignation and forgave his servility, which [was] only reverence for Lonsdale in an extreme degree. Lonsdale said he knew that if he had not had the misfortune to lose his eyes he would have been very high. Talked of his being well grounded in law—that Lord Grantley had said that law was quite gone from Westminster Hall.[8] Lonsdale said that except Gould there was not one of the judges who was a lawyer whose opinion was worth a pinch of snuff; that he was saying nothing but what he might say in the House of Lords. He called Buller a riff-raff fellow who aped the quickness of Lord Mansfield, and said that Wilson was by no means (I forget the expression, which was holding him cheap.)

[EDITORIAL NOTE. Again the journal breaks off abruptly, though Boswell continued at Carlisle and saw the election through. His role made him a target of printed placards and squibs: "BOZZI and SIR JOZZI: a Dialogue on the Art of *Procrastination* between a Certain Wor-

[6]Sixty additional freemen had voted for Stephenson this day, the eleventh day of the poll, bringing his total to 335, while Knubley's still stood at 145, no additional freemen having voted for him since the seventh day. But the mayor had already admitted 191 "mushrooms," and Lonsdale must have been well pleased the next day, 13 December, when another 130 were added.

[7]Refined, clarified.

[8]Fletcher Norton, first Baron Grantley, sometime Speaker of the House of Commons, had held judicial office since 1769, but he was not one of the twelve chief judges of England (of the Courts of King's Bench, Common Pleas, and Exchequer), some of whom Lonsdale mentions next.

shipful Mayor and His Learned Counsel"; "At the Corporation Long-Room, Market Place, Carlisle, SIR JOSEPH, Knight of the SMILING COUNTENANCE, will display his Great ART of DUPLICITY. He, contrary to nature, surprises the spectators by swallowing BOZZONIAN PILLS, each the full size of a HEN's EGG, enough to choke any other man." One stanza of a ballad entitled "The Mushroom Garland" runs as follows:

> Let not your hearts in such a job[9]
> The fears of hanging awe,
> My Lord shall guard you with his mob
> And Boswell with his law,
> A-voting we will go, etc.

A letter in the *London Chronicle* (3 September 1785), signed "A Westmorland Freeholder," asks how Boswell, the "defender of the rights of mankind in the case of the injured Corsicans," could stand forward, in the *Letter to the People of Scotland*, 1785, as the "public adulator" of the tyrannical Lonsdale.

The outcome of the poll was 554 votes for Knubley, 407 of them from "honorary freemen," and 405 for Stephenson, who promptly petitioned against the return; Boswell, who was in London again on 22 December, attended the meetings of the Carlisle Committee of the House of Commons on at least five days, 16 to 21 February 1787, and took notes, among them nine folio leaves, written on sixteen sides, of Thomas Erskine's witty address to the Committee on the last day. On 26 February Knubley was unseated and Stephenson declared elected.

For his service as Counsel to the Mayor, Boswell was paid a fee of £157. 10s. But the annual "View of My Affairs" which he drew up 1 January 1787 shows that his financial status was as alarming as ever. In the first two months of the year he wrote the usual careful letters concerning the management of Auchinleck, condoled with Temple on the loss of his eldest son, and presumably worked on materials for the *Life of Johnson*. The journal opens again on 1 March.]

[9]A cheat.

THURSDAY 1 MARCH. Breakfasted with Langton and got from him his letters from Johnson. Dined home. Some of the *Life*.

FRIDAY 2 MARCH. Home all day; the *Life*.

SATURDAY 3 MARCH. Home till the evening. The *Life*. Drank tea with Malone. Had a visit in the forenoon of General Paoli.

SUNDAY 4 MARCH. Home forenoon. Afternoon with Veronica, Euphemia, and Alexander at Broad Court Chapel. Had a visit of T.D. The children said divine lessons. In the evening at a conversation at Sir John Sinclair's: maps, prints, etc., etc., of the different countries he had visited.[1] Tea, lemonade, etc. Supped between Sir Adam Fergusson[2] and Seward. Was pretty well. Had not tasted wine since Wednesday. Took it now too liberally, but not to excess.

MONDAY 5 MARCH. Somewhat low; home all day. The *Life*. In the evening Langton came and supped. Wife very apprehensive and desirous of returning to Auchinleck.[3]

TUESDAY 6 MARCH. Very bad morning. Langton came and took up a considerable part of it, chiefly in consultation how to relieve a debtor in Newgate. A little of the *Life*. Was melancholy and fretful. Resolved to stay at home all day, but Courtenay beseeched me to come and meet Lord Townshend at his house at dinner. My wife most obligingly pressed me to go. I went. Lord T. being detained in the House of Lords did not come. There were only Courtenay and Jack Devaynes and I. They kindly sympathized with my perplexity and uneasiness how to resolve, when my wife wished to go to Auchinleck, which would sadly disturb my plan of passing some time in London to try my fortune in Westminster Hall. I was miserably cast down. Devaynes suggested her trying Brompton, Kensington, or one of the spots thereabout. I

---

[1]An agricultural improver with a passion for statistics, Sinclair had just returned from extensive travels on the Continent. He is remembered as the editor of the first *Statistical Account of Scotland*, 21 vols., 1791–99.

[2]Fergusson, M.P. for Edinburgh, was a political and personal *bête noire* of Boswell's. They had been long embroiled in a financial dispute.

[3]She had had a return of her "alarming complaints," and though her health improved over the next few days, she did not think she could be fully restored "but by the air and comforts of Auchinleck" (Boswell to Robert Boswell, 8 March 1787).

grew better as we advanced in good cheer. Did not get home till half past eleven.

WEDNESDAY 7 MARCH. Was restless. Paid a visit at Sir Robert Strange's. Wrote a little of the *Life*. Dined at Lord Lonsdale's with Lord Eglinton, etc., etc. But I need not mention any names except General Clerk, who chattered incessantly and prevented conversation. His *Scottishness* (in Macklin's sense of it) was very disgusting.[4] Satterthwaite and Knubley, with whom I had been so hearty at Carlisle, were here. It shocked me that my gloom at present prevented me from feeling as I did then. I however dined well and drank a good deal of wine. Was drowsy. Walked home between eleven and twelve; a clear night.

THURSDAY 8 MARCH. This and the two following days are blanks in my memory, as I have not marked them at all. Only I recollect being at the opera on Saturday, tiring, and coming away soon.[5]

SUNDAY 11 MARCH. In the forenoon the children said divine lessons. In the afternoon had Veronica and my two sons at Queen Street Chapel with me. Dined at Mr. J. Devaynes's with Courtenay, Mr. Glover (son of *Leonidas*),[6] Mr. Ramus, the King's page. Had a great deal of anecdotes from Ramus not to the credit of the King's generosity. He asked me to come and see him at St. James's and promised me mutton. Formerly I should have jumped at such an opening. I am now too far advanced. Yet I may go. I felt my gloom dispelled by wine and drank a great deal. Devaynes was obliged to go and said Mrs. Devaynes expected us to tea. I said, "Leave some wine," and Courtenay and Glover and I drank a bottle of madeira more. This *freedom* cannot but offend. I was sorry for it afterwards. But thought it better to say nothing. Courtenay came home with me and we supped dully. This disturbed my dear wife, who was very ill.

MONDAY 12 MARCH. Was very ill and very vexed. Lay till one. Thought of sending an apology to Dilly, to whom I was engaged to dinner, but went as I heard Wilkes was to be there. He did not come. There were only some Americans and Bushnan,[7] the City Comptroller. I was sadly low-spirited and came home early.

---

[4]Alexander Carlyle says Clerk attacked the opinions of others as he would a castle. Macklin created two unpleasant stage Scotsmen, Sir Archy MacSarcasm and Sir Pertinax MacSycophant.

[5]He saw *Il Tutor Burlato*, a new comic opera by Giovanni Paisiello, performed by an Italian company at the King's Theatre in the Haymarket.

[6]Richard Glover, M.P. for Penryn, the younger son of the poet and Greek scholar of the same name. *Leonidas*, an epic poem first published in nine books in 1737, was considered a political manifesto in opposition to Robert Walpole.

[7]MS. "Bushnel." Boswell heard the name incorrectly.

TUESDAY 13 MARCH. Breakfasted with Seward. We hypochondrized mutually. He walked with me to Brompton to look for a well-aired house, in case my wife should be persuaded to go to it. We found Dempster. He assisted me. I found him easy and kind, though I had not seen him for I believe more than two months. Dined at Langton's with Sir Joshua, Malone, Windham, and Rev. Mr. Clarkson. I was dull.

WEDNESDAY 14 MARCH. Some of *Life*. Dined at Malone's to meet Hon. Major Francis North, who proved to be indeed very lively and joyous—a Falstaff, as Malone said. There were Dean Marlay,[8] Kemble, and Courtenay. I stayed till twelve. I relished the heartiness much. My wife was rather better.

THURSDAY 15 MARCH. Rev. Dr. Barrow, Dr. Bourne of Oxford, my brother and wife and Mrs. Green dined with us. In the forenoon my wife and Phemie and I looked at houses but saw none that would do. I made out the day well enough.

FRIDAY 16 MARCH. [*Nil.*]

SATURDAY 17 MARCH. Did a good deal at *Life*. In the afternoon went to Malone; drank a glass of wine with him (St. Patrick's Day) and tea comfortably.

SUNDAY 18 MARCH. A charming day. Walked beyond Blackfriars Bridge. Went a little into Mr. Rowland Hill's chapel.[9] Did not like it. In the afternoon went with Phemie and my sons to Queen Street Chapel. Dined at General Paoli's; quite in Italy. Drank tea at Cosway's placidly with Cavallo.[1]

MONDAY 19 MARCH. Dined at Sir Joshua Reynolds's with Mr. and Mrs. Hastings, etc. Admired her much;[2] found him a sensible, reserved man, and no more at first. I sat next him. Felt how everything human tends to diminution. Here was a man who had been an oriental emperor. In the evening additional company and cards. I lost two guineas at commerce.

---

[8]Major North was the second son of Lord North, the former Prime Minister, whom he eventually succeeded as Earl of Guilford. Richard Marlay, Dean of Ferns (and a member of The Club), was consecrated Bishop of Clonfert on 30 December of this year.

[9]Hill was a famous evangelical preacher who remained in communion with the Church of England though denied advancement beyond deacon's orders because of his irregularities. His chapel at Little Charlotte Street, Blackfriars Road, held three thousand people.

[1]The pioneering physicist Tiberius Cavallo, F.R.S., an Italian by birth.

[2]Fanny Burney described Mrs. Hastings as a "pleasing, lively, and well-bred woman" who aimed always at being the most conspicuous figure wherever she appeared (Burney's journal, 25 May 1792).

TUESDAY 20 MARCH. Malone, who had dined at Sir Joshua's the day before, advised me to push him to get Johnson's diary, etc. from Sir John Hawkins, that I might see them. I breakfasted with him today and he promised to write for them.[3] Then breakfasted with Sir Joseph Banks, and was pleased with his library and literary company.[4] Was in fine spirits. Sat awhile with Courtenay, who had been ill. Looked at many houses in vain. Found Sir George Osborn. Called on Mr. Knubley and on Mr. Hastings. In his present situation, to pay him a visit I thought was a liberal compliment: "Valeat quantum valere potest."[5] I had a great inclination to go to the Literary Club, but resisted it and dined quietly with my family. Was a little angry that my wife would not praise me for this. She with a high spirit said she wished me to do what was most agreeable to me. After dinner took her a long walk to look at houses. I drank tea at Sir Robert Strange's. Was in perfect serenity and cheerfulness. Had a cold, and took some pleasant punch at night, and felt "*hope* travelling on"[6] with me very briskly. Thought that at last some fortunate incident would come and raise me. Felt that returning to the Court of Session would be soon intolerably dull and contracted. My wife was easier. ———.

WEDNESDAY 21 MARCH. Was restless. Went to the Temple and inquired for chambers, but none were to let. Did some of *Life*. Sandy was ill again with his rupture. Mr. John Hunter visited him and found that Squires, the truss-maker, was right in his discovery that one of the testicles was not come down. This interrupted the cure of the rupture, as no truss could be applied till the testicle should come down. This was hard, especially as he could not go to his academy for fear of being hurt. I resolved to make him read, and to examine him myself till I could find one to come in and teach him. My wife was a good deal better. Mr. Hunter thought she looked greatly better. Passed the evening at the Essex Head Club with Brocklesby, Wyatt, Calamy.

THURSDAY 22 MARCH. Rose in delightful spirits. Breakfasted at Malone's. He said if I should quit London and return to Scotland, I would hang myself in five weeks. I begged he would prevent me. All dreariness was quite vanished. Douglas having (weakly as I thought) taken offence at my mentioning a lively saying of Dr. Johnson's against his filiation in my *Tour to the Hebrides*,[7] and as I thought it unpleasant

[3]Reynolds, Hawkins, and Dr. William Scott were Johnson's executors.
[4]The library, which was rich in scientific works, became the property of the British Museum after Banks's death in 1820.
[5]"Let it count for whatever it is worth."
[6]Pope, *Essay on Man*, ii. 274: "Hope travels through, nor quits us when we die."
[7]See above, 2 March 1786 and n. 1.

and unbecoming that he and I should be on bad terms, I had written to him a handsome letter on Sunday, to which he on Monday had returned a cold note. I read both to Malone, who advised me to have nothing more to say to him. I was conscious that he had never shown me any generous gratitude, and thought nothing could be made of him. I found Lord Eglinton, who was quite indifferent. Met Sir Andrew Cathcart there. Imagined that all my countrymen almost shunned me, from an overcharged representation of my partiality to England. Went to the House of Lords, and Clarke, the door-keeper, allowed me to stand in a corner and hear the prayers, the decency of which pleased me much. Did a little of the *Life*, having been occupied a good while in searching for Johnson's letters to Dr. Warton, which I feared were lost.[8] Mr. Lumisden drank tea with us.

FRIDAY 23 MARCH. It had been a very wet night. I awaked ill. After breakfast found Colonel Montgomerie and talked with him as to additional Commissioners of Supply for Ayrshire. Was disgusted by hearing of narrow local topics. Found Colonel Stewart of Stair. Had the same impression. Was angry at myself for being so *unlairdly* fastidious. Was quite relaxed and uneasy. Sauntered about, wishing for any object. Called on Courtenay; not at home.[9] Dined quietly with my family, the fourth day, one after another, but was not complaisant. In the afternoon, by my showing discontent that my dear wife did not feel as to England as I did, she was agitated and again spit blood. I was sadly distressed. She seemed to have no comfort in view but being at home at Auchinleck. I was clear for taking her down directly. She was miserably apprehensive. Did a very little of the *Life*.

SATURDAY 24 MARCH. Called at Mr. John Hunter's with Sandy. Wrote letters. Dined with the Rev. Dr. Douglas at the chaplain's table, St. James's, along with General Paoli, Mr. Cavallo, Mr. Bryant,[1] Dr. Lort, Mr. Wilson, solicitor in Chancery. I felt quite comfortably. Drank coffee at the General's and tea at Malone's.

SUNDAY 25 MARCH. Having resolved to hear Dr. Douglas preach in the early service at St. James's, rose easily and was there at eight. He gave a good plain discourse on Christ crucified being to the Jews

[8]The two letters which the Rev. Dr. Joseph Warton, poet, critic, Headmaster of Winchester, and member of The Club, had sent him recently were published in the *Life of Johnson*.

[9]There is at this point another wavy line something like that recorded at the end of the entry for 15 November 1786.

[1]In September of this year, John Douglas, D.D., a member of The Club, was appointed Bishop of Carlisle. Jacob Bryant, fellow of King's College, Cambridge, was an eminent mythographer and antiquary.

a stumbling-block. I partook of the Holy Sacrament with about twelve, Dr. Heberden one.[2] Breakfasted with Earl Fife, and felt my spirit roused as a landed gentleman. Went to Dr. Kippis's Meeting; was pleased with his able and decent mode both of praying and preaching, though I had more mysterious belief than he. His text, Malachi 3, v. 8: "Will a man rob God?" I came home and took my two sons to Queen Street Chapel and heard the Rev. Mr. Bevil preach on the frailty of man, from the words, "Behold the lilies of the field, how they grow."[3] My children said divine lessons to me at home, and having had so much of religious exercises this day, I actually felt myself *full* of comfortable religion. My wife was better. I dined with my family, though invited to Malone's. But knowing that steady Reed was with him, I went after dinner, drank wine and tea, and eat cold beef and drank negus; at night had a great deal of literary talk and was quite in a London frame. I was sorry that I did not get home till one o'clock.

MONDAY 26 MARCH. Wrote letters. Went into the City to put some into the East India letter-box. Dilly had Dodsley, Walter, and Hughs to dine with him, and asked me. I could not resist so many of *the trade*.[4] Home early and quiet. But no *Life* done today.

TUESDAY 27 MARCH. Some *Life*. Dined and played whist at Mrs. Bosville's.

WEDNESDAY 28 MARCH. Drank chocolade with Malone. Called Garforth and Lord Lonsdale. Went to the door of the House of Commons, intending to go in and hear the debate on repealing the Test Act; the House was full.[5] Dined at home. Some *Life*. In the evening my old acquaintance Dr. Wright, who was going to settle as a physician at Oporto, sat some time with me. I took him as my guest to the Essex Head Club. Present: Jodrell, Cooke, Wyatt, Brocklesby. I was drowsy.

THURSDAY 29 MARCH. Laboured at *Life* all day, yet did no more than seven pages. Supped at Lady Strange's with Veronica and Phemie. Sir Robert was gone to Paris.[6] Counsellors Strange, Mure, and Park were there, and Mr. Lumisden.

FRIDAY 30 MARCH. Wished to labour at *Life* as I did yesterday. But it is dangerous to go out in the morning. After breakfast went to Malone's to consult him whether I might stay to dine at Dr. Lort's on

[2]William Heberden, the eminent physician who attended Johnson in his last years.
[3]Matthew 6:28: "Consider the lilies of the field, how they grow."
[4]Publishing and bookselling was known as "the trade."
[5]The Test and Corporation Acts required Dissenters to take Holy Communion in an Anglican church if they wished to hold public office. The motion for repeal was defeated.
[6]Robert Strange had been knighted on 5 January.

the day on which the Commission was to open at Kingston on the Home Circuit. He told me that if I was not there that day, to appear when briefs were to be delivered, I need not go at all. I might have some chance business. As I had gone to none of the other towns, and resolved to go only into Surrey, for the assizes of which I had a general retainer of five guineas for Lord Portmore and Mr. Langton,[7] it was clear that I should make my appearance on the Home Circuit in the fullest form, so far as might be at one town only. The advantage of that circuit is that a counsel may take what part of it he pleases and save appearances.

I called on Courtenay, who insisted that we should take a long walk, and that Malone and I should dine with him. I was very sorry to have an idle day, yet I could not resist this cordial invitation, in case Malone should agree. He did, and said he would let me off from my task of Johnson's *Life* for today. Courtenay and I went and sat an hour with Wilkes, who had a bad cold, which made me think with concern of our losing him. But he was lively as usual. He expressed his opinion freely of Pitt's folly as a politician, as it appeared to him: "By going against Hastings he has offended the Queen and the German women. By going against the Dissenters he has offended the people of principle, and by his shop-tax he has offended the people without principle— the low shopkeepers all over the kingdom. And the City of London will never forgive him."[8] He was properly keen against Hawkins's *Life of Johnson*.[9] Courtenay and I walked in Hyde Park. For an hour before dinner I read Taylor's Preface to his translation of Orpheus. It fanned my mind to perceive him quite absorbed in the wildness of ancient metaphysics.[1] We dined at six and sat very happily till past twelve. I relished it much. No memorabilia.

SATURDAY 31 MARCH. Was in bad spirits. Called on Const and fixed to go with him to Kingston on Monday. Dined at home. A little *Life*.

[7] For business related to the Wey River Navigation in Surrey. Langton and Portmore had each inherited a moiety of the company and were closely associated in developing it.

[8] Mrs. Hastings was German, and the Queen (also German) and the German ladies of her entourage were warm supporters of Hastings. Pitt had alienated the Dissenters by opposing the repeal of the Test Act on 28 March (above). The shop-tax, which imposed a duty upon all shops according to the rent paid by the shopkeeper, was put in force in 1785.

[9] The book had appeared ten days before.

[1] Taylor's *Mystical Initiations, or Hymns of Orpheus*, which had also been published recently, contains a dissertation on the life and theology of Orpheus.

SUNDAY 1 APRIL. My wife was much indisposed. Colonel Craufurd went to Queen Street Chapel with me and some of my children, and dined with us. They said divine lessons.

MONDAY 2 APRIL. Went to Kingston in a post-chaise with Const and Venner. Crowd of counsel at dinner. Went a little while into Crown Court.[2] Played whist and sat till past three. Won, but was uneasy and vexed that I was so irregular.

TUESDAY 3 APRIL. In *nisi prius* court, and was pleased with old Gould. After dinner, whist, and won. Home early. Felt myself quite a Home Circuit man.

WEDNESDAY 4 APRIL. A little while in *nisi prius* court, but there being a long dull cause concerning a common, was chiefly in Crown Court, and heard Baron Thomson try prisoners remarkably well. The counsel dined with the judges. In the evening played whist and lost part of what I had won.

THURSDAY 5 APRIL. A little while in Crown Court. Had now been enough on the circuit for appearance. Was dissatisfied that I had nothing to do. Took a post-chaise and went to Richmond Lodge. Mrs. S. so indifferent could not bear it. Walked, and read in Sheridan's *Life of Swift*, and *Life of Arthur Mainwaring*.[3] Colonel returned from London. Lord and Lady Binning and Lady Jane Hope dined. I was *retenu*, but sat over claret till (I believe) near nine. Home late. Wife had been very ill.

FRIDAY 6 APRIL.[4] I am not sure how I was employed. My wife's illness was sadly alarming. She had feverish heat and cold and sweatings in the night. Colonel Craufurd went with me to Queen Street Chapel. I fasted, and went into the City and visited Mr. Dilly.

SATURDAY 7 APRIL. Courtenay and I dined at Malone's; just we three comfortably and soberly.

SUNDAY 8 APRIL. Colonel Craufurd and I met at the Chapter Coffee-house and breakfasted, and then attended worship and communicated in St. Paul's Church. I called on Lord Somerville. Colonel Craufurd dined with us. The children said divine lessons.

MONDAY 9 APRIL. Though Colonel Craufurd and I had drunk only a bottle of claret, I awaked sick and gloomy. My benevolence had made me hunt out a poor man, Cochran, who used formerly to write for Lord Eglinton, that I might give him the little advantage of writing a presentation to Kilmaurs, with which the Earl had favoured me, to

[2]The criminal court.
[3]By John Oldmixon. Mainwaring was one of the principal Whig controversialists opposing Swift.
[4]Good Friday.

Mr. Millar, my chaplain.[5] I had found him in a garret in Flower de Luce Court, Fleet Street. He brought it to me today. I dined at home. My wife was very ill. I cried bitterly. Sandy comforted me like a man older than myself, saying, "O Papa, this is not like yourself."

TUESDAY 10 APRIL. Waited on Lord Eglinton, who signed the presentation to Kilmaurs and asked me to dine with him. Mr. Bosville was with us. I drank not a great deal, but was disturbed by it. I had breakfasted at Sir Joshua's.

WEDNESDAY 11 APRIL. Was shockingly ill. Walked in the streets and grew better. Went with my wife and daughters in a coach to the Green Park and walked and sat there. Captain Bruce Boswell and Colonel Craufurd dined with me. My wife was not able to appear. I was much sunk. I upbraided myself for not having made her set out for Auchinleck before, as she now thought she would not be able to go. I was overwhelmed with dismal thoughts of death. She had lamented her poor children when I talked how melancholy I was.

THURSDAY 12 APRIL. She was a little easier and went with me and Veronica and Phemie in a coach to Hyde Park Corner; walked in the park and home again. Dined at home.

FRIDAY 13 APRIL. A bad day. Captain Boswell's wife dined with my wife. I dined at Dilly's, where Wilkes should have been but sent an excuse, which offended Dilly much. There were Americans, Rudd the attorney, etc. Played whist and lost. Home between eleven and twelve.

SATURDAY 14 APRIL. Time passed away. Left a card at Lord Chancellor's. I found Jack Lee at home and heard him talk with contempt of honours, but felt very differently from what I once did in his company, for I was now convinced he affected this. I complained of my having no practice in Westminster Hall. He seemed quite indifferent, though he had been my great encourager to come to the English bar. Sir Joshua Reynolds, Windham, Courtenay, and Malone were to dine with me and go afterwards to the first night of Jephson's tragedy of *Julia*.[6] I asked Lee, and he accepted. We had a truly good short day of it. Lee was engaged to a card-party at six. We went to Drury Lane. I sat in Mrs. Burke's box, where was Edmund. It was awkward and uneasy to me to be cold with people with whom I had once been on the easiest footing. I was not enough entertained with the play, though

---

[5]The presentation was strongly opposed by the people, who drove him out of his manse when he first appeared. Burns's gibes in *The Holy Fair* as to his preaching orthodoxy only because he wanted a parish could hardly have helped his cause. He was finally accepted by the congregation and served at Kilmaurs until his death in 1804.

[6]Malone had written the Prologue and Courtenay the Epilogue to their friend's play.

some passages struck me. I thought of the shortness and uncertainty of life. But my wife was better today and seemed pleased at dinner. I thought that I had now great points of satisfaction: a house in London—such company at dinner with me—being one of the distinguished men at a new play. But there was an insipid dreariness about me. Malone and Courtenay came home with me, and we had cold meat and port and sat socially till two. I should have mentioned that in the morning I had visited Mrs. Bedford, Claxton's mother-in-law, a fine old lady above four score, quite entire, quite English.[7] I was much pleased. General Paoli visited us.

SUNDAY 15 APRIL. Colonel Craufurd breakfasted with us. My wife was up before me. This was cheering, and I really hoped that her complaints might not yet be fatal. Visited Serjeant Adair[8] in the morning. The Colonel went with me and some of the children to our chapel.[9] Then my wife and Veronica and Phemie and I walked to the other side of Blackfriars Bridge and back again, and she went with me to chapel. I dined at General Paoli's; quite *foreign*. Home late.

MONDAY 16 APRIL. Visited Mr. Lumisden and Lady Strange and Mr. Malone. Dined at home. I remember no more.

TUESDAY 17 APRIL. Did some *Life*. Dined at the Literary Club; present: Lords Ossory, Palmerston, Macartney,[1] Bishop of St. Asaph, Dr. Burney, Sir Joshua Reynolds, Mr. Malone, Mr. Windham. I remember no more but a story which Lord Palmerston told of Christie, the auctioneer, who in selling an estate mentioned a garden with excellent walls luxuriantly covered with fruit trees. The purchaser, having found nothing of this, complained to Christie. "Sir," said he, "I ask your pardon. I was credibly informed there were walls. I confess the clothing was my own." I told the dispute between Johnson and Taylor as to the attachment to the Stuart family, with good applause.[2] From

[7]John Claxton, antiquary and an old friend of Temple's.
[8]James Adair, Recorder of London.
[9]Great Queen Street Chapel.
[1]Henry Temple, second Viscount Palmerston, father of the future Prime Minister and himself M.P. for Boroughbridge; and George Macartney (later first Earl Macartney), Baron in the Irish peerage, former Ambassador to Russia and Governor of Madras, later Ambassador to China and Governor of the Cape of Good Hope; a diplomatist with a fine reputation and scholarly tastes.
[2]Well deserved, if the account was comparable to that in the *Life*. The dispute had occurred at Dr. Taylor's house at Ashbourne (17 September 1777), when Johnson maintained that if England were fairly polled, George III would be "sent away tonight, and his adherents hanged tomorrow." The Stuarts would be restored to the throne, he insisted, because the people respected hereditary rights, and the advancement of laws now protected them from tyranny. Taylor, an ardent Whig, was "roused by this to a pitch of bellowing."

mere apprehension of not having enough of wine from the genteel sobriety of The Club, I drank too much. Sir Joshua and Malone and I sat about an hour after the rest. I walked about some time. Then supped at Lord Eglinton's; saw the Countess after her in-lying, and was easy with her.³ Lord Elphinstone and Colonel Small there. I was upon my guard and drank port and water. But I did not get home till two and was a good deal intoxicated. My dear wife rose and came down and saw me. She had again been spitting a little blood.

WEDNESDAY 18 APRIL. Rose a good deal uneasy. Walked out for air and exercise through the streets and about *Westminster*.⁴ Called on Wilkes. Dined at General Paoli's quietly with his Excellency, Mr. Gentili, and Mr. Cavallo. Braced myself with wine and coffee. Had one of my friendly consultations with Gentili, who was against my quitting London.

THURSDAY 19 APRIL. Was pretty well. Did some *Life*. Drank tea with Malone. Only water. I think visited Lord Eglinton.

FRIDAY 20 APRIL. Did some *Life*. Only water. Drank tea at T.D.'s and was pleasant in the old fashion, talking of early ideas. I am not sure how far one should carry the example of "When I became a man, I put away childish things."⁵

SATURDAY 21 APRIL. Was a little restless and walked out, which when I do, the forenoon is lost. Walked into the City; found Dilly; sat some time with Mrs. Forbes and got good accounts of Mrs. Carlisle and Este's boarding-school in Queen Square, to which I resolved to send Veronica. Only water. Was with Malone in the forenoon. Called General Ross (who had visited me), Mr. Walpole, Mr. Fullarton.⁶ Visited Lady Grant.

SUNDAY 22 APRIL. By taking a course of water and tasting no fermented liquor, I felt myself wonderfully easier; that is to say, I had no high enjoyment, but neither had I any horrible melancholy. I was calm and patient and had such a life as I suppose is meant for man in

³She had given birth to a daughter, Mary, on 5 March; the following February the Earl divorced her on grounds of adultery with the Duke of Hamilton. She bore a second daughter, Susanna, in May 1788. A scurrilous song found among Boswell's papers, which was probably written about the time of the Eglintons' marriage in 1783, when he was fifty-seven and Frances Twisden, his second wife, no more than twenty-two, prophesied that she would bear him sons not of his begetting.
⁴Underlined by Boswell, contrary to his usual practice. Probably a reference to something he does not care to record. See also below, 6 June 1787.
⁵I Corinthians 13:11.
⁶Walpole, who disliked Boswell, does not mention this call. Fullarton is probably William, laird of a large estate in Ayrshire, hero of successful military campaigns in India, and author of a pamphlet published this year, *A View of the English Interests in India.* He became M.P. for Haddington Burghs this June.

this state. I was quite convinced that our spirits depend chiefly upon what we throw into the stomach. I was at our chapel with my wife and some of the children forenoon and afternoon. Colonel Craufurd was with us forenoon. He and I and Sandy visited Lord Eglinton. He and Bob Cuninghame dined with us. Only water. The children said divine lessons. My wife had been better for some days. Returned to sleep with her. ——.

MONDAY 23 APRIL. Only water. Some *Life*.

TUESDAY 24 APRIL. Mrs. Young and her sister[7] had come from Bath last night. My wife and I visited them this morning. It was very consolatory to my wife to meet them. Some *Life*. Only water.

WEDNESDAY 25 APRIL. Easter term began. I took my seat in Chancery calmly to try what it would do for me. Mrs. Young and her sister and Miss Abercrombie and the Rev. Mr. Abercrombie, son and daughter of General Abercrombie,[8] dined with us. They had come from Bath, and lodged here in the same house. Only water. At Essex Head Club with Brocklesby, Cooke, Wyatt, Sastres.

THURSDAY 26 APRIL. In Chancery. It was unedifying, as the voice of the counsel is not well heard, and consequently I did not understand much of what went on. I dined at Malone's with Lord Sunderlin, Windham, Courtenay. After seven days only water, indulged again in wine. It intoxicated me soon to an unpleasant degree and seemed harsh. I attended in the House of Lords an appeal upon the question of what is a nominal and fictitious vote.[9]

FRIDAY 27 APRIL. In Chancery. Heard more on the appeal concerning a nominal and fictitious vote. Drank tea at T.D.'s one day this week.

SATURDAY 28 APRIL. In Chancery. Met in the street the Treasurer of the Navy and young Arniston;[1] told the Treasurer that young Arniston had promised to dine with me one day; would he come? He said *certainly*; so we fixed it for Wednesday 9 May. I dined with the Royal Academicians.[2] Malone, Courtenay, and I and Burke sat together. I drank pretty well, but not to excess.

[7] Miss Gibson. They were Edinburgh people.
[8] The indecisive Commander-in-Chief (nicknamed "Nabercromby") of the British forces in the bloody battle at Ticonderoga; now dead.
[9] A vote created by legal manoeuvres in Scotland to circumvent property qualifications. The case had been appealed from the Court of Session. Boswell had long opposed nominal and fictitious votes and had recently attacked them in his *Letter to the People of Scotland*, 1785.
[1] Henry Dundas and his nephew Robert Dundas of Arniston, the Lord President's son.
[2] The glittering event which opened the annual exhibition of paintings, sculptures, and designs held at Somerset House. Reynolds's portrait of Boswell was exhibited this year.

SUNDAY 29 APRIL. The wine having been bad, I was ill. It was as heavy a rain as I ever saw. In the intervals of heavy showers, I walked to St. Paul's and saw the judges at divine service with the Lord Mayor and aldermen the first Sunday in term, a very decent custom revived lately. Read the Edinburgh *Mercury* and *Courant* at the Chapter. Was disgusted by narrow ideas. Colonel Craufurd went with us to our chapel in the afternoon. He and the Rev. Mr. Bevil (quite a genteel clergyman and *in character*),[3] Sir Joseph Senhouse, my brother and his ladies, and Major Green[4] dined and drank tea with us. I drank good port and felt myself quite comfortable and in propriety. The children said divine lessons.

MONDAY 30 APRIL. In Chancery. Had wonderful soundness of mind, I know not how. My wife had been a great deal better for some days. Lord Chancellor made a most able speech against votes held not freely but to support another's political interest.[5] Sandy was with me.

TUESDAY 1 MAY. Breakfasted with Mr. Malone as usual on the first of a month, and read the reviews and magazines on Dr. Johnson's *Life* by Hawkins.[6] In Chancery. Dined Literary Club with Malone, Sir Joseph Banks, Bishop of St. Asaph, Lord Palmerston, Dr. Fordyce, Dean Marlay, Colman (the first time since his paralytic stroke, as lively and shrewd as ever),[7] Windham. A good pleasant day, but nothing recollected. My wife not so well today. She had again spit blood.

WEDNESDAY 2 MAY. In Chancery. Attended in House of Lords appeal on a Writ of Error from the King's Bench.

THURSDAY 3 MAY. Too late for Chancery either yesterday or to-day, having walked about making visits. Heard the Writ of Error in House of Lords finished. Mrs. Siddons was to have played Isabella,[8]

---

[3] That is, his gentility was of the sort appropriate to a clergyman; perhaps, his character is like the upright and genteel young Bevil's in Steele's sentimental comedy *The Conscious Lovers*.

[4] T.D.'s brother-in-law. A veteran of extensive service in America, he rose to the rank of general.

[5] That is, Boswell attended the House of Lords this day to hear the appeal from the Court of Session on the question of nominal and fictitious votes. The appeal was remitted for the re-examination of witnesses and evidence and another determination.

[6] He was no doubt cheered by finding the reviews uniformly hostile. The book was condemned for malevolence and spitefulness, as well as for inaccuracy, legalisms (Hawkins was an attorney), and wearisome digressions.

[7] George Fordyce, M.D., a Scot settled in London and "speciali gratia" a Fellow of the Royal College of Physicians; and George Colman the Elder, dramatist and proprietor of the Haymarket Theatre. He had suffered a stroke in October 1785.

[8] Sarah Siddons, Kemble's sister, the most famous actress of the day. Her performances in Garrick's *Isabella* (a version of Thomas Southerne's *Fatal Marriage*) in 1782 had assured her triumph on the London stage.

and I had taken places for Mrs. Young, my wife, etc. The play (on account of Mrs. Siddons being suddenly taken ill) was changed to *The Winter's Tale*. I was not for going, but Mrs. Young chose to go. My wife and Veronica and Euphemia went with me. I was in bad humour at first but got the better of it. There was a new farce, *The Distressed Baronet*, which I liked very well, though some ill-natured creatures hissed.[9] My wife looked quite well and was entertained, but on her return home found herself much worse and spit a great deal of blood, which alarmed her much.

FRIDAY 4 MAY. Wife continued ill. Chancery and House of Lords, hearing another Writ of Error.

SATURDAY 5 MAY. Visited Malone. In Chancery. Dined General Paoli's. A little heated with wine. Wished to show Jamie Macklin in Sir Archie MacSarcasm. But we found the house so crowded we could not get in.[1] Wife still spit blood.[2] This whole week had done no *Life*.

SUNDAY 6 MAY. At our chapel, Colonel Craufurd and two Miss Coutts with us. On return home found Mr. George Wallace. His Edinburgh ideas and misanthropy displeased me. My wife was better. Lord Advocate visited us. He[3] and Mrs. Young and her sister dined with her. I was so engaged to General Paoli to meet various foreigners I could not resist. Dining with him on Sunday is dining on the Continent. I was voracious; eat a great deal and drank all the wine I could contrive to get. Was much intoxicated. Walked among the crowd in St. James's Park. Then sauntered, but *innocue*.[4] Home sadly disguised.[5]

MONDAY 7 MAY. Awaked very ill. Rose and visited Mr. George Wallace at the White Bear in Piccadilly. In Chancery, and understood pretty well. Saw Cockell admitted a serjeant. Walked with Mr. Robert Sinclair in the Hall and said if I did not get practice here, I would return to my old station in the Court of Session. My wife did not spit blood. Rev. Mr. Bevil drank tea with us. I was sunk and dreary at night not knowing what to resolve as to my family, whether to keep them here or send part down. In short, I was very unhappy. My straitened circumstances vexed me. I felt a warm longing after old Auchinleck,

[9]By Charles Stuart. It was customary to perform a farce after the main piece.
[1]Macklin was also playing Sir Pertinax MacSycophant. The two performances, at Covent Garden, were a benefit for him.
[2]On this day Boswell sent letters to the Rev. Mr. Dun and the Rev. Mr. Auld asking their prayers for Mrs. Boswell.
[3]Probably George Wallace. The preceding sentence is an interlinear addition.
[4]Innocently.
[5]Drunk.

but could not bear the thoughts of receiving all company that might come, and many other circumstances.

TUESDAY 8 MAY. My wife better. In Chancery. Mrs. Young and Miss Gibson, General Paoli and Mr. Gentili, Sir Joshua Reynolds and Miss Palmer and Earl Fife and Fullarton dined and drank tea with us. I was easy and happy. Mrs. Young advised sending Veronica for a year to a boarding-school. We still hesitated.

WEDNESDAY 9 MAY. In Chancery. This being fixed for the great debate on the impeachment of Mr. Hastings, the Treasurer of the Navy and Lord Advocate were prevented from dining with us.[6] We had young Arniston, Sir John Dick, Lord Provost of Edinburgh (Grieve), Colonel Craufurd, and Mr. Lumisden. The two last drank tea with us. I was very well, and felt the *credit* of having proper company at my table. The expense indeed was a drawback. I went to Essex Head Club (present: Barrington, Cooke, Brocklesby, Wyatt); and then, from the fancy of reviving old sensations, I went to the Temple Coffee-house and had a glass of punch and a toasted biscuit. Enjoyed the scene much.

THURSDAY 10 MAY. Visited Mr. George Wallace. In Chancery. It was a wet day. I had for eleven days done nothing to Johnson's *Life*. Wrote some of it today.

FRIDAY 11 MAY. In a full suit of black clothes went to His Majesty's levee, where I had not been since I brought my family to London.[7] I wished to observe how he behaved to me, as I thought of presenting a memorial to him to have some mark of his royal favour to me. It was a delightful day. I was in fine spirits and full of courtly ideas. There were not many present. The King accosted me with a pleasing look: "How does writing go on?" BOSWELL. "Pretty well, Sir." KING. "When will you be done?" BOSWELL. "It will be some time yet. I have a good deal to do to correct Sir John Hawkins." KING. "I believe he has made many mistakes." BOSWELL. "A great many, Sir, and very injurious to my good friend." KING. "I do not believe Dr. Johnson was so fond of low company in the latter part of his life as Sir John Hawkins represents" ("describes," or some such word). I visited Malone. Mr. George Wallace dined and drank tea at my house, and then I sauntered about with him. Was disgusted with his Edinburgh manner.

[6]Dundas (Treasurer of the Navy) and Wilkes, among others, spoke against the impeachment and defended Hastings; Pitt and Courtenay, who made a notorious speech comparing Hastings to Cortez, favoured it. On the following day the motion for impeachment was carried and Burke was instructed to pronounce it at the bar of the House of Lords.

[7]The sober garb was the court suit of a barrister.

SATURDAY 12 MAY. Breakfasted with worthy Langton. He complained of the King's indifference to him, and he stated my claim to royal favour so strongly that he raised my opinion of myself and made me indulge lofty hope.[8] I was really happy with him this morning. In Chancery. I do not recollect how the rest of the day was passed.

SUNDAY 13 MAY. At Queen Street Chapel forenoon and afternoon. The children said divine lessons. Mrs. Young and Miss Gibson, who were to set out for Scotland next day, dined and drank tea with us. My wife was wonderfully better.

MONDAY 14 MAY. In Chancery. I recollect nothing more except breakfasting with Sir Joshua Reynolds.

TUESDAY 15 MAY. Called on Mr. G. Wallace. Called with him on the Bishop of St. Asaph, and visited Malone. Dined at the Bishop of Chester's. Counsellor Bower was good company. Seward talked some; so did Dr. Vyse. It was an ineffective day, and we got so little wine (the safest side, I own, and most proper for a bishop) that Seward and I were quite dissatisfied and went to the Cocoa-Tree and had cold meat and punch. We were very comfortable till unluckily Stewart Shaw came in, and I having invited him to join us, his talk was so rapid, noisy, and brutal that we were glad to make our escape. Seward said it would not be borne by carmen in England.

WEDNESDAY 16 MAY. A little uneasy. In Chancery. Dined at Malone's with Lord Sunderlin, who was to set out for the Continent next day. I was quite full of pedigree and Irish ideas. Drank tea and supped; all moderation.

THURSDAY 17 MAY. Malone and I and my son Sandy took a coach to Knightsbridge; then walked to Kensington Coffee-house and breakfasted, and afterwards heard Dr. Thomson's scholars recite. Sandy walked with me to town. We visited Sir Michael le Fleming, and dined at Malone's with Courtenay and his son and Kemble. It was a truly agreeable day. Sandy behaved as I could wish. I enjoyed life, and got home in good time.

FRIDAY 18 MAY. I went to Captain Preston and paid him three years' interest of my note to him for £500 and made an apology for not having yet got the principal.[9] Though he had asked the money last year, he frankly said he would not push me so I got myself free from apprehension.

---

[8] The King regarded Langton with special favour, often going out of his way to talk to him, but never offered him a post in his household. Boswell's claim to notice seems to be his support of Pitt and his Ministry in his *Letter to the People of Scotland*, 1783, and his praise of the King on all occasions.

[9] See above, 9 June 1786.

SATURDAY 19 MAY. Dined at home; went with my wife and two daughters to a concert at Mrs. Hunter's.[1] Veronica played by General Paoli's entreaty. When we came home, my wife was seized with another severe fit of spitting blood, so that Mr. John Hunter was called. She grew easier soon.

SUNDAY 20 MAY. I am sorry to say I sauntered all the forenoon; called Lord Eglinton, Ross Mackye, Mr. Ward, General Paoli, Malone, Courtenay. Visited Mrs. Bosville and engaged to dine with her and the Captain. When I returned I found the Captain was engaged at Ward's, so I had to dine tête-à-tête with the lady. Mrs. Ward, the Captain, and Miss Chisholm came, and we walked and then had tea. I went home quietly after visiting General Paoli.

MONDAY 21 MAY. Mr. Hawkins, Member for St. Michael, and Mr. George Wallace dined and drank tea with us.

TUESDAY 22 MAY. My daughter Betsy and I dined and drank tea at General Paoli's; Seward and Masseria there. She was quite happy.

WEDNESDAY 23 MAY. Treesbank dined with us. I took Mr. George Wallace to the Essex Head Club; Barrington, Brocklesby, and some others there.

THURSDAY 24 MAY. Dined at Malone's with Burke, Windham, Courtenay, Langton, Sir Joshua Reynolds, Palmer. A great day.

FRIDAY 25 MAY. A little feverish from yesterday. Jamie and I drank tea at my brother David's.

SATURDAY 26 MAY. Giuseppe, General Paoli's servant, had procured me a client, Mrs. Harriet Winyard, against whom an action of Trover was brought by another woman.[2] Mr. Samuel Naylor, the attorney, had called on me and talked of the action and sent me a brief (I took no fee), but did not send me notice when it was to come on at the sittings in the King's Bench, Westminster. I this morning thought I would call at his house and inquire. I found it was to come on today. I went down, but found that it was over. This vexed me, though I affected not to mind it. Bearcroft was the leading counsel, and had nonsuited the plaintiff. Some of the counsel told me I had been called for, and Bearcroft turned round and said, "I was obliged to you for your assistance this morning." I followed him into Alice's Coffee-house and asked an account of the cause. He looked gruff and said he had forgot. I marked him for a *bear*. It occurred to me that this visible neglect might hurt me much in my chance of getting practice. I called

[1] Probably Anne Home Hunter, minor poet and literary hostess; wife of the great surgeon who attended Mrs. Boswell. Haydn set some of her songs to music.
[2] A common-law action to recover the value of goods wrongfully converted by another to his own use.

on Malone, and he soothed me by saying notice should have been sent to me.

SUNDAY 27 MAY. Enjoyed the thought that the General Assembly was now sitting at Edinburgh, and that I was a distance from it.[3] I was too late for church. The children said divine lessons at great length. I visited Dr. Adam Smith, who had been ill; found Lord Loughborough with him. Felt a little awkward.[4] Visited my landlady, Mrs. Kneller. Called Lord Exeter, Sir George Howard, Mr. John Home.[5] Sat awhile with Malone. Dined at home. Walked out to Chelsea College. Found Captain Grant alone. Drank coffee with him, and was comfortable as at Auchinleck. Home, quiet and placid. M.M. very good. ——.

MONDAY 28 MAY. Sir George Howard having written to me to let him know fairly if General Paoli would like to be at the Anniversary Dinner on the restoration of Charles II at Chelsea College, I breakfasted with the General, and he agreed to go, of which I informed Sir George. Visited Malone. Courtenay came, and as he was retiring to Bath this week, it was agreed we should dine at Malone's today at half past five, when he hoped to get from the House. He could not get away, so Malone and I dined tête-à-tête, well, *ut semper.*[6]

TUESDAY 29 MAY. Quiet at home forenoon. Then went to General Paoli's and accompanied him to Chelsea College; General Trapaud, General Tonyn, Colonel Skene, etc., there. Old Captain Grant seemed glad that we met. There was no high glee, but I liked my annual feast. Night before I had dreamt of M.M. and M.C. contending for me. This heated my fancy, and the flame being increased by wine, I very improperly (after having declined any more intercourse) called at the house to which she had removed. Fortunately she was not there. Two old gentlewomen, sisters, to one of whom the house belonged, gave me a sad account of her contracting debts, saying she had an estate in Ireland and one in Scotland, and being now in the Fleet Prison. They complained much of her; were desirous to know who I was, and asked

[3]The General Assembly of the Church of Scotland, that *"vulgar and rascally* court" (Journal, 26 May 1777) at whose bar Boswell used to practise.

[4]Smith, wasted to a skeleton by a chronic obstruction of the bowel, had come from Edinburgh to consult John Hunter. Boswell, a pupil and admirer of Smith's at the University of Glasgow (1759–60), had gone out of his way in the *Tour* to rebuke him for what he considered excessive praise of Hume's wisdom and virtue. This may well have been Boswell's first meeting with Smith since the *Tour* was published.

[5]Howard, general and M.P., was Governor of Chelsea Hospital (*c.* College) for aged and disabled soldiers; Home, a Presbyterian minister and dramatist (quoted by Lonsdale above, 5 December 1786), is chiefly remembered for having written a successful historical tragedy, *Douglas.*

[6]As always.

if my name was *Rawdon*.[7] I said no. When I went away, I desired them (absurdly enough) to mention to her that Mr. *Parr* had called.[8]

WEDNESDAY 30 MAY. Mr. and Miss Wilkes, Malone, Courtenay, and my old acquaintance General Stopford and Miss Buchanan dined with us. Wilkes and Courtenay very improperly attacked General Paoli. My wife, with a just warmth, drank his health, declaring her high respect, and desired there might be no more of it. Malone and Courtenay stayed tea and coffee, after which I went to the Essex Head Club; Barrington, Brocklesby, Murphy, Devaynes, and some more there. I had paid Mr. George Wallace the compliment to ask him to dinner today, and for that purpose called on him, but he was engaged. It was not a pleasant day. It was curious, however, to see Wilkes dining with my family.

THURSDAY 31 MAY. Visited General Stopford and saw his lady.[9] My wife and two daughters dined at Sir Joshua Reynolds's with Courtenay, Malone, Sir Gilbert Elliot, Batt.[1] I liked to recollect former days, and now see my wife and two daughters actually where I used to be so highly enchanted. But this was not a brilliant day. Courtenay was to set out next day. Malone and I saw him into his house. I then strolled with Malone in Berners Street[2] in moonlight, and I thought *solidly* of returning to Auchinleck, feeling for the moment that I was inconsiderable in London. Would not go and sup with him, but went home quietly.

FRIDAY 1 JUNE. Breakfasted at Malone's as usual on the first of the month and looked at reviews of Hawkins's *Life of Johnson*. Poor Courtenay was with us and set off. It was somewhat dreary to see him depart, not to return for months. Captain Grant and son, Captain Bruce Boswell and wife, and Mr. Lawrence Hill from Edinburgh dined with us, a dinner of duty. It was disagreeable, when my wife said to Mr. Hill she wished I would return to the Scotch bar, to hear him say, "It is a great pity he left it."

SATURDAY 2 JUNE. Dr. Adams of Pembroke College and his daughter were now in town. He had called on me and I had called on him and seen him. This forenoon my wife and daughters and I called

---

[8]This is the last mention of Mrs. Rudd in the journal. She lived until 1797.

[9]Boswell had not seen Stopford since his marriage in 1783, at the age of fifty-one, to a much younger woman—at least she lived until 1841.

[1]Elliot, M.P. for Berwick, later Envoy to Vienna and Governor-General of India, was created first Earl of Minto in 1813. John Thomas Batt, barrister, was auditor for the Irish accounts during Pitt's Administration.

[2]Where Courtenay lived.

on Miss Adams. We heard the music in Westminster Abbey pretty well on the outside of the rails.[3] I took them into Westminster Hall and showed them it. Dined at home, and did some *Life*. In the evening Mr. Lumisden and Lady Strange sat some time with us.[4]

SUNDAY 3 JUNE. Visited Malone in the forenoon. The children said divine lessons. Was at our own chapel in the afternoon. In the evening, walked in the fields beyond Queen's Square with my wife and children.

MONDAY 4 JUNE. Mr. Ramus, the King's page, upon a note from me had obligingly promised to get my two daughters into a good place at St. James's to see the company going to Court. I went to him this morning at Buckingham House to ask as to particulars and found it would be proper their mother should accompany them, which she did. I was agreeably agitated by being in the house where the King actually was, and I indulged longings of ambition. Sir George Howard had kindly asked me to dine this day again at Chelsea College. I went, and found General Paoli, Colonel Leland, Colonel Skene, Mr. Drummond (son of the Provost), whom I had never seen before, a sensible, well-behaved man.[5] Came to town in the General's chariot. Wandered into the City to look at the illuminations.[6] Was somewhat heated with wine. Sat awhile with Dilly. Eat cold beef and drank small beer at the Chapter Coffee-house.

TUESDAY 5 JUNE. Dined at Malone's with Mr. and Mrs. and Miss Byng, Miss Forrest, Mr. John Kemble. We stayed the evening and supped, and Malone, Kemble, and I grew so cordial that time passed insensibly. I once or twice endeavoured to get away but was persuaded to sit down again. When two struck, I thought my wife would now be quiet, and I resigned myself to my fate. We sat till near five. I felt great remorse when I got home and found my dear wife sitting up.

WEDNESDAY 6 JUNE. As I was engaged to breakfast with Dr. Adams half past nine and was not sleepy, I did not go to bed but walked to Westminster, St. James's Park, *etc.*[7] I grew somewhat drowsy and un-easy. Heard mass in Bavarian Chapel. Breakfasted with Dr. and Miss

---

[3]This was the third day of the annual festival of Handel's sacred music, held in the Abbey. It was announced that the "band" would consist of eight hundred performers. Tickets were a guinea for each performance; the profits went to charity.

[4]They were brother and sister.

[5]George Drummond's father, also named George, was six times Lord Provost of Edinburgh.

[6]For the King's Birthday.

[7]Heavily underlined by Boswell. See above, 18 April.

Adams. Thought what a strange variety my life was. Home and dressed. Went to Malone's and walked with him to Kemble's lodgings beyond Brompton and dined. Major North and Byng there. I was sober. Yesterday's ladies came to tea. We gentlemen all walked to town. I was somewhat low-spirited.

THURSDAY 7 JUNE. Called on Malone. Both he and I were very well today. Dined at home. I recollect no more.

FRIDAY 8 JUNE. The term began. I went again to Chancery. Dined at home.

SATURDAY 9 JUNE. In Chancery. Dined at home. Did some *Life*.

SUNDAY 10 JUNE. At Queen Street Chapel forenoon and afternoon. Did a little *Life*. The children said divine lessons. I dined at General Paoli's; Seward there and T.D. It is being on the Continent to dine there on Sunday. But I felt it wrong to be there, because the dinner is intended for foreigners and today the company amounted to seventeen. I eat and drank fully. Seward and I walked in the evening and proceeded on to Bagnigge Wells, where we had some punch.[8]

MONDAY 11 JUNE. Was somewhat uneasy. Sauntered in the forenoon. Sat some time with my brother T.D. and was satisfied of the propriety of carrying my family home, unless I should in one other year get by practice or place some additional hundreds. He pressed upon me the discreditable appearance which I made here, not being either in Parliament or in practice at the bar or having fortune sufficient to enable me to make a figure suitable to the rank of my family. I resolved to quit London as a residence at the end of two years from my being called to the bar, should no fortunate event raise me. But my brother was desirous that I should send down my family directly, except my son James, to whom an English education might be of consequence. He pressed upon me the consideration how many people kept aloof from me, supposing me a man going to ruin. I was vexed that I could not unite Auchinleck and London fully, yet I indulged hope. I was too late for Westminster Hall. Sat awhile with Malone.

TUESDAY 12 JUNE. In Chancery. Dined at Literary Club with Lord Macartney, Dr. Adam Smith, Mr. Steevens, Dr. Fordyce, Mr. Malone, young Burke, Dr. Warren, Sir Joshua Reynolds. There was no force, no brilliancy; nothing as when Johnson, Goldsmith, or Garrick were with us. I was pleased with Warren's cheerfulness, which, though David Hume erroneously calls a *virtue*, is certainly a valuable quality.[9] I took care not to introduce Johnson. But Sir Joshua did, and I observed that

---

[8]A popular place of public entertainment north of the city.

a great part of our conversation was about him. I indeed took a part, though I would not lead. I drank too much wine, though Malone admonished me to stop. I grew drowsy and stupid. Sauntered, but *innocue*.

WEDNESDAY 13 JUNE.[1] In Chancery. I think breakfasted at Langton's. Some *Life*. At night Essex Head Club, last night this season. Present: Murphy, Cooke, Barrington, Devaynes, and I.

THURSDAY 14 JUNE. In Chancery. One of the days of this week (I think this), supped at Malone's heartily.

FRIDAY 15 JUNE. In Chancery. Some *Life*. Took my two sons to the gallery of Drury Lane playhouse and let them see *Love à la Mode*, that they might talk of having seen Macklin play Sir Archie Mac-Sarcasm. I was much entertained and in a most placid frame.[2] Perhaps some people are always thus. I had this evening taken my wife and two eldest daughters to see Westminster Abbey, but it was still encumbered with the scaffolding put up for the musical performances.

SATURDAY 16 JUNE. My unwillingness to return to Scotland was great, from an apprehension that I should be oppressed with the same dreary ideas which used to make me miserable. I however considered that the death of worthy Grange and of a great many others and the progress of buildings, etc., could not but produce a considerable variation upon my ideas when there. It is not possible, I think, for me to put in words my feelings upon the subject. I was vexed to think of returning without having attained honour or profit visibly in England.

[9]" 'Tis evident, that the conversation of a man of wit is very satisfactory, as a cheerful, good-humoured companion diffuses a joy over the whole company, from a sympathy with his gaiety. These qualities, therefore, being agreeable, they naturally beget love and esteem and answer to all the characters of virtue" (*Treatise of Human Nature*, bk. iii, pt. 3, sec. 4). Richard Warren, Physician to the King, attended both Johnson and Boswell in their last illnesses.

[1] On this day Boswell wrote to Lord Lonsdale reminding him of his application to be Recorder of Carlisle. He received from Lonsdale on the 27th "a very gracious letter . . . that he wishes to talk with me as to the Recordership of Carlisle—inviting me most politely to pass some time with him."

[2] The journalist John Taylor tells the following anecdote, presumably of this occasion in spite of deviations in detail: "The first time I ever saw Mr. James Boswell, Junior, was in the first gallery of the Haymarket Theatre, at the benefit of the widow and family of Dr. Glover. He was then quite a boy, and stood on the bench while his father held him round the waist. The play was *The Merchant of Venice*, and the farce *Love à la Mode*. . . . My late friend Jack Johnstone sung a song in character, each verse ending with the word *Whack*, which he gave with great power of lungs. Little Boswell was so delighted with this song that his father roared for a repetition with a stentorian voice, to please the child, and Johnstone readily sang it again" (*Records of My Life*, 1832, i, 219).

I had indeed acquired an accession of ideas. My wife was strongly of opinion that it would be of consequence to my family to have them in Scotland. I recollect no more.

[EDITORIAL NOTE. The fully written journal breaks off here and is not resumed until mid-July, but rough notes for the interval show the usual round of activities. "A little cloudy" or "dreary" much of the time, Boswell on six days made no notes at all. On 20 June the cryptic entry "watch-house" after a note of dinner at Sir Joshua's may mean that he was picked up for a disturbance in the street. His lack of practice at the English bar drove him to send two letters on 29 June which he summarized in the Register of Letters as follows: "Lord Rockville that I had last session of Parliament but a small share of Scotch appeals, which I think very wrong. He should *remit* causes to me, as is done to an accountant who is a *friend* and worthy of the trust. *Verbum sapienti.*" "Rev. Mr. Temple that I will write him a longer letter soon. I *now* beg he may send me a draft on his Indian acquisition for the money he owes me. This year I am particularly straitened and shall *relish* the sum. Neither he nor I know the precise amount of what he has paid; I suppose about £10. Let that go for interest, and of *that* no more. Let me have the neat principal, £45. Let us not be like Addison and Steele, have a difference small or great, real or apparent, about money. He would *give* me the sum were I in want of it. It cannot be wrong to ask him to repay it." (On 3 August he registered a letter from Temple and his own reply of the same date: "A short letter, happy that money matters are settled between us.")

The Register of Letters also discloses amidst the mental turmoil a steady pursuit of Johnsonian materials and a stream of responses to applications Boswell had already made. On 10–12 July he attended the Chelmsford Quarter Sessions, took notes on the trials, and got one client on the last day. "Felt *well*," he wrote, and reanimated by the activities of court and counsel, his spirits continued high after his return to London. Six days later he resumed the journal.]

WEDNESDAY 18 JULY. Dr. Brown of Utrecht breakfasted. Curious thoughts.[3] Was in high spirits. Met Sir J. Dick, and talked of getting something from Government. Sir Joshua, Dr. Scott, Malone, Langton,

---

[3]Presumably Boswell is remembering his stay in Holland, 1763–64, when he must have known William Laurence Brown, D.D., then a child of eight or nine. His father was a close friend of Boswell's.

Dr. Burney, Miss Buchanan, Mr. William Gordon dined. Miss M.,[4] Malone, and Langton supped. Quite cheerful.

THURSDAY 19 JULY. Thorpe breakfasted, and I went with him to Hertford.[5] Charming day. At church. Saw with Fielding[6] the Castle. Good dinner. Fine spirits. Well in court. At ball; admired Lady Salisbury. Agreeable supper. Got acquainted with Ibbetson, genteel man. Sober.

FRIDAY 20 JULY. Cheerful breakfast. Well in court. Off at twelve. Saw gaol; very clean and ornamented with fruits and flowers. To town half past three. Dined with my family. Then to Nichols; just going to Hawkins. Went and waited in Storey's Gate Coffee-house till treasure brought. Went to Malone's. Not at home. Sir Joshua's; gone from thence. Home with the papers.[7]

SATURDAY 21 JULY. Breakfasted well home, then Malone's with some of Johnson's papers. Home and wrote letters. Dined Malone, most firm and spirited, and viewed English bar as at least great accession of ideas. Tea. Home. Dr. Brown made an excuse for not coming; ill-bred. Langton with us. Very comfortable. Little James feverish from sore hand.

SUNDAY 22 JULY. Awaked well. Wife and I called Colbecks. Children said divine lessons. Queen Street Chapel. Dined home.

MONDAY 23 JULY. Up early. Off for Chelmsford with Richardson and Thorpe.[8] Richardson a fine fellow. He gave us the history of his duel with Parson Bate. I "liked not *such* honour," but felt it might be necessary.[9] Joined Phillips and Adair at Romford. Found Chelmsford most agreeable again, but not so comfortable as at the Sessions. Sat up late drinking with Phillips.

---

[4]Presumably Boswell's error for "Miss B.," that is, Miss Buchanan.

[5]For the summer assizes, where he took notes on two trials.

[6]William Fielding, barrister, eldest son of the novelist.

[7]Boswell had persuaded Francis Barber to copy and sign letters to Johnson's executors instructing them to turn over to Boswell Johnson's diary and any other of his manuscripts in their possession. The action was directed at Hawkins; John Nichols, Johnson's devoted friend and the printer of the *Lives of the Poets*, served as intermediary.

[8]To attend the assizes.

[9]Boswell is quoting Falstaff (*1 Henry IV*, V. iii). The Rev. Henry Bate (who added the name Dudley in 1784), a journalist and writer of comic operas, was known as the "fighting parson" from his readiness to defend his honour in the field. He had fought a duel with Joseph Richardson, a fellow proprietor of the *Morning Post*, who had been wounded in the arm. Bate was tried at the assizes on 25 July for profiteering on the sale of coal, but the plaintiff was nonsuited, and though the evidence appears substantial, the judge and jury declared the charge "most scandalously founded in malice" (*Chelmsford Chronicle*, 27 July 1787).

TUESDAY 24 JULY. Uneasy somewhat. All day in court, excellently entertained. Early home and to bed.

WEDNESDAY 25 JULY. Very well. Court, still most entertaining. Dined with Judge Gould. Then Fielding and I and a few more went to the Black Boy to have a little more claret. A number joined, so we had port. I was voted into the chair, and "Jove in His Chair" was sung.[1] We were very jovial for some time. Then I went to court. Then returned and played whist. Lost about nine guineas once, but got it all back again and a guinea with it. Sat till (I believe) four in the morning.

THURSDAY 26 JULY. Court in the forenoon, trial on Swindling Act.[2] Then Leach, Knowlys, and I set out. Dined jovially at Romford; were very happy. Home in high spirits.[3]

[EDITORIAL NOTE. Again the fully written journal gives way to brief notes. For some dates there are no entries at all. On 31 July Boswell dined at William Scott's with Sir Joshua Reynolds, Malone, Langton, and Dr. Burney, an informal committee for raising funds for Dr. Johnson's monument. Much the same company dined at Langton's the next day, 1 August, at Reynolds's on the 6th, and at Malone's on the 7th. On 8–10 August Boswell attended the assizes at Croydon, where he was "much entertained" by the hearings. "Erskine wonderfully lively." After Boswell returned to London late on the 10th his notes become more expansive and begin to read like journal.]

SATURDAY 11 AUGUST. Major Green breakfasted. Col. James Stuart, Sir Joshua, Langton, Windham, T.D. dined. The Colonel brought out only one disagreeable thing—he had heard of me at Chelmsford very drunk. *Not true.* N.B. Windham called Gibbon an odious fellow, and he and I said a solemn coxcomb.

SUNDAY 12 AUGUST. Quiet forenoon. Afternoon Queen's Street Chapel. Dined at Sir Joshua's with Col. James Stuart, who came to me, Malone, Lord Sheffield,[4] Gibbon, Windham, Dr. Burney, Devaynes, Batt, Langton.

MONDAY 13 AUGUST. Awaked *somewhat* dreary for the first time (I think) for several months, owing, I imagined, to my having drunk *too little* at Sir Joshua's. Sad slavery, if it was so! Soon grew better.

[1]A chorus from *Midas*, a burletta by Kane O'Hara.
[2]The defendant, charged with defrauding a bookseller of almost £346, was sentenced to be transported for seven years.
[3]There is here in the manuscript something that looks like a triangle, possibly a private symbol.
[4]John Baker Holroyd, first Baron (later first Earl of) Sheffield, Gibbon's friend and literary executor.

Resolved I would take my wife with me to Auchinleck. She might die, and I should upbraid myself for not having given her the benefit of travelling, change of air, and rural amusement. Besides, her good sense and activity would be of essential service to me. I also resolved to take Sandy, as his heart was quite set on it. Devaynes called and talked well, and my wife was much pleased. Sorted papers in the forenoon. Dined at Devaynes's country-house with Sir Joshua, Murphy, Counsellor Hodgson, Governor Devaynes, a fine fellow.[5] *Jack* made us gay and kept us moderate, all but *Mur.*[5a] Drove with Sir Joshua and saw illuminations for Prince of Wales's birthday.

[EDITORIAL NOTE. The notes break off here and do not resume until the Boswells—James, Margaret, Veronica, and Sandy—arrived at Auchinleck the following Monday, 20 August. They had expected to spend a week en route at Lowther Castle, near Penrith, on Lonsdale's invitation, but they learned at Kendal that he had gone to London on a "matter of high importance" (Boswell's words). Having travelled to Auchinleck for the purpose of collecting his rents, Boswell remained there a little over a month, visited and entertained company as usual, and in particular saw a good deal of the Alexander family, his new neighbours at Ballochmyle (Sir John Whitefoord had been forced to sell). Shortly after Boswell's return home the nearby parishes which united for the annual Sacrament met at Auchinleck. On the Fast Day, Thursday 23 August, he heard "Black" Russel, whose "piercin words, like Highlan swords,/Divide the joints an' marrow,"[6] preach to the crowd from a "tent" (portable pulpit) in the open air. On Saturday, Sunday, and Monday, the 25th to the 27th, Boswell listened to two preachers daily in his own church. On Tuesday the 28th he attended the Auchinleck Lamb Fair, which drew farmers from the whole west of Scotland, and dined and danced at Ballochmyle.

On 13 September Lord Hailes and Lord Braxfield arrived to open the circuit court at Ayr. Boswell, "well with the gentlemen and in court," was croupier, or assistant chairman at the foot of the table, at the circuit dinner. A week later he concluded a contract with the Glasgow Iron Company for mining the coal and minerals at Boghead, but it came to nothing. On 22 September he gave a dinner for his tenants and wrote of it, "all wonderfully well." He was sorry to leave Auchinleck, he noted the next evening, but on 24 September, accompanied by Mrs. Boswell and the two children, he started back to London. The first

[5] Jack Devaynes's brother William, M.P., Director of the East India Company, later Chairman of the Board.
[5a] Johnson's nickname for Murphy.
[6] Robert Burns, *The Holy Fair*, ll. 185–86.

night was spent at Dumfries, where he wrote the following memorandum:

> Recollecting my worthy friend Grange and many former ideas connected with this place, how wonderfully well am I tonight. The very wish of my heart in early years, when I used to read *The Spectator* with Temple, is realized. I am now a barrister-at-law of the Inner Temple, have a house in London, am one of the distinguished literary men of my age. And at the same time have an extensive estate, a number of tenants all depending upon me; in short, have, when I please, the *potentiality* of a prince. Yet persevere in attending the Essex Sessions.

SATURDAY 29 SEPTEMBER. Arrived in London about two. The children rejoiced at our return. Dressed and walked out. London seemed not at all strange but connected with Auchinleck. Malone gone to Cambridge. Dined at General Paoli's; only Mr. Gentili.

SUNDAY 30 SEPTEMBER. At Temple Church.

MONDAY 1 OCTOBER. Dined at Sir Joshua Reynolds's with Admiral Vincent. In the morning had been at Dilly's, who in the most friendly manner *offered* me a loan which I wanted.[7]

TUESDAY 2 OCTOBER. Off early in Colchester coach to Chelmsford to attend the Sessions. A two-guinea brief welcomed me.[8] Good meeting with my brethren. Old Mayhew not able to attend. Benson also absent. Thin bench. Lived rather too full.

WEDNESDAY 3 OCTOBER. Well in court. Lived too full.

THURSDAY 4 OCTOBER. Rose low-spirited and very anxious to see my family again. Drove to London in the Chelmsford coach. Not at all well.

FRIDAY 5 OCTOBER. [*Nil.*]

SATURDAY 6 OCTOBER. My wife and two eldest daughters and I dined at Mrs. Bosville's. Quite London. But I was not well.

SUNDAY 7 OCTOBER. At Queen Street Chapel forenoon and afternoon. Dined at General Paoli's. Still not well.

MONDAY 8 OCTOBER. [*Nil.*]

---

[7]Boswell was under constant financial pressure during these years. At this moment, Robert Preston was asking for repayment of his loan of £500 (see above, 9 June 1786 and 18 May 1787). Dilly offered £300, and Boswell finally also borrowed £200 from Henry Baldwin (see below, 15 and 26 October 1787).

[8]He also earned a total of another guinea from two other cases at these Sessions (and had time to write a whimsical dialogue in verse entitled "On Geese" with another lawyer, James Trower).

TUESDAY 9 OCTOBER. Visited Mr. Coutts. Sir Joshua Reynolds, Mr. Courtenay and son, Mr. Langton and son, Mr. Devaynes, Mrs. and Miss Buchanan dined with us. All but Devaynes supped. I was not well.

WEDNESDAY 10 OCTOBER. At *Life*. T.D. dined. N.B. Understood *not well* till a change is marked.

THURSDAY 11 OCTOBER. T.D. and Masseria dined. At *Life*.

FRIDAY 12 OCTOBER. Sadly depressed. Walked to Hackney and visited Dr. Price. He obliged me with the rate of an annuity on money sunk. Vexed that I did not relish his conversation.[9] Dined at Sir Joshua Reynolds's with Courtenay and son, Langton and son, and Hoole. Revived somewhat.

SATURDAY 13 OCTOBER. The fit not gone. Called at Malone's, who was to return today. Found he had ordered dinner. Walked about, listless and uneasy, till near five, when I went to him and complained of depression. He kindly said, "We'll set you up again." Had a little dinner and a cordial glass and tea comfortably. But still not well.

SUNDAY 14 OCTOBER. Rose restless. Breakfasted with Sir Joshua. Envied his activity and placid disposition. Sat awhile with Courtenay. Then to Malone's, who insisted on my meeting Courtenay and Kemble at dinner. I agreed. Went home and heard the children say sacred lessons, and was at Queen Street Chapel afternoon; and thus *quieted*, dined most heartily and drank a great deal of wine and came home late.

MONDAY 15 OCTOBER. Dilly called. I was sadly sunk. He said a fine day was like a dram to him. Walked out. Called on Baldwin, my honest printer, and asked him frankly for £200 for four months. He said he had some inquiries to make into his affairs, but believed I might depend on having the loan. Felt just as I have done formerly when at the worst. Sat awhile with T.D. Shrunk from the thought of returning to Edinburgh, yet did not see how I could go on in London. Some *Life*.

TUESDAY 16 OCTOBER. *Life* all day. Note from Baldwin that I might have the loan.

WEDNESDAY 17 OCTOBER. Breakfasted with Malone and read to him some of the *Life* which I had lately done. He animated me by commending it. Home and continued. General Paoli called. I told him of my depression. He said, "You must not think of it," and asked me to dinner with some foreigners of rank. But I kept to *Life*.

[9]Richard Price, D.D., a Nonconformist minister, had become famous for his pro-American stand during the American Revolution. Yale awarded him the LL.D. in 1783. He was an authority on actuarial statistics.

THURSDAY 18 OCTOBER. *Life* all day. Sad depression. Vexed to find this in London. Thought of returning to Edinburgh. Wife spit some blood. Uneasy that Sandy's health was such that it was thought not safe to board him at school or academy, as I perceived him growing unruly. Was so dreary that I could not perceive the just distinction between good and evil, so that I was inwardly *indifferent* as to the success of my children. Little James, however, engaged me much by his vivacity and love of learning. Kemble sat awhile with me in the forenoon and fixed me to dine with him Sunday sennight with Malone, Courtenay, etc. I *felt* in some degree being asked as a man of literature. He told me that at a school in Lancashire he had translated my *Account of Corsica* into Latin as an exercise. In the evening T.D. visited us. My only comfort at present was eating and sleeping. I had drunk nothing fermented since Sunday.

FRIDAY 19 OCTOBER. *Life*. T.D. and Mrs. Green dined with us. Miss Buchanan supped. I was quite relaxed.

SATURDAY 20 OCTOBER. Kemble had sent me a note at my desire to inform me when he could dine with me, which was *Monday*. So I hastened to secure Malone, Courtenay, and Sir Joshua. Breakfasted with Malone and was well entertained with some old letters giving an account of his grandfather and other family particulars. Some *Life*, but still hipped.[1]

SUNDAY 21 OCTOBER. Very cold. At Queen Street Chapel forenoon and afternoon. Some of the children said sacred lessons. After some hesitation, dined at General Paoli's. An Italian countess and several foreigners there. Could not relish it fully. Came home early.

MONDAY 22 OCTOBER. Some *Life*. Mr. Kemble, Mr. Malone, Sir Joshua Reynolds, Mr. Murphy, Dr. Brocklesby, Mr. Langton, and Miss Buchanan dined, and all but Brocklesby supped. I was not at all in spirits.[2] I talked privately to Malone of my being afraid that I had done wrong to come to the English bar. He consoled me, and said I

[1] Morbidly depressed (from "hypochondriacal").

[2] But they were all "much entertained," he wrote to Sir William Forbes on 7 November, by a copy of the "Round Robin" to Dr. Johnson which Boswell had opportunely received from Forbes this day. The *jeu d' esprit* had been composed by Burke, put in a fair copy by Forbes, and signed in circular form (so that no one would be blamed as instigator) by all the guests at Reynolds's in spring 1776. The petitioners humbly requested Johnson to make some changes in the epitaph for Goldsmith's monument, primarily to write it in English, the poet's language, rather than Latin. Forbes reported to Boswell that Johnson had received the document from Reynolds's hands "with much good humour" but said that he would " '*never consent . . . to disgrace the walls of Westminster Abbey with an inscription in English*' " (From Forbes, 19 October 1787).

had in the mean time this life of enjoyment; that he did not expect that I would get into great practice at the bar, but that fortunate things might happen through Lord Lonsdale or otherwise; that I was a prudent man as to expense, was not involving my circumstances, and had always a solid property to retire to. Excellent friend!

TUESDAY 23 OCTOBER. Some *Life*. Dined at Dilly's with Dr. Lettsom, Mr. Millington from Barbados, and Mr. Cobb, author of *The First Floor*, etc.[3] Was very low, and very injudiciously had recourse to too much wine to raise my spirits.

WEDNESDAY 24 OCTOBER. Some *Life*. Breakfasted with young Sibthorpe, just returned from France.[4] Felt as when at Glasgow College. He drank tea with us. Was very ill.

THURSDAY 25 OCTOBER. Some *Life*. Young Sibthorpe and Mr. Mabon dined with us. I was gloomy and in absolute pain of mind.

FRIDAY 26 OCTOBER. Very ill, but obliged to hurry into City to settle Preston's note. Got £200 from Baldwin and £300 from Dilly, and settled with Martin, Preston's clerk. Then (by my dear wife's prudent advice) paid a visit to Preston not to have a quarrel with him. It went off very easily. Met Mrs. Knowles at Dilly's, who told me she knew the cause of my uneasiness: the want of reconciling the soul to GOD. I thought so. Met Sharp, who cheered me as to my *Life*. Was wonderfully relieved. Evening some *Life*.

SATURDAY 27 OCTOBER. *Life*. Was easier

SUNDAY 28 OCTOBER. Not so well. Was restless. Went to Malone's and read him an year's journal of Johnson's conversation for *Life*, which I feared was of little value. He cheered me by praising it. Dined at Kemble's of Drury Lane with Sir Joshua, Courtenay, Malone, and a Dr. Pearson. Was tolerably well. All but Pearson stayed supper. I did not get home till half past one.

MONDAY 29 OCTOBER.[5] *Life*. Was better. Breakfasted with Sir Joshua with Mrs. Wells, who gave us some of her imitations, which were exquisite.[6] Duke of Rutland's death agitated my blood by making me *feel* the changes in human life and *fancy* that I might one day perhaps

---

[3] John Coakley Lettsom, a Quaker physician who became a good friend; James Cobb, whose farce *The First Floor* was highly successful.

[4] A young Irish cousin of Boswell's whom he and Mrs. Boswell had come to like very much when he was attending the University of Edinburgh.

[5] His forty-seventh birthday.

[6] A beautiful and popular comedienne at Covent Garden who earlier this year had presented imitations of Mrs. Siddons and other actresses at the new Royalty Theatre, a variety house.

rise to some eminence.[7] Went to Malone and talked that perhaps there might now be an opening in Ireland for Courtenay. In the evening heard Sheldon lecture on anatomy at the Royal Academy. *Who* sat at Sir Joshua's right hand but Edmund Burke! Sir Joshua carried him and me home in his coach. We had cold meat and some wine. I was sorry to perceive Burke shy to me. But my loyal zeal against the India Bill was a *letalis harundo*[8] in his side. I spoke with indignation of the prosperity of men who did not deserve it. He justly observed that this was the nature of things: activity will have its reward; and he repeated from Pope some lines to that effect, which I found were the *original* of an observation which had struck me in Smith's *Moral Sentiments.*[9] He said *Fingal* was the clumsiest imposture; that when the fragments came out, he could not say whether they were ancient or not, but when there was a mass of it, he saw clearly.[1] He said that it was culpable to carry on a literary imposture upon which *facts* could be founded, so as that the world should be deceived as to manners and ancient history. He said he wished to have a good library. He did not believe all his books were worth £100. He had never seen a good Civil Law library in England, though no doubt there must be some; he had seen several in Scotland. He would have a complete library of voyages and travels, which would now come to a great deal of money, and he would have a Shakespeare library, all the old English authors from whom he had borrowed. He said Foote had not only a number of old stories but a great deal of ready wit; that he was like all people who entertain

---

[7]The Duke had just died at the age of thirty-three of a liver complaint apparently brought on by a life of excess. A descendant of the sister of Edward IV, Knight of the Garter, Privy Councillor, Lord Privy Seal, and finally Lord-Lieutenant of Ireland (where the magnificence of his entertainments was conspicuous), he was a character who would naturally fire Boswell's imagination.

[8]*Aeneid*, iv. 73: "deadly arrow."

[9]*Essay on Man*, iv. 149–56:

> 'But sometimes Virtue starves, while Vice is fed.'
> What then? Is the reward of Virtue bread?
> That, Vice may merit; 'tis the price of toil;
> The knave deserves it when he tills the soil,
> The knave deserves it when he tempts the main,
> Where Folly fights for kings, or dives for gain.
> The good man may be weak, be indolent,
> Nor is his claim to plenty, but content.

Adam Smith's paraphrase occurs in the third part of his book, chapter five.

[1]Debate on Macpherson's purported translation of an ancient epic by Ossian had been renewed by the publication of the *Tour*, in which Boswell reported Johnson's remark (22 September 1773) that *Fingal* was " 'as gross an imposition as ever the world was troubled with.' "

much—they must have cold pies and other substantial dishes always ready.[2] I felt my own emptiness sadly while I heard him talk, a variety of knowledge ten times more than I have recollected. He said there was nothing worse than not doing what a man knows to be right for fear of obloquy. This was a spirited and generous sentiment.

TUESDAY 30 OCTOBER. A good deal of *Life*. Drank tea with Malone. Had Captain Cuninghame of Thornton, his brother Archibald, young Wellwood, Captain James Dunlop, and Mr. Sibthorpe at supper.[3]

WEDNESDAY 31 OCTOBER. *Life*. Dined at Dr. Brocklesby's with *the Gang*,[4] Mr. Burke, Mr. Devaynes, Mr. Langton, Mr. Murphy, etc. As Brocklesby was cutting a piece of lamb rather awkwardly while someone who was a skilful carver kept looking at him, it was hoped it was not *an evil eye*. "What!" said Malone, "not *fascinat agnos*?"[5] There was a great deal said of which I retain nothing; nor do I of much pleasantry at Sir Joshua's where *the Gang* went afterwards and sat till about twelve over fine punch. Only that Courtenay said that Charles Fox had his India Bill, which ruined him, in his hand in his portrait, like St.———,[6] who was always painted with the gridiron on which he was broiled.

THURSDAY 1 NOVEMBER. *Life*.

FRIDAY 2 NOVEMBER. Breakfasted at Malone's, and he went with me to the Temple and looked at chambers which I had taken, but which we feared were not creditable enough. Not well, but did some *Life*.

SATURDAY 3 NOVEMBER. Walked to Chelsea College and breakfasted with Dr. Burney, who gave me some letters from Johnson to him. Sat awhile with Captain Grant. Was sadly low-spirited. Called at General Paoli's; not in. Sat awhile with Malone. T.D. dined with us. I grew so much hipped that I could not write any *Life*.

SUNDAY 4 NOVEMBER. At Queen Street Chapel forenoon and afternoon. I do not like giving dinners on Sunday, but I had engaged Squire Dilly and his brother to be with me the day after the Squire's arrival, which proved to be this day. I had with them Malone, Reed, and Mr. Burney, who keeps an academy at Hammersmith, that I might talk to him of putting Sandy under his tuition in case his mother could be persuaded to trust him from home.[7] I was gloomy, so could not

[2]Samuel Foote, famous as an actor, mimic, and comic dramatist.
[3]Except for Sibthorpe, all officers who had served in the American Revolution.
[4]Reynolds, Malone, Courtenay, and Boswell. The name seems to have originated with Philip Metcalfe.
[5]Virgil, *Eclogues*, iii. 103: "[Some evil eye] bewitches [my tender] lambs."
[6]St. Lawrence. The portrait of Fox was by Reynolds.
[7]Charles Burney, Dr. Burney's son, enjoyed a great reputation as a classical scholar.

perceive anything with clearness, and had a wretched feeling of in-difference as to all excellence. Wine did me some good. Malone, Reed, and Squire Dilly supped.

MONDAY 5 NOVEMBER. A little *Life*. Dined at Malone's with Reed, Dr. Brocklesby, Mr. Humphry the painter,[8] and Sir Joshua. Bad spirits still continued. Good eating and drinking and conversation relieved me somewhat. Went to a card-party at Mrs. Bosville's. Dull, dull, or rather insipid. Returned to Malone's, having half promised. Was mor-tified at feeling myself unable to make a good figure. Would not stay supper, as my wife had been complaining much from a severe cold. Came home a little after twelve.

TUESDAY 6 NOVEMBER. Term began. Westminster Hall seemed to me "flat and unprofitable."[9]

WEDNESDAY 7 NOVEMBER. Supposing Ross's benefit to be tonight at Royalty Theatre, took Sandy with me. It was put off. We dined at Cock Tavern behind Exchange. Tea Dilly's and oysters afterwards, Squire Dilly and Sharp having joined.

THURSDAY 8 NOVEMBER. Mr. Dundas, Sir Joshua Reynolds, Mr. Langton, Mr. Malone, and Sir John Dick dined with us. Dundas was frank and good-humoured. Malone said, "He has disarmed me." He said that power was thought desirable on account of the patronage annexed to it. But that the uneasiness was much greater than the satisfaction, for you had six or seven letters to write to people who were disappointed and probably had to give the office to one for whom you did not care, but that government must be carried on. He said that he had watched Mr. Fox, and he really believed that his wish for being in power was not for the patronage but to do public good. He said that no man would be in power were it not for the consciousness of serving his country and going down to posterity with credit. He said that about the end of the last Parliament, while the meeting at the St. Alban's Tavern was going on,[1] Fox having made some pretence to go down the House, perhaps for an orange, contrived to come up the side where he sat and said to him (if one may use a vulgar phrase), to *pump* him, "You seem so violent that I really believe you would dissolve the Parliament, though we should not pass the Mutiny Bill." He an-swered directly, "I don't know what we may do, Charles. But I am very

[8]Ozias Humphry, best remembered as a miniaturist, lately returned from a futile attempt to make his future in India.
[9]*Hamlet*, I. ii. 133.
[1]On 26 January 1784 a group of fifty-three Members of Parliament, calling themselves "independents," had met at St. Alban's Tavern to devise ways of terminating the quarrel between Fox and Pitt and forming a coalition. The negotiations fell through.

sure what you would do." Immediately upon this, Fox ran to Brooks's and told his friends that it was in vain to delay passing the Mutiny Bill, for Ministry were determined.[2] He said that a considerable time ago when Mr. Pitt and he were riding by themselves in Richmond Park, the subject of Holland occurred and he found Pitt resolved upon vigorous measures, and so far was he from being merely a peace minister that his inclination was the very reverse, and he had a notion that Britain was omnipotent in war.[3] Mr. Dundas and Sir John Dick went away before nine, Sir John indeed sooner. The other gentlemen stayed supper. Still was clouded.

FRIDAY 9 NOVEMBER. Called on Malone. Courtenay came, and I went with him and visited Langton. Then we sat awhile with Wilkes, who looked very ill and had not the same vivid gaiety that I have so often admired. He however had one sally. Courtenay said it was told that Governor Johnstone's widow danced at a ball the very night he died. Said Wilkes: "He too was dancing—Holbein's dance."[4] I thus passed the morning and did not get to Westminster Hall. Courtenay asked me to his family dinner. I asked him to mine. By odds or evens it was decided that he should go with me. Found T.D. and Mrs. Green at my house. Courtenay and I had an hour or two tête-à-tête soberly.

SATURDAY 10 NOVEMBER. At Westminster Hall. Some *Life*. Still uneasy.[5]

SUNDAY 11 NOVEMBER. At Queen Street Chapel afternoon. Dined at General Paoli's with many foreigners. Was so much sunk that for an immediate respite I took much wine. Then went to Malone's and took some more. Home late.

MONDAY 12 NOVEMBER. Very ill. Did not go to Westminster Hall.

[2] A "mutiny bill" had to be enacted annually to render legal the existence of a standing army. Fox opposed Pitt's Ministry, of which Dundas was a leading member, and feared the dissolution of Parliament would strengthen it.

[3] When Frederick the Great died in 1786, the French supported the republican party in the Netherlands, their aim being to force the resignation of the Stadtholder, William V, whose wife was the sister of the new Prussian king. If they had succeeded, Holland would have become a dependant of France. Pitt overcame the King's initial apprehensions and almost risked war to prevent this development, before the Prussian government finally took a firm stand and sent troops across the frontier.

[4] An allusion to the "Dance of Death," a fresco in Switzerland mistakenly attributed to Holbein.

[5] On this day he registered the following letter: "Rev. Mr. Temple. Of sad depression of mind and despairing of practice. Know not what to do. Dundas dined with me day before yesterday and was very frank and good-humoured. *Perhaps* he may get me a Scotch judge's place."

Dined at Malone's with Courtenay, Langton, young Jephson, and young Purdon, both Irish templars.[6] Grew better.

TUESDAY 13 NOVEMBER. At Westminster Hall. *Life*.

WEDNESDAY 14 NOVEMBER. At Westminster Hall. *Life*. Evening (first night for winter), Essex Head Club. Present: Brocklesby and his nephew and Hoole, visitors; Cooke, Wyatt, Barrington, Calamy.

THURSDAY 15 NOVEMBER. Some *Life*. Dined at Sir Joshua's with young Burke, Hoole, and Dr. Laurence of the Commons, whom I now saw for the first time and thought a fine fellow. He said Mr. Edmund Burke had not so much wit or humour as a certain sportive vivacity.[7]

FRIDAY 16 NOVEMBER. Called on Malone in the morning, and was advised by him to attend laxly this term and get on diligently with my *Life*. Did some today. Dined at Sir Joshua's with him and Northcote[8] and Humphry, painters.

SATURDAY 17 NOVEMBER. Some *Life*. The *Gang*, i.e., Sir Joshua, Malone, and Courtenay, dined with me on a pheasant (not a formal dinner) and sat the evening also.

SUNDAY 18 NOVEMBER. Was restless. Was a very little while in Covent Garden Church. Visited Lord Dumfries, then Aberdein, who had visited me some days ago. He described Edinburgh so that I shrunk from it, especially as he said my returning to the bar there would be returning to my leavings. I was very uneasy, for my wife complained of the expense of London, of the injury it did her health and that of both my sons, and of the obscurity in which my daughters must be. I was sensible of all this. But my aversion to the narrow, ill-bred sphere was very strong. I visited Malone. Dined quietly with my family and heard the children say divine lessons.

MONDAY 19 NOVEMBER. I do not mark particularly my *lax* attendance in Westminster Hall. I did *Life*.

TUESDAY 20 NOVEMBER. Did *Life*. Very dull. Visited Mr. Daines Barrington, who had called on me lately.

WEDNESDAY 21 NOVEMBER. Dined at the Devil Tavern with Mr. Daines Barrington, Mr. Dunbar, and Mr. Hulse, all schoolfellows of Royal Ross, to whose benefit at the Royalty Theatre we were to go tonight. Counsellor Graham also dined with us. It was quite solid London society. But I was sadly hipped and made worse by hearing them

---

[6]Irish members of the Inner Temple.

[7]French Laurence, D.C.L., of Doctors' Commons. He helped Burke prepare the preliminary case against Hastings, and became his close associate and literary executor.

[8]The portrait-painter who began as an assistant to Reynolds, lived in his house for many years, and wrote an influential memoir of him.

tell of an acquaintance of theirs, a solicitor in Chancery now abroad, who used to be very ill in that way. It was very cold weather. I was not much entertained at the Royalty Theatre.

THURSDAY 22 NOVEMBER. Awaked very uneasy. Lay in bed till noon and drank coffee. Then rose very low-spirited. Westminster Hall. Malone's and told him how ill, and how I apprehended at such times my friends were tired of me. He told me that Jephson had similar fits, which consoled me. Courtenay was engaged to dine with him, and he *insisted* that I should stay. I was prevailed on; and by a pleasant, social, sober, convivial interview, I was restored to serene cheerfulness.

FRIDAY 23 NOVEMBER. A great deal of *Life*. Drank tea at Mrs. Buchanan's with my wife and daughters, Rev. Dr. Burn from India, a sweet-looking Miss Swift, etc., etc. Was awkward.

SATURDAY 24 NOVEMBER. Dined at Sir Joshua's with Malone, Courtenay, Metcalfe, Sir Abraham Hume and a Mr. Ker, Dr. Scott, young Burke, Mr. Byres from Rome,[9] Rev. Dr. Lort, Mr. Batt; a very good day. Dr. Scott, Metcalfe, Courtenay, Malone, and I stayed supper.

SUNDAY 25 NOVEMBER. Was restless. Visited Malone. Was at Great Queen Street Chapel in the afternoon. T.D. and Mrs. Green dined. I was dull. The children said divine lessons.

MONDAY 26 NOVEMBER. Some *Life*. Visited Langton. Sir Joshua Reynolds sent to me to come and dine with him at four. Nobody but Mr. Marchi with him, who left us in a glass or two, and then we drew close to the fire and took a cordial glass tête-à-tête, excluding the cold, which was intense. He communicated to me in confidence Lord Ailesbury's exertions for Dr. Warton to get him St. Cross, which had been frustrated by the Prince of Wales's interfering for Dr. Lockman; and he showed me a letter which he had written to the Prince to try to persuade him to let Dr. Warton have it. This was certainly as nice a thing to do as can be conceived. He had done it exquisitely well. He told me he had shown it only to Lord Ailesbury and Gibbon. I said it must not be lost and asked him to let me have a copy of it. He said, "Some time hence I will deposit the original in your hands."[1] This flattered me much. I loved to see the warmth of his friendship for Warton.

[9]Hume was a collector and patron of the arts (he sat to Reynolds three times); Byres lived in Rome for forty years, and his classical collection had included the Portland vase.

[1]This letter has not been traced. John Lockman, D.D., became Master of St. Cross Hospital, Winchester, for poor and decayed men, in 1788 and held the appointment for twenty years.

TUESDAY 27 NOVEMBER. Some *Life*. Dined at the Literary Club with Sir Joshua Reynolds, Mr. Malone, Mr. Steevens, Dr. Burney, Sir Charles Bunbury,[2] Dr. Fordyce, Mr. Windham. Not a very good day upon the whole. But Windham was indignant against Sir John Hawkins, and expressed a strong desire to attack him. Malone suggested an admirable thought, which was to have a solemn protest drawn up and signed by Dr. Johnson's friends, to go down to posterity, declaring that Hawkins's was a false and injurious account. Sir Joshua alone hesitated. But it was generally approved. I resolved it should not sleep. Sir Joshua, Windham, Malone, and I sat a long while after the rest and drank tea, and then adjourned to Sir Joshua's and eat oysters and drank some punch very pleasantly. I was quite well.

WEDNESDAY 28 NOVEMBER. Very cold. Breakfasted with Lord Graham by appointment and talked over Wilson of Kilmarnock's claim of relief for a vessel captured.[3] Visited Malone. Heard at Garforth's that Lord Lonsdale was come; called and found his Lordship. Was well received and asked to dine. Knowing his very late and uncertain hour, dined with my family quietly between four and five. Went to his Lordship between seven and eight, as to sup. Only Mr. John Lowther and Satterthwaite there. Strong conversation and good wine. He agreed that the Northern Circuit was best for me. Satterthwaite, who walked so far with me on my way home, said (though he had no *direct* authority) that Lord Lonsdale would give me the Recordership of Carlisle. But it must be all his own doing. Was *elevated* but no more.

THURSDAY 29 NOVEMBER. Visited Captain Preston and talked to him of James Cuninghame, etc., and found him in good humour.[4] Some *Life*. Dined at Lord Lonsdale's with Bishop of Carlisle, Rev. Dr. Grisdale, Sir Philip Jennings-Clerke, Captain Satterthwaite, Mr. John Lowther, Mr. ———,[5] Member for Lincoln, Governor Penn;[6] much the same as yesterday. Had tea in compliment to the Bishop, and less

[2]Brother of the caricaturist and friend of Fox; ultimately M.P. for a total of forty-five years. He was co-founder of the Derby in 1780, and the first winning horse was his.
[3]James Wilson and Son shipped shoes, woollens, and other products of its great tanneries and factories to the West Indies, Nova Scotia, Quebec, and other distant points. Wilson's goods may have been seized during the American war. Boswell discussed his claim with Graham because, as we have said previously, he was a Lord of the Treasury.
[4]Cuninghame was one of Mrs. Boswell's nephews, who had gone to India to make his fortune. He had not been doing well, and Boswell wanted Preston, with his powerful East India Company connections, to help him.
[5]John Fenton Cawthorne.
[6]Richard Penn, grandson of William Penn; deputy-governor of Pennsylvania from 1771 to 1773. He was M.P. for Appleby, Westmorland, one of Lonsdale's seats.

wine. The Bishop set me down at my own door. I was now grown insensibly free from gloom.

FRIDAY 30 NOVEMBER. Did a great deal of *Life*, having laboured all day. For some days a very keen frost.

SATURDAY 1 DECEMBER. A thaw. Some *Life*. Dined at Metcalfe's with Sir Joshua, Courtenay, Malone, Colonel Musgrave, Lord Wentworth. An elegant *repas* and excellent wines. I was too much heated.

SUNDAY 2 DECEMBER. A rainy day; visited Langton and wished him joy of being elected Professor of Ancient Literature in the Royal Academy. Was pleased with his conversation as usual. Afternoon was *alone* at our chapel. Had virtue enough to refuse an invitation to dine at Kemble's with Major North, Malone, etc. Kept quiet at home. The children said divine lessons.

MONDAY 3 DECEMBER. Had dreamt some weeks ago of seeing Dr. Johnson cursorily but without having any conversation. Of late had dreamt frequently, though not with any great continuation. This morning attended the last meeting of the partners of the unfortunate *London Magazine*, to settle accounts. Was sorry that it was no more, but was consoled that instead of having something to pay, I received £44.1.[7] Felt that *res angusta*[8] was a principal cause of my uneasiness. Was vexed that I could not afford to send my daughters to a boarding-school to give them elegance of manner. Yet still *thought* of doing it. Had on Saturday sent a memorandum to Lord Lonsdale showing of what consequence to me would be the Recordership of Carlisle. This I considered as a ticket in the lottery. I despaired of business at the English bar. My wife's asthma alarmed me. Visited Malone. He pressed me to dine with him, which I did, with young Jephson and Baker, another young Irishman.

TUESDAY 4 DECEMBER. Some *Life*. Earl and Countess of Dumfries, Mr. Langton and Lady Rothes, Mr. Windham, Sir Joshua Reynolds, Bishop of Carlisle, and the Rev. Mr. Bevil dined with us. This was a good creditable day, and I was very well, though not bright. Langton and his lady, Windham, and Sir Joshua supped. We talked of the country life, which Windham said was more agreeable in reality than one could conceive from a description of it. He said a set of people, agreeable to each other, being for a week at a house in the country was quite a different kind of society from anything to be had in London.

[7]Boswell owned a sixth share in the *London Magazine*, which had ceased publication after fifty-three years in June 1785. His seventy *Hypochondriack* essays had been published in it, 1777–83. In 1782 he had valued his share in the magazine at £250.
[8]Juvenal, *Satires*, iii. 165: "narrow circumstances."

Yet he agreed with Sir Joshua as to the superior zest of London conversation.

WEDNESDAY 5 DECEMBER. Mrs. Buchanan, young Craigengillan, Mr. Manners, who was to travel with him to France, and Mr. Whitefoord, son of Sir John, dined with us. Some *Life*. I visited Malone in the forenoon.

THURSDAY 6 DECEMBER. T.D. and his wife (now happily much recovered),[9] her mother, and Major Green dined with us. The Major's conversation entertained me. I visited Duke of Montrose, called General Paoli's, Mr. Courtenay's, and Mr. Osborn's. Felt myself more contracted in my London society than formerly.

FRIDAY 7 DECEMBER. Some *Life*. Was dull in the afternoon. On a sudden went to Covent Garden Theatre and saw *The Tender Husband* and *The Farmer*.[1] Was somewhat cheered.

SATURDAY 8 DECEMBER. Some *Life*. In the evening went to the first night of a new club, instituted for every Saturday night by Windham.[2] Only he and I there. We had oysters, malt liquor, and punch, and having got upon the extensive and interesting subject of Johnson, did very well.

SUNDAY 9 DECEMBER. Was restless. Visited Malone; found Courtenay there. Malone asked us to dine. Each was engaged at home with his family. I refused. Courtenay would not agree if I did not. I desired we might walk into the street and hold a conference, and if we agreed to dine, we should immediately return and give notice. I opposed it, saying, "It is kind to dine at home." "But," said Courtenay, "it is much pleasanter to dine abroad." I persevered, and we walked on. I put it inwardly upon *a die*, resolving that if Courtenay asked again, I would consent. I meditated on *human will*, watching the ultimate decision. He did ask, and I agreed. I was at our own chapel in the afternoon, and then at Malone's dinner, young Jephson with us.

MONDAY 10 DECEMBER. Restless. A debate on the augmentation of the army was to come on in the House of Commons. Captain Macbride took me in. It was dreary to sit from one to four, then be turned out twice by divisions of the House, and be squeezed getting in again, all before the debate began.[3] I expected to have heard Barré and

---

[9] Her mental health was unstable.
[1] By Sir Richard Steele and John O'Keeffe, respectively.
[2] We find no record of this club, which appears to have attracted few members (see below, 15 December 1787).
[3] The Commons met for legislative business at a quarter to four; the House had to be cleared of strangers before a division could take place.

Sheridan. But heard only Sir G. Yonge, Fox, Pitt, and others.[4] I was heartily wearied. Came home about eleven, eat a couple of eggs and drank port with relish. Parliament appeared to me much of a farce.

TUESDAY 11 DECEMBER. Some *Life.* Jephson's tragedy of *Julia* was to be renewed the second night. Courtenay and I were to have dined at Malone's on a haunch of venison and gone to the play after. But Courtenay most judiciously insisted that we should dine *after* the play. I did some *Life.* Went to the pit. Was not interested as in younger days. After it was over, found Malone in the box-keeper's lobby and went with him to Kemble's dressing-room. I did not feel *all* that imagination at a distance figures to be felt *behind the scenes of old Drury, etc., etc.*[5] But imagination figures too much. At Malone's, whither he and I and Kemble and young Jephson went in a hackney-coach, Courtenay was found waiting. We had a noble haunch of venison, a brace of grouse from Auchinleck, and a barrel of oysters; port, sherry, claret, hock, burgundy. We had a most jovial meeting and sat till between four and five. I walked home, but was much intoxicated.

WEDNESDAY 12 DECEMBER. Was very ill and very much vexed; more so, I calmly think, than was reasonable. But it is shocking to be in such a state in the eye of one's family. *I made a vow for three months; viz., till 12 March.* I lay till half past three and had coffee, and rose just in time to dress and go with my wife to dine at Mr. Langton's. Lord and Lady Dumfries, who were to have been there, could not come, my Lady being ill and the Earl having gone to Scotland to an election.[6] So there was only Sir Joshua Reynolds. It was a dull day.

THURSDAY 13 DECEMBER. Breakfasted with Sir Joshua Reynolds. Visited Malone. Some *Life.*

FRIDAY 14 DECEMBER. Some *Life.*

SATURDAY 15 DECEMBER. Some *Life.* T.D. and wife and Mrs. Green and old Macklin dined with us. Macklin went away early. T.D. and I walked awhile in Covent Garden. I had some bad fumes in my head which affected me gloomily, and observed that the high admiration of London went off. He was of a different opinion and said that even a shoeblack felt a kind of pride here. Went to the second meeting of

---

[4] Isaac Barré was a bold and melodramatic speaker against North and Pitt. Now totally blind and less active in debate, he reserved his big speeches for opposing the extensive increases in fortifications. Sheridan's speech on 8 February presenting the fourth charge against Hastings had created an immense sensation, and his speeches were eagerly awaited.

[5] This seems to be a quotation, perhaps from a song, but we have been unable to identify it.

[6] He failed of election as a Representative Peer in the House of Lords by one vote.

Windham's Club. Only he and I and Dr. Laurence of the Commons. All East Indies.[7]

SUNDAY 16 DECEMBER. Had last Sunday in my restlessness stepped into a chapel in Berwick Street, where I heard a Dr. Chandler preaching with animation, but was not composed enough to stay. Felt a kind of impulse to go again today when rather better, but not in good spirits. Heard him for about forty minutes lecture on the —— Psalm, and I do declare, was relieved and animated. At our own chapel afternoon. The children said sacred lessons.

MONDAY 17 DECEMBER. Some *Life*. Was somewhat uneasy at a doubt suggested by Grange's trustees as to a bill by him to me for £70 being still due, when I was sure it was. But his transactions and mine had been by no means accurate. *I saw that with the most intimate friend there should be clear states of money matters.* I wrote to Robert Boswell an explanation of the doubt.[8] Dined at Langton's with Sir Joshua Reynolds, Mr. Courtenay, Dr. Brocklesby. We were better than last day but not brilliant. Sir Joshua and Courtenay and I went in the evening and sat an hour with Malone, who was indisposed.

TUESDAY 18 DECEMBER. I recollect nothing.

WEDNESDAY 19 DECEMBER. I recollect nothing; only I think I was at the Essex Head Club.

THURSDAY 20 DECEMBER. Visited Malone in the morning. Then called at Mr. Garforth's, where I heard Lord Lonsdale was still in town. Called to leave my card. But the servant said his Lordship would see me. So I waited, and by and by was shown in. He told me that he had considered my application for the Recordership of Carlisle. He had turned it in his mind upon his pillow; he had many applications—one from Lord Darlington.[9] He did not wish entirely to deny them all. But as I wished for it as an opportunity for returning to the Northern Circuit, he had resolved that I should have it for some time and then I could resign it; and he talked as if he had appointed me to come that morning. When I appeared not to understand this, he said, "Have you not had my note?" I told him no. Said he: "I sent a note to you

[7]Since both Windham and Laurence were much involved in Hastings's trial.
[8]The trustees continued to raise doubts, and Boswell wrote several more letters to Robert Boswell insisting on the validity of his claims. In February 1788 he registered the following letter: "Mr. John Gordon, that he is satisfied Grange's bills to me are justly due, but as his [Grange's] brother is a very troublesome man, the trustees have raised a multiple poinding [an action requiring all the claimants to come together and settle their claims in court], that they may pay mine and other debts with safety." The business was still unsettled seven years later at the time of Boswell's death.
[9]Lonsdale's brother-in-law.

Alexander Macdonald, ninth baronet and first Baron Macdonald of Sleat. This portrait (c. 1770–80) by an unknown artist hangs in the Scottish National Portrait Gallery, on loan from Lord Macdonald.

REVISING FOR THE SECOND EDITION.

"Revising for the Second Edition," 1786, an engraving by Thomas Rowlandson, after Samuel Collings. The caption quotes the second edition of Boswell's *Journal of a Tour to the Hebrides* (p. 527): "Having found on a revision of this work that a few observations had escaped me the publication of which might be considered as passing the bounds of strict decorum, I immediately ordered that they should be omitted in the present edition." This passage is followed by lines from Peter Pindar's *Poetical Epistle to James Boswell*:

Let Lord Macdonald threat thy breech to kick,
And o'er thy shrinking shoulders shake his stick.

"The Biographers," 1786, an engraving by James Sayers, shows Mrs. Thrale, John Courtenay, and Boswell seated under the seemingly watchful gaze of a bust of Johnson. Mrs. Thrale's *Anecdotes of the Late Samuel Johnson* and Courtenay's *Literary and Moral Character of Doctor Johnson* had both been published in 1786, shortly after the second edition of Boswell's *Journal of a Tour to the Hebrides* appeared.

vecchio, Harrison — Amara di
sentir giurisprud inglese techni-
calmente — A letto di buon ora

Giovedì 30 Novr

Tutta la mattina e sin al vicino
a 5 in Palazzo. Aveva gran
piacere di ricordar viva-
mente il tempo quando
era primo a Carlisle in Cum
berland — melanconico — e ammi-
rante tutto che era inglese
Adesso era counsellor at law
on Bench wh. Mayor deciding on
english election law. Pranzava
con il Mayor. Th deaf brother
e due reple gentle gales. La
sera tea Ld. Lonsd.

Venerdì 1 Decr.

Aveva sognato di M. M. Era
innamorato di ella, e sentiva
teneramente, the want. Ma
l'occupazione mi animava
Pensava come curiosa era
che

che il Laird of Auchinleck era a Carlisle directing english proceedings. There was un a certa elevazione che era come Ally del gran Lowther di Westmorland. In Court shocking border barbarity upon Harrison's blindness let him feel at Act dec. He to Wyb.! An insult upon an infirmity. I hope sir you shall not be deprived of your eyesight — Tedious Poll by protracting purposely the long oaths. I read Douglas; elections. Pranzo con ... Col. Whelpdale &c — Lui harangued e grande alcuni commenciava a parlar, anche a espingere conservo — dicea; you shall hear! Un certo Saul con lengua ... nera, quando ... trattava un argomento che narrava, con contempto — rifflort. Somme un Bis. So era prudentissimo. ... brandy water & pipe wr. Col. ... church in bar — Church had been

Journal entries for Thursday 30 November and Friday 1 December 1786 show the "macaronic" mix of Italian and English that Boswell used to record his experiences while serving under Lord Lonsdale's patronage as Counsel to the Mayor in the Carlisle election of 1786.

James Lowther (1736–1802), first Earl of Lonsdale, wears the fancy dress of a member of the Hell Fire Club in this portrait by Thomas Hudson, painted in the 1750s or 1760s.

A watercolour by John W. Archer of Nos. 55–56, Great Queen Street, London, as it appeared in 1846. No. 56, the house Boswell and his family moved into in 1786, is the middle building.

Sir

    I inclose you, for Mr Boswell, the Ballad you mentioned; and as I hate sending waste paper or mutilating a sheet, I have filled it up with one or two of my fugitive Pieces that occurred. — Should they procure me the honor of being introduced to Mr Boswell, I shall think they have great merit. — There are few pleasures my late will-o'-wisp character has given me, equal to that of having seen many of the extraordinary men, the Heroes of Wit & Literature in my Country; & as I had the honor of drawing my first breath almost in the same Parish with Mr Boswell, my Pride plumes itself on the connection. — To crouch in the train of mean, stupid Wealth & Greatness, except where the commecial interests of worldly Prudence find their account in it, I hold to be prostitution in any one that is not born a Slave; but to have been acquainted with such a man as M.r Boswell, I would hand down to my Posterity as one of the honors of their Ancestor.————

I am, Sir, your most obedient
& very humble serv.t
Rob.t Burns

Mauchline Nov. 13.th
1788

A letter (dated 13 November 1788 from Robert Burns to Bruce Campbell, Boswell's cousin and estate overseer. Boswell and Burns never met.

Edward Thurlow, first Baron Thurlow, Lord Chancellor. In this portrait, painted by Sir Joshua Reynolds in 1781, he wears his chancellor's wig and robes, and his mace sits on the table.

this forenoon desiring to see you. I own I have some notion of communications being made to people in a way that we cannot explain. For here you have come of yourself just at the time when I wished to see you. I am to set out tomorrow morning for Lowther, where I shall be only for a day, and then go to Whitehaven Castle, where I am to have a great deal of company, and if you will go with me, I will introduce you to them, which will be of advantage to you as returning to the Northern Circuit, and you shall go to Carlisle and be elected."

I was agitated at finding now that LOWTHER really had resolved publicly to befriend me, but I was somewhat embarrassed. I told his Lordship that I was very much obliged to him; that I should be very happy to have the honour of attending his Lordship. But that I had several engagements, and Johnson's *Life* to finish. However, I would try, and I begged that his Lordship would allow me till the evening to consider of it. He did so. I ran home and talked with my wife, who was for my going. So was T.D., who thought *it could do no harm.* Messrs. James and Cumberland Wilsons dined with us. At night I returned to Lord Lonsdale's and told his Lordship that I would wait on him. He kept Mr. Garforth and me late, and then Mr. Garforth and I walked through Berkeley Square cordially. He said this was a feather in my cap. (For the jaunt, see separate sheets.)[1]

FRIDAY 21 DECEMBER. In a great hurry to be with Lord L. at nine *to a second.* Disturbed my family and was quite uneasy as I did not reach his door till twenty-five minutes after nine. Garforth smiled and said I would be time enough two hours after. Was shaved in the hall.[2] Satterthwaite came. Mr. John Lowther came about eleven knowing how it *might* be. I went to Partlet's Coffee-house in Shepherd's Market and had a pot of coffee and a muffin comfortably. Between twelve and one Colonel Lowther came and told me the coach was at the door. We talked of the Great Man. He said the way to get anything from him was not to ask it but rather to have somebody to oppose it, such as saying, "What! would you bring Boswell into Parliament?" He seemed to think I might have a chance for Cockermouth in room of Senhouse, who hated being in.[3] I objected that I should not choose to be a Member of Parliament without any will of my own but merely to utter Lord L.'s inclination. He said, "He was very honourable to his Members and did not require this." But Satterthwaite afterwards told

---

[1] The entries for 21 December 1787 to 7 January 1788 are now published for the first time.
[2] The servants' hall.
[3] Humphrey Senhouse, M. P. for Cockermouth, eldest brother of Sir Joseph Senhouse.

me sagaciously that it was *understood* in all cases where a Member was brought in by any person that he should not go against him.

When I returned there was no appearance of his coming out of his room. The uncertain waiting was very unpleasant. Governor Penn came, and asked if that was the first set of horses, for he had known a set changed at the door, the first having waited very long. It was frost this morning. Penn said he knew him well, and when he was with him, he just eat, drank, and slept as it might happen, without any thought about the matter. "It is a school," said he, "to which people must be broke in." I laughed and said, "Harder than that of Pythagoras."[4] All the things were put into the coach. He ordered them all to be taken out again and, I suppose, packed in some other way. At length he came to us and first took Penn into another room, and then Garforth, who had been waiting since half past seven.

At last Satterthwaite was desired to go into the coach and to wait in it at the corner of Davies Street, to which it drove *down* Charles Street. Soon after, the Earl, accompanied by Mr. John Lowther and Penn and me, walked *up* Davies Street and turned into Hill Street, and so got to the coach. What this round-about mode could mean was a mystery. But they told me he never went into the carriage at his own door, but had it waiting at some place out of sight. He and I sitting frontwards, and Satterthwaite and Mr. John Lowther backwards, drove off. He felt himself hungry but did not stop till we came to Stevenage.[5] There, in the kitchen, we had beefsteaks, a fowl with mushrooms, porter, and four bottles of port. He and I this day sang several of the songs in *The Beggar's Opera*. We stopped at night at Buckden[6] and had tea and white-wine whey.

SATURDAY 22 DECEMBER. Satterthwaite and I had colds, his the worst. We breakfasted at Stilton. Victor, his Norman servant, rode always on and had horses at the door each stage. He made the boys drive excessively hard. We dined at Grantham but poorly, there being what is called the squires' monthly dinner in the house,[7] which took all their best things. Ale and two bottles of port. At night we stopped at Doncaster.[8] We had sung less today. He felt himself ill in his stomach. Would take only tea and eggs, and Satterthwaite only an egg and white-wine whey, and Mr. John Lowther only tea and a jelly. There was a

[4] In which novices were not permitted to speak during a probationary period of five years.
[5] About twenty-eight miles north of London.
[6] About sixty-one miles from London.
[7] No doubt the George, an excellent inn recently built at great expense.
[8] About a hundred and fifty-six miles north of Buckden.

comfortable supper put down and I eat some veal cutlet, a grey plover and a bit of another, and a tart, and had ale and gin and water. We had sung some more *Beggar's Opera* today, and he had talked a good deal of bawdy.

SUNDAY 23 DECEMBER. Excessively cold. A good deal of snow had fallen for two days. He had been very ill in the night and taken forty-four drops of laudanum.[9] He was in my room before I was up, as I had disbelieved the maid's report, and indeed Satterthwaite had put me on my guard that, after the horses were put to and his company all up and ready, he sometimes would not come down for two hours. We had breakfast before setting out. Satterthwaite was worse. He did not seem to mind him but made him go and see his things put into the coach. Victor was exceedingly sick and seemingly unable to go on and hinted piteously to get into a carriage, but in vain. He was ordered to stop at Boroughbridge and have some dinner ready for us. When we got there (Mr. John Lowther having gone out at Ferrybridge), Victor said he could go on. But He *of his own accord* desired he might be put into a warm bed and come in the stage-coach next day, and ordered a man from the inn to ride on and order horses and send one on from next stage. The landlord, Rushton, was a stupid, miserable-looking old man.

He damned and scolded about bad beef, etc., and was irritated that a bolt of the coach was broke and had to be mended, which took some time. Two shillings were charged. He would give only one; and because the Wetherby boys had not come in less than an hour and twenty minutes he gave them only sixpence apiece and nothing to the ostler,[1] nor would he take back a guinea in the hire, which they said was light. His way was to call, "Boys, I'm in a great hurry. Make haste or I'll give you nothing. I am not to waste my lungs calling to you. I have looked my watch.[2] If I have to call to you again you shall have nothing. If I must waste my lungs I must save my cash."

Only one bottle of port today, porter, and ale. Then Gretabridge. Hard driving. Sad work for the last part of the road near to Lowther.[3] Had asked me on road, "What will you have?" I said, "Only a little warm milk." Satterthwaite said the same, but when L. was out of the room complained seriously to me of giving such a precedent,

[9]About three grains, three times the usual dosage.
[1]The postboys from Wetherby had driven a distance of eleven and a half miles to Boroughbridge.
[2]A contemporary idiom; now dialectal.
[3]They had driven about a hundred and twenty miles from Doncaster to Lowther Hall, just south of Penrith.

and said, "When we had had a damned bad dinner, we should have had something good at night." George Saul, whom we found here, had come from Lancaster and hardly eaten all day. He durst not say he would have anything till L. was out of room, and then said if he could have had but a piece of bread and cheese. I mentioned his wish and he had it. L. took warm milk. Dreadfully cold in the waste[4] dining-room, and there was a railing of iron painted green to keep us off the hearth that it might be clean. In this whim He was obstinate. Bedroom cold, cold.

MONDAY 24 DECEMBER. Satterthwaite took care that each of us should have some tea and roll and butter in our rooms, but beware telling. Breakfast not till about one. I sat a long time with Satterthwaite in his room, where he had a good fire and bid me take care to have the same, as it was the most comfortable thing I would have here. He said there was a total want of all comforts. A man for instance might be days without having his shoes cleaned. Garforth sometimes wiped his with the carpet. He spoke strongly of the Earl's want of attention to make people happy about him, and told how a gentleman observed how great a man he might be if he were but commonly civil. "Nay," said another, "if he were but commonly *un*civil." He said no man of parts had ever submitted to go along with him. He said he did not wish to put those attached to him into good situations because that would make them independent. Yet, from his great fortune and influence he ought to have a Lord of the Treasury, a Lord of the Admiralty, and a Commissioner both of Customs and Excise. Yet he said for himself he could not complain, for He had done very well for him. He said he talked freely to me as looking upon me now as attached to Him, and he would be glad to communicate with me.

All this struck a damp upon me, and I saw how fallaciously I had imagined that I might be raised by his interest, for I never would submit to be dependent. Satterthwaite said he thought all along that He would make me Recorder of Carlisle, for He had praised my conduct at the election[5] and said I had gone as far for his interest as my character in my profession would allow. I now foresaw many difficulties in being Recorder, as he could not bear even decent attention to be paid to his opponents in the Corporation.

We were kept long hanging on for dinner even after it was on the table, and I believe sat down about seven. Tolerably well. Port, hermitage, frontignac, rather too much. In the forenoon He had a visit

[4]Empty, unfurnished.
[5]The disputed election at Carlisle in November–December 1786.

of Thomas Whelpdale, Colonel of the Westmorland Militia and High Sheriff of Cumberland, a rustic mortal. He was ordered to go to White-haven. After dinner L. read aloud, I think three acts of John Home's *Alonzo*.[6]

TUESDAY 25 DECEMBER. Rose somewhat uneasy. Saul had been in the housekeeper's room and had tea. I went too. Found Mrs. Elwood, a large, stately woman who gave me breakfast very civilly and talked of my Lord doing things just because other people did differently. It snowed heavily. But I have not for thirty years been absent from public worship on Christmas Day. So went briskly to Lowther Church. Very, very cold, and Dr. Lowther very inanimate. Raised devotion as much as I could. Received the Holy Sacrament.

We were to have gone to Whitehaven today and much I wished to get away. But He, thinking roads would be better next day, sent off Satterthwaite and the cook in post-chaise that Satterthwaite might be at election of coroner next day. We had at dinner Mr. Nicholson, Clerk of the Peace for Westmorland, a little, humpbacked man. I had read some in Boyd's *Justice of Peace*. A pretty good dinner. But he talked all himself, long, tedious accounts. After five bottles I improperly asked for another. He took none of the third part of it, and it was too heavy upon me. We had tea. I was drowsy and stole away to bed.

WEDNESDAY 26 DECEMBER. The day not looking well, He put off setting out, and sent a man with letters ordering roads to be cleared, and *resolved* to set out early next day. He talked to Saul and me in the forenoon, I believe three hours without intermission. We dined about six. His camp *butcher*[7] dressed for us ox-cheek broth, tripe, and a bit of venison. Moderate drinking, but though I said I preferred not, he gave chiefly hermitage, which I disliked. Each day at breakfast he had honeycomb, which he took all to himself. I was quite dull and dispirited and gloomy, for we all sat in vile, timid restraint.

Saul told me that he had not yet paid his bills of the Lancaster election. About £2,000 remained.[8] For one, Saul was bound and would soon be sued if not paid, which he always put off. And what he had paid he had so cut down that the people were considerable losers and

[6]The improbable historical tragedy Lonsdale had quoted earlier (see above, 5 December 1786).

[7]The butcher who accompanied Lonsdale on encampments of the Westmorland Militia, of which he was Colonel.

[8]Lonsdale's candidate for Lancaster, his cousin John Lowther, having been defeated in the General Election of 1784 stood again at the by-election held in 1786 after the incumbent was made a peer. Lonsdale, who owned no land in Lancashire, spent at least 20,000 guineas creating freemen but Lowther was narrowly defeated.

called him all the swindlers' and bad names that can be conceived. *This was shocking*. Poor Saul told me that some time ago he had desired him to pay the chaise hire from Whitehaven, but to this hour Saul had never been repaid.

I paused and asked myself what I had to do with such a man. All the way down I had been uneasy and anxious at being away from my dear wife and children, and to look forward to a much longer absence overwhelmed me. I also felt how unworthy it was of the Laird of Auchinleck to hang on thus upon a savage. I thought I heard my worthy father say, "James, I left you independent." I wished to elope from him and was quite impatient to be gone, and I studiously meditated how I should decline the Recordership. It was dismal always when I went to bed. He slept a good deal after dinner, never minding his company, and we never had wine but from his own hand.

THURSDAY 27 DECEMBER. Tom Jarker, his gamekeeper, whom he had sent with orders to clear the roads, returned and reported that they would not be passable till Saturday. This quite sunk me. I now resolved to be off with the Recordership but knew not how to communicate it. The day was painfully cold. The dry logs, we were told, were all done, and we had some abominable green ones which he persevered in maintaining he would make burn, while Saul and I stood shivering. At last he left the room, when Saul got plenty of coals and, mixing them with the green wood, made an excellent fire, which He was glad to see when he returned.

George Saul is a merchant in Lancaster. He was nine years in America. He is a large, stout man with a ruddy, good-humoured countenance and a black scratch-wig. Being in America has taught him the management of wood fires. He has for seven years been zealously attached to the interest of Lowther and has lived much with Lord Lonsdale, whom he respects and fears, yet sees his faults. There is a remarkable naïveté in his manner. He holds down his head and shakes it and winks when he talks of the Earl's opponents, calling them dogs who want to pull down the king if they could. When he looked at the cold, green wood which his Lordship had insisted should burn, he said, "If this be your fifty thousand a year, my service to it." The Earl inquired, and good dry logs were found in the servants' hall. We had them and the fire blazed, and we were warm at last.

Dinner was between six and seven, ox-cheek broth, tripe, plum pudding, which he said no man cook could make well, but the camp butcher did. We had Nicholson today at dinner. Only two bottles of wine, I forget which. But the grievous thing was that no man could ask for a glass when he wished for it but had it given to him just when the fancy struck L. The glasses were large, eight in a bottle.

While LONSDALE was drowsy after dinner, we sat in stupid silence, and I groaned inwardly. I could not help showing impatience at this treatment. I turned myself some time restlessly upon my chair and then went up to my room, where I meditated sullenly what I should do, sometimes thinking of setting out on foot for Clifton, a village two miles off through which the mail-coach comes, and from thence getting off for London this very night, sometimes of going to bed. The immediate pressure of uneasiness was terrible, and the dreary waste of the cold house, with nobody but Saul, a sycophantish fool, to talk to made me almost desperate. I fancy my mind was in a state very similar to that of those wretched mortals who kill themselves. I did not stay long but resumed resolution and went back to the dining-room, thinking to go off next morning in daylight. No notice appeared to have been taken of my absence, and I weathered out the night till about twelve, when I got to bed.

FRIDAY 28 DECEMBER. I had been very uneasy and hardly slept at all, but tossed and vexed myself during the night. It was galling to me to find that I was so miserably deceived in the notion which I had formed of the high honour and great advantage of being connected with LOWTHER. I viewed with wonder and regret my folly in putting myself at such an age as my forty-sixth year into a new state of life by becoming an English barrister. I saw that it was not a life of spirited exertion, as I had supposed, but of much labour for which I had ever been unfit, and of much petulant contest, which in some states of my changeful mind I could not bear. Being made Recorder of Carlisle *to bring me back to the Northern Circuit*, as I had put it in my application to L., I considered as again involving me in a tiresome, expensive, ineffectual struggle to get business which I had no probability of obtaining; whereas by cutting short at once, after a fair trial of two years, I could return to Scotland and resume my place in the Court of Session as an advocate, and perhaps obtain a judge's place, and, if not, could certainly make my affairs easy by care and regular attention, and have my family in a much more creditable situation than I could afford for them in London. I looked upon this painful discovery of L.'s being the worst man in the world for a patron to be in effect a most beneficial event for me; and thus I reasoned. I resolved, however, not to fly off from him with a sudden violence but to accompany him and see his greatness at Whitehaven, which I had celebrated,[9] and then to tell him that I

[9]In his *Letter to the People of Scotland*, 1785, Boswell had exhorted Lowther to "come forth, and support us! We are his neighbours. . . . We all know what HE can do: HE upon whom the thousands of *Whitehaven* depend for three of the elements: HE whose soul is all great—whose resentment is terrible; but whose liberality is boundless" (p. 28).

declined the Recordership, and to return to London without any appearance of disappointment. I saw in Him that vast wealth and influence do not produce proportionate happiness. I thought of a judicious saying of Commissioner Cochrane's that it was a misfortune to a family to become too rich, for then the representative went to London and became an alien.

I had a headache in the morning, and as I had no hope of being warm but in bed and wished to escape the dreary waiting for breakfast, I resolved to be ill and lie in bed all the forenoon. Now I meditated calmly on the infatuation of a gentleman of a large estate, fine Place, and excellent house dooming himself to trouble and servile vexation. I felt at my heart my absence from my dear wife and children; I upbraided myself for it, when there was no sufficient cause for it. Yet my *mistake* might excuse me. For Dempster had said to me on my getting acquainted with L. "that one card played well is enough to raise you," and the Bishops of Killaloe and Dromore had both written to me concerning him as one who would bring me forward in England.[1] But the thought that I had hurt the health probably both of my wife and children by bringing them to London, and the dismal apprehension that my wife might die and how I should then see how little of that rational, creditable happiness to which our situation in life entitled her she had enjoyed, but had without repining sacrificed it to my spirit of adventure—all these considerations made me deeply miserable.

Between ten and eleven I grew weary and rose. Saul had gone early to Penrith to see his mother-in-law and his daughter and was to return to dinner. I walked in a troubled frame between the dining-room and my bedroom and upon the gravel before the house till it was one o'clock, and still there was no appearance of L. or of breakfast. I *felt* the insolence so as to meditate writing to him in the keenest terms that he did not seem to know who I was. My impatience to be gone increased. The servants, a parcel of negligent wretches unless when the Lion roared and frightened them, were always solacing themselves in their hall and other places, so that none of them were to be seen, and

[1]"If you had been permitted to choose out of the British dominions a patron the most capable of conducting you to honour and profit you could not have pitched upon one more fit your purpose than Lord Lonsdale: he has wealth, he has interest, he has business enough to keep you employed" (Barnard to Boswell, 23 January 1787). Thomas Percy, Bishop of Dromore, best remembered as editor of the *Reliques of Ancient English Poetry*, and, like Barnard, a member of The Club, praised Lonsdale as "a nobleman distinguished for the zeal and spirit with which he serves his friends," and thought his bringing Boswell into Parliament "an event . . . no less certain than splendid to your fortunes and establishment in England" (6 March 1787).

consequently they did not observe when anyone went out or came in. I got my travelling-bag all packed, and taking it in my hand, I walked off.

When I came to the porter's lodge, the good civil old man with the C*oo*mberland d*ee*alect looked rurally kind, and when I asked how far it was to Clifton and how far to Penrith, suggested, when he saw my bag, that I wanted to have some linen washed.[2] The snow, which was lying deep, discouraged me somewhat; so I put my bag into his lodge, told him I was going to take the coach for London but I was afraid my Lord would not let me go; so charged him to say nothing, and perhaps I would take my bag in the evening.

I returned again for a little while to the house. But observing two men with carts going out at the gate, I went to them and was informed they were going to Clifton. So I put my bag into one of the carts and walked on before till I was out of sight of the house, and then got into another of them and sat upon a sack and drove along. Having had no breakfast, being very cold, and being sadly fretted, I was quite gloomy and could look upon nothing without disgust. A gleam of felicity came across my mind when I thought of being again with my wife, and I thought that nothing upon earth could make up to me for being absent from her, even for a week or two at a time. All my fondness for Miss Peggie Montgomerie, all her admirable conduct as a wife and mother were before me in a warm glow. But I feared that she would despise my impatience and flight, and that I should be made ridiculous on account of thus forfeiting my expectations from the Great Lowther, whom I had celebrated in lofty language. I was also not without apprehension that he might resent my abrupt departure as impertinent to him. But I thought I could write to him declining the Recordership in very smooth, respectful terms. And keep my own secret, never mentioning his intolerable behaviour.

The carts went towards Temple Sowerby, and I quitted them where they turned off from the Penrith road, and then walked on to Penrith carrying my bag, which was pretty heavy.[3] I had seen no inn at Clifton which looked comfortable, so luckily did not stop there. At the end of Penrith I bought some paper at a shop and there left my bag, and then walked into the town uncertain what I should do. I got notice at the George Inn where Mr. Saul was and, having found him, told him that I feared Lord L. might put off from day to day going to White-

[2] The distances were about one and a half miles and four miles respectively.
[3] He had travelled about three miles in the cart and walked another mile and a half to Penrith.

haven; that He had told me we were to be there on Tuesday, and I had come from London in that belief, as I was obliged to be back again on the 6th January, if I could, but certainly by the 8th or 10th; and that I now saw my time at Whitehaven would be so short it was not worth while to go, and I had better return directly; so I was come here to take the coach. I sounded him if he thought Lord L. would take it amiss if I went off. He was clear he would. So I being by this time somewhat better by exercise, resolved I would return and speak to him, and I could get off by the coach any day.

I went to the George and had a pot of coffee and muffin and toast, the first comfortable meal I had enjoyed for some days, and I insensibly felt myself restored. It struck me to compare my poor state at this house now with what it was when here last with my wife,[4] etc. The cold and dark weather was gloomy, and for two days I had been troubled with one of my foreteeth being half broken off yet the root of the broken part not separated from the gum. It was a mouldering memento of my mortality.

I walked to Lowther with Saul and carried my bag all the way. I was fully tired and all in a sweat, so went to my room and changed myself from head to foot and felt stout. I was glad that I had avoided writing a letter to Lord L., for a strange one it must have been. I went down to the dining-room and sent a message to his Lordship that I begged leave to speak with him for a few minutes. He came instantly. I said to him in a flurry, but composing myself as well as I could, that I took the liberty to speak to him what I was going to have written, that I had lain awake all night thinking of the Recordership which his Lordship had been so good as to promise me, and that after much wavering it did appear to me that I ought not to accept of it. That his Lordship's having given me the preference had done me great honour; that I was conscious of this and had the honour as much as if I had been elected. (He very politely said it should be as I pleased and there was no appearance of his being displeased.) I said it was happy that the matter had not been communicated. "No," said He, "it is entirely between you and me."

I said I would presume to speak freely. The truth was I had been of a very good standing at the bar in Scotland. I had been flattered and persuaded that I might succeed in England, in a wider sphere. My ambition had led me to make the experiment. I found I had been

[4]When they emigrated from Scotland in September 1786 (Penrith is on the road from Carlisle to London). Boswell kept no journal for the period and the surviving papers make no reference to the visit.

deceived. Jack Lee and others who had encouraged me had told me that the difference of practice in the two countries was not great, that I had only to acquire a few elements and forms. But that I had found the difficulty very great at my time of life. That I had tried the Northern Circuit in vain, and had then gone the Home Circuit with as little success. That this of the Recordership was a *dernier ressort*, a forlorn hope, but that upon thinking it over and over again, I thought that my returning to the Northern Circuit and still having no business would make me appear in a much worse light; and that as one great motive of my wishing for the Recordership was to do what I could to promote his Lordship's interest, I thought my unfitness for the office was against that, for I should discredit his Lordship's recommendation. That there were many gentlemen who could be of much more use to him in that way, and that my being appointed, one newly come from the Scotch bar, might raise a clamour. I sincerely thanked him, was ashamed of my weakness, but thought I was now resolving for the best.

"Sir," said he, "you applied to me for this several times, and at last mentioned your returning to the Northern Circuit as a reason for your having it. I thought of it deliberately for some time. I never consult, neither the *officer*[5] nor Garforth nor one of them. They may be partial or they may think themselves right. You applied to me several times.[6] I gave no answer. I considered. I thought not only of myself and the Corporation but of you. It is said it is easier to get into a situation than to get well out. If a man does not get out well it is a reflection on the person who put him in. I considered your being Recorder of Carlisle. You could say to a Minister, 'Here I am,' and make it a step. I don't know your views. But you might go into Scotland or into some other situation. I may say without disparagement to you that there are many gentlemen on the Northern Circuit who know English law better than you. But what I should say to the Corporation: 'Here is a man of great sense, of talents, who when a thing is properly prepared can judge of it with ability.' And the business is all prepared by the Town Clerk. Besides, when the Recorder is consulted, other counsel are consulted at the same time."

"Your Lordship is very kind. You put it in the most favourable light. I am now ambitious to have it. And as to the Circuit, there is no necessity for my beating the whole round. I may take more or less of it as I please. To be sure, you have many who go only to particular

[5]Presumably Col. James Lowther.
[6]In letters dated 9 November 1786 and 13 June 1787 as well as that of 1 December 1787.

places. Why, Scott does not go all round. My Lord, I am very much obliged to you. Your Lordship has not only the power to give me the place but you have given me fortitude to take it. I am of an anxious temper." "You can think of it for four or five days or a week, and it shall be as you please. If you had had as much to do in life as I have had, you would not have that anxious temper."

This conversation gave quite a new turn to my spirits.[7] The Rev. Dr. Lowther came, and our dinner was his supper, and he was very placid and, being a new being in our sphere of existence, gave relief. We had cow-heel soup, very good, as I now thought, cow-heel dressed with white sauce, and something else; a double bottle of a rich Spanish red wine and a bottle of port; and a pint of —— wine and a pineapple, which pleased my senses, and I felt myself wonderfully well. I told how I had got a good dish of coffee at Penrith. "Why," said Lord L., "could not you have had it here?" "I should be very glad to have it, my Lord," said I. Upon which the bell was rung, and Payne the butler was directed to have it well made and, just as it bubbled, to have a little hartshorn put in.[8] So minute! It was indeed very good. Saul, who said he liked coffee, told me he never had seen it here, and that the housekeeper told him she knew of none in the house except some of her own. The relief as to the Recordership, the novelty of Dr. Lowther, the little comforts of the stomach, and the prospect of moving next day to Whitehaven Castle, which I was assured was warm, made me go to bed in tranquillity. Such is the human mind. Tell it not.

SATURDAY 29 DECEMBER. Rose well, and expected to get off about nine; but Lord L. *trifled* away the time, as Satterthwaite well expresses his way, till after eleven. Then He and I and Saul got into the old ship, as he calls the coach which brought us from London, and away we drove with four post-horses which He keeps, I know not how long at a time, at a guinea a day; but we soon had a couple more put to, and now, I think, for the first time in my life was I driven in a coach and six. I saw that Jarker's report was true, for the snow was high-piled up on each side where the road had been cut. We drove to Keswick, where we had six fresh horses. I could scarcely distinguish two of the lakes from the surrounding snow. But Saddleback and other mountains and the famed Skiddaw looked sublime. Lord L. now as upon the road from London kept both glasses up, so that the thick, heated air was

[7] A memorandum in the margin of the manuscript reads, "Think of Moffat and Carlisle long ago and persevere patiently. It *will* be a *station*. You will be Lowther's charge." For Moffat and Carlisle, see above, 30 November 1786 and n. 6.

[8] Spirits of ammonia, presumably added to enhance the taste and aroma, possibly for a supposed increase of the stimulating effect.

disagreeable and gave me a headache. But he must have all his own way.

We went over the great steep of Whinlatter and so proceeded to Cockermouth, where I recollected having often thought of it before I saw it, or rather was at it, for it was too dark for me to see it. We then with four horses came to Whitehaven. Being again in a town and seeing lamps and shops was agreeable after the cold imprisonment at Lowther. The Castle, a large house originally built by old Sir James of Whitehaven,[9] but new-faced in the Gothic style and augmented to three times the size by Lord L., stands at the upper end of the town. When we entered we found Whelpdale and Satterthwaite. Lord L. soon had me through the house, which he took great pleasure in showing. Its great extent, numerous and spacious rooms, and good furniture filled my mind. The kitchen was magnificent and the fire immense. I soon felt we were in a mild climate, and the large coal fires made me quite comfortable.

I expected that Lord L., Saul, and I, and the two gentlemen whom we found here should have had a full social meal and plenty of wine. But we three had only a small cod, a beefsteak and potatoes, and a bottle of port and a bottle of madeira, while they two sat by and were never offered a glass, though many hints were given and though Saul and I both offered a glass to them from our share. This was shocking. L. put it off by saying with an appearance of heartiness, "There is little enough for ourselves, eh? And you would not have me go to the cellar again tonight." Saul had resolution to say *he* would take the *trouble* of going, willingly. But nothing would do. I wondered at the patience of the two gentlemen. Lord L. harangued away and would not let me go to bed till about one in the morning. I went once away and he followed, diverting himself with my not being able to find my room. At last he accompanied me to it politely. It was an excellent one in all respects. I relished it.

SUNDAY 30 DECEMBER. When I went down in the morning, Whelpdale asked me if I had ever seen anything so *savage* as Lord L.'s behaviour to him and Satterthwaite last night, and said it was *lunacy*. Satterthwaite also spoke strongly, and said that all the time they had been here before us they had no dinner in the castle, but went and found it, till the day before, when they had some and one bottle of wine; and he said if such behaviour had happened before anybody but those who know his Lordship well, he would have left the room. Whelp-

[9]Sir James Lowther, Bt., who died in 1755 in his eighty-second year, and in addition to the Castle left Lonsdale, his second cousin once removed, a fortune estimated at £2,000,000.

dale said nobody submitted to keep company with him but needy people for the good of their families, or people who had some view of self-interest. He told me he never had a shilling from him, but he kept three of his sons at Eton School. He had paid £700 for Satter-thwaite's company[10] and kept a son of his at Eton. And Saul had a view to the office of Collector of the Customs at Lancaster. I felt myself very awkward amidst such people. But I thought, "What does the world *imagine* as to the *consequence* of living intimately with the GREAT LOWTHER, the powerful proprietor of £50,000 a year?" And in the world's esti-mation one wishes to exist high.

We had at breakfast Whelpdale's wife, a pretty, pleasing woman only thirty-four, though she has had eleven children. She is daughter of Green, the stage-doctor,[1] who is still alive. Whelpdale ran off with her to Gratney Green[2] at sixteen. The Earl commissioned Saul to make the tea and had himself a pot of currant jelly, which he spread thick on his buttered toast but offered nobody a tasting of it. Mrs. Whelpdale, Satterthwaite, Saul, and I went to the old church, a very good one; and Huddleston, the parson, officiated very well. The Rev. Mr. Church sat awhile with us after the forenoon's service, but did not see the Earl. I felt much as at Edinburgh.

Near three we had a tolerable dinner, and the seven officers of the Cumberland Militia now here were with us. No hob or nobs.[3] The Earl distributed the wine, just four glasses each, about a pint. At four we rose and saw the militia parade behind the castle, a fine body of men. The Earl looked nobly in scarlet and showed me great attention, taking me with him along the ranks. We then had tea and a true, quiet Sunday evening. Then a little supper, eggs, roasted potatoes and slices of cold beef, and some port (a bottle among us). I mixed water with it. Went to bed a little after eleven.

MONDAY 31 DECEMBER. It was showery. After breakfast Lord L. took me into what he calls his evidence room, where all his papers are kept and he writes, and talked a long time of I do not remember what, and showed me the map of Cumberland. I asked when he thought my election might be. He answered, "I cannot tell. I have sent for Jackson.[4] I have not thought of it yet." This was teasing to my impa-tience to be back to London. I was anxious to be with my family. I was uneasy to be absent when the Wartons came to town and there are

[10]Satterthwaite had become a captain in the 30th Foot in September 1786.
[1]A mountebank who practised in public, on a platform.
[2]Gretna Green. Boswell's spelling shows the contemporary pronunciation.
[3]No drinking to each other alternately, with clinking of glasses.
[4]Richard Jackson, alderman of Carlisle and mayor at least six times.

many valuable literary meetings,[5] and I was vexed that I had no settled time to go on with Johnson's *Life*, though I had the notes of the year 1778 with me. Time was wasted till past one, when He took me and Saul with him that I might see the harbour, for he would let nobody show it but himself, nor would he allow me to walk out and look about the town. The regular building of the streets and many good houses pleased me, but families living in cellars seemed very bad. Lord L. thinks so and is to build a great many more houses that it may be so no longer. He dragged me on so slowly along the quays in the thick rain that I was heartily wearied. I was surprised at the quantity of shipping, though we saw but a part.[6] We dined tolerably and had tea and supper.

[5]The Club held special meetings when the Wartons were able to attend.
[6]The Lowthers of Whitehaven were aggressive entrepreneurs. From Sir John, second baronet (d. 1706), to the Earl of Lonsdale, they had steadily consolidated and extended the mines and developed the harbour until their coal trade was second only to Newcastle's. Their mines were unique, moreover, in running under the sea, as far out as one and a half miles. The Lowther fleet carried iron ore, pig iron, salt, and lime as well as coal to ports throughout the British Isles. As a consequence of such activity, the former hamlet of Whitehaven had grown to have three times as many inhabitants as Carlisle.

TUESDAY 1 JANUARY. It was a very wet day. So we only went through the house. When he came into my room, which had once been his own, "Here," said he, "is a room which may be celebrated. It may be said such and such things were written here." When he chooses to pay a compliment nobody can do it more graciously. At dinner we had the militia officers and Captain Harris and Lieutenant Willox of the 40th Regiment. The Lieutenant was an Aberdeen man. The northern accent is so broad, and his superfetation[7] of English was so thick, that I could not be quite sure he was Scotch, till he talked of the wind being in a particular *airt*,[7a] I suppose *àrd-point* in Erse.

Today, as on Sunday, we dined in a large room below. We had a coarse dinner. But madeira, of which I had four glasses. There were besides either three or four glasses of port. I took only one. The second was quite thick, for he never decants wine and, as he said himself the other night, the fire before which he always sets it brings off the crust. The other night he made Saul drink a thick glass which I declined. I let my thick one today stand before me, and when he observed I did not drink, I said, "No more, my Lord." I had no doubt he knew why, but said nothing. At last he said, "Squire Denton will drink that glass."[8] I said, "It is thick, my Lord." So we all rose and away to tea. I wondered that the great Lowther, Lord Lieutenant, etc., etc., did not entertain the officers with more credit to his dignity. Such entertainment, and a total suppression of animal spirits by his talking all himself, fretted me, and I was sulky though I did not show it. Evening went on as last.

WEDNESDAY 2 JANUARY. A still wetter day. After breakfast Lord L. abused Burke as an unprincipled, wrong-headed fellow and would not allow that public speaking had any effect in Parliament. He was heated that I did not acquiesce and, to obviate my instancing Lord Chatham, said that I certainly did not know the history of this country. Even Smollett could have informed me.[9] He then with a wonderful

[7]Superabundant overlay (a Johnsonism).
[7a]Direction.
[8]Thomas Denton held a pedigree which went back to the twelfth century. Lonsdale had purchased the family manor, Warnell Hall, from Denton's father and now leased it to the son.
[9]Tobias Smollett, the novelist, like Boswell a Scotsman, was the author of *A Complete History of England*, 20 vols., 1757–65.

reach of memory gave the state of parties,[1] and how Pitt had bowed to Lady Yarmouth, with whom he had often seen him, and had veered about against and for the German war, and, in short, had all kinds of political intrigue, and so had got on.[2]

He told us how he had been the man who quashed the prosecution against Rumbold,[3] that he thought it oppressive and cruel, and when Dundas moved to put it off for a short time because Burke could not attend, he rose and said he should move to have it put off for six months. Dundas, seeing the House thin, went off with those that were with him, thinking there would not be a House. His Lordship, however, knew of several of his friends above stairs and near the House and talked on till he had them collected; and, having then a House, put the question for six months and carried it, and thus Rumbold was relieved. He knew nothing of him. *This shows that the report as to Dundas's being bribed to stop the prosecution against Rumbold is not true.*[4]

My Lord said if he had been in the House of Commons he would have quashed the affair of Hastings too. He called Dundas a swaggering fellow, and said he saw that Hastings was so great at St. James's and his wife such a favourite with the Queen that he would be put at the head of the Board of Control. Therefore he did all he could to get him kept out from that situation.[5] Pitt, said he, is proud and selfish, and having nobody to speak for him but Dundas, who in a profligate

[1] In the eighteenth century a term often synonymous with "factions," political groups gathered around a specific leader and sometimes referred to as his "friends" ("Rockingham's friends").

[2] While in Opposition, the elder Pitt had advocated strengthening the British navy and firmly resisted George II's policy of German alliances, costly subsidies, and troops for Hanover. In 1756, when war with France appeared imminent, Pitt conciliated the King by cultivating his mistress, Lady Yarmouth, and explaining his policies through her (as other Ministers had done regularly). During the Seven Years' War, Pitt formed a ministry with the Duke of Newcastle, furnished vast sums to Prussia and other German states for their fight against the French, and later declared that he had conquered America on the plains of Germany.

[3] Sir Thomas Rumbold, Governor of Madras, dismissed from the service of the East India Company in 1781 and charged with responsibility for the war in the Carnatic because of corrupt and oppressive dealings with native Indian rulers.

[4] Henry Dundas, head of the Secret Committee to investigate the war in the Carnatic, pursued the inquiry ruthlessly at first, but it languished and was finally abandoned in December 1783. Rumours of bribery were widespread, but it is also asserted that the evidence against Rumbold was neither sufficient nor trustworthy. Lonsdale is not named in the debates on Rumbold; he was teller for the affirmative, however, in the motion to adjourn the proceedings.

[5] That is, Dundas tried to keep Hastings from heading the Board of Control, whose six members were ultimately responsible for the government of India.

way gets up and says, "It is all who shall be in, who shall be out. You want to have my place, I want to keep it," therefore obliges Dundas in this.[6] His Lordship described Pitt's Treasury Bench with just, contemptous vivacity.[7] But his insensibility to Burke's talents was amazing. He said the Marquess of Rockingham was killed by three men, Sir George Savile, Lord John Cavendish, and Burke.[8] He had no mind of his own. But Sir George would come, "This must be black." Then he saw Lord John. "Don't you think it should be black?" "Black! No, no. It must be white." Then Burke would be with him, and he'd tell how he was puzzled. Said Burke, "It should be yellow. But suppose we make a mixture of all the three." He said on "the hereditary virtue of the whole House of Cavendish"[9] that they were always fools.

Before dinner came Mr. and Mrs. Senhouse and a boy, their eldest son. This diversified the scene a little. In the evening came two young Mr. Richardsons from Penrith, the eldest, who had been in India and had now succeeded to be squire, and the other Mr. George, lieutenant in the 54th, who had not joined;[10] and their sisters, Miss Mary and Miss Margaret, and Miss Lowther, sister of the Reverend Doctor, and Miss Dun from Lowther, daughter of the surgeon-apothecary, and her aunt, Miss Adamson, and Captain Postlethwaite. To describe them all would take too much time. Let me only observe that it occurred to me one wonders what is the use of many insects in the universe; I now see that fops and fantastical misses may be of great use in dissipating melancholy. But it's fair to add that though they seemed as I have mentioned at first view, they proved on better acquaintance cheerful,

[6]Pitt voted to censure Hastings for the fine of £500,000 he had levied on the Zemindar of Benares, a motion that made impeachment almost inevitable. The trial freed Pitt from defending all the mistakes made in India and increased Dundas's control over the East India Company.

[7]In 1788, Lord Chancellor (Lord Thurlow), Lord President of the Privy Council (Earl Camden), Lord Privy Seal (Marquess of Stafford), First Lord of the Admiralty (Viscount Howe), Foreign Secretary (Marquess of Carmarthen), Home Secretary (Lord Sydney), Master-General of the Ordnance (Duke of Richmond): on the whole, not an impressive list. For *contemptous*, see 7 December 1786, p. 111, n. 6.

[8]His staunch friends and associates, although Savile, an independent, refused appointment in both of Rockingham's Administrations. Rockingham died of influenza less than four months after he had formed his second Administration, in 1782.

[9]Edmund Burke, *A Letter to the Sheriffs of Bristol*, 1777: "If I have wandered out of the paths of rectitude into those of interested faction, it was in company with the Saviles, the Dowdeswells, the Wentworths, the Bentincks . . . with the temperate, permanent, hereditary virtue of the whole house of Cavendish" (*Works*, 1849, ii. 239). The Cavendish family is headed by the Duke of Devonshire.

[10]Not joined his regiment.

pleasant people. No doubt they had not wit and such circumstances. We had a supper (slight enough) in the large, low room, and the Earl exerted himself wonderfully. I had today a packet of letters, from Bruce Campbell, James Bruce, Sir William Forbes, and Veronica that her mother's cough had been severe; but I hoped it was no worse than formerly.[1]

THURSDAY 3 JANUARY. By nine o'clock we were at breakfast in the room where we had supped. Coffee, tea, chocolade—all pleasant. I forgot all anxiety and thought I could live for ever in this manner. The *Gazette* announcing Miller President, Macqueen Justice Clerk, and Maclaurin a Lord of Session.[2] The *changes* produced an agitation not unpleasant, but I felt *somewhat* uneasy to think that had I steadily remained at the Scotch bar I might have had the judge's place. But I considered that I should not have relished it while under the strong delusion of hope at the English bar. Nay, yet I doubted if I should relish it. Then how much more enjoyment have I had than if I had been in Scotland! It was still rainy. My Lord took me and the two Richardsons to see his timber-yard, which is extensive, and a young bear sent to him from the Baltic. His slow progress and insensibility to rain fretted me. We went with him also and viewed Trinity Church and St. James's Church.

At dinner all was quite as it should be: two soups, fish, various dishes, a dessert as last night, hobbing nobbing. But no claret. The moderation in drinking, however, was commendable, and of great advantage to me. The conversation was quiet and decorous. I began to think that this was the best style, for though there was no vivid enjoyment, neither was there struggling—and then languor. Mr. Peter Taylor, a merchant here, dined with us. At five we were at tea and coffee. Then the Earl and I and Saul and Taylor played whist till supper, between nine and ten. To bed between eleven and twelve.

FRIDAY 4 JANUARY. Every night almost during this jaunt, or whatever it may be called, I have dreamt a good deal, which is not my custom. I must therefore be more agitated. A letter from my dear wife today, written so that I could perceive that what was contained in a

---

[1] James Bruce, overseer at Auchinleck since Boswell's youth, sent him weekly reports on the estate. Boswell replied to Veronica at once, expressing his anxiety about Mrs. Boswell.

[2] The changes followed on the death, 13 December 1787, of Robert Dundas, Lord President of the Court of Session. He was succeeded by Thomas Miller, Lord Justice Clerk. Lord Braxfield (Robert Macqueen) became Lord Justice Clerk, and John Maclaurin, Boswell's contemporary and friend, an occasional author, was elevated to the bench as Lord Dreghorn.

letter from Veronica which I received yesterday, as to her being ill, had a more serious foundation than was expressed. But what could I do? To break off now, when I was confident my election must soon come on, would have been losing all my time and expense and sore labour, as *hanging on* most certainly is to me. I again reminded his Lordship how inconvenient it was to me to come down and that I *must* be in London again next week. He said, "I am *thinking* of it."

The weather was mild as in summer. He carried me and the Richardsons and Saul and viewed the harbour fully, and his great receptacle for coals,[3] and the mode of loading the vessels with them by what is called a *hurry*, being a conduit of wood through which each wagon-load is tumbled from a great highth into the hold of a ship. The other night he took me under the arm while we walked in the house. He did the same today when we were out. I said, "This is most comfortable living. I don't care how long it last, were I not obliged to be in London on business." He seemed pleased and said, "And I am sure I shall be the happier the longer you stay." We had again dinner, coffee and tea, whist, and supper. It is a waste of time to be minute in writing what will afterwards be of no moment. I won at whist both last night and this. His play was only a shilling, and he and I betted a crown the rubber.

SATURDAY 5 JANUARY. Another fine day. He and I and the same gentlemen as yesterday went and viewed what is called the Northwall, a very good pier; also his great steam engine. The same course as yesterday, only I lost at whist part of what I had won, and after supper came Sir Michael and Lady Diana Fleming. I felt how a numerous company may be very happy at a house in the country. But then, to be sure, this is not intellectual and literary enjoyment. I speculated on what could be the intention of human beings thus created. "Wait the great teacher Death," says Pope.[4] The detection of Lady Eglinton with the Duke of Hamilton made a fine agitation. *His* cold, ungrateful neglect of my valuable spouse, to whose brother he was under great obligations, and *her* being, I suppose, the insolent cause of it, made me rejoice at this event.[5] I felt here a kind of calm seclusion from life, and, as I experienced that I could live in perfect moral practice, I

[3]The major part of it, which was covered to protect the quality of the coal, was 115 yards long and nineteen yards wide and held more than 5,200 wagonloads.
[4]*Essay on Man*, i. 92.
[5]See above, 17 April 1787, n. 3. Boswell wrote for particulars at once to his friend Alexander Fairlie. Lord Eglinton was Margaret Boswell's "Chief" and should have called on her and introduced her in London. We do not know why he was under obligation to her brother James, who died in 1766.

trusted that I should henceforth assume a steadiness in that respect. The half of my foretooth which was loose came out a day or two ago, but it did not affect me so much as I supposed it would have done.

I discovered much jealousy among the Great Man's minions. Postlethwaite said Satterthwaite liked to lead the life he did, and allowed him no merit for his patience. Satterthwaite said Whelpdale was a drunken, foolish body and so vulgar that it was a disgrace to have him appear as High Sheriff of Cumberland. Whelpdale said of Satterthwaite, "I might have been in his place but would not, as it would ruin my constitution to keep such late hours. He has had no education and been little in company, but he is a very cunning man." The truth is Whelpdale, though long in the army, is a coarse *Coomberland* squire with no knowledge or talents, creeping before Lord L. and abusing him behind his back. Satterthwaite as to the Earl is pretty much the same, but having served his time to an attorney is an understanding man in many things and has a certain depth of shrewd sense, and is also a well-bred man.

Lord L. told me what I must not forget, that when the present Duke of Norfolk was going to present a petition against him in Parliament concerning the Westmorland Militia, he took him upstairs to Bellamy's[6] and told him, "You have nothing to do with Westmorland. The petition is false, but your presenting it may make an impression. I tell you that I shall consider your doing it as personal to me. You shall answer for it. And if you have any affairs to settle, don't delay, for one of us shall die." He at first shilly-shallied and talked of a Member's having a right to present any petition, then said, "I can say nothing, for is not this a threat?" Lord L. said, "I do not threaten. I only tell you what I am resolved to do," upon which he said he would consider of it, and next morning said he would not present the petition. "But," said he, "this is not to be mentioned." Lord L. said, "No. You won't mention it; I shall not."[7] Some such words of course passed. He bid me not mention it. I was satisfied that the Duke of N. was a coward. Lord Lonsdale said as to "all the blood of all the Howards," the family

[6]A celebrated chop-house adjoining the House of Commons.
[7]Charles Howard, Earl of Surrey, was M.P. for Carlisle from 1780 until he succeeded his father as eleventh Duke of Norfolk in 1786. He and Lonsdale were fierce political opponents, as we have seen in the disputed Carlisle election of December 1786, and rivalry between their families was long-standing. In 1780, Lonsdale had criticized duelling between M.P.'s in a speech in the House of Commons: "If free debate were to be interpreted into personal attack, and questions of a public nature which came before either House were to be decided by the sword, Parliament would resemble a Polish diet" (A. S. Foord, *His Majesty's Opposition*, 1964, p. 358).

of Howard was not very ancient. Their lustre was by great marriages.
"Then," said I, "'all their blood' means the blood thus acquired."[8]

Satterthwaite told me today that by Lord L.'s directions he had
written to Alderman Jackson at Carlisle to come directly, and he supposed that my election would be ordered as soon as he arrived. I had
before said to Lord L. that I did not wish he should take the trouble
of going, but I had again stated that I wished it much as a great honour.
His Lordship said, "We shall see." Satterthwaite was of opinion I should
express a great desire to have that honour but not to insist upon it,
that there might not be a reason for delay. Such *management* must there
be. His Lordship attends to the most minute article of his domestic
economy.

SUNDAY 6 JANUARY. A very cold day. I received a letter from my
brother David written by desire of Mr. Devaynes, without my wife's
knowledge, acquainting me that she was not at all well, and that though
there was no immediate danger, I should return as soon as I conveniently could. The letter was prudently worded, but it alarmed me much.
I mentioned it to Lord L., whose indifference as to my tranquillity was
shocking. He said he had written for Jackson that he might settle as
to my election, but if I were called away he would keep the place open
and I might be elected in summer. I was in a miserable state of indecision. I was agitated even to trembling and quite impatient to be
with her. Yet I was vexed to lose all my time and trouble and vexation
for the difference of a day or two. Satterthwaite assured me Jackson
would come on Monday and advised me to wait. I told Lord L. I would.

I was at Trinity Church in the forenoon. Mr. Church read the
service very well, and a Mr. Thomson from Ireland preached well on
Christ's having come to destroy the works of the Devil. I was pleased
to hear the influence of evil spirits asserted in these days of *narrow*
thinking, as *unbelief* certainly is. Wild, hurried, distracted thoughts
concerning my dear wife darted through my mind. We had dinner,
tea, and supper, and it was a dull evening. So necessary are cards to
people in general.

MONDAY 7 JANUARY. Had tossed and dreamed a great deal. Lord
Lonsdale carried me and Saul out to ride with him on the roads towards

---

[8]Pope, *Essay on Man*, iv. 215–16:
> What can ennoble sots, or slaves, or cowards?
> Alas! not all the blood of all the Howards.

The Duke of Norfolk is the Premier Duke and Earl of England, and descends through
the female line from Edward I (1239–1307). The Howards have indeed made some
splendid marriages.

St. Bees, from whence I had a full view of the town, of the bay, and also saw the Isle of Man and Scotland. He took us above a quarter of a mile into his Howgill colliery.[9] To see the strata of coal and stone and the water conducted from where it issues and the methods by which air is circulated underground entertained me. But there was something horrid in the thought of being under the earth. He had at dinner today the trustees for the harbour, some creditable-looking, well-dressed merchants and ship captains: Mr. Dixon, Captain Shamman, Mr. Walker, etc., etc., Rev. Mr. Church, Rev. Mr. Huddleston; and in the evening came their ladies and daughters and Miss Fleming to tea and coffee in the great drawing-room, where were cards, and at the same time in a saloon opening on the staircase, which made it cool, we had a ball. I roused all the animal spirits I could and danced several country dances. Lord Lonsdale danced with a wonderful complaisancy. We had, I think, for music two fiddles, a bass, a tabor and pipe, and two clarinets.

It was *impossible* not to have my mind somewhat shaken loose from its anxiety by all the circumstances of gay variety. I meditated with a kind of fluttering desperation not quite unpleasant upon human existence in general and my own in particular, wondering "through what new scenes and changes must we pass,"[1] considering that sooner or later, if I did not die sooner than from my constitution I supposed, my dear wife must be removed from me into the next state of being, and trying in imagination how I could bear it, sometimes thinking to retire to a convent, sometimes to live private at Auchinleck, sometimes to hide myself in London, sometimes to be as much as possible in company. But when I considered my duty to my children, particularly my three daughters, who would much require a father's protection, I thought to force myself to bear the troubles which I feel under a course of ordinary life and to weather it out at least till they should be able to take care of themselves. Sometimes ambitious stirrings to add wealth and consequence to my family by a second marriage, altogether free from that tender connection of hearts which I now experience. Thus was gloomy delay of the object for which I had left London forgotten for a while.

Between nine and ten we went to supper, handsomely served upon six tables in the great dining-room. Dividing us into separate *companies* had an admirable effect to produce ease and cheerfulness. His Lord-

[9]Twenty-three hundred acres in area, it was by far the largest colliery in the kingdom and included the deepest pit, Thwaite Pit.
[1]Not identified,.

ship desired me to hand Mrs. Dixon and sit by her at his table, which was the centre one next to the fireplace. She was sister to Mr. Hamilton, surgeon here, and wife of Mr. Dixon, merchant, to whom she had been married four or five years. She was a woman of manners more than common, had seen a good deal of the world, was refined yet not affected. I felt myself improved by talking with her. She had read my *Tour*, she told me, and was going to read it a second time. She admired the vivacity of Dr. Johnson's ideas. Her husband had purchased an estate in Scotland, *Fairgirth*, near to Mr. Maxwell of Munches's. They went to it every summer by sea, but she stipulated to return always by land. She talked with an elegance about everything. She was Mr. Dixon's second wife and seemed to be pretty well advanced in years and somewhat paralytic, for her head shook. On my other hand sat a Miss Walker, one of two sisters, with hair black as ravens, without powder, a very pretty, pleasing girl. I took a fancy to the *Coomberland* pronunciation. There was a rural simplicity in it.

[EDITORIAL NOTE. The "separate sheets" end abruptly here, and the entries which Boswell may have made for 8 and 9 January have not been recovered. On 10 January the journal was resumed on sheets uniform in size with those which have borne the entries from 29 September 1787. Boswell is still at Whitehaven Castle.]

THURSDAY 10 JANUARY. Was to go to Carlisle. Lord L. proposed to give me a convoy on horseback, so I sent forward my chaise, and his Lordship, who most obligingly regretted my going away, and Messrs. Satterthwaite and Saul rode with me so far, and then I rode on to ——, where my chaise waited. I had a dull day alone after so much society, and being anxious about my wife. Got to Carlisle by ten. Had Alderman Jackson first with me, and heard how all was prepared. His shrewdness and address pleased me much. I had the mayor and him and Alderman Wherlings to sup with me, and could not but think within myself how wonderful it was that I was now so easy and even confidential in an English town.

FRIDAY 11 JANUARY. Rose remarkably well, and dressed as well as I could. Had a message to come to Joseph Porter's, where all Lord L.'s friends of the Corporation had breakfasted. I shook hands with them all and thanked them. They went to the Moot Hall and, after they had resolved, sent for me. I walked down and, being introduced, was told by the mayor of their intention to choose me Recorder if I would accept of the office. I said I should think myself much honoured. Only Mr. Harrington (called "Sword" Harrington) objected, and pro-

posed Counsellor Clark. Four others would not hold up their hands
for me. But there was so great a majority, I was declared duly elected.
I then made a speech, thanking them and saying that my only uneasiness was that I should not be able to discharge the duties of the office
as I wished to do. But it should be my sincere endeavour to do it to
the best of my abilities. That I was sorry there were party dissensions
among them, but with these I had nothing to do. My business was with
the law and the solid prosperity of this ancient city. I then shook hands
with all my electors. Sword Harrington walked off. I went up to Borriskill,
one of the opposite party, and with a frank, good-humoured look said,
"*Will* you give me your hand, Sir?" He was won; gave me his hand and
said, "I wish you joy, Sir." I then (after having been sworn in, which
I believe was before my shaking hands) asked my electors to go to the
Bush with me and drink a glass of wine. The mayor, with me at his
left hand (my *place*), walked up the street, followed by all my friends.
I sent an invitation to the five of the opposite party, but they would
not come. We did not sit down, but drank a few toasts in sherry: I
their health, they mine; "Prosperity to the Ancient City of Carlisle";
"The King, the Earl of Lonsdale, and may His Majesty long have such
an able supporter of the just rights of the Crown." I was really elated,
and could not but inwardly muse how extraordinary it was that I had
obtained this promotion. Mine host, Howe, with wonderful gravity
addressed me, "Mr. Recorder," as if I had been seven years in the
office.

I set out in the heavy coach for Penrith between one and
two, having secured a seat in the mail-coach, and at Buchanan's I had a comfortable supper and sleep, and was taken
up about three in the morning by the mail-coach. I had a
very good journey to London, and arrived at the General
14 JAN.   Post-Office about eight o'clock on Monday morning. When
I got to the door of my house, I was glad to find the knocker
tied up, as this proved that my dear wife was not dead, as
my anxious mind had frequently figured. Mrs. Bruce informed me that she was a good deal better, but I soon saw
from her appearance that she had been at the gates of death.
She was, however, now so far recovered that I dismissed Sir
George Baker,[2] who visited her in the forenoon. I went to
Mr. Malone's in the evening, and was cordially social. From
this day till Wednesday 20 February, when I am now writing,

[2]President of the Royal College of Physicians and one of the King's doctors.

I kept no journal, so that a portion of my life is a mass with some prominencies in it, such as dining at Malone's on

6 FEB.

Ash Wednesday with Hamilton, Flood,[3] Windham, Courtenay, Langton, young Jephson, when we had a great deal of conversation about Johnson, and Hamilton well observed what a proof it was of his merit that this company had been talking of him so long, as probably other companies were. He said, "There is no such man; 'Nec viget quicquam simile aut secundum.' "[4] He told us that Johnson called Addison the Raphael of essay-writers.[5] That he told Johnson that ———— had observed that everything might be expressed in English in words of two syllables; that Johnson paused some time and then said he believed it might. He quoted in favour of Johnson's style a passage in one of Dryden's Prefaces, how a nerveless style is sheltered under the praise of being natural. (I believe he meant a passage in the Preface to *The Fall of Innocence*, but he made it much better—*if* there be not another.)[6] When I mentioned Johnson's saying he formed his style on Sir William Temple, Mr. Hamilton said that Temple had as strangely imagined that he had formed *his* style on ———— *History of All Religions.*[7] Flood praised the *Dictionary* highly, and said on *that* Johnson's fame must rest.

There was another day before this at Malone's (I think Saturday 19),[8] where I dined with Burke, Courtenay, Sir Joshua, Palmer, Metcalfe, Dr. Scott, Dr. Joseph Warton, Mr. Thomas Warton, young Jephson. Burke was as usual fertile and playful. Being placed near a *ham*, he said, "I am *Ham-Burke* (Hamburg)." Then he gave a luminous dissertation on

19 JAN.

[3]Henry Flood, the Irish statesman and orator, since 1783 a Member of the English House of Commons.
[4]Horace, *Odes*, I. xii. 18: "Nor lives there anything like or even next in rank." Boswell quotes this remark of Hamilton's at the end of the *Life of Johnson*.
[5]So Arthur Murphy also reports in his *Essay on Johnson*.
[6]"I cannot but take notice how disingenuous our adversaries appear: all that is dull, insipid, languishing, and without sinews in a pom they call an imitation of Nature." From "The Author's Apology for Heroic Poetry and Poetic Licence," *The State of Innocence and Fall of Man, an Opera*, 1677 (*Dryden: The Dramatic Works*, ed. Montague Summers, 1932, iii. 421–22).
[7]Presumably Alexander Ross's *Pansebeia; or, A View of All Religions in the World*, 1653. The diplomatist Sir William Temple (1628–99), Swift's patron, was noted for his essays.
[8]MS 16; but 16 January was a Wednesday. Everything considered, Saturday 19 seems most likely.

farming and showed that farming with all its labour and all its chances is a poor business. He maintained, and particularized how, that a farmer should have seven rents to be well.

20 JAN.   The day after (Sunday 20[9] January) I dined at Sir Joshua's with the two Wartons, Malone, young Jephson, and I forget how many more.

22 JAN.   I dined at the Literary Club on the 22, when Charles Fox, who had not been there for some years, came in unexpectedly when dinner was half over and was exceedingly agreeable. I had never seen him before but in Johnson's company, and he then did not talk frankly. He this day was quite easy and good-humoured and talked of literary matters. He observed that the auxiliary verb *have*, as *have done*, which was common in modern languages, was a strange circumstance in language. He wished to know if it was in *all* modern languages. Hawkins Browne's imitations of Pope, Cibber, etc., being mentioned, he told us that Burke had contrived very happily to introduce the first nonsensical line of the imitation of Cibber so as to give it the effect of sense. At Admiral Keppel's trial they had a good deal of difficulty about the *line of battle*.[1] At length that was cleared, and then Burke exclaimed in triumph,

Old battle-array big with horror is fled.[2]

There were present Sir Charles Bunbury, Mr. Malone, Mr. Steevens, Mr. Warton, Mr. Gibbon, Mr. Langton. I was pleased with Fox's naming me when he observed upon something that I said. There was no appearance of supercilious resentment.[3]

[9] MS. 17.

[1] Admiral (later Viscount) Keppel had been tried by court-martial in January 1779 for misconduct and neglect of duty in an indecisive action against the French fleet in July 1778. The prosecutor was Sir Hugh Palliser, one of the Lords of the Admiralty, who had commanded the rear and had ignored Keppel's order at a critical juncture of the engagement to form the line of battle. Keppel was in Opposition and on bad terms with Lord Sandwich, the First Lord of the Admiralty, but he was completely exonerated and Palliser and the Admiralty, especially Sandwich, were widely criticized. Burke was part-author of Keppel's defence.

[2] "And olive-robed peace again lifts up her head" (Browne's "A New-Year's Ode").

[3] Because of Boswell's attack on Fox's East India Bill in his *Letter to the People of Scotland*, 1783.

12 FEB.   I dined two different days at Malone's with only young Jephson. On Tuesday 12 February (I think) I had a shocking day and night at Dilly's, having dined there with Dr. Mayo, Mr. Fell, Mr. Cutting, and Colonel Smith, American secretary,[4] and my brother David, and drank and played at whist till four in the morning, so as, in the fever of attempting to get back what I lost, to grow desperate. The result was losing *nineteen pounds seven and sixpence*. And my keeping my dear wife from rest a whole night did her much harm. In

13 FEB.   short, I was very miserable. I next day went and saw the opening of Mr. Hastings's trial.[5] On the Saturday before

9 FEB.   I had on a sudden gone with Courtenay, who called on me, and dined with Colonel James Francis Erskine in a noble house at Paddington Green; a German lady, four children,

10 FEB.   many servants. Next day (Sunday) Courtenay and I and young
14 FEB.   Jephson dined with Malone most agreeably. On Thursday I
15 FEB.   dined at Sir Joshua's quietly, nobody there. On Friday (after hearing Burke's opening)[6] I also dined with him;[7] Sir John

16 FEB.   D'Oyly[8] and Malone there. On Saturday I dined at General Paoli's (only Masseria there), and then supped tête-à-tête at Malone's. Took between the two more wine than did me good. Had for I think twelve days not written one line of Johnson's *Life*. Was quite idle and dissipated.

17 FEB.   On Sunday I again dined at the General's with Soderini, the Venetian Minister, Herschel,[9] Cavallo, etc.; not too numerous a company. Drank too freely. Sat awhile at Sir Robert

[4]William Stephens Smith, secretary to the American legation, and John Adams's son-in-law.

[5]The event of the season. Westminster Hall was entirely decorated in red except for the area reserved for the Commons. The crowd included the Queen, the Prince of Wales, and other members of the royal family. The chief charges against Hastings were bribery, corruption, and oppression of the native population.

[6]" 'He stood forth,' he said, 'at the command of the Commons of Great Britain, as the accuser of Warren Hastings' " (*London Chronicle*, 15 February 1788), and after pausing for more than a minute, expounded for two and a half hours on the significance of the case, both as to Britain's honour and the relief of India, and on the magnitude of the crimes. The speech was continued at the next three sittings, 16, 18, and 19 February 1788.

[7]Reynolds.

[8]Collector of Customs at Calcutta, later M.P. for Ipswich; one of Hastings's good friends.

[9]Sir William Herschel, the great astronomer. He had discovered the planet Uranus in 1781.

Strange's. When I came home, found Malone and young Jephson, who supped with us; and it was wonderful what a change to the better their agreeable society made on my wife and daughters, who had been long shut up in almost constant dull solitude. My wife was now a good deal better. In the forenoon, I had visited Lady Oughton (the first time since my brother's marriage, he having begged I would not visit her, as he charged her with forcing him on to an imprudent match— but he had lately gone himself), as also Lord Dumfries.

18 FEB. On Monday (18 February) I heard Burke speak astonishingly well, having breakfasted with Malone and been carried into the managers' box by Courtenay.[1] And Courtenay and his son and young Jephson and I dined with Malone. Kemble joined us in the evening. We were in great spirits, at least I was; drank a great deal, and did not get home till three—

19 FEB. another sad excess; and next morning (Tuesday 19 February) my head was inflamed and confused and I was exceedingly ill. I however, by the help of peppermint-water and good soup, both of which my dear wife kindly gave me, got so well as to sit President of the Literary Club with Lord Lucan, Lord Macartney, Mr. Gibbon, Mr. Malone, Mr. Steevens, Sir Joseph Banks. Mr. Windham came to us between seven and eight. I went home about ten, sober and well.

20 FEB. On Wednesday I was quiet at home all day, and wrote part of the Reasons of Miss Whitefoord's Case for the House of Lords.[2] At night I got a letter from James Bruce informing me that the purchaser of a bank of wood at Tenshillingside last year had failed and that I could get only a part of the value of his bill. And that he had now in his hands only £34, and the bills for ploughed land, etc., due at Candlemas would not be paid for some time. I had now only a few pounds in cash. My credit of £500 with the Ayr Bank was exhausted, all to about £50. Supposing the bills due to me to be paid, I

[1]Burke's description of native suffering and particularly of the brutalities perpetrated against women by Devi Sing, Hastings's underling, was so harrowing that many hearers were visibly agitated and Mrs. Sheridan fainted.

[2]A case concerning inheritance. Bryce Whitefoord of Dunduff left his estate to heirs male, which failing, to the eldest daughter of his second marriage, Jean, the appellant. His son James succeeded, but died without issue and left the estate to a distant relative. Jean Whitefoord challenged the succession on the ground that her brother had no right to alter the order as settled by his father, but the Court of Session had decided against her. Boswell and John Scott were counsel for Miss Whitefoord.

could not receive much above £350. Of this, £70 of interest to Sir W. Forbes and Company, and £25 of ditto to Mackilston,[3] and £76, my father's debt to Glenlee, now Lord President,[4] and at least £50 due in London, left me only £129; and I did not recollect that I could receive any more till September. How then could I maintain my family?

My dear wife, to whom I stated my situation, was seriously distressed and told me it made her feverish. She expostulated with me on the miserable consequences of keeping my family longer in London; that we were in straits, and in a mean, neglected situation, when if we were at home, we might live comfortably and creditably. She pressed upon me my worthy father's anxious wish that I should reside at Auchinleck as much as he had done, and that by living in London I was doing just what was most disagreeable to him and which he might have prevented by binding me to residence, but had put a confidence in me which I ought not to abuse. That if my living in London had any probability of advantage, I might be justified; but that I must now be satisfied that I could not give the application necessary for the practice of the English law, and that indeed I led a life of dissipation and intemperance, so that I did not go on even with my *Life of Dr. Johnson*, from which I expected both fame and profit; in short, that I did nothing; and that I found myself neglected by those who used to invite me when I came to London only for a month or two; that my circle was now confined to a very few, for that people shunned a man who was known to be dependent and in labouring circumstances. That my children must suffer in their health for want of good air and exercise and would gradually get inclinations unsuitable to their situation, as I could only leave them annuities.

In short, her arguments seemed of very great weight. But the ambitious views which I had fondly indulged, and the fondness of English manners which had made a part of my very existence from my earliest years, weighed on the other side, especially when I apprehended that my returning to

[3] Annual interest on a bond of £1,400 for which Forbes's banking-house had accepted Boswell's house in St. Andrew Square, Edinburgh, as heritable security, and on £500 lent on personal bond by John Shaw Alexander of Mackilston, a hereditary client of the Boswells'.

[4] See above, 23 April 1786 and n. 2. On 1 April 1788 James Bruce reported that he had paid the debt, which was actually £74.

the Scotch bar would be a wretched sinking and make me appear a disappointed, depressed man; and if I did not return to it, I should be looked upon as totally out of the law department and consequently be excluded from any pretensions to a judge's place in Scotland, which I still flattered myself I might attain. My wife suggested that her bad health was a very good excuse for my going down with her; that I should not declare what was my intention, nor indeed should I absolutely resolve what to do till I had found how it would be with me. That I might go occasionally into the Court of Session and, if I got business, might go on; if not, there would be no harm done. That I might come to London for three or four months every year and see what Westminster Hall would do for me. But that by having my family at Auchinleck, except perhaps for a month or two in winter at Edinburgh, and giving diligent attention to the management of my estate, I might soon make myself an independent man.

This seemed very wise, and I saw that I might keep my own counsel and float between the two countries and have a better chance for success than in my present state. But then I could not go till I had finished Dr. Johnson's *Life*, and I was sorry to take my sons away from an English education when they were going on remarkably well. James in particular I thought should be continued at it, as he might probably become an eminent barrister. I felt too a reluctance to *descend*, as I felt it, to the narrow situation of Scotland, in which I had suffered so sadly from melancholy, fancying myself excluded from any chance of figuring in the great circle of Britain. In short, I was in a sort of distraction.

21 FEB.   On Thursday 21 I was more quiet, and General Paoli having sent two opera tickets, I went at night with my daughter Phemie to *Le Schiavi per Amore*,[5] after which was a very fine dance in which devils and flames made a great figure. I

23 FEB.   heartily wearied of the entertainment. On Saturday 23 I was in better spirits, having had the day before a letter from James Bruce with an Ayr Bank receipt for £156 and a view of more money; so I found that my *circumstances* influenced the state of my mind.[6] Courtenay had proposed to have the *Gang* with

[5]Correctly *Gli Schiavi per Amore*, a comic opera by Giovanni Paisiello.
[6]Boswell inked out the greater part of this sentence, which is misplaced. See below, 25 February.

him today at dinner. Poor man, he had told me lately that all that remained to him was an annuity of £40 a year, which he was going to sell. I calculated it would yield him £240. It was wonderful to see with what spirit and serenity he lived with a wife and seven children, knowing his situation; but I trusted that his *party* would do for him. I insisted that the dinner should be at my house. He was taken ill and could not come. But Sir Joshua and Miss Palmer, Malone, Langton, young Jephson, and Miss Buchanan dined and supped with us. It was a very pleasant day. Langton was most entertaining with numberless anecdotes. Sir Joshua told us a curious particular of Dr. Adam Smith. He said he had observed people exceedingly unhappy from prejudices and resentments against others. He had taken a resolution that he would hate nobody, and if he knew himself, there was nobody in the world whom he hated. This was a new thought to me for the moment, and I am afraid it is new to most people in actual *practice*. But it is an essential principle of Christianity. Let me try it. But it does not exclude a certain degree of aversion to some compared with others.

24 FEB.   On Sunday I visited Courtenay in his indisposition, and having all along been warm for Hastings, I was in some degree tempered by his reading to me some of the circumstances of his oppression in Benares. I was shocked at the whole system of British power in India, but I supposed that Mr. Hastings would be able to give good reasons for his conduct. I however resolved not to be so loud in his defence in the mean time, especially as it would offend Burke, to whom I had formerly been much obliged, but between whom and me there had for some time been an unhappy coldness, though we met occasionally on sufficiently easy terms. I was at the chapel in our own street in the afternoon with my three eldest children and was in so placid and pious a frame that I could have died in peace. I *hoped* that at last I should be in this frame, and I *felt* that I was *now* as well as if no evil had ever disturbed me. I stayed at home all day after, and the children said divine lessons.

25 FEB.   On Monday, after a shameful interval of neglect, I resumed Johnson's *Life*. I received this day a letter from James Bruce with a receipt for £156 lodged in the Ayr Bank, so that I had now credit for £200, provided he could pay the interest to Sir W. Forbes and Company and Mackilston (£100) out of other money; and I felt that the state of my circum-

stances had much influence on my spirits. I laboured with alac-
rity at the *Life*. My wife went abroad today for the first
26 FEB.   time since her severe illness. She walked out. On Tuesday
evening I was at a *conversation*[7] at Langton's, where I met
among other ladies Mrs. Garrick, whom I had not seen since
I published my *Tour to the Hebrides*, though I had called on
her several times. I was glad to find that she talked to me as
usual.[8] I had a good deal of conversation with Lady Dumfries.
Such a society as this, which formerly used to elevate me, was
now comparatively insipid. Yet I own I liked it very well. I
had no anxious pretensions, and was calm and placid. Malone
and young Jephson, who were there, supped along with me
at young Slaughter's.[9]

28 FEB.   On Thursday I dined at Dilly's very comfortably with
Braithwaite and Reed. My wife had catched a new cold and
was again ill, so I resolved (and kept my resolution) to come
home early. I however had some good conversation with
steady Reed. I was much pleased with a practical philosophical observation of his when I said how sad it would be if a
certain acquaintance of ours at the bar should attend Westminster Hall and go the circuit all his life without getting a
brief. "No, Sir," said Reed. "He has a pretty fortune; and if
he has got over his years as agreeably as he probably could
have done in any other way, he has no reason to complain."
This is salutary consolation, but it will not satisfy a man who
has a strong ambition to rise in life or a strong desire to be
of essential advantage to his family.

SATURDAY 1 MARCH. According to custom on the first of every
month, breakfasted at Malone's and talked of anything relative to Johnson in the monthly publications. Was in wonderfully good spirits. Home
and did some *Life*. This week had done fifty-two pages. Sat awhile with
Lord Kellie.

SUNDAY 2 MARCH. Took my three eldest children to the Quakers'
Meeting in St. Martin's Lane. All silence. Sat awhile with my relation
Mr. David Hamilton, who had come up from Exeter on business.[1]

---

[7]A social gathering, often professedly intellectual or artistic.
[8]Boswell was perhaps uneasy because he had published in the *Tour* several of Johnson's
unflattering remarks about Garrick.
[9]More properly "New Slaughter's," in St. Martin's Lane, as distinguished from "Old
Slaughter's," in the same street.
[1]The descendant, probably, of Boswell's great-granduncle, Sir David Hamilton, M.D.,
physician successively to William III, Queen Anne, and Caroline, Princess of Wales.

Found Lord Advocate at home. Was *lowered* by Scotch ideas. Went to Malone's. Flood came in. Dined at home, and in the evening the children said sacred lessons. I read some of the New Testament to them with a calm fervency. Little James was particularly pleased.

MONDAY 3 MARCH. Had a bad cold. Home all day. *Life*.

TUESDAY 4 MARCH. Ditto. Ditto.

WEDNESDAY 5 MARCH. A little *Life*. My wife's illness was worse, so that she could not venture abroad at all. I and my two eldest daughters dined at Sir Joshua Reynolds's with Sir John D'Oyly, Mr. Evans, Mr. Dallas, Mr. Johnson (all East Indians), and Mr. Augustine, the great underwriter. To cure my cold, as I imagined, lived too full. Was heated with wine, but not much. Played at cards in the drawing-room, where were many ladies who had come in the evening. Lost, but it was only at commerce, so it was not more than about two guineas. My daughters and I, and Johnston and Rev. Mr. John Palmer, Sir Joshua's nephews, supped. I was quite pleased with the behaviour of my daughters, but when I got home was vexed to find myself more disturbed by wine than I had supposed, and of consequence a very unsuitable companion for my wife in her distress.

THURSDAY 6 MARCH. Awaked in sad vexation, having disturbed my dear wife much in the night and being exceedingly ill. Sent my excuse to worthy Langton, with whom I had engaged to be at Court, and lay till two. Then rose, and being somewhat better, finished Miss Whitefoord's *Case*.[2]

FRIDAY 7 MARCH. My good friend Dilly sent me this morning Mrs. Piozzi's *Letters to Dr. Johnson* a day before they were published. I read with assiduity till I had finished both volumes. I was disappointed a good deal, both in finding less able and brilliant writing than I expected and in having a proof of his fawning on a woman whom he did not esteem because he had luxurious living in her husband's house; and in order that this fawning might not be counteracted, treating me and other friends much more lightly than we had reason to expect. This publication *cooled* my warmth of enthusiasm for "my illustrious friend" a good deal. I felt myself degraded from the consequence of an ancient Baron to the state of an humble attendant on an author; and, what vexed me, thought that my collecting so much of his conversation had made the world shun me as a dangerous companion. I carried the volumes to Malone and drank tea with him and young Jephson. I was sent for home, my wife having become much more uneasy and being

[2]Boswell may have italicized the word to remind himself to use it. The Scottish equivalent, with which he was much more familiar, would have been *cause*.

very frightened. I hastened to her and found her in a complication of distress, with asthmatic and feverish complaints. I sent for John Hunter, who came and ordered some things and raised her spirits somewhat. He told *me* that she had only a bad cold, which produced all these symptoms. This relieved my anxiety.

SATURDAY 8 MARCH. Went to Sir Robert Herries's and got money.[3] Sat awhile at Garforth's and got acquainted with the famous (Bob) Mackreth. Heard of Mr. Pitt having the night before been hard pushed on his, or rather Dundas's, bill for explaining his India Bill, and that Dundas was become exceedingly unpopular. Found Courtenay at Malone's and heard particulars of the debate.[4] Yielded to an invitation to dine at Malone's next day, after some objecting, he having said that I now did everything proper but nothing pleasant. As Courtenay and I walked along, I threw out that, "Suppose I should write against Pitt's India Bill, now seeing Fox's to be not worse than it, the *Commissioners* not being allowed to act but by the King's approbation, as Courtenay stated?" This was a rash sally of a mind soured by Pitt's neglect of me after I had done so much for his cause (though as the *King's* cause, to be sure). Said Courtenay: "It would show you an impartial man and reconcile you to the other party." I recollected myself and said, "I must talk with George Rex." John Hunter called today on my wife of his own accord. She was considerably easier. My three eldest children went to a ball at Langton's, it being George's birthday, and I stayed at home all the evening. My wife being much troubled with fever in the night, I now took a separate bed in the drawing-room.

SUNDAY 9 MARCH. My wife was not so well. Was with Phemie at our own chapel in the forenoon. Then sat with my wife. Saw her in a severe fit: cough, spitting blood, high fever. Went to Godbold and got a pint bottle of his vegetable balsam,[5] but she would not try it as yet. I was very miserable. She seemed hurt from a notion that I grudged the expense of a physician because I talked of the difficulty of getting free of them. This distressed me deeply. I was sending for Sir George Baker again, but she stopped me. I was for calling Dr. Warren. She

[3]Founder of the banking-house which bore his name.
[4]The East India Declaratory Bill for explaining Pitt's Bill of 1784, which established a Board of Control on political matters, justified the decision of the Board to send four regiments to India at the expense of the East India Company and to divide the appointment of officers for those regiments between the Crown and the Company. The Company contended that no additional troops were necessary and that the selection of officers was wholly in its province. Fox spoke eloquently in the debate on the encroachments by the Crown which Pitt's Bill introduced, as opposed to his own defeated proposal of 1783 to establish an independent Board of Commissioners.
[5]This nostrum was widely advertised as a cure for consumption and asthma.

thought it better to state her *case* to him and get his opinion, but deferred that too.[6] I went, very low-spirited, to Malone's and dined; just he and I and Courtenay. I revived by good eating and wine in moderation and a good flow of talk. They both thought better of Johnson's letters to Mrs. Thrale than I did, though upon looking at some of them again on Saturday, they improved upon me. They advised me to call Warren, of whom Hamilton said, "He's a coxcomb, but a satisfactory coxcomb"; and when I objected that from his multiplicity of business he could give little time to the consideration of any one case, "True," said Courtenay, "but he brings to that case the experience of twenty similar to it on the same day." He gave us a good saying of a French physician to ———, who objected that physicians had no *principle*. "True," said he, "but we have *practice*. Suppose there were six blind men in Paris who had gone about in it all their lives, and then all the rest of the inhabitants should go blind. They could not find their way at all, and would gladly submit to be led by those six, because, though also blind, they had a practice which the others had not." Courtenay made a remark which struck home to me: that if Johnson had been born to £3,000 a year, he would have been more unhappy, because his melancholy, discontented temper would have been more at leisure to torment him. I stated seriously that a man who was unhappy because he could not speak like Fox or Burke was really unhappy, though he would not be pitied.

Sir Joshua, who had dined at Lord Harcourt's, came to us. He told us that Johnson said of Thrale and his wife, "He has ten times her sense, though she is more flippant."[7] We had a dispute with Courtenay for the soul as separate from matter, in which Sir Joshua was clear, as he was for a future state, from his notions of GOD; yet he was for religion in all countries as something in aid to morality and *therefore* divine; but he did not allow of any preference which one religion had in being *revealed* more than any other. Very loose thinking. I was strenuous for the Christian revelation as putting immortality beyond a doubt. Though resolved to come home early, I was drawn on to stay so as that it was twelve. I felt the high relish of London abated and

[6]Dr. Warren, a society doctor with a consoling manner, had the largest medical practice in the country and at this time was reportedly earning an annual income of £9,000. It was common procedure for the patient to be seen by an apothecary (in this case Devaynes), who then gave a statement of the case to a physician and received the patient's prescription. It was generally only in very serious cases that the physician himself saw the patient. See below, 18 and 23 March 1788.
[7]Fluent, voluble; an obsolete usage which the *Oxford English Dictionary* illustrates by means of this same sentence as Boswell gave it in the *Life of Johnson*.

was sensible of my diminution in it, compared with my situation as an extensive landed gentleman. I was sadly vexed to find my wife had been worse, and I had a longing wish that we were all at Auchinleck. She was fallen asleep. I went to bed dreary.

MONDAY 10 MARCH. My wife was rather better. I stayed at home all day and worked at Johnson's *Life*, except sitting a short time with Lady Strange.

TUESDAY 11 MARCH. At home all day. *Life*. My wife having become rather worse and very apprehensive, and having declared she had a confidence in Sir George Baker, I called him again in the evening, when he found that she had by catching cold had a severe relapse.

WEDNESDAY 12 MARCH. Had dismal apprehensions about my wife. By Sir George Baker's orders she was bled by Mr. John Hunter, and her blood was quite inflamed. Sir George told me that there was an inflammation upon her lungs, and that though the symptoms which now distressed her might be removed, they would be always recurring, the lungs having been once affected. He said that people died of consumptive complaints at all ages, but that the disease took longer time to consume a person well advanced in life than a young person; that my wife's complaints would soon have killed a girl of seventeen. This was pronouncing her not perfectly curable. I did some *Life*.

THURSDAY 13 MARCH. Either yesterday or the day before had a visit of Lord Kellie. The appeal, Whitefoord against Whitefoord, was to come on in the House of Lords next day. I was much occupied in looking into authorities and writing out a speech. But I had all the week been very gloomy. I had this forenoon for the first time a visit of Mr. Steevens, who animated me somewhat by his literary conversation. He sat with me above an hour. My wife was much in the same way as for some days, though somewhat easier.

FRIDAY 14 MARCH. Consulted on the appeal with Mr. Scott at his chambers and felt that kind of flutter which a man who has been some time confined by sickness does when suddenly called out. As an instance how proper it is for a counsel to look narrowly at deeds themselves, I last night discovered that one of the seisins of the late Dunduff was razed and superinduced, and so vitiated *in substantialibus*.[8] I showed it to Scott, who thought it very suspicious. I was humbled when I contrasted his clearness of head with my hurried flow of ideas. But he had fewer ideas, and what he had were better arranged than mine by his constant practice in the courts. I found in my son Alexander a judicious

[8]One of the property deeds of the late Bryce Whitefoord of Dunduff was erased and written over, and so invalid in substance.

aptitude for a law case, so I took him with me to hear the Appeal. I was frightened a good deal from not being used of late to speak in public. The weather too was excessively frosty. It was within five minutes of five when we were called in. Scott stated the cause with admirable clearness, and the farther hearing was deferred till next day. I had been one morning this week at Malone's trying if he could furnish me with any arguments;[9] and I had one morning also this week a visit of Mr. Daines Barrington, who sat some time. I was very melancholy tonight, and as I drove home in a hackney-coach, London seemed quite dull and misty. My wife was more uneasy tonight. I was very sad.

SATURDAY 15 MARCH. Rose in somewhat better spirits. Took Sandy again with me. I was kept waiting some time in the outer room, where Pitt, Dundas, Rose, and so many more Members of the House of Commons also waited to carry up the Declaratory India Bill. Dundas talked with me frankly and gave his opinion clearly against Miss Whitefoord's appeal. But Pitt took no sort of notice of me. I cannot be sure but that he did not know me in my bar-dress, though I should think he did. Dundas having said, "It is hard that we must be kept so long waiting for a bishop. Is there no Treasury bishop?" I said, "I think the Board of Control might have a bishop for themselves. Why not, considering what you have? Why not ecclesiastical powers too?" He laughed and called to Pitt, "He says the Board of Control should have a bishop for themselves." Pitt advanced and said, "They may have a Brahmin, if that would do."[1] He looked cold and stiff and proud, and I should suppose must have known me, otherwise he would have asked who I was. I felt indignation towards him. I had resolved to write a strong expostulating letter to him and meditated on it while he stood thus. When counsel were called in I had no uneasy apprehension and stated the case to my own satisfaction. I soon was satisfied that the Lord Chancellor saw through my reasoning, and it is very unpleasant to talk what one is conscious is mere plausibility when it is addressed to a man of sense. His Lordship said, "Mr. Boswell, you state your case very ingeniously. But—" and then he put a question which showed he knew the fallacy, and smiled. However, it was my business to do justice to my client, and I spoke about an hour. He affirmed the Decree without hearing the respondent's counsel. But I prevailed in having a reser-

[9]Malone had practised at the Irish bar.
[1]The business of the House could not begin without prayers, and since most bishops were appointed for political rather than ecclesiastical reasons, Dundas in effect was asking, "Don't we have one of our appointees here?" He was the leading member and later President of the Board of Control for India.

vation of the objection as to the instrument of seisin being vitiated.[2]

I went home and saw my wife, who was more uneasy today. I then dined at Courtenay's with Sir Joshua Reynolds, Malone, Langton, Palmer, young Jephson. It was a comfortable, good, moderate day. I was miserably low and dusky when I went there. I had not tasted fermented liquor since Sunday. The sensation of it today was grateful, and I soon formed external good spirits, as a stratum of fertile earth is spread on the surface of a rugged rock. Courtenay's wit sparkles more than almost any man's. When I was talking how kind Dr. Brocklesby was in attending on Dr. Johnson, "Yes," said he, "but he trusted to Heberden. He would not let Brocklesby '*kill* him with kindness.' " Langton and I came away at eleven and walked together from Bryanston Street to the bottom of Prince's Street, Leicester Fields.[3] He spoke violently against Pitt for neglecting me and talked like an *ancient gentleman* against his pride because he had a high official situation. "What!" said he, "don't we know that he was t'other day Will Pitt at Serle's Coffee-house, and are we to be awed by *him*, who have lived with Johnson?" Langton and I parted tonight in great cordiality. We had joined in thinking that Johnson in his letters to Mrs. Thrale appeared to disadvantage, as showing a studied shunning to speak of the friends whom he valued most in terms such as to make her at all jealous of them. This was a stooping in the high mind of Johnson.

SUNDAY 16 MARCH. Lord Kellie was to have dined with me today quietly in case my wife was no worse, but on account of her illness I had put off our meeting and engaged to breakfast with him at Lord Fife's, where he lived at this time. I did so, and had Scottish ideas fully renewed, and felt that wealth and rank and a fine house, etc., etc., are nothing if there be not a flow of elegant existence. It was a cold easterly storm, and the *Thames* looked no better than the *Tay* or the *Spey*. Lord Fife went out after breakfast, and I stayed and walked up and down the room with Lord Kellie for I suppose an hour and had from him a full account of his[4] appearing on the side of Opposition, which was so contrary to his Tory principles. It seems he had acted from gratitude to Lord North, who, he thought, had exerted himself with the King to get something for him. But he had now found that Mr. Dundas had put his Memorial into Lord North's hands and insisted on its being

---

[2]Although Boswell thought her case weak, Miss Whitefoord professed herself much satisfied with his handling of it. Boswell's objection concerned what was, in effect, the title-deed.
[3]From the "little house" Courtenay had taken the previous year to what is now a part of Wardour Street, about one and a half miles.
[4]Lord Fife's.

carried to the King. So the Earl was now quite well with Mr. Dundas, who had desired him to give himself no trouble. He would take care to have what was proper done for him.

I then sat some time with Mr. Mackintosh, who had lately come up, and had from him an account of the present state of the Court of Session, which he said was very respectable. I then called at Lord Lonsdale's, as his Lordship was expected in town at this time, but he was not yet come. Having thought my wife rather easier in the morning, I had left word that I might perhaps dine somewhere with Lord Kellie. So as I considered I should not be positively expected at home, and being very gloomy I accepted of a kind invitation from Malone to eat roast beef with him tête-à-tête, having called on him between three and four and felt myself relieved by his conversation. I however felt remorse afterwards, both for having neglected public worship and my children on Sunday, and for having been all day without seeing my dear wife, who had been worse. I upbraided myself with seeming indifference, and thought how very differently she would have behaved had I been ill. But my own wretchedness had engrossed me.

MONDAY 17 MARCH. Was kept idle all the morning by visits of Colonel James Erskine, Mr. Mickle,[5] Rev. Mr. Bevil, and Mr. Cuninghame of Enterkine, who came to me with a foolish application to pledge myself to vote against the coalition between Lord Eglinton and Sir Adam Fergusson at all events, informing me that Lord Dumfries was hesitating as to making more votes because he did not wish to oppose that coalition unless there was a good prospect of success; that he *would not show his teeth when he could not bite*, but that he was disposed to support the *independent* party if there was a strong union. I told him plainly that I myself was a candidate for the county; that the only positive resolution I would declare was that I would prefer myself to Sir Adam, but if I had not a majority of the *real* freeholders for me, I would not be elected. But that I would not engage not to vote for Sir Adam Fergusson, because, although I disapproved of him, there might be a candidate to whom I would prefer Sir Adam, upon the principle "Of two evils, choose the least." That, for instance, if Mr. Craufurd, a professed follower of the Opposition[6]—that party which I thought dangerous, and which our county had reprobated—should be the person who would carry it if Sir Adam did not, perhaps I might

---

[5]William Julius Mickle, poet, translator of the *Lusiad*, failed dramatist; Boswell's sometime protégé.
[6]John Craufurd, in youth nicknamed "The Fish" because of his avid curiosity; a Foxite driven from the Commons in the rout of 1784.

think it my duty to prefer Sir Adam. He said that probably Sir John Whitefoord, who was on the side of Ministry, might be the candidate who would have the best chance. Surely I would vote for *him* rather than Sir Adam. I was positive to come under no engagement whatever. I stood upon the purest independent interest. I never had solicited a peer. I thought it improper to do it. I asked the votes of the gentlemen. Whoever should think me worthy of his vote would honour me highly. If he thought another more worthy, I should not take it amiss. It was his duty to vote for him. I had told Lord Dumfries that I was a candidate. His Lordship, knowing this, might dispose of his interest as he pleased. I would not tie myself up in any way. Gentlemen might tell me, "If you had been free and unconnected, we should have been for you, but we do not like your being entangled." I thought it fair for a candidate to wait and take all the chances of a contest. Suppose me to have only ten votes. The Opposition party has nine of majority over Sir Adam Fergusson. Mr. Dundas sees that the Ministerial party will lose unless he makes Sir Adam's votes go for me. My ten being firm and resolute to stand out, I should have the election. Thus I talked, but I afterwards thought I had said too much to so foolish a fellow.

In the afternoon I did some *Life*. But my wife, who had been free of fever all night and part of the day, had a severe return, which depressed me sadly. I called Sir George Baker again at night, and he ordered a blister on her breast and that she should be blooded again next day. Poor woman, she had said to me mournfully this afternoon, "Oh, Mr. Boswell, I fear I'm dying." Sir George told me tonight that she was very ill, and that if she did not grow better, she must grow worse. He alarmed me. But my mind was so deadened by melancholy that I did not feel so tenderly as I have done. It seemed to me that, as there was no comfort in living, it was very indifferent how soon people were removed from life. I was in a miserable frame indeed.

TUESDAY 18 MARCH. My wife was rather easier, but I insisted that she should be blooded again, which was accordingly done by Mr. John Hunter. Though she had a horror at that operation, she during this illness behaved wonderfully well and submitted to it twice. She continued to be better all day. Mr. Devaynes visited her daily. I had settled with Sir George Baker on Thursday last that he should come when sent for, to which he very civilly agreed. The expense of a physician attending constantly at a guinea a day is a heavy article. Sir George was sent for both on Saturday and Monday. I had this forenoon a kind visit of Lord Kellie to inquire for my wife before setting out. He was to go next day. I had also a visit of John Wilkes, who looked very old but was better than when Courtenay and I saw him. He still talked with levity of the Christian religion, and seemed to take a mischievous pleasure in pointing out how often Johnson had written slightingly of me to Mrs. Thrale.[7] I was, however, glad to see him again, and to feel, as it were, some *revivification* of gaiety in my mind. I did *Life* with more satisfaction than for some days. In the morning had a short visit of Mr. Dilly, who was very desirous that I should put it fairly into the press.

WEDNESDAY 19 MARCH. In all day. *Life.*

THURSDAY 20 MARCH. In all day. *Life.* My wife was rather better these two days.

FRIDAY 21 MARCH. (Good Friday.) Had cross-buns to breakfast. Went to Langton's, and went with him to Whitehall Chapel, where Mr. Este read prayers and Dr. Ekins, Dean of Carlisle, preached. Felt the effect which decent apparatus has on *belief.* Walked to the City, intending to be at John Wesley's chapel in the afternoon, but it did not open till the evening. Did not dine, but had not much of the solemn sensations of a *fast.* There is no accounting for difference of feeling at different times. Worthy Langton by appointment drank coffee and tea with me. Malone came of his own accord. We had a very good literary evening, and they stayed and had oysters and ham and sat till one.

SATURDAY 22 MARCH. Breakfasted with Malone. At one, attended a meeting of the landholders of Scotland at the St. Alban's Tavern to consider of the representation of the counties. There was a respectable number of peers and commoners. I started (with great respect) a doubt as to the peers interfering. This roused them. Lord Hopetoun and Lord Kinnaird spoke, asserting their right, as did Lord Sempill, really very well. I was certainly well founded, but no gentleman joined me. There was a strange diversity of opinions. I was for explaining the old law and avoiding innovation, and this was carried by a considerable majority. I had heard that Lord Lonsdale was come, so I hastened to him and was admitted. He hailed me, "Mr. Recorder," and gave me an account how he had gone on since I left him. He asked me to dine with him on Tuesday. I dined quietly at home.

SUNDAY 23 MARCH. (Easter Day.) Breakfasted at the Chapter. Attended divine service at St. Paul's and received the Holy Sacrament with much devotion. I was pleased to observe Mr. Stewart, younger of Grandtully, communicate. My wife was now easier and this day came

---

[7]For example, "Boswell went away on Thursday night, with no great inclination to travel northward, but who can contend with destiny? . . . He carries with him two or three good resolutions; I hope they will not mould upon the road" (18 May 1776).

down and sat in the drawing-room. I called Sir George Baker, that he might give her directions how to go on. But he said little and seemed dry because his attendance was not desired. He said to me, "I am not to flatter *you*. She is by no means well yet. The fever is not gone." I dined at Malone's with Dr. Farmer, Master of Emmanuel, Cambridge (who had officiated today as a canon residentiary of St. Paul's), Courtenay, Kemble, Reed, Langton, young Jephson. We were very social and sat till between one and two, but I recollect none of the conversation.

MONDAY 24 MARCH. (See a note of this morning.)[8] Was heated and somewhat uneasy from having taken too much wine yesterday. Called on Courtenay, with whom I walked to Hampstead Heath, and got into excellent spirits, enjoying fine fresh air; then dined with him tête-à-tête on mutton broth and mackerel and drank mountain and old port moderately. We sat till eleven and felt no cessation of talk.

TUESDAY 25 MARCH. Dined at Lord Lonsdale's with Mr. John Home, Sir Michael le Fleming, Sir James Johnstone,[9] Colonel Lowther; a very excellent day. Much good wine.

WEDNESDAY 26 MARCH. Called on Courtenay, who had asked me to negotiate for him a loan of £200 from Dilly on a deposit of his books. We walked into the City together and Dilly readily agreed, in case the books should be estimated at a sum a good deal more. They were lying at the Tower in safe custody; so Courtenay, who had waited for me in Sewell's shop, proposed that we should go thither and inquire about them, which we did, and brought the catalogue to Dilly. I would have had Courtenay to come home with me to dinner, but he objected that it would disturb my family when my wife was ill. So we first went to Billingsgate to have good mackerel, but there were none left, so we contented ourselves with the variety of a beefsteak, porter, and punch at Dolly's, where I had not been, I believe, for twenty years. We then drank coffee at the London Coffee-house and ended the evening at the Essex Head Club, to which he went as my guest. Present: Barrington, Brocklesby, Wyatt. Courtenay was a valuable addition. Indeed his conversation is excellent; it has so much literature, wit, and, at the same time, manly sense in it. I wondered at his tranquillity when he talked of his having no more left than might keep him going for a year. He quoted Marcus Antoninus's sentiment that a man should think only of the present, and he would be satisfied that whatever evil is allotted to him may be borne patiently.[1] On Monday he rationally

[8]The note has disappeared.
[9]Of Westerhall, Bt.; M.P. for Dumfries Burghs.
[1]This stoic sentiment occurs frequently in the *Meditations*.

observed to me that the fortune which I had would not do more than furnish such a family as mine bare necessaries in London, and that this consideration, joined to my wife's disagreeing with the air here, should determine me to carry my family back to Scotland and just float myself between London and it. He that day, though unhappily not a believer except in a Supreme Being, owned that every other subject was nothing compared with immortality, were it but true.

THURSDAY 27 MARCH. Called on Lord Lonsdale, who asked me to dine with him, he being to go north again next day. There were Sir Michael le Fleming, Colonel Lowther, and Mr. Cawthorne, Member for Lincoln. A very good day again. I felt myself now really well with him, and Cumberland freeholds being mentioned, begged his Lordship would get one purchased for me, which he promised to do for less than £50, with this condition only: that when I chose to part with it, I should sell it to him. The more strings by which I am connected with LOWTHER, the better.

FRIDAY 28 MARCH. At home and laboured at *Life*. My wife was rather better but recovering very slowly, and my being so much abroad appeared very unkind to her, though I was *conscious* of sincere regard. At the same time let me fairly mark the modifications of feeling by time and circumstances. I certainly had not that tenderness and anxiety which I once had, and could look with my mind's eye upon the event of her being removed by death with much more composure than formerly. This I considered as humanely ordered by Providence; yet I was not without some upbraidings as if I were too selfish, from leading what may be called a life of pleasure. My enthusiasm for my *Family*— for *Auchinleck*—has abated since I plunged into the wide speculative scene of English ambition.

SATURDAY 29 MARCH. Called on Courtenay, who promised to meet me at Malone's. Lord Sempill had left a card for me yesterday. I left one for his Lordship today. Perhaps it is not wise in me to keep myself so much abstracted as I do from Scotchmen of all ranks. Malone asked Courtenay and me to dine with him, but I insisted that we should meet at my house, to which they agreed; and I ran to Sir Joshua's and was lucky enough to find him disengaged, and secured him. Malone accompanied me to the Prerogative Office in Doctors' Commons, where I inspected Alderman Atkinson's will, as to the tenor of which, so far as it respected Lady Anne Lindsay, there was a bet of a dinner at the London Tavern on the first of May, laid between Sir Michael le Fleming and Sir James Johnstone at Lord Lonsdale's.[2] Young Jephson went

[2]Boswell made a memorandum of this bet, laid on 25 March, which Johnstone and le Fleming signed, but if the dinner took place he does not mention it. Richard Atkinson

with us. He was engaged to dinner. Malone looked at the will of old Burbage, the player.[3] I was highly pleased with the order in which the wills were kept, and the tranquillity of the scene made me form a momentary wish to pass my time as one of those employed there.

The *Gang* saw my wife in the drawing-room before dinner. My two eldest daughters dined with us, and we had a very good day and sat till one in the morning. Sir Joshua maintained that there was no such thing as a natural good ear for music in one person more than in another, but that it was all art, as occasion and study operated. We all joined against him. Malone as strangely maintained that a man has the same fondness as a lover for a woman who has been for years his own as for the finest woman whom he has never possessed. Sir Joshua justly observed that admitting this was setting aside two of the strongest principles of human nature: desire of preference and novelty, which were given us for wise purposes. He said that something else very comfortable, very valuable, came in place of fondness when there had been possession; there was then affection, friendship. He said the reason why he would never marry was that every woman whom he had liked had grown indifferent to him, and he had been glad that he did not marry her. He had no reason therefore to suppose that it would not be the same as to any other woman.

SUNDAY 30 MARCH. In the forenoon was with some of my children at the chapel in our own street. In the evening tried to hear Mr. Wesley, but he was at Bristol. Called on Dilly and he and I drank a bottle of old hock.

MONDAY 31 MARCH. Some *Life*.

TUESDAY 1 APRIL. Dined at the Literary Club and was in the chair. Present: Bishop of St. Asaph, Dr. Fordyce, Mr. Steevens, Mr. Malone, Dr. Burney, Sir Joshua Reynolds. Took rather too much wine, but was in excellent spirits.

WEDNESDAY 2 APRIL. Somewhat uneasy; dined at Sir Joshua Reynolds's with Courtenay, Malone, Devaynes, Metcalfe, Sir George

---

(d. 1785), M.P., alderman of London, and West Indies planter, is variously described as having had a platonic admiration for Lady Anne Lindsay and as having been her unsuccessful suitor. In any case he left her a large fortune, including an annuity of £700. Johnstone claimed that Atkinson's will mentioned a "love correspondence" and left money to her three children (she was unmarried) and the one with which she was then pregnant. The will says nothing of any correspondence or of living children; it does make provision for any children she might have in the future. In 1793, at the age of forty-two, Lady Anne married Andrew Barnard, son of the Bishop of Limerick (formerly of Killaloe). Their marriage was childless.

[3] Richard Burbage, the most famous of Elizabethan actors. Malone printed part of the will in the Variorum Shakespeare of 1821.

Beaumont,[4] Sir Abraham Hume, Sir Harry Englefield, Sir Joshua's nephews (Mr. John Palmer and Mr. Johnston), Mr. ——— from India, Mr. Wilbraham.[5] Quite a hurly-burly, but very pleasant. Courtenay and Metcalfe and Sir Joshua and I sat till between twelve and one.

THURSDAY 3 APRIL. Some *Life*.

FRIDAY 4 APRIL. Ditto.

SATURDAY 5 APRIL. My wife had for some days been very low-spirited, but her illness was rather lessened than increased. I dined at Courtenay's with Dr. Brocklesby, Malone, young Jephson, Sir Joshua Reynolds, and Mr. Burke, hearing of the party, fell in upon us, and brought Dr. Laurence with him. Sir Joshua carried me in his coach, and as we drove along he observed how very false the commonplace observation was that there is no medium in marriage, for that the parties are either very happy or very miserable; whereas there is nothing in which there are more shades of variety. I agreed with him, and added that so far was the commonplace observation from being true, though always in the mouths of misses to show their delicate sensibility, that nothing was so rare as to find either a very happy or a very unhappy couple. Man and wife in general do wonderfully well in a kind of middle state. Burke as usual was full of talk. He gave a total denial to the authenticity of Macpherson's Gaelic translations; said he was informed in the Highlands that Macpherson had a great readiness in turning English into Erse verse, and therefore he believed every specimen of the original which was now repeated had been fabricated since Macpherson's publication. He denied that there was such a word as "Gaelic," and said "Fingal" and "Ossian" were sounds invented for English ears. He offered me a bet that I should not produce a Highlander who could repeat one line of Macpherson's poetry in Erse, provided he was fairly taken without being tutored or prepared. Courtenay said he knew a Colonel Campbell (brother of Kilberry) who could repeat some fragments. "Nay," said Burke,

> Sure the pleasure is as great
> In being cheated as to cheat.[6]

This Colonel has something in his mind which he supposes the same with Macpherson's but never has compared them." I began to think that really the whole might be a forgery. He talked of the inequalities

[4]Connoisseur and landscape-painter, patron of Wordsworth.
[5]At this point Boswell left a blank for more names. Englefield was an antiquary and writer on science.
[6]Altered from Samuel Butler, *Hudibras*, II. iii. 1–2.

which we see in this life and therefore of the probability of a future state from that consideration alone. His religion is always consolatory. I am sorry my record is so imperfect. Malone and young Jephson and I stayed some time after the rest. They accompanied me to the end of Oxford Street.

SUNDAY 6 APRIL. In the forenoon was at the chapel in our own street with some of my children. The strange mortal Stockdale preached.[7] Called on Lord Eglinton and left a card. Dined at home. The children said divine lessons.

MONDAY 7 APRIL. I should have mentioned that having read in the Edinburgh newspapers that a man had been *proved* to be the same person who had been capitally convicted and broken prison and therefore had been of new sentenced to be hanged without a jury being called to try his identity, though he demanded it, I was shocked at the illiberal tyranny of the Court of Justiciary and wished to be out of a country where such power prevailed. Though I had by no means that grateful return[8] from my country for my animated interposition to preserve the Court of Session, I again resolved to exert myself in a great question, and intended to wait upon several of the Scotch, and perhaps some English, Members of Parliament to get the execution (which was to be on the 2 April) prevented. But it occurred to me that it would be better first to call on Lord Advocate, with whom I was on friendly terms. I accordingly did so on the morning of the 24 March, and to my agreeable surprise found that his Lordship was of the same opinion with me and had sent to Lord Sydney's office to have the man (Peter Young) reprieved till 2 July.[9] I smiled and said, "How agreeable is it when we find you great men do right, that is, as we think." I should have mentioned also that Seward, who had been so ill at Bath as to be *confined,* had called on me, and I had next morning breakfasted with him and found him as well as ever. I was yesterday and today much distressed with a swelled cheek occasioned by a severe toothache. Did *Life.*

---

[7]Perceval Stockdale, army officer turned clergyman and miscellaneous writer, mixed in London literary circles. He was aggrieved that the London booksellers had engaged Johnson, who had been his protector, rather than himself to write the *Lives of the Poets,* and in general cherished grand illusions about his abilities as a writer.

[8]This sentence seems to need some such words as "I deserved" at this point.

[9]Young gained nothing in the end, for he was identified and hanged on the day set for the reprieve. Twenty-four years old, he had been condemned at Aberdeen for breaking into a shop and stealing a considerable quantity of goods. As Secretary of State for the Home department, Lord Sydney handled cases involving reprieve.

TUESDAY 8 APRIL. Mr. Hoole breakfasted with me and gave me some letters from Dr. Johnson to him and some notes of his last days. Did some *Life*. At night, though my cheek was not yet well, went to the first night of Lady Wallace's comedy;[1] sat sometimes in the gallery, sometimes in the slips.[2] It was very dull, and the insolent support of a party for her was provoking. I was at last well entertained with the tumultous contest between saving and damning it. I thought it was damned.[3]

WEDNESDAY 9 APRIL. Went to Peele's[4] and read all the newspapers on the new comedy, which was justly lashed. The Lord Provost of Edinburgh (Mr. Grieve) breakfasted with me and delivered me my diploma of the freedom of that city, granted to me in 1784.[5] I was much pleased and thought with no dissatisfaction of returning to my native city. Some *Life*.

THURSDAY 10 APRIL. Went to Peele's and read more strictures on the comedy; had met with nothing for a long time that gave me a lively agitation till this, so indulged it and went again at night, when it was again played, and again a tumultous contest ensued. Mr. Lewes begged it might be allowed to be played one night more.[6] This was great meanness in a lady.[7]

FRIDAY 11 APRIL. Dined at Sir Joshua Reynolds's with Lord Monboddo, Mr. Courtenay, Mr. Malone, Mr. Gibbon, Dr. Ash, Mr. Langton, Dr. Brocklesby, etc. Monboddo to my surprise spoke courteously to me.[8] He was as wildly dogmatical as ever on the supreme preference of the ancients. Brocklesby boldly asserted that Burke's speeches would a thousand years hence be much more admired than Demosthenes' orations, for they comprehended much more extensive knowledge and

---

[1] *The Ton, or Follies of Fashion*, by Eglantine Maxwell, an Edinburgh friend. Beautiful and high-spirited, she had divorced Thomas Dunlop-Wallace of Craigie, self-styled baronet, on grounds of repeated adultery and made an independent life in London and later on the Continent.

[2] The sides of the gallery.

[3] That is, it would not be repeated.

[4] A coffee-house on Fleet Street frequented by practitioners of the law, where, reputedly, all the newspapers published in Great Britain were taken in.

[5] On 15 September, as a consequence of his opposition to Fox's East India Bill.

[6] According to the *London Chronicle* the noise was so great that the end of the fourth act had to be performed in pantomime, and shortly after the beginning of the fifth act a quart bottle was thrown from the gallery into the pit, injuring a woman in the audience. Lady Wallace charged that a cabal which feared exposure of its vices had plotted to damn the play as indecent.

[7] Because the third night was the author's benefit.

[8] See above, 12 January 1786 and n. 3.

philosophy and allusion. I endeavoured to rouse Monboddo to speak by saying that the philosophy in Demosthenes' time was very narrow. Malone also with the same view expatiated on the richness of imagery in Burke's speeches, but Monboddo was on his guard and said nothing. I tried also to incite him by saying that a priori all things that did not involve a contradiction were equally probable, so that belief of them must depend on evidence. I had also an eye to Gibbon, who sat snug and would not venture. I said that Tertullian's expression, "Ego credo quia est impossibile,"[9] was noble in the sense in which he meant it. I was too warm in exclaiming upon the question whether the same body could be in several places at once, so as to show a *catholic* zeal. Monboddo said nothing aloud against Johnson but whispered to Langton that our nation had disgraced themselves by allowing genius to Johnson and learning to Clarke.[1] There was a pleasant circumstance when he maintained there was no rhythm in the English language, and to show that there was in Latin, quoted from Horace and altered a word so as to have a false quantity.[2] Langton and I and Malone and Courtenay sat a long time after the rest, and all of us except Malone supped. My wife's complaints were rather easier, and my spirits were pretty good.

SATURDAY 12 APRIL. Was in a great flow of spirits, so that though I had resolved to work at *Life* all day, could not settle. After breakfasting in a hurry, called on Seward and drank some coffee with him. Mr. Lysons came, and from him I filled up a great many of the blanks in Dr. Johnson's *Letters to Mrs. Piozzi*.[3] I sat awhile with Malone; dined at home, my brother David with us. Just as dinner was done, which happened today to be almost nothing but a piece of cold roast beef, Mr. Burke came in a hackney-coach and was shown upstairs. I had some days ago written to him, begging that he would dine with me next Saturday (this day) or any other Saturday, and I would get Sir Joshua,

[9]"I believe because it is impossible." The actual words are *"certum est quia,"* etc. ("The Son of God was born—it causes no shame because it is shameful; and the Son of God died—it is credible precisely because it is absurd; and he was buried and rose again —it is certain because it is impossible"—ch. 5.)
[1]Samuel Clarke, D.D. (1675–1729), regarded as perhaps the most eminent metaphysician and theologian of his time, though suspected of deism and Arianism. Editions of Caesar and Homer exemplify his versatile erudition.
[2]Boswell here left a blank for the quotation from Horace but failed to recall it. Someone (perhaps Langton) must have told him about the false quantity. Boswell knew a good deal of Horace by heart, but he never mastered the principles of scansion.
[3]Samuel Lysons, a young antiquary, had been of great help to Mrs. Piozzi in the publication of her *Anecdotes* and the *Letters*: he had read all Johnson's originals and had helped Mrs. Piozzi excise the names and passages which she did not wish to appear in print.

etc., to meet him. He wrote me a very obliging answer that he could not engage, but if I would let him know any day when I had company, he would fall in upon me as he did at Mr. Courtenay's. He had imagined this was a day on which he might do so. He asked my servant if I had friends with me and, hearing not, said he had mistaken the day, begged I might not be disturbed, and hoped he would be more lucky another time, and then hurried off. I was much vexed. But I did right not to follow him and ask him in when I had neither dinner nor company for him. It was really unlucky. After sitting a proper time, I went to Sir Joshua's, where I supposed he might be and where I found he had called, but Sir Joshua was abroad. I then hastened to Malone's to consult. He also was abroad. I called at Mr. Burke's house. He was not at home. I left my card.[4] I came home to tea. Then went to see the new comedy the third night, but it was over.

SUNDAY 13 APRIL. In the forenoon paid some visits, that is, made some calls, at Sir John Dick's, Captain Macbride's, and Mr. MacLeod of Colbecks's, whom I found at home, and sat a little while with him; also found Lord Eglinton, who seemed to me somewhat awkward and rather less proud. Was at our own chapel in the afternoon and so calmly devout that I could have died in peace. Dined at home. The children said divine lessons. Found Mr. Burke at home in the morning and explained yesterday's misfortune. He said he found he was engaged at another place.

MONDAY 14 APRIL. Breakfasted with Sir Joshua Reynolds, who told me that Sheridan had sent him an excuse and he wished I would fill up his place that day at dinner. I luckily was not engaged. I told him I was much obliged to him for so many agreeable parties. He said he should be glad to have me at every dinner he gave, but he had so many to invite. I was much flattered by his friendly attention. We had at dinner today Mr. and Mrs. Burke, Dick the brother and Richard the son, Dr. Laurence, Rev. Dr. Parr, Mr. Gibbon, Sir Gilbert Elliot, Mr. Windham, Jack Lee. Burke came late, being detained by an East India examination. I said it was a *cross*-examination. Dr. Parr told us he was to write about Dr. Johnson. He had found out forty points of

---

[4]Boswell's agitated response to Burke's call stemmed from continued uneasiness about their relations, as he had told Burke in the dinner invitation. Burke repeatedly denied any estrangement, and he wrote now, in response to Boswell's invitation, that Boswell had given a "wrong construction" to his late manner, which arose from the little command he had over his time. He closed the letter with the "most unfeigned respect and regard."

similarity between him and Plutarch.[5] Burke said Plutarch was a most
agreeable writer, indeed the only one who was read with pleasure in
a translation. Gibbon instanced also Melmoth's Pliny's *Letters*, which he
thought better than the original, for all that was valuable was preserved,
without his quaintness.[6] Burke agreed, and said that Pliny was very
ostentatious and made the most of all the taste and all the virtue he
had. Dick Burke was too rough and wild in his manner today, and I
could perceive either liked me worse than his brother did or had less
art to conceal his dislike—on account of politics. The Burkes and Windham and Lee and Gibbon and I went up to tea. Gibbon with polite
gravity, though perhaps he was laughing inwardly, made Burke give
the history of the Coalition and of their being turned out. Burke said
that no Ministry in this country could go on without the King. That
they wished to please him, but there was no being certain how to do
it.[7] Lee talked of Dunning; of his getting £8,000 a year by his profession ·
but being killed by it; that it was literally with him "animasque in vulnere
ponunt,"[8] and that he had a great contempt for lords.[9] Burke with
great propriety took up this (which was indeed *trimming* Jack Lee himself) and said there never was a man who affected to despise lords who
had not an extreme respect for them, mixed with envy. I had for some
time been quite satisfied as to the *imposition* of Jack Lee's bluntness. He
brought me home in his coach and wanted me to go to his house and
have some punch, though it was eleven o'clock. But I refused. Before
I knew him as I do now, I should have gone.

TUESDAY 15 APRIL. Dined at home. Some *Life*.[1]

[5]Samuel Parr, an erudite but pompous clergyman and schoolmaster, never wrote a
life of Johnson, but he used to say that if he had, it would have been the third most
learned work ever to appear.
[6]William Melmoth translated the *Letters of Pliny the Younger*, 1746.
[7]The Fox-North Coalition (April–December 1783) had been forced out of office partly
because of the King's intense dislike of it.
[8]Virgil, *Georgics*, iv. 238: "[Bees, in the act of stinging,] give up their lives in the wound
[they make]."
[9]Dunning, the foremost lawyer of his day, author of the famous motion of 6 April
1780 to diminish the influence of the Crown and also of a successful measure for
economic reform, was made a peer under the Rockingham Administration in 1782
and granted a pension of £4,000 a year. He died in August 1783.
[1]A letter to Temple is registered on this day: "Of my wife's uncertain state, and my
indecision. On that account alone would have entreated him to come to console me
as a friend and a divine. Entreat he may not fail, but may relieve me from the dismal
apprehension that 'my friendship with Temple has perished.' " As it happened, a stern
letter from Temple, dated 14 April, crossed Boswell's: "Certainly everything now has
appeared that can be of any use and, if not interrupted by the business of your
profession, you can have no excuse for not going forward with your great work."

WEDNESDAY 16 APRIL. At home all day. Some *Life*. Mr. Malone, who had been in the City, drank tea and supped with me. I was comforted and enlivened over a moderate glass. He animated me by the hopes of my yet having success in life, and said that the fame which my *Life of Johnson* would give me, though Lord Lonsdale did not know much of that subject, would still contribute to his valuing me more.

THURSDAY 17 APRIL. Some *Life*. Dined at Mr. Langton's with Sir Joshua Reynolds, Miss Palmer, Mr. Courtenay, Mr. Malone, young Jephson; a good quiet day.

FRIDAY 18 APRIL. I went to the King's levee, not having been at Court for a long time, not since ———.[2] I thought it would be a quiet day. But there was a great crowd. The King only asked me, "Have you come from Scotland lately?" BOSWELL. "No, Sir. I have been some time here." I dined at home.

SATURDAY 19 APRIL. Having received from Francis Barber a letter authorizing me to demand from Sir John Hawkins all books or papers that belonged to Dr. Johnson which remained in his possession, of which I had acquainted Sir John and begged to know when I might wait on him to receive them, I had received from the Knight a very civil answer, with which his second son called, and fixed this evening at six; but upon my suggesting that I was engaged and that it would be more convenient for me any morning, he politely sent the young gentleman again to give me my choice either of this day or Monday at eleven in the forenoon. I accordingly was with him a few minutes after the hour, by Westminster Abbey clock, and found him with a crimson velvet nightcap on and his eldest son with him, who stood by all the time while Sir John and I settled the business, which we did in perfect good humour. He complimented me on my coming exactly to my time. I said, "I am as regular as you, Sir John; at least, I wish to be so." There were but three pamphlets, the three diplomas of degrees from Dublin and Oxford,[3] and a few papers, for which I gave a receipt, "as witness my hand at Westminster." We sat most serenely opposite to each other in armchairs, and I declare, he talked so well and with such a courteous formality that every five minutes I unloosed a knot of the critical cat-o'-nine-tails which I had prepared for him. I stayed above an hour. How much might human violence and enmity be lessened if men who fight with their pens at a distance would but commune together calmly face to face! I sat with Sir John Hawkins above an

[2] His last recorded attendance was on 11 May 1787.
[3] The M.A. and D.C.L. from Oxford, 1755 and 1775 respectively, and the LL.D. from Dublin, 1765.

hour, and I told him that if there was any particular paper which he wished to have, I would get it for him. He defended himself, I thought very well, from the charge of the gold-headed cane which Francis's letter mentioned, but I told him fairly of Francis's complaint that he did not go at first to Mudge, the maker of his master's watch, to get it valued, as his valuation was double that of the others.[4] Sir John said to me, "You are Recorder of Carlisle, Sir." "I have that honour, Sir"; upon which he presented me with his *Charge to the Grand Jury of Middlesex*,[5] for which I returned him thanks. He desired his son to write upon it "from the author." I asked him to do it with his own hand, to authenticate it, for without such authenticity a vain man might buy the works of all the eminent men of his age and get them marked, "From the Author." He thought me right and took his pen, adding, "I will appropriate it by mentioning your name—*James* Boswell, Esq.?" Here I in good humour gave him a fair touch on his studied attempt to represent me as an obscure man, "Or in your own style, 'Mr. James Boswell, a native of Scotland.'" Said he: "There is no occasion for that."[6] We parted quite placidly. I went and sat awhile with worthy Langton, who wondered and was pleased at this interview. I thought I would spare Hawkins as much as I in justice could.

I walked through the park, and when I came to the door of the Green Park into Piccadilly and looked through the keyhole to see if anybody was coming to open it, I, to my very agreeable surprise, saw my wife on the outside, who was waiting with the same view. This was quite romantic. The Bishop of St. Asaph let her in. Phemie and Betsy were with her. We walked some time and rested on one of the seats,

---

[4]Sir John had appropriated the cane, which someone had left by accident in Dr. Johnson's house before his death, and though the other executors "in vain urged that Francis had a right to this till an owner appeared," as Malone reported, Hawkins would not restore it, "and his house being soon afterwards consumed by fire, he *said* it was there burnt." (A. L. Reade, *Johnsonian Gleanings*, 1909-52, ii. 53). Hawkins was also charged with having secured a low valuation on Johnson's watch so that he could purchase it cheaply for himself. Barber had prevented this by refusing to sell. Thomas Mudge, partner with William Dutton, was the King's watchmaker.
[5]Sir John, a magistrate, had published two pamphlets with this title, in 1770 and 1780.
[6]Hawkins's only reference to Boswell, though it perhaps does not seem so slighting if taken in its context, certainly does not indicate that Boswell was well known: "[Dr. Johnson] had long been solicited by Mr. James Boswell, a native of Scotland, and one that highly valued him, to accompany him in a journey to the Hebrides." Boswell, in discussing with Temple in the following year his own strictures on Hawkins in the *Life of Johnson*, says, "Hawky is no doubt very malignant. Observe how he talks of me as if quite unknown." He retaliated by introducing his rival as "Mr. John Hawkins, an attorney."

and then she went home in a hackney-coach which was waiting for her. It was wonderful to see her so well. Some days ago she was in dismal low spirits and mournfully exclaimed, with death before her eyes, "Oh, I am terrified for the dark passage." My heart was most tenderly touched, but I could do her no good, for all my consolatory pious suggestions were not congenial to her too rational mind. I was in charming spirits today and said I could die easily. She said she could not, but she was not in the melancholy frame which I have described.

I went to Courtenay's and found him at home, and got him to correct a letter which I had written to Mr. Pitt desiring once more to see him;[7] and I was much obliged to Courtenay's judgement. He at the same time told me candidly that he thought I had no claim for anything from Pitt, because I had written my pamphlet against Fox's India Bill from principle as against what I thought a bad measure, without regard to party; and that I had no claim from Dundas because I had afterwards opposed his measure of diminishing the Scotch judges. All this I was sensible was just. But as I had done the King's cause essential service, I thought I was entitled to a reward; and as Mr. Dundas had engaged some years ago by letter to assist me in obtaining promotion, and had declared upon his honour, in a conversation with me, that my Court of Session pamphlet had not been taken ill by him, I trusted that he would keep his word, or rather I was *determined* that by and by he *should*, otherwise he should answer to me.[8] I dined at Malone's with Mr. Byng, his lady and two daughters, Miss Cecilia Forrest, the two Palmers, Courtenay, and young Jephson. We had a very good day, though I recollect no particulars. I played two rubbers at whist and a little vingt-et-un, and upon the whole won. We stayed supper, and the ladies and Byng and the Palmers did not leave us till I suppose about two. The rest of us sat till five, but without much drinking.

SUNDAY 20 APRIL. When Courtenay and young Jephson and I found ourselves in the street, it was so very fine a morning that Courtenay thought it was a pity to go to bed and proposed a walk to Hampstead. I agreed with some reluctance, for I considered that my wife would be very uneasy about me. However, I could not resist, and was *led away*, as the phrase is, though once or twice I was for turning, as I

[7]The letter was not registered and may not have been sent.
[8]In the letter of 30 March 1785 to which Boswell alludes Dundas wrote that he should be happy if he "could produce any satisfactory result" from a promise made the previous December to make an earnest effort to assist Boswell. But Boswell's *Letter to the People of Scotland*, 1785, had changed their relationship (see above, 8 July 1786 and n. 4).

was almost asleep. I roused by degrees and was happy to hear Jephson argue very well for the truth of Christianity. His father's instructions had not been lost upon him. We found no house at Hampstead that pleased us; so we crossed over to near Highgate and breakfasted heartily on coffee, tea, and eggs, and bread and butter, in a house which had a garden, in which we walked. I know not how we got over so much time, but it was between ten and eleven when we returned to Malone's, had him called up, and took an additional breakfast with him. Old Macklin joined us. This was quite an Irish morning to me.[9]

I was sorry to find that my wife had sent to inquire for me. It was twelve when I got home. She had been informed at seven that I was not come home and was so agitated with anxiety that she was more feverish and spit more blood. This was shocking to me. I shaved and dressed and took my two sons with me and waited on Sir Thomas Miller, the new Lord President, who appeared old, but revived in my mind some comfortable ideas of my youth. On my return home Lord Advocate called on me; he had sent me the papers and opinions of the judges on the Case of Young as to identity requiring a jury trial, and he asked me to write my opinion in a letter to him, for he was getting all the light he could and consulting all the Scotch lawyers here; they differed in opinion. Mr. Dundas was against a jury; Sir Adam Fergusson for it. I dined quietly with my family, after having been at our chapel. My brother's wife and her mother drank tea with us. I was very drowsy and went early to bed.

MONDAY 21 APRIL. Wrote and sent to Lord Advocate my opinion on Young's Case. Sauntered about, I know not now where. Dined at General Paoli's; only Gentili there. Heated myself with wine.

TUESDAY 22 APRIL. Idle as yesterday. But for the first time had Edmund Burke at my table. I was very anxious to have him, and never was sure till he actually appeared.[1] He behaved wonderfully well. My wife and daughters dined at table. *She* was not so much struck with him as I wished. *They* were. She said he must be a very perfect politician who could conceal the resentment which he must entertain against me for having so keenly opposed his party, but that she believed he would show it whenever he had an opportunity. Sir Joshua Reynolds, who was engaged to be with us, was unfortunately carried off by an annual engagement to a previous dinner with the Council of the Royal Acad-

[9] Courtenay, Jephson, Malone, and Macklin were all Irish.
[1] Boswell was so anxious, in fact, that he sent Burke two reminders of the engagement, one on 16 April ("it will be a great mortification to be disappointed") and another on this very day.

emy, to taste the wines for their Exhibition Dinner. But we had Courtenay, Malone, young Jephson, and Metcalfe (first time). Burke said that it was a very bad plan to put a young gentleman who was to follow the law first to an attorney; that considering the law solely as a *lucrative trade*, it might be well to do so, for thus he would form intimacies with attorneys and their clerks and get sure business. But that it was very wrong to give narrow and contracted notions to men who might one day decide upon the lives and properties of the subjects of this country, nay, arrive at the highest honours and have a great sway in the state. He said it was proper for gentlemen at the bar to cultivate in a certain degree the acquaintance of attorneys to whom they were to owe their being employed; and he had no objection that after a lawyer was come a certain length, and had his habits formed liberally, he should go for some time into an attorney's office and perfect himself in forms.[2] All of them but Metcalfe drank tea. Malone, Courtenay, and Jephson supped. I regret that I did not attend better and record more of Burke. He was quite easy and polite and told me I had a fine family. I looked back to my first views of him as author of the *Sublime and Beautiful*[3] and *felt* that I was now wonderfully up in the scale of literary and intellectual society. I was sorry to perceive Courtenay looking dark, as I supposed from thinking on the wretched state of his affairs.

WEDNESDAY 23 APRIL. I did little or nothing this forenoon but go again to the levee, where I saw Sir Thomas Miller presented. His earnest anxiety was striking at a distance. I was not near him. I afterwards said to Langton, "How little did even the chief of the law in Scotland appear in the great world of London!" "Ay," said Langton, "and think of his going back: *reddarque tenebris*."[4] It was a crowded Court. The King was as ineffective today to me as on Friday. He said, "Have you been much in Scotland this year?" "No, Sir. I was there last year." "You have not been there at all this year?" I suggested to Langton afterwards that this might be perverseness. He said no, mere thoughtlessness; for he often began with him asking about the weather. I once thought of answering, "When was Your Majesty in Hanover?" or, "I go more to Scotland than Your Majesty goes to Hanover." Langton at first thought this might do very well, but on second thoughts he justly saw it would be improper. He owned to me that the King had one day

[2]Many law students began their training by attending in an attorney's office. Attorneys, who practised in the common law courts, held a lower social and professional status than solicitors or barristers.
[3]Published in 1757.
[4]Virgil, *Aeneid*, vi. 545: "And I shall return to the darkness"—the speech of the shade of Deiphobus, whom Aeneas has met in the underworld.

been in bad humour about my conference with him on the designation of Prince Charles, and said to Barnard and Nicol in his library, "He asked me how he should name the Pretender. I did not care how."[5] I dined at Dilly's with Dr. Towers, Dr. Gillies, Dr. Sims,[6] Mr. Lofft, Alderman Macauley. Gillies was so noisy we got no good out of the day. Home quiet.

THURSDAY 24 APRIL. Passed a part of the morning with Langton talking about the King and the drawing-room, to which I went today. A very great crowd. Could see neither Sir Thomas Miller nor his lady. Was charmed with Miss Vernon.[7] The King only said to me, "It is very warm weather; it is very close." I was weak enough to be vexed at his indifference to a zealous Tory. I called at Malone's, wishing to dine with him, but he was in the City. Came home. Was restless. In the evening found Malone and drank tea with him.

FRIDAY 25 APRIL. Was uneasy that Courtenay thought Dilly's charge for appraising and cataloguing his books too high, and that Dilly was fretted and the agreement was broke off. I called on Courtenay, who was in better humour, and desired to settle it without any reflections. The particulars would fill a page. I found Mr. Horace Walpole at home, just the same as ever: genteel, fastidious, priggish. He said he never read but one newspaper, and he did not care which, as all that he wanted to see was in every one of them—the marriages and deaths, that he might know where to send inquiries.[8] He said Johnson's letters to Mrs. Thrale were written in a very easy style and gave him a much better opinion of Johnson, for they showed him to have a great deal of affection. He said the sentiment which Johnson produced was pity, he was so miserable. It was cruel to publish his diary.[9] I said there was

[5] See above, 16 December 1785, n. 1. Frederick Augusta Barnard was the King's Librarian and George Nicol his bookseller.
[6] Joseph Towers, LL.D., dissenting minister and miscellaneous writer, author of an *Essay on the Life, Character, and Writings of Dr. Samuel Johnson,* 1786, and associate of Andrew Kippis in the new edition of the *Biographia Britannica,* 1778–93; John Gillies, LL.D., F.R.S., author of a popular *History of Ancient Greece,* 1786; and James Sims, M.D., president for twenty-two years of the Medical Society of London, author of books on medicine.
[7] Probably Caroline, aged twenty-six, second daughter of Richard Vernon and his wife Evelyn, Dowager Countess of Upper Ossory. She was one of "The Three Vernons" to whom Walpole addressed verses, and had been painted by Reynolds in his allegorical canvas, "St. George and the Dragon."
[8] As usual Walpole was not candid with Boswell, whom he thought it a virtue to deceive. He bought several newspapers and read them all carefully. At this very time he was cutting up newspapers and pasting articles and news onto folio sheets as part of his *Memoirs.*
[9] The *Prayers and Meditations,* published by George Strahan in 1785.

no man whose diary would not have weak and foolish things in it. "Yes," said he, "and therefore I wonder how any man should choose to review his own life." He said he considered the gout as a cure for other distempers, not as a distemper, and he would not be free of it if he could, for he knew how to manage it, he did not know how to manage other distempers; he thought it a kind of harlequin, for it often appeared in the shape of other complaints. *Horry's* constitutional tranquillity, or affectation of it, and the *tout ensemble* of his connections and history, etc., etc., pleased me. I marched on to Dilly's, and, as I thought, pacified him as to Courtenay's business. Dined at home. Do not recollect what I did in the evening.

SATURDAY 26 APRIL. Called on Malone and saw Courtenay there. Sauntered about. Dined with the Royal Academicians.[1] Sat between Sir Joseph Yorke and Malone. Was pleased to talk easily with Sir Joseph, by whom I was awed five-and-twenty years ago when he was Ambassador at The Hague.[2] I had also curious internal speculation on finding myself so well now, compared with my sickly state of mind in Holland. Before dinner the Lord Chancellor came up to me, shook me by the hand, and talked a word or two about a picture, and then broke off. This was a sort of *notice*, but very unsatisfactory. I told Malone I was tortured to see Lord Thurlow, Lord Loughborough, Lord Amherst, and all who had risen to high situation while I was nothing; but I trusted that my being so tortured was a sign that I was made for something great and that it would come. I relished my dinner and my wine and the show of pictures and company and the music. I *felt* myself high above anything in Scotland. As the company grew thin, I moved up to the President's table and got next to the Duke of Norfolk, who recognized me, and we drank some glasses together and talked easily enough, though I was under a cautious restraint, considering him as the violent opponent of Lord Lonsdale. I joked and said I had a mind to set up at Carlisle on the interest of the old voters; why should not they be for me as well as Christian or Stephenson, though I differed with them in opinion? He laughed at this. But I said I did not despair. He said Lord Lonsdale had given a proof that he was not of a convivial turn by not building a house at Lowther, though in possession of a great fortune for thirty years.[3] I asserted his conviviality

[1] The annual Exhibition Dinner.
[2] A stiff and pompous man, Yorke was gracious to Boswell, however, when Boswell was introduced to him in 1763, and invited him to dinners and balls.
[3] The central structure of Lowther Hall, which connected two old towers, had been destroyed by fire in 1726 and never properly rebuilt.

and expatiated on his exhibition at Whitehaven Castle. I heated my-
self somewhat with wine. I had not written one line of *Life* this week.
Sad idleness. I had one morning presented my brother David to Lord
Eglinton.

SUNDAY 27 APRIL. At home a good part of the forenoon. Was at
our own chapel in the afternoon with all my children. The calm tranquillity of a very thin congregation and Mr. Bevil's mild, elegant manner of preaching never fail to have a benignant effect on my mind. I
should have mentioned that Counsellor Scott[4] had long promised to
hold a conference with me as to what I should do at the English bar,
but he never had found time. I took my chance this morning of calling
on him. He was alone and at leisure. I stated to him that by the en-
couragement of Jack Lee and others I feared I had brought myself
into a scrape by removing from the Scotch to the English bar. His
opinion, which he said he gave upon honour, was in short this: that I
should be an universalist, sit sometimes in one court and sometimes
in another, and see where business would come; that two years could
not be reckoned a sufficient trial; that practice began by some fortunate
chance and then went on; that I should go the Northern Circuit both
spring and summer and have the fair chance of time; that my being
at the English bar for some time was no good objection to my being a
Scotch judge, and that in order to it, I should be as much as I could
in Scotch appeals in the House of Lords. He again animated me. But
my spirits were now so good that all things seemed easy. My wife went
to chapel with us, but finding herself uneasy, retired home before the
service began. I dined at General Paoli's; T.D. and a moderate company
there. Was somewhat heated with wine, but pleasingly. Walked long
in the crowd in St. James's Park. Was sorry I stayed out till it was, I
believe, past eleven. It appeared unkind to my wife, yet I was fully
conscious of affection for her.

MONDAY 28 APRIL. Resumed the labour of *Life*. Did so much.[5]
Dined at Mr. Devaynes's with a medical company: Sir W. Fordyce, Drs.
Hervey, Grieve, Garthshore (physicians), Mr. Heaviside (surgeon). Had
a tolerable day and drank tea comfortably in the drawing-room. Was
warmed with wine. Went to the Temple and walked about on the pavement with Fielding, who said immediate pleasant sensation and looking
a *little* forward agreeably constituted happiness. He expressed his belief
in a future state. I was sorry he was engaged on business, for I wished

[4] John Scott, K.C.
[5] A good deal.

to sup with him at the Grecian. I told him I intended to sit down at the Middlesex Sessions.

TUESDAY 29 APRIL. At home all day; not out of my slippers. Laboured at *Life*. At night was much distressed by seeing my wife in one of the feverish fits which come upon her at that time. She wandered and roved⁶ strangely. Her relief from them is by laudanum. Then follows a profuse sweat, which weakens her much. She has been also for some time, with a few intervals, troubled with a looseness. She was so emaciated that it was a pain to her to sit up in bed. I was in dismal apprehension.

WEDNESDAY 30 APRIL. Laboured at *Life* forenoon. Dined with Seward at a club at the Blenheim Coffee-house in New Bond Street, founded by Dr. Ash from Birmingham, of which I was admitted an honorary member, which obliges one only to attend on the anniversary or pay four shillings. There were twelve at table today. I did not like it much, but drank wine freely, which reconciled me to it. Seward said it should be called the *Fraxinean* Club from *fraxinus—ash*.⁷ Mr. Parsons the traveller, a genteel man, Mr. Trevor, Envoy at Turin, Lord Monboddo were there. The bill was called for at seven. Seward and I and a Mr. Allen, who had been educated in France, and Lord Monboddo had more wine and sat till ten. Monboddo and I were well enough, and, though crossly, he told me where he lodged when I said I intended to have the honour of paying my respects to him. Allen and I had a bottle of burgundy by ourselves and sat till eleven. How I got along I know not, for I have no recollection but of missing my ring in Cranbourne Alley and asking a watchman how I could recover it. I did not get home till two. I had but a shilling in my pocket when I left the tavern and that shilling I had next morning.

THURSDAY 1 MAY. Awaked very ill and very vexed. Walked out. Took a glass of brandy at Bedford Arms, Charlotte Street, which did me some good. Breakfasted with Malone but was quite confused. Went to the Blenheim Coffee-house and inquired if my ring had been seen. No accounts of it. Was more tranquil than on former occasions when it was lost. Malone and Seward, whom I visited, both thought the chance very bad this time for my recovering it. So did Dunn, the barber, who got it for me last year, for I had now no guess where I had lost it. I had handbills printed as soon as could be, describing it and offering

⁶Was light-headed or delirious; a Scotticism.
⁷The accepted name was the Eumelian Club, from the Homeric epithet for warriors, "armed with good ashen spear" (*eu* = well, *melia* = ash, spear). It was founded this year; Reynolds, Burney, and Windham were also members.

a guinea reward and, what was truly wonderful, the very first pawn-broker who got one produced it. He lived corner of Broad Court, Long Acre. He said a well-dressed man, who said he had found it in Long Acre, sold it to him that morning for the value of the gold—half a crown. I was exceedingly relieved.

In the forenoon when thirsty I had drank a bottle of cider at the old Cider Cellars, and then being somewhat uneasy, took another glass of brandy at Jupps's in Duke's Court, where I met Dr. Moffat, who, I found, dined here sometimes at a 14*d*. ordinary. He told me of Dundas's insolence to him. Seemed to wish I would look at his letters to Dundas, but I declined. I *felt*, as I have formerly done, that intoxication kept up makes me happy; at least not unhappy, but pleased. I dined heartily with my family on roast pork, drank a good deal of small beer and three glasses of port, and enjoyed my existence. How *material* is man! I myself am certainly much so. Signor and Signora Corri and their daughter drank tea with us, and they and my daughters really pleased me with music, and my wife seemed to be cheered by their company. I then went to Malone's and told my extraordinary good luck, saying it was a *magic ring*. He lectured me upon my intemperance and on my delaying Johnson's *Life*, on which I was to rest my fame. Young Jephson and he and I had some bread and cheese and hock, sugar, and water. Home quiet. On this first of May, felt a return of a certain warmth which had not disturbed me for some time. I experience all changes of constitution.

FRIDAY 2 MAY. Perceived that in my late intoxication I had sprained my ankle. At home all day. *Life*.

SATURDAY 3 MAY. My sprain was very uneasy, and what was worse, my wife was very ill and very low-spirited. Yet I could not resist dining at Devaynes's with Lord and Lady Townshend. I was inwardly shocked at my rage for pleasure, which made me leave a distressed wife, who never would have left me, even in the slightest illness. But I braved all tender checks, and truly I came to be satisfied that I had done right; for I added to my stock of pleasing subjects for recollection, and had I stayed at home, should have fretted and done my wife more harm than good. Lord Townshend was lively and droll and short today. His lady's beauty and affability charmed me, and his daughter, Lady Elizabeth, was very agreeable. The rest of the company were Courtenay, Sir Joshua Reynolds and Miss Palmer, and the Rev. Mr. Beauvoir, the clergyman, well advanced in life, whom Miss Sharp, a very great fortune, took a fancy to marry.[8] It was a very pleasant day. I really felt

[8]She was twenty-nine and he close to sixty when they were married in 1782. He died in 1789.

how uneasiness may be perfectly removed for a time by variety of ideas. Courtenay and I went home with Sir Joshua and had cold beef and punch. I came home in good time soberly and found my wife somewhat easier.

SUNDAY 4 MAY. Was at our own chapel in the forenoon with some of my children. Dined at General Paoli's, where was Seward. I was very moderate in drinking today. Tiberius Cavallo told me that his mother was nine years ill of a consumption of which she died; that she had a cough and spitting and sweatings; in short, she had the symptoms with which my wife is afflicted. I was very anxious and came home early. Found T.D. and his ladies.

MONDAY 5 MAY. Had not been in Westminster Hall this term. Resolved I would be there once, so went today, being the last of term, but without my wig and gown. The courts seemed much crowded, and I felt as if I could not contend with those whom I heard speaking with a perfect English accent. This was a temporary *nervous* shrinking. I am sure my accent is better than Jack Lee's.[9] I had another return of warmth of blood; was cautious against it. Had wavered much how to resolve as to my dear wife's going down: whether to go with her at all; whether to go only part of the way; whether to pay her the respect and satisfy my own anxiety by going all the way. She said that my going would be of no service, but I could not help thinking that if I did not she would feel very uneasily and that it would have the appearance of uncommon neglect. I thought I might go half way, or as far as Lowther for certain, and perhaps go on to Auchinleck. And I thought that by carrying with me my journals of the years 1783 and 1784, and what I had still to copy out and expand of 1783,[10] I might finish Johnson's *Life* in the country, go the Northern Circuit, or part of it, and after holding the Michaelmas Sessions at Carlisle, return to London and revise and correct and get all the work printed. Thus I considered, recollecting however that my wife might grow worse and detain me more. In short, I could not be precise in my plan. I hesitated also as to taking all the children down; but considering that it would be medicine to her to have them all with her and that they would be much the better for it, I fixed that they should all go. Her temper was so much hurt by her sufferings and her apprehensions that it was extremely difficult not to fret her. I had now for some time had wonderfully good spirits. T.D. and his ladies dined with us. I was comfortably rational with him and warmed myself moderately with wine.

[9]Lee was from County Durham.
[10]1781? Boswell did not meet Johnson in 1782.

TUESDAY 6 MAY. Fitzgerald dined. Martin came; sad day—*perdidi.*[1]

WEDNESDAY 7 MAY. Ill; to Westminster Hall with children. Dined home.

THURSDAY 8 MAY. Went to various places; night, opera of *Olympiade* and heard Marchesi with Ve and Euphemia.[2] Still resolved on setting out.

FRIDAY 9 MAY. Walked about with sprained ankle much, having determined to publish Johnson's supposed Nuptial *Ode.*[3]

SATURDAY 10 MAY. Went to Tower with all my children, T.D. accompanying.

[EDITORIAL NOTE. A manuscript found among Boswell's papers and inscribed in his hand "A Reflection by My Daughter Veronica at London, 10 May 1788" reports the excursion in detail. Because it is also an unaffected picture of the relationship between Boswell and his eldest child, who was now in her sixteenth year and much like him, we print the composition as she wrote it, except for the silent correction of a few obvious slips of the pen.]

on the 10th of May 1788 We went to the Tower to see that celebrated Building We saw The Wild beasts which are thought to be the most Worth seeing The first we saw was a Leopard a lioness given as a present to the king by Lord McArtney The Jackalls a Black Leopard which the keeper said was a very wonderful Animal that no historians had ever mentioned their having met with one of them We saw afterwards a most beautiful Lion he is quite the King of Animals when We came to him The Keeper said it shewed the power of the almighty in creating so many creatures for our inspection It surprised me to hear a man in his low station make so good a remark For my part I think the Characters one meets with in life are more worth attending to than Wild Beasts though they are less attended to. We paid 6*d* each

---

[1] "I have lost [a day]"—a remark of the Emperor Titus.

[2] A benefit performance of Cimarosa's *L'Olympiade* at the King's Theatre for Luigi Marchesi, the castrato who sang the lead.

[3] *Ode by Dr. Samuel Johnson to Mrs. Thrale upon Their Supposed Approaching Nuptials,* a parody of Johnson's style in which Johnson is presented as the accepted suitor of Mrs. Thrale, lustfully anticipating the delights of marriage; the first version of it was almost certainly composed at Sir Joshua Reynolds's on 12 April 1781 (for the text and a full account of its composition, see *Boswell, Laird of Auchinleck, 1778–1782,* ed. J. W. Reed and F. A. Pottle, 1977, pp. 316–21). Boswell back-dated the *Ode* to 1784, the year of Mrs. Thrale's marriage to Gabriel Piozzi and Johnson's death, promoting it by a teasing paragraph in the *Public Advertiser* (12 May 1788) and a vulgar set of verses entitled "A Thralian Epigram" published in the same newspaper the next day.

We saw a Lioness who has got a dog who lives with her The keeper said she was miserable if he was absent from her half an hour I cant tell with how much regret I leave this place but trust that Mamas health will be reestablished and then we must not complain. When I was at the Tower this morning I plucked a branch from a tree that I might preserve the leaves. When at Auchinleck I shall deposit them in my cabinet I cant forbear sighing at the thought of leaving this beloved Place If I had been told that I was to like this Metropolis the third part as well as I do I should never have believed it could be possible. how often have I blamed my father for his Love for this place and Now I am as bad

I remember now that I was very peevish this Morning at the Tower. When My Brothers were going into the Tower to see the Armoury Phemie and I were not allowed to go upon which we were very sulky and said we had as good a right to go as them after going on for a little time and refusing to go into a boat we went to the Place where my *Too* indulgent Father said the best armoury was. We sat down on a seat below the tree I huld the inclosed leaf from and he went to get us admittance I having come a litle to myself said I would not wish to go. and we did not go

Leaves from the Tower

May 10th 1788

He[4] dined with us. I was a little heated. Went to Dilly's and had some calcavella. Home; was asked unpleasingly, had I been drinking? Glad of an excuse to go out. Went to Piazza; beefsteak and brandy punch. Quite English.

SUNDAY 11 MAY. Visited Forbes; was in usual spirits as to London. Had more and more desire to give Ve advantage of Queen Square, now or never.[5] Wife came to consent. Dined General's with Baron Baciocchi of Cologne, fourth generation from Corsica, Marchesi, etc. Moderate. Then Mrs. Macbride and talked as to Veronica, as to whom I now *hoped* I had carried my point. Home quiet; wife a little easier.

MONDAY 12 MAY. Had resolved to go next day but put it off till Wednesday. Was in great flow of spirits. Dined at Sir Joshua's with Mr. Stables, Metcalfe, etc.; an inefficient day. Waited on Mrs. Stevenson. Was much pleased with her manner. Stated my difficulties and

---

[4]T. D. Boswell.

[5]The fashionable boarding-school kept by the Misses Stevenson at two houses in Queen Square. In 1786 the number of young ladies in their charge was 220 and the fee over a hundred guineas.

how she should have come sooner. She would not take her till she had seen her. In the evening my wife went with her. She said she'd take her on her face. Then Malone's to meet Courtenay and drink some farewell hock. Seward came; was a little alarmed that my *quarto* might not sell. Called, "Seward, where are low spirits now?" "*In mare creticum,*"[6] said he. Stayed till two.

TUESDAY 13 MAY[7]. Resolved not to go till Thursday, that I might have full time. Mrs. Stevenson told my wife, as *she* was uneasy as to Veronica's having once spit blood and having a cough, she hesitated as to taking her. But my wife assured her she should be easy, and Mr. Devaynes, who visits the school, had promised to attend to her health. I do not recollect what more passed before we set out, only that either this evening or Wednesday evening I went with Veronica and saw the young ladies at Mrs. Stevenson's dance. I felt a strange kind of tender irresolution, as if it was cruel to leave *poor* Veronica. But as she appeared quite satisfied, I hardened

15 MAY. myself. On Thursday, I as usual before setting out on a journey, even when I have delayed it, had a number of things to do, so that we did not set out till after five, I think, which was too late for my wife, who was very ill and sadly moved at parting with Veronica, seeming to apprehend that she should never see her again. We lay at Welwyn, where my wife was much fatigued and dispirited. Next night we lay at

16 MAY Stamford, where she was so ill as to rove and say she would remain there.

[EDITORIAL NOTE. Because of Mrs. Boswell's illness the trip north had to be made by easy stages, and the family (all except Veronica) did not arrive at Auchinleck until 21 May. Boswell appears to have kept no journal from the time he left London until 1 July 1788, when he went from home upon his own horse to join the Northern Circuit. The gap is covered by a section of a particularly informative letter to Malone written from the Circuit.]

---

[6] Horace, *Odes*, I. xxvi. 1–3: "[A friend to the muses, I shall give dejection and anxiety to the wild winds to carry] into the Cretan sea."

[7] A letter to Temple of this day is registered as follows: "Of my wife's uncertain state; that I am to set out with her for Auchinleck next day or the day after; that I am in great spirits, which I can no more help *now* than being gloomy in November; that I finish the rough draft of my *Life* in the country, return to London, polish and put to press, and get out about Christmas. He must write as usual, etc., etc."

[Boswell to Malone]

York, 12 July 1788

MY DEAR MALONE,—Before I set out from Auchinleck my wife had a very favourable remission of her severe and alarming complaints. The country air, ass's milk, the little amusements of ordering about her family,[8] gentle exercise, and the comfort of being at home and amongst old and valuable friends had a very benignant effect upon her;[9] and I would fain flatter myself that she may recover, though not full health, yet such a degree of it as that she may enjoy life moderately well. Her preservation is of great importance to me and my children, so that there is no wonder that I suffer frequently from anxious apprehensions, which make me shrink. I sometimes upbraid myself for leaving her; but tenderness should yield to the active engagements of ambitious enterprise. I am not sure whether I shall go all round this Circuit, though I rather think I shall, unless I hear that she is worse.

But you will be very angry when I confess to you that I have not yet advanced a single page in Johnson's *Life* since I left London. The truth is that during the six weeks that I was at Auchinleck I was in some degree indolent or rather averse to sedentary exertion; I had a great deal of business to settle in the management of my estate, and having been a declared candidate for the county ever since the last election, I found such an appearance of stirring, that it was proper for me to begin my canvass directly, in which I tell *you*, not ostentatiously, that I have met with more success than I expected. You know that in the Scotch counties there are comparatively speaking few freeholders, I suppose not above 300 in any county; and if the votes which I and many others call *nominal and fictitious votes* be struck off according to the Lord Chancellor's opinion, I suppose there will not be above four-score in Ayrshire. But the uncertainty as to the *sincerity* of each of those votes (as Lord Thurlow well expressed himself), that is to say, being really and true the freehold of the voter and not a vote *by* the *grantor through* the voter, will make our county elections curiously dubious if no law be made to ascertain with more precision the legality of our votes.

I stand between two parties: the State Coalition interest,[1] which is to support one candidate, and a strange coalition between Lord Eglin-

---

[8]That is, household.

[9]"The mind has much influence over the body," she herself wrote to a friend on 22 November 1788. Boswell's Book of Company shows a modest number of dinner guests during the first months of their return, with large parties again in September.

[1]The coalition of the Earls of Dumfries, Cassillis, and Glencairn, the local followers of the Fox-North Coalition.

ton and Sir Adam Fergusson, who are both with the present Administration, but which has given great offence to many of their friends,
who will therefore prefer me, who am of the same political way of
thinking without having the exceptionable circumstance of being in a
confederacy to enthral the county.[2] Thus I am; and I assure you the
business of what we call *riding the county* and being as civil and agreeable
to everybody as possible is fine training. I return to Auchinleck from
the Circuit that I may complete my round of the freeholders and
arrange a variety of matters concerning my estate. Now do not scold
me, for I promise to set apart so much time for the *Life* that the rough
draft will be all done and brought with me to town early in October.

[EDITORIAL NOTE. The journal that Boswell kept on the Northern
Circuit, 1–29 July 1788, is the other medley of English and macaronic
Italian to which we referred in the Editorial Note above, 25 November
1786, p. 102. This journal also is reduced into idiomatic English and
now printed for the first time.]

TUESDAY 1 JULY. Set out easily, thinking curiously that an English
circuit was to me quite as natural now as a Scots circuit in time past,
and that in fact the people in the vicinity look upon a circuit as nothing
out of the ordinary. Sandy accompanied me nearly to Cumnock. It
rained a little but stopped almost at once. At New Cumnock I spoke
with Captain McAdam, who was leaving his inn but did not invite me
to join him. At Sanquhar Provost Whigham sat with me when I took
breakfast, gave me newspapers to read, and talked in a very sagacious
way of the state of the Scots burghs and of the proper influence of the
peers who won popular support, but gave an appropriate instance of
opposition to the Duke of Queensberry, who thought that he held
counties and burghs in Scotland as an outright fief.[3] My horse was sick
and caused me great concern. I had let him drink too much water. At
Brownhill he had all possible care, and after that he went well. In the
evening at Dumfries I was in strong spirits and at the same time recalled
the weakness of my mind in years past. I wrote well an Address to the

[2] Boswell found the Eglinton-Fergusson alliance offensive because they had been on
opposite sides from 1774 to 1784, when they struck a deal to divide control of the
Ayrshire seat.
[3] William Douglas, fourth Duke of Queensberry (later known as "Old Q"), debauched,
eccentric, and indifferent to opinion, held the commanding interest in Dumfriesshire
and Peeblesshire, but in the General Election of 1784 his candidate for the Dumfries
Burghs, George Augustus Selwyn, an Englishman, was defeated. Sanquhar (which the
Duke did control) was one of the five Dumfries Burghs and only eight miles from
Drumlanrig, his seat.

Real Freeholders of Ayrshire[4] and letters to Robert Boswell and Mr. Bushby. Dined well and refreshed myself, but no more, with port.

WEDNESDAY 2 JULY. Set out early. Had for travelling companion John Fawcet, tenant of Dr. Barlow, apothecary of Lancaster, at Kellet, between Burton and Lancaster, a mile off the road. He guided me through the water, but from our crossing it too early it was deeper than I liked.[5] It rained a little sometimes. At Carlisle Alderman Jackson went with me and saw that I got the best lodgings. Dined alone. It rained hard. I felt a little hipped but knew why. Took coffee at Mrs. Alkins's, and she sat with me. Had some conversation with Mr. Mounsey, an attorney. In the evening Mr. Barnes with me. Was quite the Recorder.

THURSDAY 3 JULY. Set out early. Arrived at Penrith thinking how I had been there in 1760.[6] After a good breakfast Mr. Buchanan accompanied me on the road to the Beacon.[7] I stopped at Appleby, which I saw for the first time, and took some cold ham with good tasting water and a little brandy. Spent the night at Brough. Walked with Mr. Aungier[8] about his lands. Supped well, and had Lord Lonsdale's room on condition that I would get up the instant his Lordship should arrive.

FRIDAY 4 JULY. My horse went on well. It rained heavily when I passed Stainmore. I got very wet and was a little unhappy, but it stopped and I arrived in good spirits at Gretabridge. I saw Andrew Stuart there and spoke to him in passing; he told me he had a post-chaise and horses with him. I answered lightly, "But you are a greater man than I am."[9] His nephew, James Cochrane, the minister, and another minister, Dr. Tidy, nephew (i.e., married to sister's daughter) of Lord Adam Gordon, and I breakfasted together. Later, when I went into a

---

[4]Dated 30 June, from Auchinleck, and published in the *Edinburgh Advertiser* for 1–4 July 1788, it announced that Boswell had begun his canvass but was called away to England for a few weeks by "professional engagements." He entreated those gentlemen to whom he had not yet spoken personally to refrain from engaging their votes until they had given him a fair hearing.

[5]The Solway Firth reaches inland for about forty miles between Dumfries and Carlisle and is remarkable for the rapidity with which its tides ebb and flow over the broad sands.

[6]When he ran away to London in March of that year.

[7]A stone structure with an extensive view situated on a hill about a mile north of the town; it was used to raise an alarm in times of public danger.

[8]James Aungier, proprietor of the Swan, the inn at which Boswell was staying.

[9]Stuart, W.S., had been Keeper of the Signet, Commissioner for Trade and Plantations, M.P. for Lanarkshire, and King's Remembrancer in the Court of Exchequer; he was now Keeper of the Register of Sasines.

room where I had left my hat, I was surprised to find Sir Adam Fergusson. He came to see Mr. Cochrane and spent some time with us, and then I walked with him in his room discussing Sheridan's speech,[1] the best way of having trees sown or planted, etc. Went on to Catterick Bridge and had excellent ham and roast beef, both cold, with gin and water, and the landlord sat with me. I saw there Maconochie the writer with his wife, and said, "I believe the Douglas Cause is about to begin again. I met Andrew Stuart this morning and, lo, he is followed by Mr. Maconochie."[2] In the evening I arrived at Boroughbridge: fifty-five miles. A little too much gin and water had made me sick to my stomach. But with coffee and having my head shaved I was soon quite well; I felt as easy at Boroughbridge as at Hamilton,[3] and the landlord (Fretwell) sat with me.

SATURDAY 5 JULY. Having a day free, I went to Knaresborough, where I had learned at Catterick Bridge that I should find Mr. Murray of Broughton. I went directly to his house to surprise him. He was walking about. I met him, and he seemed to me much aged both in face and manner of speech. He said to me, "I have been long out of the world." "But your friends don't forget you." "They are much better to me than I deserve." Poor man.[4] I begged him to go with me to my inn, and he went, saying very politely, "I would have asked you into my habitation were it not for the situation in which I am." Feeling for him, I said, too laxly, "Such things have happened since the world began." "But," said he, "you know the saying. 'There is no fool like an old fool.'" I however spoke on other subjects, just as we had in time past. This was a romantic interview.

Mr. Batt appeared unexpectedly on horseback, and he and I were much surprised to see each other here. He invited me to dine with

---

[1]Sheridan began his speech at Hastings's trial relating the mistreatment of the Begums of Oude on 3 June 1788, continued for several hours on three additional days, and fell exhausted into Burke's arms when he finished on 13 June. The speech was the topic of the day.

[2]Stuart had been agent for Hamilton and Maconochie for Douglas in the Douglas Cause.

[3]Possibly Hamilton on the Glasgow–Edinburgh road, where he had felt "fine sensations" in his youth (Journal, 10 November 1783). Boswell seems to mean that he felt as easy in England now as in Scotland.

[4]James Murray, formerly M.P. for Wigtownshire and Kirkcudbright Stewartry, Boswell's acquaintance at least since 1762, was married in 1752 to his cousin, Catherine Stewart, daughter of the sixth Earl of Galloway. But in July 1785, at the age of fifty-eight, he eloped abroad with the sister of Peter Johnston, a family friend and former protégé. Murray gave up his political ambitions and had now settled down with his mistress.

him at the Green Dragon at Harrogate. I went and, when I arrived, I saw together with several gentlemen who had their hats on a young man without a hat, to whom, thinking him one of the servants, I called out, "Waiter, can you tell me where Mr. Batt is?" "No, Sir," said he, "but you are in a mistake if you take me for a waiter." I begged his pardon, saying, "They all look so smart now, and your being without your hat made me hastily conclude so." He accepted of my apology very good-naturedly. And who was this but Mr. Montagu, Lord Hinchingbrooke's eldest son. He looked much older than he really was, being just of age. At tea I again hoped he would excuse me, and said, "Well, I shall one day have it to say of Lord Sandwich that I called him waiter."[5] I dined very well as Batt's guest. Near us were Captain Townshend from Chester, of the 54th Regiment, Major Boyd, Lieutenant Kinsey, adjutant to Lord Pembroke's regiment; Mr. Glynn, the banker who had been at Knaresborough with Batt, which made me take him for a lawyer, so I called him Serjeant Glynn;[6] Mr. Arbuthnot, a Scotch gentleman, I believe an officer; and a Mr. Leigh, an Irish M.P. We grew wonderfully hearty, and after some port had several bottles of claret, for one of which I called, saying, "I like this Green Dragon. I don't think you are greenhorns; [rather you are] *Dragons* for drinking.[7] You are said to have the reputation for it." I was asked why I had gone to the *Bell* at Knaresborough. Said *Kinsey*, who had got the name of *Mc*Kinsey, "You have joined today *Bell* and the *Dragon*."[8] A great deal of heartiness and mirth went round, and felt an elevation in finding how much I could promote festivity.

Bankrupt John Fordyce was there with his wife and daughter, provokingly strutting as usual.[9] I took no notice of him, and I found that Batt and Glynn knew his character well. They walked with me on the common, and then we had tea. A gentle Miss Jarratt of Hull made it. I returned to Knaresborough hoping to have had Murray to sup with me. But Keith Stewart, whom he had not seen for three years, had

---

[5] John George Montagu died in 1790, without having succeeded his grandfather as Earl of Sandwich.

[6] John Glynn, serjeant-at-law, was a well-known radical M.P. and Recorder of London.

[7] Boswell is temporarily using French, in which language "dragon" and "dragoon" have the same spelling (*dragon*). In Boswell's puns a little goes a long way.

[8] An allusion to Bel and the Dragon, one of the apocryphal books of the Old Testament.

[9] A partner in Fordyce, Grant, a banking-house which failed in the Ayr Bank crash of 1772, supposedly for the immense sum of £243,000. Fordyce, however, suffered little and, through influential connections, now held the post of commissioner of the Land Revenues.

come, so he excused himself.[1] I went with him to the Crown and sat
a little while with Keith, who seemed dry and rather sarcastical when
I talked of my being a candidate for Ayrshire and catched at every
one of my pleasant sallies, attempting to twist them unfavourably. I
knew his cold, selfish character well and did not mind him. As we
parted (he having only punch on the table, till a pint of white wine
was brought for me) he said, "If you mean to be serious, I can say
nothing (from my connection with Lord Eglinton) till I know what he
is to do." I returned to my own Bell, supped very comfortably, and
went to a good bed quietly.

SUNDAY 6 JULY. I set out early and arrived at York, where I found
my counsellor's clothes which were sent from London; breakfasted,
and then secured a good apartment recommended by the landlord of
the York Tavern, Pulleyn, to whom I had written; and I had from him
a good two-horse stall for my own. I went to the Cathedral, but felt
ill, and I was not so elevated as I should have wished. To my great
surprise there came in Hamilton of Grange and Reid of Seabank, with
a Mr. McCormick from America, with his wife, newly married. I stayed
and took the Holy Sacrament. The Archbishop conducted himself with
great decency, and I observed that when he repeated the solemn words
he spoke in a low voice, which had a very proper effect.[2]

At the inn were I think ten counsellors at dinner. I suddenly discovered among some of them a rude intention to make me serve again
as Junior. I resisted, however, and when they showed a determination
to force me in their half-impertinent, half-ludicrous way, I got up from
the table and walked out. At the moment I felt how much I was lessened. But I kept myself firm by the reflection that in making the
experiment which I had resolved to make fairly, by which I should at
least get some improvement in legal knowledge and accuracy and ex-
pertness in doing business, I must undergo disagreeable things. After
walking for some time I went to Ringrose's, where I took several glasses
of wine and coffee and tea with the Scots company which I had met
at the Cathedral. Suddenly I felt myself raised. Hamilton and I walked
together beside the river, and then I went early to bed.

MONDAY 7 JULY. I went immediately to Mr. Chambré and told
him that I should speak to him as a ward of the court, as a gentleman,
concerning the intention to make me serve again as Junior, and begged
him to be my friend. He received me with great politeness and assured

---

[1]Stewart was Murray's brother-in-law. He was a captain in the navy.
[2]The Archbishop, William Markham, D.C.L., was a High-Churchman from Co. Cork.
Boswell here records one of his "High Church" practices.

me that I should not be plagued. I told him I was determined not to be so used. Visited the judges. Grose had gone into court.[3] Saw Thomson. I felt tender anxiety concerning my dear wife. But the bustle of the court kept up my spirits. At dinner I was moderately well; and after dinner I evaded with good humour the foolish and unpleasing attempt to make me again Junior, and was made easy by the two youngest barristers who had been called the same term drawing cuts and one of them being installed. In court after dinner. Supped with the Circuit.

TUESDAY 8 JULY. Court morning and after dinner. Dined with Circuit. Evening to bed.

WEDNESDAY 9 JULY. Court morning. The Seniors dined with Lord Thomson. We Juniors dined together, and having taken much claret I was decidedly intoxicated. I was a ninny to go into court in the evening, because I went to sleep. However, I went home quietly.

THURSDAY 10 JULY. Waked without feeling great discomfort and was quite well in court. We Juniors dined with the two judges. Then I went into court. This was *Grand Night*. I was somewhat afraid that the Circuit would make me pay heavily for the privilege of returning, but I escaped with a fine for each court I had been absent from, *two guineas and a half*, and going through the ceremony of riding on S. Heywood as a *black ram* and repeating,

> Here I am
> Riding on a black ram,
> Like a deserter as I am,
> Etc., etc.,

the words I had prescribed for young Burke if he should return to the Northern Circuit.[4] The din and the foolishness did not please me as much as the first time, when there was novelty and hopes of success

[3]Sir Nash Grose, Puisne Judge of the King's Bench.

[4]Richard Burke had removed to the Oxford Circuit in March 1786, and Boswell, then Junior on the Northern Circuit, wrote the official but facetious letter acknowledging his resignation. (A copy of Boswell's letter, in his own hand, is entered in the records of the Northern Circuit.) Burke could return, Boswell wrote, upon performing the ancient ceremony by which unchaste dowagers in Berkshire were restored to the estates they had forfeited (an allusion to *Spectator* 614). He also adapted the indecent verses the widow was required to speak as she rode a black ram backwards into court, and concluded the lines quoted above as follows:

> My contrition sincere, O Grand Court, don't disdain,
> But good Mr. Junior let me have my place again.

Boswell got the original verses from Voltaire, who recited them (no doubt from the *Spectator*) on 27 December 1764.

as an English counsellor. I appeared to myself to be in a situation which did not suit well with my age and the circumstances of my family; and indeed, my heart was touched with tender feelings for M.M. But I thought that in a great part of the causes I could do well, and that the putting myself forth as candidate for Ayrshire and the friendship of Lord Lonsdale and various other particulars would avail to keep me up in the world for some time. The sad apprehension of losing *my valuable friend*, whose good sense and kindness had so long been my comfort, shocked me sadly. Got home at a good hour and quite sober.

FRIDAY 11 JULY. In court before dinner and enjoyed the accuracy and animation. The day before yesterday Wickham had carried for me a note of recommendation from Batt to the Archbishop of York, and I had an invitation to dine at Bishopthorpe this day.[5] Wickham and I went in a chaise. I was politely received. Mrs. Markham, her daughters, three sons: one returned from India, a captain in the navy, a clergyman of £500 a year. All prosperous. Several young children. Foljambe, Hon. and Rev. Mr. Lumley, etc., etc. An excellent dinner and good wines. Rev. Mr. Waddilove sat near me, and we talked a good deal together. After dinner his Grace obligingly showed me the house and walked with me through his pleasure-ground.

I was surprised to find him a mild, cordial, venerable man, so as to interest me with a degree of affection. I perceived nothing of the haughtiness or scholastic roughness which I had figured. He spoke in a gentle, pleasing tone, very slowly and distinctly; and I wondered how he could take the trouble to be so minute in his accounts of everything about the Place. There was no learned or intellectual talk. Talking of the Scotch nonjurors now praying for King George, he said, "We must be glad that they are now become such good subjects. But they, I find, point at some protection. I own I do not see my way. We know not what may be agreeable to the people of Scotland, what to the people of this country."[6] I accompanied his Grace and most of the company after tea and saw his gardens, greenhouse, etc.—all abundant, all excellent. I returned to York in the evening, and went to bed in good time. I should have observed that when one of his Grace's little daughters called to him from a window with easy frankness, "Papa," I ob-

---

[5] The Archbishop's residence near York.
[6] Nonjurors, those clergymen who refused to take the oath of allegiance following the deposition of James II in 1688, included the majority of the Episcopalian clergy in Scotland. Earlier this year their bishops met at Aberdeen and agreed to swear allegiance to George III. As Boswell had reminded Johnson on their Hebridean jaunt, Episcopalians were only "tolerated" in Scotland, where Presbyterianism was the established religion.

served that they were not afraid of him. "No," said he, "I have always lived with them as with brothers and sisters." When I said significantly that by his leaving London he had lost a great deal of the eloquence upon Mr. Hastings's trial, he answered, "I have escaped it. I heard all the evidence, but not what Mr. Sheridan called his summing-up. I thought I could sum up as well for myself." He said, "They have erected a theatre for themselves," and he gently remarked how foreign nations must wonder that the man who had done so much for his country should be so treated when he came home.[7]

SATURDAY 12 JULY. I was in court only a little while because there was very little instruction. Fearnley told me that he had made ninety-nine guineas in one session; that that did not lead to any eminence in the profession, but it was nevertheless very comfortable, for he got above £300 a year by it, and whenever there was any law affair in any part of the country all round they came to him. "Well," said I, "you know it was Caesar's resolution to be 'primus Mantuae quam secundus Romae.'[8] All cannot get into eminent situations, and it is well when a man sees what will do with him." He said it was very difficult to get into business as a lawyer in any situation, and that a lawyer was made by practice, without which no abilities, no knowledge would do. A man without practice must be awkward in cross-examining witnesses and in many particulars. I told him I really liked business; it amused me.

At dinner I had a great deal of good conversation with Mr. France, a very young barrister who was in a question of pedigree but candidly told me he had no pedigree. He said of Wedderburn that when he did business as a judge it was not like a tradesman who had served his time but like a gentleman who had taken it up of himself, so that one wondered that he did it so well. He said, however, he wished he had been made Chief Justice, because for that high office there was something more requisite than being a mere lawyer like Sir Lloyd Kenyon; there should be an elegance of manners and a knowledge of the world.[9] And he was convinced that if Wedderburn had been appointed Chief Justice he would in a year have made himself a much better lawyer; that he was a dissatisfied man and thought his merit had not been sufficiently honoured. "What!" said I, "when I remember him not worth a shilling and now see him Chief Justice of the Common

[7] The Archbishop was a staunch friend of Hastings's. The trial ended his friendship with Burke.

[8] "To be first in Mantua rather than second in Rome"—a version of what Plutarch reports about Julius Caesar (see "Caesar," *Lives*, section 11).

[9] Kenyon, coarse and parsimonious, but a learned and industrious judge, had been sworn in as Lord Chief Justice of the King's Bench the previous month.

Pleas?" "But your remembering that," said France, "does not limit his ambition."[1] I declared my hearty approbation of the appointment of Kenyon. To have preferred another to him would have been a discouragement to the real lawyers, the laborious men of the profession, and he would be a good fuller's mill to thicken and consolidate the law, which was very necessary after the loose texture which Lord Mansfield had given it.

I played some rubbers at whist, but felt a kind of wandering which I have often experienced, so that I had not any distinct recollection of the cards, and being also not lucky I lost, which always vexes me, so that I believe I should not play. But still I like it. I went to the Green, the only summer amusement at York. There is a tolerable room belonging to the bowling-green, in which there is dancing and card-playing after walking in the Green. But this being a rainy evening there were only four ladies and very few gentlemen, so that there was but one card-table, and I had nothing to do. I however saw for the first time a very curious fact in natural history, which was shown us by Dr. ———, physician, I believe; which was a very great number of worms all over the bowling-green, stretched out in the damp on the surface of the turf, and as we made them sensible of our approach, either by touching them with a stick, or by giving a concussion to the ground by our tread, or (it was maintained by some of the company) by the sound of our voice, they as it were darted themselves into their holes with an agility which was very surprising. Several pairs of them appeared to be in the act of coition, being joined together, some said, by two ties and even by a sort of rings, their heads being turned away from each other, and the junction or junctions being towards their tails, so that they put one in mind of "canes post coitionem sed nondum separati."[2] I must read concerning this.

The weather having grown fair, I sauntered some time in the street with Park, who told me a good deal about the watchful jealousy and envy of barristers, notwithstanding the liberality in communicating knowledge from a principle of mutual advantage, as the first lawyers might at times be helped by the Juniors; and he said a great deal in

[1] Alexander Wedderburn, originally a Scots advocate, had an insignificant practice at the English bar until his friend Lord Bute came to power in 1760. He later made a notorious shift from the Opposition to Lord North, held office in his Administration (see above, 26 July 1786 and n. 2), and took a place on the bench when North's fall seemed imminent, at which time he was raised to the peerage as Baron Loughborough. He parted company with Fox over the French Revolution, and Pitt named him Lord Chancellor in January 1793.
[2] Dogs after coition but not yet separated.

favour of Buller, with whom he had lived much, and indeed thought he owed his life to him, by being taken by him into Devonshire when in bad health. He gave me a concise account of his rapid advancement, to account for his provoking much enmity, and he assured me that he was a very humane man, nay, so tender-hearted that he has seen him weep at an affecting story, and that his mind was often severely worked by applications for mercy.[3] That his principle was to support the law in all cases, and therefore to endeavour that verdicts should be in conformity with the law, however severe; but that whenever there were alleviating circumstances in a case, he was ever desirous that relief should be granted, as the Constitution allows, by the King, the Fountain of Mercy, or by his judges, to whom he delegates that prerogative when upon their circuits. Park reasoned very well that even allowing my notion to be right, that jurymen are judges of law as well as of fact, they are bound by their oaths to find according to the law when it is clear, although they may disapprove of the law in the case before them. For they are not legislators. They must not take upon them to repeal laws. I went home quietly. I thought tenderly of M.M. But my mind was quite fixed.

SUNDAY 13 JULY. I went to make an experiment whether it was possible to get the least hospitality from Burgh. I was at his door about nine. The servant told me he would not be down for two hours. I went to the Cathedral, and felt much more devotion than the last Sunday. In the course of this week it had rained many times. Today after the service in the church it rained with extraordinary force. As I had resolved to go on horseback to the Archbishop's and could not get room in a post-chaise since they were all full, I was afraid that I should miss the scene of a dinner given by the Archbishop for the judges and counsel. Luckily the rain stopped, and I went very well, feeling myself stronger and more at my ease in coloured clothes and boots. I was pleased with the formality and with making a part of it. The dinner and dessert were splendid and the wines truly good. I sat next to Withers, who told me he had heard Wallace say that by the Northern Circuit he had got £1,500 in a year, that is, by retainers, by money got on the circuit, and by business in Westminster Hall in consequence of it. He told me how he[4] had fixed himself as a *provincial* and what an advantage he had in point of health and amusement, which he enjoyed

---

[3]Buller was made a judge of the Court of King's Bench in May 1778, when he was thirty-two, and was Lord Mansfield's choice to succeed himself as Chief Justice. Though quick and clear, he was also criticized for haste and prejudice.
[4]Withers, who was later Recorder of York.

progressively with business, whilst London lawyers looked for these at a distant day, and when it arrived were not able to enjoy them. When the judges retired to the drawing-room, young Markham entertained so many of us as sat with him with additional wine, but not to excess. I however *felt* it.

As the company went off in their carriages and Fearnley on horseback, the Archbishop asked me to stay, saying, "There's a bed for you." I hesitated a little whether to accept, as I was heated with wine, but I could not resist an archiepiscopal invitation. By and by Mrs. Markham said, "Had not you better order your horses to be put up?" I told her I was to have the honour of staying all night; his Grace had been so good as to ask me. We went and walked in the garden, the family and Law[5] and I. The Archbishop talked a great deal of antiquities and etymology, how the Saxons had been long in Britain before the Celts, how single captains had made incursions and settlements, without there being for a long time national invasions, etc., etc. He said names of places were either descriptive or historical. He suggested that Auchinleck might be Saxon. *Aik*, a flow of water, and *leck*, where it falls at some point.[6] I must get this correct, for it struck me at the time as applicable to the *Lugar* meeting at a point with the *Dippleburn*.[7]

It was remarkable that he never talked to me as a writer, nor of Johnson, except that he merely asked if I had been in any of the Western Islands besides those in which I had been with Johnson. I behaved myself with great decorum of reserve, and did not forwardly introduce any topic. As we walked about, I reflected curiously with what ease I now saw the great Markham, the Master of Westminster School, etc., etc., of whom I had often thought with distant awe. We had a little plain supper, a leg of roast lamb and some cold dishes. When the ladies were gone a servant came and helped his Grace to put on a night-gown and black nightcap, and he then said, "Mr. Boswell, will you walk this way?" I begged he might not take the trouble. He said, "I go this way," and he accompanied me to the door of my apartment, a handsome bedroom and dressing-room looking upon the garden and river.

MONDAY 14 JULY. Awaked well. Walked out. Then had the decent ceremony of morning prayer in the beautiful old chapel, Mr. Wad-

[5]Edward Law, K.C., counsel to Warren Hastings; named Lord Chief Justice in 1802 and created Baron Ellenborough.
[6]The Archbishop's etymology is as wildly inaccurate as his account of early Britain ("the Saxons had been long in Britain before the Celts"). The name Auchinleck is from the Gaelic, *achadh-na-leac*: the field of flagstones, or of the (flat) stones.
[7]Boswell spelled it Dupolburn, indicating the Scottish pronunciation.

dilove, the chaplain, who had known my brother at Madrid, officiating, and a good part of the family being present. Then a good breakfast and easy conversation, in which he agreed with Dr. Johnson's doctrine that there is a moral obligation upon a man born to an estate to take care of it and of the people upon it.[8] His hospitality not only to masters but to their servants and horses, even hacks, was extraordinary. I told him I was sorry to find this see was not worth so much as I supposed. "How much did you suppose?" said he. "Why," said I, "about ten thousand a year and I am told it is only six." "It is better," said he. "It is worth seven, and if there be no foolish expense, one may do all that is right and lay up money too. But I do not depend on it solely. I got a good fortune with my wife. I got £20,000, and that accumulates. And I have told my sons they must not trust to what I can do for them; they must do for themselves." The frankness of this from so high a dignitary and so stately a man pleased me exceedingly. He showed us his court of offices, and a pigeon house which he had built exactly as I project, or rather as my dear wife has projected, and he showed us some fine horses. Law, in whose chaise I was to go to York, quoted from Juvenal.[9] To my surprise, the Archbishop said he had read Juvenal but once and was not fond of him. Statius he had read once, and Lucan once. *Him* he thought a fund for French tragedy. And then he added, "When one has read the true simple sublime, other kinds of writing will not be relished. I have read Homer again and again."

Law and I went in his carriage to York. There, having met with Garforth, I arranged my little affairs and set off. Arrived at Thirsk and found some of the counsellors after dinner. Instead of joining in a roar or being loudly conspicuous, I proved the solid truth that I wish I had sooner felt, that a man is much better to be quiet unless when something worth while calls him to exertion; and I was quite free from the unhappy, mistaken apprehension that prominent mirth was expected from me. I was *sure* on trial that it was not, and it never is unless when a man by habitual indulgence accustoms people to expect it. If one who has been used to do so stops of a sudden, he may be stared at. But if he gradually fills the void with more rational subjects, he will keep his consequence. I had cold ham and chicken and a pint of port in a corner. Then I rode briskly nine miles to Northallerton, and expecting that several of the counsel would shun Hirst's, where the

[8]"He spoke of a gentleman who has an estate being called in duty to reside so much upon it, and do good there," Johnson's pointed advice to Boswell himself (*Journal*, 9 April 1773).
[9]Boswell left a blank of nearly half a line for the quotation, but did not recall it.

judges were, I put up at the King's Head, Bulmer's newly fitted up. His wife had been Mrs. Shaw, at the Golden Lion, Durham, and recollected me. None of the counsel came to this house, so I was quite alone, but read some of Juvenal, and was in amazing soundness of mind; drank my coffee, supped well, and had the landlord to drink a glass of port with me, and went to bed sober and serene.

TUESDAY 15 JULY. Set out between seven and eight. The road was very bad. The heavy rain in the night had made it quite miry. But this should not be on a turnpike road. Mr. Allan, attorney at Darlington, is one of the trustees. I understand gravel is at a great distance. Near to Darlington I was overtaken by the cavalcade of the judges. They were both on horseback, their carriages following. I rode some time along with them and then fell back. I should have mentioned that last night I rode part of the way with Winslow, now servant and crier to Justice Grose. He had gone the Oxford and Chester Circuits many years as servant to a lawyer. He was seven years butler and many years crier to Judge Willes and attended him in his last illness. He told me that the Judge was cheerful to the last and always endeavouring to say something to make people laugh. He said, "I am not in pain. It is only death that is working with me." He regretted that a complaint which he had made it prejudicial to him to go often to church, but he was a most sincere Christian in private and very attentive to his religious duties. He made Dr. Warren tell him fairly his situation, declaring that he was not afraid to die. He had no clergyman with him but his son. He was quite serene, and expired without any struggle. His countenance was very little altered. This was a pleasing and interesting account. Willes was always very kind to me, and I loved him sincerely.

At Darlington I found several of the counsel, and I breakfasted well. I had said I would dine there but found I should be too late, so I did not see my cousin, the Rev. John Cochrane, who had gone out of town and was not yet returned, though he had told the parson with whom he lodged that I was to meet him here this day. Lambe and I rode on to Durham, leaving a number of the counsel dining at Rushyford. Some of them, Holroyd, a special pleader, and two fine young men, Wilkinson, son of Jacob, and Gregory, son of the East Indian Gregory who has purchased an estate in Connaught, rode part of the way with us. I liked Lambe better when I had him out of the bustle of the circuit. He told me his inclination was "——— et fallentis semita vitae."[1] I put up my horse at the Golden Lion, Durham, and Fairest,

[1]Horace, *Epistles*, I. xviii. 103, trans. H. R. Fairclough, Loeb ed.: "An secretum iter et fallentis semita vitae: a secluded journey along the pathway of a life unnoticed." Boswell left a blank for the beginning of the line in case he recovered it.

the landlord (an excellent name for a land*lady*), helped me to lodgings at Mrs. Robinson's, milliner's. Lambe and I then repaired to Shotton's good inn and had a comfortable dinner, after which I drank tea with him and looked at some of his briefs. Then sauntered with various counsel, and went to bed in good time.

WEDNESDAY 16 JULY. Went out early and walked almost to St. Giles's Church. Went a little to the Cathedral and heard good music and an excellent sermon by the son of the poet Anstey. In the square where the prebendaries live I was accosted by a gentleman who asked if my name was Boswell. This was Mr. Ambler, the Recorder, a Johnsonian indeed. He had been frequently with Johnson and admired him greatly. He had been along with the Hon. Andrew Erskine and me at the Queen's Head in Holborn when we supped with Flexney and the printer of our *Letters*.[2] This had totally escaped me. After hearing part of a cause which lasted the whole day concerning the property of two pigs, I dined well at the mess. After dinner I was called out, and to my surprise saw Mr. John Gordon, Clerk to the Signet, and an attorney with him. I asked what had brought him here. He answered, "To give you a fee." It seems he and Mr. Forrester, two directors of the Bank of Scotland, were come to prosecute a woman for uttering forged notes. So I had my brief and three guineas and was elated a little, and as it was soon found out, saw the *feelings* of some of the Circuit, but did not mind them. I was in wonderful good spirits.

Ambler obligingly walked with me to the race-ground and to the fine romantic walk near the Cathedral. I had my literary ardour revived after it had been dormant for some time. He told me that I did not know what a great man I was at Durham, where the ladies were exceedingly fond of Johnson and of all my writings and would be eager to see me. I *took* all this, and I was sure that he was acquainted with some of my works from the account he gave of them. I went to his house and got *European* and *Gentleman's* magazines which I had not seen and drank a glass of wine and some wine and water. We agreed to sup with Wood, who was my senior in the forgery cause and with whom I was to confer about it this evening. I went to him accordingly, and then came Ambler, and we all supped with Wood's landlord, Ebdon the organist, easy and well. Ambler had been long at special pleading under his father in London, at the same desk with Wallace and Jack

[2]William Flexney, bookseller, who published Boswell's *Critical Strictures on Elvira* as well as his correspondence with Erskine; and Samuel Chandler, printer. Boswell records supping with them at the Queen's Head on 8 July 1763 but he does not mention Ambler, and his reference to Erskine is a rare lapse of memory, for he wrote to him about the supper.

Lee, and he had also lived with wits, Wilkes, Lloyd, Thornton, etc.[3]

THURSDAY 17 JULY. In the criminal court heard some cases very well conducted by Justice Grose. Had a little internal trepidation when I opened the one in which I was engaged, but repressed it and suddenly was under way. We lost it by a *variance* from the *record*. Dined well at the mess. After dinner insensibly sat after the rest with Ambler, W. Scott, and Gerrard, and we had a couple of bottles of very pretty burgundy. I was somewhat elevated. Ambler drank tea with me. Made wonderful professions, and said he would exert himself to get business for me here and that he had extensive influence. We had last night drank coffee at Mr. Andrews's, who had been surgeon to the Duke of Cumberland both in his foreign campaigns and in Scotland. He was a civil, gentleman-like old man and had five young daughters, to each of whom he could give at least £15,000. He had a great resemblance to Sir James Campbell of Ardkinglass. This day before dinner, I called on Forrester and Gordon at their inn with very civil attention. *Felt* (and it is all as one feels) a superiority in my *English* situation.

Ambler and I went to the assembly. I danced with Miss ——— Salvin a little awkwardly, being confounded by the figure of right and left, which I never could learn, and with Miss ——— Andrews, better. Ambler's prodigious celebration of me to my face among the ladies was *too much*. I avoided it as well as I could without offending him. The Rev. Sir Harry Vane was very polite to me; mentioned our having met at Burke's and kept up literary talk very well. He presented me to his daughter, a very fine woman. There were several good-looking girls at the assembly. We had tea on tables brought into the room, and I played a rubber at whist with some of my brethren and won, and got home before one. I thought within myself, "This is a very good way of getting over life to a man who has often struggled in 'the miry clay'[4] of a melancholy existence." There was a manly steadiness about me which I enjoyed much; and I was animated with thinking that I was in a *great* lottery.

FRIDAY 18 JULY. Called on Sir Harry Vane; not at home. Was some time in Thomson's court, where he sat all day to hear a process concerning the boundaries of a coal-pit. I was also in Grose's court but did not profit much, the cause being long and involved in point of fact. I amused myself all morning after the first by taking coffee and

[3] Robert Lloyd, poet, and Bonnell Thornton, parodist and miscellaneous writer, members with William Cowper and George Colman the Elder of the high-spirited Nonsense Club. Boswell himself had "got into the middle of the London Geniuses" when he met Wilkes and Lloyd at Thornton's on 24 May 1763.
[4] Psalms 40:2: "He brought me up also out of an horrible pit, out of the miry clay."

reading a newspaper at the Golden Lion. Justice Grose and the counsellors who were not in the process in Thomson's court dined at the
Bishop's.[5] I loved being in the Old Castle. My imagination brought
strongly to mind the days when the prince of an independent palatinate
was here.[6] The Bishop, although he was not a little like his brother in
countenance, was not rough in manner like him but took me by the
hand, saying, "I am very glad to see you here." However, he said nothing more to me. I know not how much conversation he was capable of.

The dinner was announced by the sound of wretched music, apparently of violins. The Bishop sat at the head and his chaplain, Dr.
————, at the foot. Next to him Dr. Bever, whom I had seen at Bishopthorpe, and I next to him. His *civil polity* in eating and drinking was
very good.[7] He had, I believe, some office under the Bishop; at least
he took a superintendence of the entertainment, for he informed me
first that fish was coming, and afterwards that venison was coming,
and having asked me to drink a glass of wine with him, he named what
wines were to be had. We were so *totus in hoc*[8] that we had no leisure
for any conversation, except that he had made a pretty extensive tour
in Scotland thirty years ago and that the Bishop of Carlisle, from what
he computed by long acquaintance with him since they were at Oxford
together, must be now sixty-five or sixty-six. Bever's book, from the
extracts which I have read, is, I think, an able performance and duly
seasoned with Toryism. We had madeira, port, sherry, hock, burgundy,
champagne in the time of dinner; and after it I drank very good port
and very good claret from Bates, Smith, and Co., to whom Dr. Bever
told me the Bishop at one time gave an order to the extent of about
£800. It struck me with wonder to think of the chances of this great,
free country. Here, by the powerful mind of a brother, Lord Thurlow,
was a man of no birth and no eminence of talents raised, I may say,
from a loom to a throne.[9] We sat a short time after dinner and the
wine did not circulate quick. It was right that there should be proper
decorum. I sat at the Bishop's table. There were two other tables of

[5] At Thomas Thurlow's, younger brother of Lord Thurlow.
[6] The Bishop of Durham (a County Palatine) had the authority to create barons, appoint
judges, convoke parliaments, raise taxes, coin money, and grant pardons of all kinds
until his powers were abridged by Edward I and Henry VIII.
[7] Thomas Bever, D.C.L., Judge of the Cinque Ports and Chancellor of Lincoln and
Bangor, had brought out *The History of the Legal Polity of the Roman State* in 1781.
[8] "Wholly absorbed in this."
[9] Neat, but not to be taken literally. The Bishop came from Norfolk, long a centre of
the woollen industry, and was indeed of humble origins, but his father and grandfather, both also named Thomas, were obscure country parsons, not weavers.

good size in two windows. Gregory sat on my right hand, and his conversation pleased me. His notion of the peculiar advantage of the British government was good, viz. that although it cannot be said that *all* the people are represented, there is such a check upon the executive power as is to be found in no other government.

Michael Angelo Taylor and I drank tea with Mr. Recorder Ambler, whose lady and daughter were from home. Michael was now in violent indignation on account of his being refused a *patent of precedency* after being promised it.[1] He was very warm and very communicative. He said that his intimacy with Pitt did not begin at college, as I had supposed, for Pitt was of Cambridge, he of Oxford, but they had lived next staircase to each other in Lincoln's Inn and used to sup together at Serle's Coffee-house, and thus became friends. He said he used to say to Pitt, "It is on your account alone that I support Administration, for I look upon them all but yourself to be sad fellows."[2] That he wished to have rank on the Northern Circuit. He was senior both to Law and Cockell. He went to Lord Thurlow and desired to have a patent of precedency. Thurlow said he would consider of it. After six weeks he went again. Thurlow said he had no objection, but added, "Go to Pitt, for he has named to *all* the law offices of late." He went to Pitt, who seemed quite satisfied and pleased, but said, "I shall see Thurlow." When he again saw Pitt the answer was, "I have been with Thurlow and you must have misunderstood him, for he says he *cannot think* of recommending you to the King." Michael upon this fired and said, "He is a liar and a scoundrel. Either he or I must be a liar after what I told you of his sending me to you, and I desire that you as my friend may do me justice." Pitt again talked of a law promotion being to be recommended by the Chancellor. "Why, damn it," says Michael, "the fellow told me that you had made a Master of the Rolls and an Attorney-General without consulting him.[3] And will you not take upon you a paltry patent of precedency?" Pitt kept cold and stately.

"Now," said Michael, "I have stood by him always when he was in the right, and am I to be treated so? I have now £2,000 a year given

[1]Letters patent formerly granted to barristers as a mark of distinction which enabled them to rank among the King's Counsel.
[2]Michael Angelo Taylor, of Bawtry, Yorkshire, was M.P. for Poole on the recommendation of Pitt and Lord Howe. Though he declared himself a supporter of Pitt, he had voted to seat Fox for Westminster in 1785, was now a manager of Hastings's trial, and opposed Administration on various important issues in the Commons in 1788–89.
[3]Richard Pepper Arden, M.P. for Aldborough, Attorney-General, 1784–88, had succeeded Kenyon as Master of the Rolls on 18 June; Sir Archibald Macdonald was made Attorney-General on 28 June 1788.

me by my father, and shall have £6,000 a year" (I am not sure if an *additional*) "at his death. I need not care a damn. But what am I to do? This is my profession. My father when he heard of it gave me £15,000 and said, 'It depends upon yourself whether you sink or not in character upon this occasion.' " What a curious thought is it to an *ancient* gentleman that all this intimacy with a first Minister and all this bouncing (whether right or wrong) against a Lord Chancellor came from the son of a *builder*.[4] Such is the *consequence* of wealth in our nation. I was apt to suppose that honest Michael had *mistaken* the Chancellor, from his *constant* and *never dubious* notion of himself. He said, "I cannot challenge Thurlow (he being Chancellor) as I should do another man. But whenever I meet him, I will greet him with marked contempt. Instead of turning my face I will turn my a—e to him, and I will everywhere proclaim that he is a liar and a scoundrel. If," said he, "Pitt had handsomely told me that this savage is necessary to Administration and must be humoured, and that he would take a proper opportunity to show his regard for me, good and well. But for him to tell me coolly, Thurlow says he cannot think of recommending you, which is, in other words, you are a fool, I did not understand." This was a high scene, an exhibition of state arcana.

We went and walked in the romantic park and then to the concert at the Red Lion, not numerous in company but very good music. After it was a dance. I was at first disconcerted by having no good partner and particularly by missing Miss Vane, so did not dance, which I was sorry for. Ambler was somewhat troublesome by pressing me, and by way of being on Johnsonian familiarity he called me (in northern broad dialect) *Bozzy*, which I did not like, so I would not sup after the dance. Young Gregory came to me with a message (as he said) from Miss Dolly Wilkinson, a very pretty young lady, asking me to dance with her. I doubted if it was genuine and evaded it. I was sorry afterwards, for *if* genuine it was a great want of politeness to refuse; and at any rate, joke or not, a man cannot but be a gainer if he has a fine girl for his partner. Amidst all this I was a *thinking* man, and I went home quietly. It is impossible to put upon paper all the sensations and combinations. The *mind* will retain and revive them to myself, and that is quite enough. Perhaps it is idle to write so much. I won a rubber at whist.

[4]Sir Robert Taylor, Michael Angelo's father, was one of the principal architects of his time (Bank of England); *his* father, however, was a London stonemason. Sir Robert died later this year and most of his fortune eventually went to establish the Taylor Institution of Modern Languages at Oxford.

SATURDAY 19 JULY. A damp day. Was in court only briefly. Then visited Chambré and Park and felt myself idle. Set out for Newcastle and went a part of the way with young Gregory and Wilkinson, whose vivacity diverted me. Was pretty thoroughly wet. But suddenly it cleared, and I entered Newcastle in good humour. Dined well alone and drank a bottle of good port slowly, and then drank coffee. Few barristers arrived this evening. Mr. Leighton came and received me with much respect and cordiality. Supped at his house with one of his daughters, his son the bootmaker, and a Miss Cole, daughter of a tenant of Lord Scarbrough. Had a good room.

SUNDAY 20 JULY. Set out early for Benton, the seat of my old friend Bigge, who with his lady received me very agreeably at breakfast;[5] after which (as he was not to go to church this day) he and I walked about his Place, which is very pretty, and had a great deal of good conversation, then an excellent family dinner, and then I went with him in his coach to Heaton, the seat of Sir Matthew White Ridley by the father's side (Blagden, [eight][6] miles to the north, being his grand seat by the mother's side).[7] On the Sunday in the assize week he gives an evening entertainment to the judges and a number of ladies and gentlemen. We had tea and coffee and cake in the house, and wine and fruits in tents. We walked about, the band of music of the —— Regiment played to us, and there was what I called a living hedge of common people who behaved very well. How far such an exhibition is perfectly agreeable to the notions as to Sunday in this island I shall not inquire. Here I was very politely received. I renewed my acquaintance with two rich Miss Harrisons, and engaged Miss Betty, the youngest and much admired at Newcastle, to dance with me at the assembly next night. Here I met Mr. Cramlington, the mayor of Newcastle, who is a celebrated punster. At one assizes, when the *law* was given as a toast he said, "And let us add—the *profits* (prophets)." I was at him tonight upon the shocking steep road up and down what is called the *side*.[8] "I have heard," said I, "of *divisions* at Newcastle, but it appears to me you have been all *of a side*, and that the *wrong side*." "But," said he, "we are now to alter the road, but you must not call us *out of the way* people." I returned well to Newcastle, and paid a visit to Dr. Hall, whom I found so much worse with an unknown complaint in his throat

[5] Thomas Charles Bigge, whom Boswell had met on his tour of Italy in 1765, and his wife, Jemima Ord. Benton House (spelled Bentinck in Boswell's manuscript) was two miles east of Newcastle.
[6] Boswell had left a space for the distance.
[7] Ridley, a country gentleman of great wealth, was M.P. for Newcastle-upon-Tyne.
[8] The descent to the Tyne, the busiest part of the city.

than when I saw him last that he was hardly intelligible. It was painful to be with him, so I declined an invitation to sup with him and ended the evening with my good landlord and his two sons.

MONDAY 21 JULY. Breakfasted at the Rooms. In court forenoon. Dined at the mayor's, a prodigious crowd; sat by Bigge. Assembly at night; fine room. The ladies very elegantly dressed. Danced with Miss Betty Harrison, a very agreeable woman, though not very lively. Supped below stairs with one or two of the counsel and of the grand jury, amongst whom was Mr. Askew of Pallinsburn, to whom Flodden Field belongs. He promised me leave to erect on it a monument to my ancestor Thomas Boswell, who fell there. We were very hearty, and he and I and the Rev. Mr. Steevens sat till near four in the morning. I did not drink to excess.

TUESDAY 22 JULY. Lambe and I dined tête-à-tête at the mess, after being in court. I had suffered much anxiety on account of my dear wife. A letter from her that she continued a good deal better revived me. I went to the concert and talked with Betty Harrison and other ladies, but was chiefly pleased with Miss Wilson, an heiress of the county of Durham who had a great deal of conversation and was very well-looked. I should have mentioned that on Monday night young Gregory introduced me at my desire to Sir Henry Liddell, who had for a wager done a very spirited thing. He had gone to Lapland and brought over two of the natives, two young girls, and two reindeer, of which he had now a breed at his estate in Northumberland. He told me that before he set out he knew he had upon that estate the kind of moss on which that animal feeds. He politely asked me to come to his seat at Ravensworth Castle and see some reindeer horns and other Lapland curiosities. I went home quietly tonight and took some little refreshment with my kind host, who insisted on my drinking a glass of his claret. He talked well on physic, and gave me good hopes of my wife's recovery.

WEDNESDAY 23 JULY. A charming morning. I rode out about four miles to Ravensworth Castle, and was much pleased with its antiquity and good condition, with the grand woods and pretty walks, and with the easy politeness of Sir Harry, who is about the age of the Duke of Buccleuch, and of his lady, sister of Steele of the Treasury.[9] Young Gregory was there. I was shown several Lapland curiosities, and Sir Harry rode into Newcastle with me. I was disappointed at not finding three causes here which had been promised me by Mr. Currie, attorney in London. Today I received a truly original letter from him from

[9]Liddell, born in 1749, was almost three years younger than Buccleuch. Thomas Steele, joint Secretary of the Treasury, was an intimate of Pitt's.

Belford, mentioning that upon his coming down he had found the parties *inflexibly bent on arbitration,* which he gravely regretted, but had secured my fees for me. I dined at Mr. Hopper Williamson's, a barrister here, with a number of *the Circuit.* The coarse jocularity disgusted me much. I had sent off my clothes by the baggage-man so could not go to the assembly. But in the afternoon I called on Miss Wilson, who, while I sat with her mother, sent me a polite note that she was sorry she could not have the honour to wait on me, being under the hands of the hairdresser. I however had found her so uncommonly agreeable that I was resolved if possible to see her and said I would call again, which I did. After drinking coffee at the Rooms, saw her, drank a glass of wine with her and her mother, paid some compliments, and took leave. I then sat awhile with Mr. Fawcett, the Recorder, who had asked me to dinner today. I found him a sensible, well-bred old gentleman of seventy-five, the oldest barrister in England, having been called very young. It seems Lord Mansfield had driven him out of Westminster Hall, he having given information of his Lordship's famous drinking of a certain health on his knees.[1] I supped at my landlord's, where was a Mr. Bell concerned in manufactories in London and in Dundee. It was a placid evening. I was to set out early next day.

THURSDAY 24 JULY. Counsellor Gregg had very obligingly fixed to carry me this day to Naworth Castle. We breakfasted at Chollerford and dined at Glenwhelt, and during our ride he repeated more of Horace than I ever heard from any one man. He also spoke French with great fluency. In short, his company was very refreshing after the rough vulgarity of *the Circuit,* as the body of counsel is called. Gregg's father, the great attorney in London, being the Earl of Carlisle's agent, his son has a plenary power at Naworth Castle, where we were most hospitably received by the steward, Mr. Ramshaw, his wife, and son. It is precisely in its ancient state.[2] I had heard my friend Grange describe it.

FRIDAY 25 JULY. I was shown the Castle. A number of the counsel came, and their vulgar jocularity disturbed the ancient feelings which I had indulged. Some of them went on to Carlisle; some stayed and

[1] In 1753 Mansfield (then Solicitor-General and Newcastle's spokesman in the Commons) was examined before the Cabinet and the House of Lords on the charge that he had toasted the Pretender years before in the house of a London mercer. His denial of the charge was accepted. Mansfield's brother and sister were both prominent in the Pretender's court and many stories were circulated about his supposed Jacobite leanings.

[2] Erected on an impressive site north-east of Brampton around 1335, it was altered and enlarged extensively in the sixteenth century and contained many Roman antiquities dug up along Hadrian's Wall. It is still the seat of the Earl of Carlisle.

went as I did to see the Abbey of Lanercost, and dined. Ramshaw showed on the sideboard glasses which hold above a quart and said that to be free of the Castle a man drinks one of ale. I absurdly offered to do it and actually performed it. I stood it very well for some time; nay, I had a curious fancy that having a *breastplate of ale*[3] I could drink port with impunity. We drank very hard, and at last Ramshaw and I drank each a glass of brandy. To such wild excesses I have too often resigned myself. I was pretty well when I first mounted my horse but soon became quite intoxicated, and others of the counsel being also much in liquor, we rode very violently. Though I could hardly sit, and once, when I was trying to alight, tumbled over without being sensible of it, I got safely to Carlisle, where my friend Knubley very kindly supported me from the Bush to my lodgings at Mr. Hodgson's, a surgeon.

SATURDAY 26 JULY. Awaked ill. Trembled when I recollected the danger I had been in, and was particularly uneasy that I had made such an entry into the city of which I was Recorder. However, I quieted myself and attended the *nisi prius* court. Lord Lonsdale came to town in the forenoon. I waited on his Lordship and was well received. I dined at the mess, went to the card-assembly at night, played at whist, and lost. Supped there with two or three of the counsel. The familiarity and petulance and coarseness hurt my feelings exceedingly. I was not as when in London with Sir Joshua Reynolds, Malone, Courtenay, etc., nor as when at Auchinleck as an ancient Baron. But I resolutely endured the disagreeable circumstances of an ambitious, though I feared now, an ill-judged experiment.

SUNDAY 27 JULY. Attended at the mayor's with other members of the Corporation and had a glass of wine and cake according to custom, and then walked as Recorder in the procession to church. I resolved to have either a gown on purpose or my bar-gown next time. I felt myself very serene in the Cathedral and looked back to former days. I went with Sir Joseph Senhouse and visited his new-married lady at his mother's; then went to my lodgings and read in the *History of Cumberland and Westmorland.*[4] And then dined along with many of the Corporation and other gentlemen at a venison feast given by Lord Lonsdale at the Bush Inn. I sat next old Mr. Potts, the mayor, who was now eighty-three. He had been nine years at a grammar-school and retained a good deal of Latin. He then was bound to a grocer in

[3]Ephesians 6:14: "Having on the breastplate of righteousness."
[4]Joseph Nicolson and Richard Burn, *The History and Antiquities of the Counties of Westmorland and Cumberland*, 2 vols., 1777.

Carlisle and had carried on that business. He had £100 of his own and got £100 with his wife, and his trade had never exceeded £200 a year. But he had acquired land in Cumberland of £100 a year and houses in Carlisle of equal value and had educated three sons, one to his own business who unhappily fell into drinking, a major in the army, and a banker's clerk in London. He showed me what a long tract of economy may do. I found him a healthy, cheerful old man who had lived very soberly, taking, however, a hearty glass now and then. I was moderate today and went home in good time. I was unlucky again as to business here, for a cause of Lord Lonsdale and others was withdrawn.

MONDAY 28 JULY. A great deal in court. Dined at the mess, the style of which seemed irksome. Waited on Lord Lonsdale forenoon and afternoon. He went home at night. I went to the assembly and engaged Lady Senhouse to dance with me; but Sir Joseph having hinted that it might be *dangerous* for her, I let her off but had thus no partner, which I regretted as I wished to share in the gaiety of my own city. I had played whist at the inn and lost. I played it at the assembly tonight and won. Major Clarke, a decent, hard-favoured veteran, the town-major,[5] cut into the party of which I was. I wished him to be with me as I was in luck, and I understood that his funds were not ample. Finding he was against me, I proposed playing for a trifle, but he named half a crown, and as I was against him (by cutting) two rubbers, I won from him 17s. 6d., much against my will. I was really very much pained but I could not help it. I went home at four in the morning with a sore heart for him. Perhaps there was no good reason, but it proved that my disposition was humane and generous. I thought of making him a present equal to the value of his loss. I should have mentioned that old Dr. Coulthard introduced me this afternoon to Sir James Graham, and that Sir James was exceedingly courteous to me at the assembly, insisted on my coming to his house, said he should be happy to be of service to me with Mr. Bushby in my election, professed a warm regard for Lord Lonsdale, and said they will find me of more consequence in the county of Cumberland than they suppose. [SIR JAMES.] "I intend to make all my people of Longtown freeholders." [BOSWELL.] "I shall be glad to have a conversation with you upon the subject." I liked to be talked to as a friend of the Lowther interest.

TUESDAY 29 JULY. In court. Dined at the mess. Had visited the Rev. Dr. Grisdale in the morning. Played whist a long time at the inn and lost a good deal, which vexed me, as losing at play always does,

---

[5]Chief executive officer of a garrison town or fortress, a remnant of the time when Carlisle had been a Border stronghold against the Scots.

and then I began to reflect on the expensive dissipation of this *circuiting* and how unjust it was by an imprudent experiment to deprive my dear wife of the comfort of having her husband and children always with her, as she was entitled by marriage to expect. I was very uneasy. I went into the court, which sat late, and was somewhat entertained. Home before twelve.

[EDITORIAL NOTE. At this point, except for a brief fragment of 18–24 May 1789, there is a gap in the journal of more than a year, the longest period of silence since the lean years of 1770–1771. It is possible, however, to reconstruct events in considerable detail because of the preservation of the Book of Company, the Register of Letters, and an unusual number of letters filled with news. Seventeen letters to Mrs. Boswell form as satisfactory a substitute for the journal as we could have had. We intersperse with them related correspondence and other documents of special interest.

Boswell returned to Auchinleck from the Circuit on 15 August 1788, and as his note in the Book of Company shows, "was much from home canvassing the county." With his friend Alexander Hamilton of Grange he called one evening at the home of Robert Baillie of Mayville, whose daughter Leslie, in her own words, "instantly fell a sacrifice to the charms of his wit, vivacity, and humour." "I am *charmed, fascinated, bewitched*," she wrote to her friend, Jean Campbell Reid, "beyond the power of language (at least any language *I am mistress* of) to express, and wish, most devoutly wish, that I had a dozen votes at my disposal for his sake." The account of a meeting that Boswell sent to the newspapers suggests that he also won considerable practical support, but the reader will notice that it mentions no numbers and only two allies by name.]

[From the *Edinburgh Advertiser*, 26–30 September 1788]
Extract of a Letter from Kilmarnock, 25 September

This day was held here the meeting of *real freeholders* of *Ayrshire* called by *Colonel Craufurd* of *Craufurdland* by public advertisement, when the Colonel being put into the chair, he stated to the meeting that an attempt was making to introduce Mr. McDowall of Garthland, a gentleman from another county, as representative for Ayrshire, upon a vacancy which was soon to be declared; that Mr. McDowall was supported by that coalition in this county, which, if permitted to be effectual, would entirely annihilate the freedom of election; and therefore he thought that the independent gentlemen of Ayrshire should unite against it. *Mr. Boswell* of *Auchinleck* said that it was well known that he was a candidate to represent the county at the General Election, which was an object of great importance to him; that he heard, with surprise and indignation, of the attempt which had now been mentioned, which was declaring to all Scotland that there was not, in this respectable county, any gentleman worthy to represent it, so that it was necessary to *import* a representative; that he, therefore, feeling for the honour of the county, had laid aside all cold considerations of prudence as to the influence which his struggle now might have upon the General Election, and had resolved that if there should be only his own vote for himself, he would stand forth and vindicate the county from the disgrace of submitting unanimously to so humiliating a measure, which was a pretty specimen of what the county were to expect from the strange coalition between Lord Eglinton and Sir Adam Fergusson; that he wondered that Mr. McDowall, to whom he had personally no objection, but the contrary, should choose to undertake so ungracious a task; that it was of no more consequence to him than to any other independent freeholder; and, to convince the meeting of his sincerity, he engaged that if another candidate whose residence was in the county should appear to them more likely to succeed in defeating the invasion, he would cheerfully resign his pretensions and heartily support that person. *Sir William Cuningham* of *Robertland* expressed himself with becoming spirit against the attempt, and said the county were much obliged to Mr. Boswell for standing forth in so handsome a manner; and he therefore moved that Mr. Boswell should be supported upon this occasion.

The meeting then unanimously resolved, "That the attempt to introduce Mr. McDowall of Garthland, a gentleman from another county, as the representative in Parliament for Ayrshire is derogatory to the honour of this county; and they therefore pledge themselves to oppose the same to the utmost of their power.

That Mr. Boswell of Auchinleck having stood forth for the honour of the county, they unanimously make choice of him as a proper candidate to represent the county upon this occasion, and engage to give him all their interest and support."[6]

[EDITORIAL NOTE. Thus distracted, Boswell had still made no progress on the *Life* when he wrote to Malone on 18 September and begged for comfort instead of a scolding. ("Your neglect of Johnson's *Life* is

[6]As it turned out, Hugh Montgomerie, the sitting M.P., was appointed Baggage Master and Inspector of the Roads in North Britain on 27 June 1789, and McDowall was returned for Ayrshire at a by-election held on 3 August 1789.

only what I expected," Malone replied, "Scotland is not the place for it.") On 3 October Boswell set out for the Michaelmas Quarter Sessions at Carlisle, where Lonsdale joined him on the 5th. On the 7th he made a speech to the Grand Jury in his official capacity as Recorder, but there being no criminal business, he was back at Auchinleck again on the 9th. It appears to have been his original intention to continue on to London from Carlisle, to make one more trial of the English bar and to finish the *Life*, but by the time set for the Sessions he had not succeeded in raising £500 owed to Charles Dilly ("which *must* be paid in London about the first of November," he told Malone, 7 October). Consequently he had to go back for it. He sold the timber of Templand Wood for £650 and used three of the four promissory notes which he received in payment as collateral for a loan of £300 from the bank of Hunter and Company, Ayrshire, and for an additional £200 from the Bank of Scotland, Kilmarnock. On 20 October, with Sandy and Jamie, he set out for London.

En route Boswell stopped at Lichfield, where he continued an unsuccessful attempt to involve Anna Seward in an affair. On 26 October he arrived in London. There he worked feverishly on the *Life* through the winter, groaning because of the apparent endlessness of his task. Veronica remained with Mrs. Stevenson, but the placement of the boys was unsettled when he wrote the following letter to Mrs. Boswell, who had been very ill and anxious since he left Auchinleck.]

[Boswell to Margaret Boswell]

London, 9 November 1788

MY DEAREST LIFE,—Yesterday morning I was alarmed in a terrible manner. The postman's loud rap shook my nerves (which for a week and more had been very bad), and a letter with the mark Mauchline, sealed with black and directed by Phemie, was delivered. The circumstance of its being sent directly and not under Mr. Garforth's cover seemed to imply unusual haste and added to my fears.[7] I was almost afraid to open it, which I did in great agitation, and when I saw your handwriting, I fervently thanked GOD. The poor boys were in the room, and you may imagine how they were affected. How came it to be sealed with black, and how directed by Phemie, and why not under cover of Mr. Garforth, whose letters are all opened at his office, so that his being in town or not makes no difference? I was so much relieved by finding that you had written me any letter at all that I bore with much tranquillity certain passages which otherwise would have

[7]Since Garforth was an M.P. letters to him went free.

pained me a good deal. Sensible as I am of conduct which I so sincerely blame that I can scarcely believe it to be true, and of which I have repented most seriously and with vexation of mind, I cannot but think it hard that the regard which I express should be doubted, or rather not credited, when I am sure that, notwithstanding many culpable deviations, there never was a more lasting attachment, more true esteem, or more tender love. During this last separation I have felt it deeper than ever; and when I have been depressed by a return of melancholy joined with contrition, how distressing must such reflections as are in your letter be to me! The creature to whom you allude I told you was totally dismissed from my attention, and I solemnly protest that I have not corresponded. How shameful would it have been if I had, after what I assured you, or indeed in any view! If you can, for this one time more, generously and wisely forget and forgive, I think my feelings have been such that there shall never again be any occasion for just complaint.[8]

Veronica is now in a more composed frame. Yesterday Miss Palmer brought her in the coach to Sir Joshua's to dinner, where I had the pleasure of meeting her and being pleased with her behaviour. Miss Palmer afterwards carried her to the play (to a private box) and set her down at home. Last Sunday she dined with me, and I had her Uncle David and Mrs. and Miss Buchanan to meet her. This day I brought her to breakfast, and she dined and drank tea with me and her brothers, and I took her home at night. She was quite rational today, and though she talked of her situation being disagreeable, did not as before whine and foolishly ask to be taken away before her year being out.

I wearied of the *country* at Mr. Malone's and stayed only a day and a half and two nights.[9]

My friends with whom I have advised as to the boys all agree that Sandy's complaint[1] would make a great school dangerous for him, but that James should be sent to one, and Westminster seems to have most votes. I am still wavering very uneasily. Sandy seems inclined for Westminster, while I am thinking that Dr. Thomson's would be best for

---

[8] The "creature" was probably, though not certainly, Mrs. Rudd. There is no record of Boswell's having seen her since 23 April 1786 (see above), but Mrs. Boswell was with him in London from the end of September 1786 to May 1788. During that time he attempted to call upon Mrs. Rudd at least once that we know of, 29 May 1787 (see above).

[9] Malone had been living at Cobham Park, Surrey, since 14 August because his house in London was being painted inside and out.

[1] An inguinal hernia.

him; and I cannot quite resolve to part with Jamie. In the mean time Mr. Slee is doing a great deal for them. As to accommodation, the chambers in the Temple which I have yet seen are dreary, and I shudder at solitude. Mrs. Wrother sent me a polite message that her lodgings were disengaged and that she would be very happy to have me in them. But I have a notion that a small house would be best, if I cannot find cheerful chambers. In case of my selling the furniture, be so good as to write—[2]

(I am now writing on 11 November, having been much occupied yesterday in inquiring at various places about the King, who was positively reported to be dead.[3] But thank GOD he is still alive and *may* recover, though there are very faint hopes. Some say the disease is a dropsy; some that it is a severe nervous fever. He has been quite delirious. The Queen is in the most miserable distress. You cannot imagine how much real concern there is here amongst all but the Opposition party.)

Be so good as to write if you would have any of the furniture sent down, except *our own bed* (which I would not give for its weight in gold), the large mirror in the parlour, and the bed and table linen and blankets and your chest of drawers. The man who has taken the house (who seems to be an odd mortal) said to me he would take several pieces of furniture at a reasonable valuation. But Bell says he estimates everything very low.

I have seen Sir John Dick since I began to write this page and was informed by him that the King was better last night; that his pulse, which was once at 120, had fallen to 75, but that he was still delirious, and it is thought he may perhaps remain so, even if he should live. This would be quite a new case and occasion much difficulty.

I have been sadly afflicted with low spirits. I was so sunk on Sunday evening that poor Veronica cried and said, "How melancholy is it to see you so ill and that I cannot help you!" I am a little better, but I think myself very bad company for my children. Oh, that I had never come to settle in London! Miserable I must be wherever I am. Such is my doom. Oh, if I could but have the boys placed under proper care! They are behaving very well. Jamie had a bad cold for a day or two.

---

[2]Boswell picks up and completes this sentence after his parenthesis.

[3]He had been ill again since the middle of October and on 5 November became so much worse that his life was believed to be in imminent danger. He was thought to be violently insane and was confined until his recovery the following February. In 1966 Dr. Ida Macalpine and Dr. Richard Hunter diagnosed his condition as the hereditary illness, porphyria, which seems to have been aggravated mentally and physically by incompetent treatment.

He in particular mourns his absence from his Mama. Sandy seems to be well reconciled to be sent to some school.

Your account that the tenants refuse to gravel the avenue provokes and vexes me. But perhaps it comes *misrepresented* to you through a certain medium, that *hands* may be *hired.*[4] I beg that you may take the trouble to exert as to this. Their tacks bind them to repair the road "from the *House* of Auchinleck to the church thereof." It is an obligation to *me*, and I will enforce it. If you please, let Mr. Bruce Campbell see to it. (I have received a packet from him round by Bath and shall write to him tomorrow.) Some of the tenants are bound to furnish only a man, some also a horse and cart. I will hire no man whatever for this work; and they shall be compelled to work year after year till the road to the head of the avenue is completely done.

I could write a long time but must send to the post. My love to Euphemia and Betsy. I paid a visit to Mrs. Green yesterday. She regrets much your absence. She says T.D. starves the child, in her opinion, for there is not milk enough and he will not let it be fed. This may be a grandmother's whim.[5]

Assure Euphemia that she is much happier than Veronica, whose letters as to her situation were written, you know, under the Mistress's eye. But she is wonderfully improved—quite a lady. I ever am yours most gratefully and affectionately,

J.B.

[EDITORIAL NOTE. It is to be hoped that the clouds over Boswell's spirits were lifted, at least momentarily, by a letter which he received from Bruce Campbell and endorsed "13 November 1788. Mr. Robert Burns, *the Poet*, expressing very high sentiments of me." There is no evidence that the two great Ayrshire authors ever met. Boswell was little in Scotland after the date of this letter.]

[Robert Burns to Bruce Campbell]

Mauchline, 13 November 1788
SIR,—I enclose you, for Mr. Boswell, the ballad you mentioned, and as I hate sending wastepaper or mutilating a sheet, I have filled it up with one or two of my fugitive pieces that occurred. Should they procure me the honour of being introduced to Mr. Boswell, I shall think

[4]Boswell probably means James Bruce.
[5]This child of David Boswell's seems to have been born only a few days before the date of this letter, though the papers now preserved make no direct allusion to the event.

they have great merit. There are few pleasures my late will-o'-wisp character has given me equal to that of having seen many of the extraordinary men, the heroes of wit and literature, in my country; and as I had the honour of drawing my first breath almost in the same parish with Mr. Boswell, my pride plumes itself on the connection. To crouch in the train of mere stupid wealth and greatness, except where the commercial interests of worldly prudence find their account in it, I hold to be prostitution in anyone that is not born a slave; but to have been acquainted with such a man as Mr. Boswell I would hand down to my posterity as one of the honours of their ancestor.[6] I am, Sir, your most obedient and very humble servant,

ROBERT BURNS.

[Boswell to Margaret Boswell]

London, 24 November 1788

MY DEAREST LIFE,—I wrote you a long letter on Friday,[7] on which day I dined at Sir Joshua Reynolds's with Mr. Burke and a good many more. On Saturday I dined at home with the boys and in the afternoon went into the City, read the Scotch newspapers, and passed the evening with Mr. Dilly. A few minutes after I had walked out, who called but Lord Lonsdale, who came into the parlour, James[8] having imagined I was at home. Sandy did not hear his name and talked to him, he says, quite easily, but takes credit to himself for perceiving something grand in his countenance. Jamie had heard who it was and stood in a corner frightened. He left word that he wished to see me next morning. I accordingly went to him and had some hours with him, partly by

---

[6]Burns had published the first edition of his *Poems* in July 1786, and the winter following had been the literary and social sensation of Edinburgh. He was now married and had returned to being a farmer. The enclosure has disappeared, but there can be little doubt that the "ballad" was *The Fête Champêtre*, which Burns had recently composed to commemorate an ambitious open air festival held on the banks of the Ayr in July 1788 by William Cuninghame of Enterkine. (Euphemia Boswell was one of the guests. See below, p. 269, n. 5.) The ostensible purpose of the entertainment was to celebrate Cuninghame's coming of age, but the real object was to discuss the politics of the county, as to which Cuninghame had sounded Boswell in the preceding March (see above, 17 March 1788, p. 200). Burns therefore begins by mentioning the three candidates for Parliament from Ayrshire: Sir Adam Fergusson, Col. Hugh Montgomerie, and Boswell:

> Or will we send a man o' law?
> Or will we send a sodger?
> Or him wha led o'er Scotland a'
> The meikle Ursa-Major?

[7]21 November.
[8]James Ross, Boswell's servant.

himself, partly in company with a gentleman of good political intelligence. The situation of public affairs is very strange. Pitt and his friends are labouring to carry a Committee of Regency. The Opposition is as hard at work making interest to have the Prince[9] chosen sole Regent. It is said the Chancellor joins the Prince; and I should think that His Royal Highness will carry it in Parliament. They will be bold or desperate men who will set themselves against the heir apparent, whose right of governing may be soon put beyond all question. Lord Lonsdale is much courted by both sides. He assured me yesterday that he had not declared himself, but he did not check me or seem displeased when I spoke warmly in favour of the Prince. His preferable claim appears natural and attended with less danger of cabal and trouble than placing the monarchical power in the hands of several ambitious strugglers for power.[1] What Lord Lonsdale wanted with me yesterday was to concert our defence against a groundless prosecution brought against us in the King's Bench as Justices of the Peace for Carlisle for not granting licences to some publicans. We are fully in the right, so there is no fear; and if you should see anything about it in the newspapers, laugh at it. His Lordship gave me another dinner tête-à-tête and was exceedingly kind. He goes for Lowther tomorrow but returns again before the meeting of Parliament. I am to dine with him again today with Governor Penn (one of his Members) and Sir Joseph Senhouse. I have no right to expect that he is to do me any eminent service. But I surely may be allowed to indulge hopes. I took it truly kind yesterday that he took more wine to himself than he gave me, saying placidly, "You'll excuse me. You cannot drink as much as I can do." What you write as to my being ill-suited to *dependence* is excellent. But where I have a high respect, and look up to superior strength of mind, I am greatly assisted.

Do not be uneasy about Veronica. There is no fear of her. I saw my sister-in-law for the first time today.[2] Mrs. Buchanan is indefatigable in looking for a house for me, but we have not as yet found one. Being confined to the *law district* makes a great difficulty.

I regret the poindings,[3] but such things are unfortunately necessary.

---

[9]Of Wales.

[1]Boswell later wrote to Temple that he was at first so "carried away with the notion of the *right* having *devolved* to the Prince" that he had almost written one of his "very warm popular pamphlets" on the subject. His notes for it are preserved among his papers.

[2]Presumably, for the first time since she gave birth.

[3]To *poind* means either to seize and sell the goods of a debtor or to impound stray cattle.

Courtenay is come and is in high spirits. I remain very well and most affectionately yours,

J.B.

I shall be in no hurry as to the boys.

[Boswell to Margaret Boswell]

London, 28 November 1788

MY DEAREST LIFE,—I wrote to you on Monday, when I was going to dine at Lord Lonsdale's. There was nobody there but Governor Penn and myself. His Lordship was to set out *alone* for Lowther next morning and to be in London again in ten days. He asked me to accompany him and expressed it so that I could not refuse. Accordingly I was at his house on Tuesday by nine o'clock. He did not appear for some time; and, when he did, he mentioned to me a matter of moment in agitation which would require my being in London, and therefore said that he would not carry me to Lowther, but I should go a day's journey with him to Buckden; we would talk the matter over, and I should return next day. Upon this I sent a note to Sandy to let it be known that I would be in town next day, and set out with the Earl. The business alluded to is highly flattering to me but is a *secret*, which I might communicate to *you*, were we together, but would not put in writing.[4] We went at night to Buckden. Next morning, finding that I could be in London again as soon by going another stage with his Lordship, I went on with him to Stilton. There we parted, and I returned in the mail-coach and brought with me a Stilton cheese to produce to Sir Joshua as a proof that I had been there. I had an invitation to dine with him yesterday, which I claimed upon my return, and the Stilton cheese appeared after dinner. I was fatigued by travelling in the mail-coach in a cold, frosty night and coming home from the City at four in the morning; but a warm bed and then Sir Joshua's revived me. Today I have dined at home with the boys very comfortably. I am wonderfully well, so be no longer uneasy about me. Poor Jamie said to me just now, "Papa, you say that I'm a great charge trusted by Mama to Sandy and you. But you are the charge trusted to us, for she writes to both of us to take care of you."

I am sorry that little Betsy has any complaint. I hope riding will make her well. Robert Paton's[5] illness gives me real concern. I beg that you may order a man to work for him, that he may be kept quite easy,

[4] Boswell nowhere reveals the secret. It may have concerned Lonsdale's manoeuvres with regard to the proposed Regency.
[5] A labourer on the estate, usually in the garden.

and have a horse to ride, or even a sail from Ayr if that is thought good for him.[6]

Be entreated to take the greatest care of your own health, and pray go out in the chaise every day. I am quite sorry to leave our Queen Street house and as yet have found none that I could possess with any satisfaction. However, one *must* be got.

Mungo's wife had a daughter some time ago.[7] They are very quiet in the house.

I am so late that James must run to Holborn after the postman.

My love to Euphemia and Betsy. I wish to hear often from Euphemia. Enclosed are letters to you and Betsy from the Chancellor Doog.[8] The boys are very well. I am ever most affectionately and gratefully yours,

J.B.

[Boswell to Margaret Boswell]

London, 5 December 1788

MY DEAREST LIFE,—When I called on Mr. Courtenay yesterday morning I had the pleasure to find your letter of the 27 November with two for Veronica—excellent ones indeed. The boarding-school one shall be sent this afternoon; the private one shall be delivered to her next Sunday morning, when she comes to us. The butter, cheese, etc., have come safe, all in good order. I wish my old scratch[9] which James forgot had been sent with them. But nobody would know of it. Bell wonders that she has not heard from you for a long time. Your last letter, it seems, hurt her much. She has done so wonderfully well since I came up and is in such prodigious good temper with us that she really deserves your countenance, and a good letter from you will soon put her into humour again.

On Tuesday I went to Mr. Malone's in *the country*, which was a great compliment from me. I returned on Wednesday, but so late that I could not write to you, as I had to hurry home and bring the boys to General Paoli's, where we dined. I then went to Lord Lonsdale's, his Lordship having returned that afternoon. I sat with him and Sir Mi-

---

[6]A "sail" is dialectal for a ride in a vehicle of any kind, but if "a sail" here means a vehicle we have not found it attested.

[7]Probably Mungo is Boswell's servant.

[8]The enclosures having disappeared, we are unable to identify the person concealed in this bit of family jocularity. Jamie had already been destined by his father for the exalted post of Lord Chancellor of England.

[9]Scratch-wig.

chael le Fleming and Mr. Satterthwaite over good wine till it was pretty late. But I came home very decently. Yesterday and today I have dined at home.

This is not much of a *London life*, as so highly painted in my imagination. But being *upon the spot*, and within reach of greatness and gaiety and variety, I fancy myself better than if I were anywhere else. But the *separation* distresses me more than I can tell, and I often say to myself, "Is there anything in this world equally valuable to *me* as being with my dear M.M.?" It is truly unfortunate that I have such a restless ambition and so little tranquillity. But if Lord Lonsdale should prove a real friend to me, I may yet have it to say that I did well to try my fortune here. I am now resolved to take another house, that I may have one year more for consideration. It is amazing how difficult it is to find one. I have today seen a neat small one, in good air, near to Bedford Square, and am just going to call on the landlord, as I am told he has an offer for purchasing it, which he may prefer to letting it. I hope in GOD that a winter in the country and a particular time of life being fairly over may make you healthy, so as to be able to come to London, if necessary. I almost despair now of getting practice at the English bar, yet I still flatter myself with visionary hopes that it may come all at once. Though there is too strong a consideration, which you suggested, and that is that my ignorance of the *forms* might expose me. The *rank of barrister* is however something, and may be turned to account.

I paid Mr. Kerr's interest at Martinmas by a draft on the Ayr Bank.[1] I had a letter from him thanking me for my punctuality, which, he says, is very rare in Scotland. I have now, I think, no more credit in the bank but £11. We live here with the utmost economy, but after Christmas I shall require some supply. Pray let James Bruce take care that my £200 bill to the bank at Kilmarnock be regularly paid. I am sorry for Andrew Arnot, but I hope he will be able to go on, and he shall be indulged. The Fosters cannot remain unless they find good security. Mr. Dun's behaviour is to be regretted. I feel for you as to *preaching*. I do not intend to settle anybody till there is a vacancy.[2] Ever most affectionately yours,

J.B.

[1] He had borrowed £2,000 in 1777 from James Kerr of Blackshiels, a money-lender, and used part of the loan to complete payment for the property of Dalblair adjoining Auchinleck, which he had bought in 1767.

[2] The Rev. John Dun, Boswell's sometime tutor, and minister of Auchinleck since 1752, had become increasingly cranky and quarrelsome with years (occasionally, it appears, with good cause), but we do not know the reason for the present complaint against him. Boswell's remark about settling someone means that he does not intend to appoint Dun's successor until he retires or dies.

My love to Euphemia and Betsy. Sandy says he will write soon, but as he is busier than Jamie, he cannot write so often. Poor James is very fond of writing to you. He has shown me the enclosed, which is truly characteristical.[3]

I am much concerned about Robert Paton. Let him be told that I desire he may want for nothing that can do him good.

The state of public affairs is very dark. The Opposition are in high expectation.

The post-days from hence by *Dumfries* are Monday, Wednesday, and Friday. So I cannot write oftener unless by *Edinburgh*, which would go to Kilmarnock.

It is surer and nearer for my letters to come to Mr. Garforth's, where they are no trouble.

Now and then one may be sent to Mr. Courtenay's, to keep up the connection.

[James Boswell, Jr., to Margaret Boswell][4]

London 5 December 1788

Dear mama,—I hope you are well as you said nothing about it in your letter to papa which he recieved yesterday. the day before yesterday we were at the generals to dine where was one Tiberius cavallo an exceeding curius man as can be. on Sunday last, we were all at Mrs. Buchanans Veronica not excepted so we past together an agreable night of it. Mrs. Buchanan invited one Dr. Burn to keep papa company and drink a bottle or two with him, he is an odd sort of a fellow for he refuses every thing and then take evry thing, they drank about two bottles together but neither of them was the worse of it which you know was a lucky thing indeed. pray how does Betseys stomack do I hope it is better if not well and how does Euphemia do. I forgot to tell you that general Pioli has his kind complements to you phemie and the leetle Buaety,[5] and I am sure I have the same oh, I wish I saw you all again, I believe papa writes to you to day Pray write me soon again for you cant think how much pleasure it gives me and I cant expres it Pray how does all about auchinleck do and poor wealside, and Jacobus Welch, not forgetting the chaise horses. so Driver is in a good way and tartar and Mr. swan I hope he is fatter poor creature[6] Pray ask phemie

[3]See the next letter in this series.
[4]Jamie's capitalization, pointing, and spelling have been preserved. He was at this time a little over ten years old.
[5]"Beauty." Jamie had difficulty with the word and wrote it twice over. In his letters to Temple, Boswell refers more than once to Betsy's good looks.
[6]Weelside was a tenant on the estate at Auchinleck and Welch was Mrs. Boswell's coachman. Mr. Swan seems to have been a colt or pony.

if she can run yet without tumbling, is she oblidged to go on horseback doun to the old house or head of the avenue. Farewell give my compliments to effie[7] and all in Auchinleck howse, papa is continuing to write his life of the great Dr. Johnson[8] and hopes to have it done by Christmas. we are not fixed upon what School we go to, nor have we found a house yet but I hope soon will Believe me my dear mama your most dutiful and affectionate son

JAMES BOSWELL.

[Veronica Boswell to Margaret Boswell][9]

Great Queens Street, 7 December 1788
My Dearest Mama,—Your kind letter which I had the pleasure of receiving this morning was a great treat to me. I am sorry that I wrote anything of my disliking School as it has made you uneasy but really my heart is so full when i have an opportunity of opening it that I have not prudence to hide what it contains your tender manner of reproving me shews the heighth of your affection but I am sorry you should upbraid yourself for indulging me it is not your fault if I should not behave prudently you have acted your part with the utmost attention and if I follow your example I shall never be wrong. I shall hope to convince you when I return home that your poor Veronica although appearances are at present against her is as dutiful and affectionate as you can desire and pray to God that that time may not be far off this is my constant prayer every morning when I pray for the preservation of you my dearest mama my father and Sisters and Brothers if it please him to grant my prayer and if we all meet again I hope to pass some more happy days. I see in one of your letters to my brothers that Betsey had been complaining of a sourness in her stomach I shall be happy to hear that she is quite well You cannot think what pleasure it will give me to instruct her in any branch of education which I am mistress enough of myself Music and french I think I can undertake her in as that is what I know most of does Phemy practise her singing it will be a great pity if she loses what she has got pray tell her I shall expect her to have a *fine* shake[1] when I return I have not begun painting as it takes such a time those who have made any progress have learnt five or six years and as it is very expensive I thought it was better to

---

[7]Probably James Bruce's daughter Euphemia, named for Boswell's mother.
[8]Jamie first wrote "Jonstone," and then corrected it, probably at his father's bidding.
[9]Veronica's capitalization, pointing, and spelling, like Jamie's, have been preserved. She was now sixteen years old.
[1]Trill.

defer that till I return to Scotland. What they excell in here is dancing, the Master is such a capital one that it gives me great pleasure to receive any instruction from him. You mention as a means to make me reconciled to my situation that Auchinleck is not so agreeable as it was but all places with your company are alike to me while you was here I was happy and if you return and I am received back again to be one of the family from whence at present I am like an outcast I shall never wish to change. That you may be long preserved as a blessing and comfort to your very Affectionate family is the fervent prayer of your very affecte. and dutiful daughter,

VERONICA BOSWELL.

P.S. Sandie and Jamie join me in duty to you and love to Phemy and Betsey. I have told Papa about Mr. Corri and Mr. Rose. Love to George Campbell and compts. to J. Cunninghame.

[Margaret Boswell to Sandy]

14 December 1788[2]

MY DEAR SANDY,—Every letter which you write me is so fraught with tender affection that I cannot help indulging the pleasing hopes that the Almighty will bless you and make you a comfort and credit to all your friends. I hope the proper sense you have of your father's goodness will have a suitable effect with regard to your behaviour towards him. The improving your mind by study and application will be the most lasting proof you can give him of your gratitude towards him, as it will manifest to the world that he judged rightly in yielding to you, contrary to the opinion of all his friends, in giving you a private tutor. At the same time I must entreat as you value me that you will not neglect regular necessary exercise. You cannot enjoy health without attending strictly to this, and without health I can with truth assure you that little good can be done. I hope to hear that your father is fixed in a house. I shall be uneasy till I am assured of it, as I know how inconvenient he will find it to remove in so short a time. Little Swan seems not well, but nobody here can find out his disease.

I had wrote so far when the Countess of Dundonald and her retinue arrived. We were all in sad plight; obliged to get James Bruce's maid as every other creature was confined. I am better, but any violent illness lays fast hold of me. The weather is so severe there is no drink to be had for the cattle but what is pumped from the well. I must bid you

---

[2] The letter was begun on the 14th and ended on the 19th. It was enclosed in a wrapper inscribed in Boswell's hand, "Three letters to my son Alexander from his mother."

adieu as I am just stepping into bed. May that merciful Being who neither slumbers nor sleeps take us under His divine care and protection. Farewell, my dearest Sandy, and believe me your very affectionate mother,

M. BOSWELL

[Boswell to Margaret Boswell]

London, 31 December 1788

MY DEAREST LIFE,—I cannot express how uneasy I am that I have had no letter yesterday or today, as a more than ordinary anxiety depresses my mind, as the season in this place is almost intolerably severe, and, if it be the same at Auchinleck, must be very hard upon you. I wish you had resolved and persevered in keeping constantly within the house during the cold weather. We have had an intense frost for some time, and this day there is a heavy fall of snow. The boys and I are very well, but shall be very anxious till tomorrow's post arrive. May GOD in His mercy preserve you to us. This dreary distance is terrible. We join love to Euphemia and Betsy. The boys send their duty and love to you, and I ever am most gratefully and affectionately yours,

1789

[EDITORIAL NOTE. On 3 January 1789 Boswell drew up his usual "view" of his affairs. It was as disheartening as ever: the annual interest alone on his debt of £4,670 amounted to almost £235. His income, he told Temple in November 1789, was only £850 clear. But also on 3 January he had completed the Introduction to the *Life of Johnson* and the Dedication to Sir Joshua Reynolds, and though they both "had appeared very difficult to be accomplished," he was confident that they were "well done." By 10 January he had sublet a "very small but neat" house at No. 38, Queen Anne Street West, Cavendish Square. He was in a "most *illegal* situation," his landlady being herself in arrears to the owner, and the dwelling would not accommodate the whole family; but houses were scarce, the neighbourhood was "genteel," Malone lived close by in Queen Anne Street East, and he was glad to be settled, even precariously.]

[Boswell to Margaret Boswell]

London, 23 January 1789

MY DEAREST LIFE,—On Wednesday I dined quietly with General Paoli. Yesterday I dined at Mr. Dilly's with steady Reed, my brother David, and a number more. Today I dine at Dr. Burn's, the trustee for Mrs. and Miss Buchanan, to meet them. I had no desire to accept of the invitation, but they were desirous I should, and they have been very obliging. My observation of Veronica's restraint at Mrs. Stevenson's on Monday made me so anxious about her that I could not be at rest on Wednesday without seeing her. To my no small satisfaction I found her by herself for some time and was convinced that my concern had been imaginary. She had begun geography with my consent, and at her own real request I agreed to her learning to paint flowers, for which there is no entrance. She was quite cheerful, and after seeing Mrs. Stevenson, who soon joined us, I departed quite relieved. If I had Sandy and Jamie placed in as good situations for *them*, I am convinced I should not be uneasy. Mr. Langton's Uncle Peregrine has agreed to pay for the education of his name-son, and the worthy man has sent *Greeny* to Mr. Burney's, where he is quite happy. Lady Rothes rejoices at this and wishes more of the boys were as well settled.

Your observations on the state of politics are admirable, and I *naturally* agree with them. But considering what myrmidons are about the Prince, it is certainly right to limit his Regency considerably, at least for some time. I have heard it asserted with much probability that he is *secretly* pleased at the restrictions, that he may get rid of many importunate beggars. Sir Adam Fergusson's having gone against Pitt is *capital*, as the phrase is. He means to prevent the Regency Ministry from being against him in Ayrshire.[3] But he will find himself mistaken. I shall consider calmly whether to avow myself against *both* the *Coalition candidates*, as they both now are.

I am better pleased with the house now that the frost is gone. There is room enough in the back parlour for the military exercise. I am longing to see James Bruce's account, which I have desired to have.

David and I, after consulting together, have agreed that unless poor John be worse, it would not be justifiable to force him into confinement, but that a careful man should attend him.

The boys, who are sitting by me, send you their kindest love (Sandy's words adopted by Jamie); and hoping to hear better accounts still of your health, and wishing much to be with you, I remain most affectionately yours,

J.B.

[Boswell to Margaret Boswell]

London, 26 January 1789

MY DEAREST LIFE,—Dr. Burn's day turned out exceedingly well: a handsome, plentiful dinner, excellent wines, and most of the company new to me, and of course I new to them, which, you know, I generally feel to be good company, and often the best. On Saturday I dined quietly at home with the boys, having really a longing for a quiet day. I had another yesterday, Veronica having been with us, and I assure you in so rational a frame as to prefer remaining in Queen Square even after the 15 of May, in case of not going directly to Scotland. You will find no complaints in her letters, which I enclose.[4]

Today I have received your *business letter* dated the 16th. No doubt what it states is, as you foretell, *not pleasant*, but that is not your fault. I am very much obliged to you for the trouble you have taken and for the advantage of being put upon my guard. James is really a strange

---

[3] Fergusson's momentary adherence to the Opposition is not noted elsewhere. He voted twice with Pitt and Dundas during the Regency crisis, on 16 December 1788 and 19 January 1789, and he did so again on 11 February.

[4] The enclosures have disappeared.

man.[5] I have written to him to send me an exact state of his accounts, as also a rental for 1789. The farming rental does not much exceed £467 half-yearly, because several of the tenants at present pay grass-rents by bills at Candlemas.

I am very sorry for James Murdoch in Whiteflat's family. I had no notion he was in so bad a way. If I recollect right, his tack provides that if he does not lime a certain proportion yearly the crop shall be answerable for it, by which means I am secure.[6] Pray make it be shown to you. The unstamped notes to Nanny Warden and Jenny Watt[7] are good for nothing. Why did they not take them on stamps? By saving twopence apiece I fear they will be in danger of losing their debts altogether. Had he been alive, they had only his oath for the money; but now he is gone, that is lost as to his children, who certainly do not know that he owed these sums. The only chance for them is that his widow *does* know; and if she takes anything by him, so as to be one of his representatives, she may be made liable upon her oath. Let them be quiet and see what she does.

I have *company* today, so am fluttered somewhat, according to custom, of which you are happy enough to know nothing, having been better used to entertain in early years. I have an earl and a bishop and a knight and the poet laureate, etc., etc.[8] Bell does wonderfully. Mother Smith assists today. The kitchen range is so small that to make my two roasts do she must *turn* the spit. As to James, I will not give him the wages of an English servant. I intend to look out for one for myself and let him go where he can have better wages, which indeed he deserves, but I cannot be pleased with him. I *must* have an English one, if I can be sure of an honest one.

Jamie is this day entered to Soho. You shall hear again on Wednesday, but I fancy I need no more mind the Dumfries post. Ever most affectionately yours,

J.B.

[Boswell to Margaret Boswell]

London, 28 January 1789

MY DEAREST LIFE,—My Wednesday's[9] dinner did wonderfully. My earl was our own Lord Moray, who lives in the same street with me; and

---

[5] James Bruce.
[6] "Grass-rents" are rents for pasturage. A tack is a lease.
[7] Janet Warden and Agnes Watt, servants in Auchinleck House.
[8] In his next letter Boswell names his guests.
[9] A slip; Boswell should have written "Monday's."

he having done me the honour of a visit on Friday, I wished to have the credit of one of the nobles of Scotland and to let his Lordship see my sort of society; and upon my honour, he played his part well, showing both sense and variety of knowledge. I had the Bishop of Killaloe, Sir Joshua Reynolds, Mr. Warton the Poet Laureate, Mr. O'Reilly, a gentleman of ancient Irish blood recommended to me by our cousin Mrs. O'Reilly, Mr. Seward, who has been very obliging in getting me materials for Johnson's *Life*, Jack Devaynes, and Windham. The bill of fare is enclosed.[1] Everything was well done, and full praise was given, so Bell had her reward. *Nine* sat with sufficient ease in my parlour. After cheese, we moved up to the drawing-room, where was a large table with oranges, nonpareils,[2] raisins and almonds, wine-biscuits, port, sherry, claret. Here the two boys appeared and had their share of the dessert and a glass of wine. Lastly came coffee and tea. The dinner was for my much valued friend, my Lord of Killaloe, and we had a good day, as I *felt*, and as Sir Joshua *confirmed* to me this forenoon.

Yesterday Sandy and I dined on excellent fragments, of which Jamie on his return from Soho had some. He is quite pleased with it and will be much the better for being there till I resolve to send him to a great school, if I should live on bread and water.

Today I have hospitable Dilly and one or two of his friends and my brother David to plain roast and boil, with my remains of turkey, and one of the chickens in a caponata,[3] and the blancmange. I *must* show him some return.

Yesterday evening there was a *disagreeable surprise*. When the boys and I were sitting quietly *who* entered but the wretched *Lawrie*, who had come from Edinburgh, partly in the wagon, partly on foot. He had been here some days and is lodged at some *friend's* house in the borough of *Sooth*wark, near London Bridge. He cannot or does not tell what his errand is. He says nobody knows of his coming but his wife and Lord Dunsinnan. He looks miserably. My notion is he has run off for debt. I asked him to come and dine here tomorrow. I am to be at Lord Sunderlin's by an engagement *since*, but I will *see* him fed. Poor creature, I can do nothing for him, and, from what you know, have no great heart to it. I will keep as clear of him as I can. He quite sunk my spirits by renewing former coarse, vulgar sensations: the Parliament *Hoose*, etc., etc.[4]

[1] The enclosure has disappeared.
[2] A kind of apple.
[3] A Sicilian speciality, a vegetable dish prepared in oil, which may accompany meat.
[4] We also do not know why Lawrie (Boswell's former law clerk in Scotland) was in trouble.

Oh, if this book of mine were done! Job says, "Oh, that mine enemy *had written* a book!" I shall rejoice when I can speak in the *past* tense. I *do* hope to be at *Finis* in ten days.

How hard is it that you are not here! I flatter myself that your constitution will be strengthened so as you may be able to live in a well-aired street *with a carriage*, to defray the expense of which I *must* contrive. Fortune, I trust, will at last favour me, for I am sure I deserve it.

I have had a long and most kind letter from Sir William Forbes, who sends you his best respects. I have answered it suitably.

Veronica now puts on her clothes neatly, which Mrs. Stevenson justly considers as a valuable habit. I assure you when she appears with her large muff, which is now fashionable, she is quite the lady. Mrs. Stevenson does not wish to have Miss who has been at the *Fête Champêtre*, but is very desirous to have Betsy.[5] I, however, am of opinion that *twelve* or *thirteen* is the age when real improvement in *manner* may be had in Queen Square, and much earlier than that a girl gets no more than she can get in any good house in *England*. If Euphemia will go willingly, I may *prevail* on Mrs. Stevenson to take her, and it would do her much good to be under elegant discipline. I enclose one of her letters as a specimen of her writing, which I approve.[6] You may either show it to her or tell her what I mean.

Pray take the greatest care of yourself. As to money matters, my comfort is that the rental grows better, and in proportion as it increases my children's provisions are enlarged.

Sandy sits by me and sends his affectionate duty. My love and his to the two with you. I ever am most affectionately yours,

J.B.

Lord Lonsdale is still confined to his room with a rheumatic fever.

[Boswell to Margaret Boswell]

London, 9 February 1789

MY DEAREST LIFE,—Your kind letter of the 2nd was received by me on the 7th, and I was glad to see from it that mine of the 23, 26, and 28 had all come safe. So you like my dinner. But Sandy says Bell should write to you with what difficulty she persuaded me to have it as it should be, my first plan being by no means so plentiful and genteel. The

[5]See above, Robert Burns to Bruce Campbell, 13 November 1788, p. 256, n. 6. A letter from the Countess of Crawford to Mrs. Boswell shows that it was Euphemia who attended and that Lady Crawford gave her a new hat for the occasion. She was now almost fifteen years old; Betsy was eight and a half.
[6]This letter has disappeared.

whole cost £2.10.9, and you must consider how dear fish is. Mine that day cost sixteen and sixpence. But how *can* you say I am better without you? Be assured that I feel our separation more than you can imagine. At this very time I am much in the frame that I was in the summer that we returned from Ireland, and you recollect what *that* was.[7] I get into fits of extreme impatience to be with you and sometimes into fits of sad fear. Yet I am upon the whole wonderfully well, owing, I do believe (though perhaps I should be sorry for it), to my living very *heartily* and being in much variety. I am, however, struck with a serious remark in Johnson's *Prayers and Meditations*, upon reviewing a portion of his time: "This is not the life to which heaven is promised." Let me endeavour to do better. All last week I did none of my Great Work. This vexes me, for it will be a week longer delayed, and I cannot *absolutely* see when I shall be done with it. Were you but here I should be less uneasy on that account. Sandy and Jamie, who speak of you with the warmest and most constant affection, are much against your coming up, for fear that London should do you harm again. But I would fain flatter myself that the air on this side of Oxford Street would not affect you like the air of St. Giles's parish.[8]

Bell is, I really think, happier now than ever I saw her. Working is her element, and she is much better fitted for a life of labour than for that of a superintendent. I have never once seen her in bad humour. The boy Ross is sober and honest and can serve very well; but even Sandy now says that he is grown more negligent and impertinent. If I could but get a genteel, active lad that I could depend upon, I would recommend J.R. to a place where he would get more wages and be kept in better order.

In about a month hence the Northern Circuit for the spring begins. It is a very disagreeable thing to me, lasts about thirty days, and costs about fifty pounds. I wish to make my *book* an excuse for shunning it. Yet if I *am* trying my chance as a barrister, ought I not to *endure hardships*?

I had luckily written to Smith in Glenside's brother-in-law before I received your account of his shameful behaviour. I will certainly show him no favour. I am afraid that without *writing* I cannot fix a *tack* upon them. But I will try to get either that or damages.[9]

[7]Their love for each other had become apparent in May 1769 during a visit to cousins in Ireland, Boswell as suitor of their heiress daughter. Disquieted by a separation from Margaret after their return to Scotland in June, he wrote to her on 20 July offering himself in marriage with all his faults and was nobly accepted two days later.
[8]The Boswells' house in Great Queen Street was in this parish.
[9]Smith left Glenside (a farm at Auchinleck), but we know nothing about his behaviour.

On Friday I dined quietly at General Paoli's. On Saturday, being in the City buying my lotteryticket out of my Recorder's salary, Mr. Dilly laid hold of me and made me dine tête-à-tête with him, to talk on business. Yesterday it rained, so that I kept the boys at home and made them read the Bible and say sacred lessons. I dined at General Paoli's feast of foreigners, at which Don Titus (as he calls Uncle Davie) is, I believe, a constant guest now, which is a happy thing as it brings him out. Poor man, he has a dreary life at home. He seems to feel it more than ever and is more violent against Lady Oughton. This child is not a small addition to his troubles. When I call on him, I hardly ever see his wife. Poor creature, she cries when she speaks of your great kindness to her. Mrs. Green is not often invited to the house. I paid her a visit one day, and I am thinking to have her here the next time that Veronica comes. Major Green has called on me once, and I on him, but we have never met except in the street.

Sandy is going on with his Latin and Greek as well as I could possibly wish, and Jamie is doing excellently at Soho. They are very good companions for one another and have great brotherly love. But I could wish to have them more in life. There is however time enough. Jamie is at the head of his class.

Lord Lonsdale is now out of danger but still distressed. I have never seen him yet. He is for the *Prince*, but how *far* he will support the *Opposition party* I cannot say.

The Queen will have considerable power. Sir Joshua and I hope she will give something good to Langton. But I really now believe that the King will recover.

I am very anxious to see you. For less than £20 I could go down and return. I should like to come and stay ten days or a fortnight with you, without its being known till I was gone. I could fix my day with you and come in the dark.

I saw Veronica on Saturday, very well and quite content. But when I whispered to her about her continuing longer than the year, she did not seem to relish staying beyond the 15 of May. I shall talk to her more fully after hearing from you. I have today an answer from Mr. Bruce Campbell to a letter of 30 January, on which one to you was dated.

The boys join in most affectionate duty to you and love to Euphemia and Betsy, to whom I send mine. Bell is to write to the young hussy in a day or two.[1] I ever am, my dearest M.M., most affectionately yours,

J.B.

[1] Betsy?

London, 11 February 1789

[Boswell to Margaret Boswell]

London, 11 February 1789

MY DEAREST LIFE,—Yours of 4th *current* came today. It gives me much concern to find that you have had another feverish fit. I read your letter to Mr. Devaynes, who sees that your constitution is not yet confirmed. It is to be hoped that it will be so by degrees. Your letter of 28 *January* came yesterday, and as it said nothing of your complaints I flattered myself that you were much relieved. You cannot be too careful, and as the weather grows milder you will have more air and exercise.

The letter which came yesterday surprised me as to Veronica. She certainly had been writing strange complaints, just from *habit*, for I protest she has for a considerable time been quite satisfied. I shall have her here on Saturday and consult with her as to remaining till the holidays. Euphemia in her last letter seems willing to go to Queen Square, and I dare say Mrs. Stevenson's might be *persuaded* to take her. The expense no doubt is considerable. But I really think the advantage great. Miss Langton thinks her[2] quite free of the Scotch accent.

I am vexed that I did not order the acorns to be sent directed to yourself, but you did not, as I recollect, desire this. I wonder they are not arrived. Hair must have been somehow negligent.[3] I will speak to him. I am very much obliged to you for your attention about the thorns. What a *trimming* was Mr. Alexander's to a certain person![4] It is impossible not to see how unfaithful he has been. Nothing shall be taken in the nursery way from the *farmer*.

It will not be necessary to give Sandy what you mention. I bought a magic lanthorn which cost a guinea and carpenter's tools which cost nine shillings. His turn for mechanics is strong and will be a great amusement to him. Jamie is quite a *genius*.[5] Mr. Slee says he never saw such a boy and that he will certainly be a great man. At my desire he is writing down his comedy. It is amazing both as to plot and dialogue, though imperfect, and how he can carry it all in his head I cannot conceive.

What think you of this verse in one of his songs to the tune of "The Broom of Cowdenknows"?

[2] Veronica.
[3] Hugh Hair, a workman at Auchinleck.
[4] Probably James Bruce. Claud Alexander was Laird of Ballochmyle; we do not understand the allusion.
[5] Boswell seems to be using this word in the restricted sense of "talented writer."

> Despair has seized my throbbing breast,
> And I'm oppressed with pain;
> And I cannot have any rest
> Until I see thee again.[6]

He has written to the young hussy. Sandy *"would not write to maids!"* How different they are. Sandy will make an excellent worthy gentleman. If James does not rise high, I shall be disappointed. I am resolved to send him to Eton, but not for a year or more. I am perfectly satisfied with Soho. There are now two lords' sons there.

I have paid Corri four guineas, being the exact sum due. He keeps his coach, has great employment as a teacher, is quite happy, and says he would not return to Edinburgh for the Duke of Buccleuch's estate, he should tire so.

Mr. Seward has presented Sandy with Hooper's *Rational Recreations* in four volumes, a book which teaches all sorts of sleight of hand and magic; and he has given Jamie a book to teach him universal history. They are both much pleased.

Lord Lonsdale and I and others were acquitted from the charge against us yesterday.[7] I refused an invitation to Malone's, and could not resist the *immediate* impulse to dine at a shilling ordinary which I saw advertised in Brook Street, and was truly well entertained with decent yet curious company. I have no more room than to add, most affectionately yours,

J.B.

I have made Bell write to her daughter to assist Sandy's nurse for me as far as three guineas.

[EDITORIAL NOTE. Though letters were surely exchanged between Auchinleck and London during the next month, so far as we know none of them has been preserved. Margaret's health had deteriorated alarmingly since the autumn of 1788, but her indomitable will carried her on. James Bruce told Boswell more than once that she was much too active and fatigued herself dangerously, "but it's her disposition that cannot be helped." His report of the cold she had suffered at the end of January was also ominous. Boswell, near the end of the rough

---

[6]Jamie's "comedy," entitled *The Siege of Carthage, a Comic Opera in Five Acts*, is indeed very clever for a ten-year-old. (The manuscript is now at the University of Glasgow.) The verse that Boswell quotes appears in the manuscript, greatly revised, as part of one of the songs of Philomela, a fair Carthaginian.

[7]See above, Boswell to Mrs. Boswell, 24 November 1788, p. 256.

draft of the *Life*, could not make up his mind to leave London. He wrote to Mrs. Boswell's physician, who no longer attended her professionally (she having decided that doctors could do her no good), and asked him to call "as if on a visit (being in the neighbourhood)." Dr. Campbell did as he was asked, and prefaced his report, made on 8 March, by observing that he had seen her six times (he thought) and in varying degrees of health since her return from London; at no time would he have said that she could live a month "had she been anybody else than my old friend Mrs. Boswell." The weather was now milder and she was somewhat better; both he and a friend of hers thought that Boswell might wait to see what turn things would take.

He remained in London and continued his political manoeuvrings. Convinced that Dundas, in spite of his professions of friendship, had no intention of assisting him, he appealed directly to Pitt, sending "at intervals" several letters requesting an interview. The Great Man did not even condescend to acknowledge them. At last Boswell risked everything on a letter which, if it failed, would make further appeals impossible. Pitt's behaviour was "certainly not generous—I think is not just—and (forgive the freedom) I doubt if it be wise. If I do not hear from you in ten days, I shall conclude that you are resolved to have no farther communication with me; for I assure you, Sir, I am extremely unwilling to give you, or indeed myself, unnecessary trouble." He did not hear from Pitt in ten days—or ever.]

[Boswell to Margaret Boswell]

London, 9 March 1789

MY DEAREST LIFE,—Your long letter dated February but not mentioning the *day*, which I found this morning at Mr. Courtenay's, gave me a good deal of uneasiness, not upon my honour that it offended me that you should write freely, but because it pained me to think that after your humane and generous conduct you should be agitated with any suspicions that what I am truly sensible was very bad indeed is not totally at an end. Be perfectly assured that it is and that you shall have every proof that can possibly be given of sincere regret. You really do not know me well enough; otherwise you would give more credit to me. I entreat, then, that all remembrance of this unfeeling and criminal conduct, for such I from my heart allow it to be, may be banished from *your* breast. As for me, I consider it to be my serious duty to be for ever sorry for it and to be more and more upon my guard.

I am quite of your opinion now as to Smith in Glenside, and also as to the tenants who have made rich upon the estate and will not agree to a reasonable rise of rent. Reid in Thirdpart is not an old tenant. I remember his coming to that farm.[8] My brother David approves of my following this rule with old tenants: when the fair rent is ascertained and they are sensible of it, I will give the land to them at two shillings an acre less. Thus I intend to give Hapland his at eight for three, ten the next three, and twelve the remainder of a lease, in case ten, twelve, and fourteen be set upon it. I consider that an indulgence to old tenants to the extent of a thousand acres would at this rate be a deduction of only a hundred a year. There are in reality not many old tenants upon the estate, I mean such as have possessed for generations. This I mention to you to be considered.

Veronica dined with us yesterday. I have made her easy by assuring her that I will not go to Scotland without her. Dr. Barrow says Jamie may go down for six or seven weeks about the beginning of June. He is a charming boy. Today David comes and dines on our cold veal, bacon, and apple-pie. Tomorrow the General sends his carriage, and Veronica and I and the boys dine with him and in the evening drive about and see the illuminations.[9] I was asked to Sir Joshua's dinner yesterday forenoon but would not leave Veronica. I went in the evening and found a very agreeable company.

My love to Euphemia and Betsy and very best compliments to Miss Macredie.[1] I hope she will stay some time with you. But I am sorry to hear that one of your chaise-horses is lame. Pray get another or another pair without delay. I entreat of you to spare nothing that can be of any service to you.

I enclose a foolish letter from Mr. Dun which came today, and my answer to it, of which I desire Euphemia may make a fair copy for me, and let them both be returned to me.[2] He seems to grow worse and worse. It is painful that an old preceptor and parish minister should

[8]Boswell was proposing to raise the rents on the estate, as Fairlie had advised, but to reward old tenants by lowering theirs a little.
[9]Celebrating the King's recovery.
[1]Jane Macredie, a cousin by marriage.
[2]Register of Letters, 9 March 1789, Received: "Rev. Mr. Dun insisting that Dr. Johnson did not use the word *Hottentot* to him, and *expecting* that I will say I am told so by him in another edition of my *Tour* or in my *Life of Johnson* to prevent his publishing a denial of it"; Sent: "Rev. Mr. Dun that I am perfectly certain as to the *Hottentot*. To let the matter rest as it is." Boswell had reported in the first edition of the *Tour* that at dinner at Mr. Dun's on 5 November 1773 he had talked of "fat bishops and drowsy deans," and that Johnson, highly offended, said to him, "Sir, you know no more of our church than a Hottentot." In the second edition of the *Tour* Boswell retains the exchange but attributes Dun's remark to an anonymous member of the "Presbyterian clergy."

be such a man. May GOD be pleased to grant you better health, for indeed you are of more consequence to us all than I can express. I ever am most affectionately yours,

JAMES BOSWELL.

The poor wretched being, Weelside, would make a sad figure as a servant in any gentleman's family. If he is miserable at home, let him renounce his tack and take service in the country. I really wish you had a decent servant in the house. I am thinking, if you choose it, to bring down James Ross and leave him. My *real* motive (which is perhaps not right) for wishing to have another is my preference of an English servant about myself, but my brother David must find me an honest one.

[Boswell to Margaret Boswell]

London, 11 March 1789

MY DEAREST LIFE,—Yesterday's illumination was, I dare say, the most brilliant show that ever the metropolis exhibited. After being most politely entertained at General Paoli's at dinner, I took Veronica and Sandy and Jamie in a coach and drove slowly through Grosvenor Square, Berkeley Square, Bond Street, St. James's Street, Pall Mall, the Strand, Fleet Street, and up as far as to the India House in Leadenhall Street. The general blaze of light was very fine, and many particular places were conspicuous by ingenious arrangements of coloured lamps, transparent figures, etc., etc. We returned by Newgate Street, Snow Hill, and Holborn, set Veronica down, and then drove home through various streets and Cavendish Square, in which Lord Hopetoun's great palace made the grandest appearance of the whole. All the end of it towards the Square was covered. There were in rich transparency the Royal Arms above Britannia, on each side a whole length emblematical figure, and an altar flaming, and all around was a profusion of coloured lamps disposed in festoons. We had the parlour and drawing-room lighted with candles, curiously placed upon pasteboard supporters by Sandy, who had also a crown in each window of the drawing-room, and G under one and R under another, really very well cut out and rendered transparent by himself, the crowns having a mixture of colours. How much do I regret that we were not all here to see it together. Every street was crowded with people all rejoicing. The effect was to make me forget all anxious uneasiness for the time. But alas, when it was over, my former feelings recurred, and though they distress me, I should be most unworthy if I had them not.

May God send better accounts. I ever am most affectionately yours,

JAMES BOSWELL.

[Boswell to Margaret Boswell]

London, 17 March 1789

MY DEAREST LIFE,—Having a frank for today, I write two lines, merely to let you know that we are well but that we are very anxious that there has been no letter from Auchinleck for several days. The weather here is very cold, and I am frightened to think of its being the same with you. Best compliments to Miss Macredie and love to the two girls. I ever am most affectionately yours,

J.B.

[Boswell to Margaret Boswell]

London, 24 March 1789

MY DEAREST LIFE,—This morning I had the pleasure to receive your truly kind letter of the 18th. I am now at Mr. Dilly's and have only time to thank you, Lord Lonsdale having sent for me this morning and detained me so long that I have just time to dress and be in time at the dinner of the Humane Society for recovering persons apparently dead. My love to the girls. Ever most affectionately yours,

J.B.

[Boswell to Margaret Boswell]

London, 25 March 1789

MY DEAREST LIFE,—The meeting of the Humane Society yesterday was a grand show: about 350 people at dinner, after which the persons recovered from drowning, etc., during last year, nine grown-up people and about twenty children, marched and were carried round the room to a slow, solemn tune.

This is one of the worst days I ever saw, both for snow and wind. I tremble to think of there being such weather with you. I was with Lord Lonsdale two hours this forenoon. The severe season prevents him from going to Bath.

Tomorrow the Queen is to have a prodigious drawing-room. I have taken a suit of clothes for the occasion,[3] as I really think every gentleman who is at all in the way of going to Court should show himself at this time.

It is painful to find that an old servant as Johnnie Wylie is can be guilty of such dishonest practices. Poor old creature, I have much pity

[3]"A suit of imperial blue, lined with rose-coloured silk and ornamented with rich gold-wrought buttons" (Boswell to Temple, 31 March 1789).

for him, but I am satisfied he *must* not keep a cow. I would however allow him £5 instead of that perquisite because his wages are only £3. But I did not advert to his having also meal, so I will make the allowance £4. Mr. Bruce Campbell has engaged a man to look after my woods and hedges, etc., etc., who is to live at Brackenhill and to have a cow's grass. I would not break the bargain for one year, but I mean to cut off the cow afterwards. Workmen should be accustomed to buy milk.

I am still wavering as to coming down sooner than May. I solemnly protest that my love for M.M. is perpetually pressing on my heart. But I am not *rational* enough. One happy circumstance I can mention, which is that I have all this time been free from *any* such *folly* as I look back on with regret.

I am very careful to write nothing to Mr. B. C.[4] but mere business. I once only wrote that the Chancellor was with the Prince, and when I found I was misinformed I wrote to him that I should not again mention *politics*.[5]

The boys are both quite well and send you their most affectionate duty, and love to their sisters, to whom pray give mine. I ever am most affectionately yours,

                                        JAMES BOSWELL.

                    [Boswell to Margaret Boswell]

                                        London, 27 March 1789
MY DEAREST LIFE,—Your letter of the 21, which I received yesterday, gives me such a view of your distress that I cannot help being in great anxiety and very impatient to be with you. Yet as I would fain hope that the season, which is milder today, may recruit you soon, and am very unwilling to take Veronica from the boarding-school before her time, I still hang on here. She is to dine at Mr. Langton's the day after tomorrow with me, and if by Lady Rothes's help I can persuade her to free me from my promise of taking her with me, and to stay peaceably, I will run down to you, were it but for three weeks.

The crowd and splendour of the drawing-room at Court yesterday was great indeed. I went early, even before the doors were opened, so saw it all. I was there from twelve till between six and seven, when Sir Michael le Fleming took me home with him in his coach to a family

---

[4]Bruce Campbell.
[5]Thurlow, Lord Chancellor and the King's confidant, manoeuvred to desert Pitt for the Prince of Wales and Fox during the King's illness, but shifted back to Pitt when the King started to recover.

dinner with him and his lady, and then he and I paid a visit to Lord Lonsdale.

I was made very happy at Court by a speech of General Bland, lieutenant-colonel of George Campbell's regiment. He said to me in the hearing of several people, "You have given us a fine recruit—your nephew. He is the best young man I ever knew. He has every good quality. I assure you I have as much pleasure in telling this to you as you can have in hearing it." I have written it to George today to encourage him, and said I may one day have the honour to have a general for my nephew.

Lady Rothes has found great relief from having a constant blister on one of her arms. I hope you continue that good, though painful, remedy.

What can we do but look up to our merciful Creator? I had a long kind letter lately from Dr. Blair, who says he is grown prodigiously old and expresses himself as if willing to die. But, alas, I do not suppose he apprehends that death is near.

I have dined quietly at home with Sandy. I ever am most gratefully and affectionately yours,

J.B.

[Boswell to Margaret Boswell]

London, 30 March 1789

MY DEAREST LIFE,—From the view which I have of your distress, I can have no peace day or night at this distance from you; and therefore am to set out tomorrow or next day and bring Veronica, with the entire approbation of Mrs. Stevenson.[6] Veronica is resolved to be a *teacher* to Betsy, and I hope will be of great use to her as she has been accustomed to act in that capacity to the younger ladies in Queen Square. I hope in GOD we shall find you better and be of some service to one to whom we owe so much. Your generous conduct in not even suggesting a wish that I should leave London cannot be enough admired. I come, I own, from a selfish motive: for my own relief. Sundrum[7] and his son have called on me, and I this morning found them and sat a good while with them in very *good bounds*, as we say.

Pray tell James Bruce that Robert Murdoch's son shall have the piece of ground on which he wishes to feu.[8] I shall, I trust, do *some* good to my affairs when I am with you.

---

[6] He had received "alarming accounts" of her the previous day from Dr. Campbell.
[7] John Hamilton of Sundrum, fellow student with Boswell at the Universities of Edinburgh and Glasgow, and his near neighbour in the country.
[8] To let.

Please also to let Mr. Bruce Campbell know that he is totally wrong as to Captain Preston, of which I shall talk with him when we meet. I do not write to Mr. B. C. nor James Bruce, as I am much hurried and am to see them so soon.

Sandy and Jamie send their affectionate duty to you and join me in love to their sisters. I ever am most gratefully and affectionately yours,

JAMES BOSWELL.

[EDITORIAL NOTE. On April 2nd he started north with Veronica and on the 6th arrived at Auchinleck. He found Mrs. Boswell worse even than he had expected: unable to digest her food, by his own description "emaciated and dejected" as well as "very weak." Her sufferings were painful to witness, and Dr. Campbell told him frankly that she could not recover, though she might live some time. Although he had come to Auchinleck "on purpose to soothe and console her," from the day after his arrival he was repeatedly away from home, engaged in canvassing or in other political schemes. On 5 May, as preses (chairman) of the General Quarter Sessions at Ayr, he proposed and carried an Address to the Prince of Wales, "expressing" (as he wrote to Temple), "a grateful sense of his *public* conduct with regard to the Regency."[9] On 16 May, dining at the Laird of Drongan's, where he "was eager to obtain political influence," he got drunk, and as he was riding home in the dark fell from his horse and bruised his shoulder severely. While confined to bed with the injury, he received word that Lonsdale wished him to come at once. He was to accompany Lonsdale to London and there appear as Recorder of Carlisle in an action brought against the Corporation in the Court of King's Bench. "My wife was now exceedingly ill of that fatal disease the consumption," he later noted in the Book of Company, "but I flattered myself she would grow better as summer advanced, as she had done for the three former

[9]The emphasis on *public* indicates Boswell's awareness of reports that the *private* conduct of the Prince was said to have been shockingly bad. Boswell praised him for leaving the matter of the Regency to the "deliberations of Parliament" and for accepting it with restrictions that "however thought necessary could not but be ungracious . . . and irksome." As he wrote to Temple, he carried the Address with him when he set out for London on 19 May, to be presented by Lord Eglinton "accompanied by such of us justices as may be in London. This will add something to my *conspicousness*—will that word do?" But a report that Mrs. Boswell was sinking rapidly recalled him to Auchinleck almost at once, and the Address was presented in his absence. Not many of the Justices of the Peace in Ayrshire signed the Address because they saw that it was a stupid move: indirectly it was an attack on Dundas and Pitt, who were firmly in command of the government, and whom Boswell himself still felt bound to support.

years; and both she and I thought that there was no fear of a sudden change to the worse. I was in great agitation and very averse to go. But she generously pressed me to be resolute" ("as my English connection must be *jealously* cultivated," he explained to Robert Boswell).]

MONDAY 18 MAY. Shoulder somewhat easier. Rose; severe conflict in view of parting. Admired her superior firmness. Drove to Cumnock, accompanied by Veronica. Found mail-coach passed Douglas Mill at four o'clock, so was too late. Returned. Wife did not seem surprised. Found Mr. Bruce Campbell. Was in old style of the family at tea. Yet what a passing scene is this world! Talked with him of various particulars concerning my estate.

TUESDAY 19 MAY. Fluttered. After breakfast bid adieu tenderly, yet less in agitation than yesterday. I never shall forget her saying, "Good journey!" Veronica went with Mr. B. C. and me in chaise to Cumnock, where I took Swan's, and Mr. B. C. went on with me. Stopped at Muirkirk and viewed the ironwork on the outside.[1] On the road was sadly dejected, so as to shed tears. Mr. B. C. suggested that in case of sudden emergency I should leave orders whether to wait for my return to funeral. I said, "By all means." I was tenderly shocked. Dined at Douglas Mill. Mail-coach came up. Travelled with a Mr. Macpherson, a Glasgow student from Sutherland, very civil and intelligent. At Moffat felt impressions redolent of youth.[2] At Carlisle could not hear with certainty
20 MAY whether Lord L. was gone to London or not. At Penrith heard he was not. Breakfasted there. Took chaise to Lowther. Found Satterthwaite, Colonel Lowther, Denton, Knubley, Hill. Not yet breakfast. The Earl appeared; gracious reception. Much talk. Walked in garden a little. Dinner and wine hearty. Sir Joseph Senhouse came. Coffee, tea, and cards and supper. I to bed, in great pain with shoulder.

THURSDAY 21 MAY. Breakfasted about ten. Shoulder worse. Rheumatism wide[spread]. Much talk. Dr. Lowther and sister, Mrs. Dun, three sisters and daughter dined; tea, cards, and supper. Had written letters. Covering mares.[3]

FRIDAY 22 MAY. Read Anderson against slave trade. Harrison of Appleby breakfasted, and then came several ladies and gentlemen. I wrote letters. L. walked about with them. Then we had sweet wine,

---

[1] The ironworks begun by Lord Cathcart in 1787, consisting principally of three blast furnaces, a forge, and a foundry.
[2] Thomas Gray, *Ode on a Distant Prospect of Eton College*, l. 19: "Redolent of joy and youth."
[3] That is, he had been at the stud.

etc. Were to have gone next day, but after dinner came turbot of 23 pounds caught that day, so resolved to eat it. Was all this time in repeated tender agitation about M.M. Shoulder a little better. Mares again. Hill always helped me on and off coat and waistcoat. OLD MACLEOD: "He[4] does not know one half he has, but worthy of all." (This on my seeing huge leathern cases in garret.)

SATURDAY 23 MAY. Breakfasted late. No matter. Letters and always four newspapers.[5] Rode out a little way. He had let me off from it, but I did not like to be *out*, and would be on horseback again within the week. Saw his village. He bounced into every house, bedrooms and all. "How many children?" Very populous. Woman, eleven.[6] Had given field of potatoes. She blessed him. Home to turbot; luxurious, three sauces but no lobster. Good deal of wine. Left us, yet after all we had three bottles port from Colonel's snug bing.[7]

SUNDAY 24 MAY. About two in morning L. came into room. Alarmed as if coach at door. "You need not get up these two hours." He had not been in bed. Headache from additional port and being disturbed. Broken sleep. Up early. Tea in *still room*[8] from Mary Dawson from Foundling Hospital, seventeen years in his service. Was acknowledged by relations in Shropshire and had been there; now wife of *orphan*, also from Foundling Hospital,[9] one of Lonsdale's stable-men, now in London. Wrote to Sir W. Forbes in alarming state of agitation. Tea again in steward's room with Mrs. Nuthal the housekeeper, Wheatley, Warker, Denton, Satterthwaite, Victor Scott, upholsterer—a guinea a week and half board wages. Strange chance; had been with Hamilton, Canongate, and worked in furnishing my first house, in Chessels's Buildings.[1] Talked away with great pleasure. Felt a sparkling of ideas. Then with Earl on square. Satisfied me he did well not to sell his seats in Parliament. American war might have been carried by his votes, or any other bad measure. "Well, my Lord. But I will not be satisfied that your Lordship does not take a part in administration of this great

[4]Lonsdale.
[5]That is, "Lonsdale spends much time with his letters and always reads four newspapers." See the end of the entry for 24 May.
[6]Some defects in the bottom of a leaf, affecting the entries for 20 and 23 May, have been silently restored. This sentence is the only one concerning which there is any uncertainty as to what Boswell wrote.
[7]Dialectal for *bin*.
[8]A kind of pantry; formerly the place where perfumes and cordials were distilled.
[9]Since 1760 the children accepted at the Hospital were generally not orphans but illegitimate children whose mothers were known.
[1]Also in the Canongate. The Boswells had lived there for one year, from May 1770 to May 1771.

country. I would have it to say, 'Went volunteer to St. Cast, afterwards humbled France as Minister.' "[2] He did not *take* this ambitious hint. I mentioned his ancestor, first Lord Lonsdale, Secretary of State;[3] the dignity to a family in having it recorded how such a one was a great statesman. I perceived he was only on a provincial scale. I regretted this much. Found I was too late for church; was sorry and not easy, as Judge Gould says. It was a very heavy rain, which was some excuse, though Colonel Lowther and Knubley were there. The other day L. talking of life, said, "There is no doubt it is a burthen." I said, "If *you*, my Lord, say so, it *must* be so. It is *my* opinion, and that we only divert the feeling of this by various means."

This morning he burst forth against Lord Macartney; run over his history as an adventurer who got in with Lord Holland when he was much failed, and with Lady Holland, who got him into Lady Bute's good graces (there being a great intimacy), and so a match was made between him and Lady Jane, who had been disappointed of another. Lord Bute was very angry; asked Lord L., "Have you heard of this match that is going on in my family?"[4] "Yes, my Lord." "I never heard of it till yesterday. What a sad thing that my favourite daughter should throw herself away on such a *fellow*." Lonsdale described Macartney as effeminate, foppish, ostentatious; no learning but only pretence. One day Lord Lonsdale called on him when he had been reading and left his book till he should be powdered. It was *Anecdotes*. Lonsdale chanced to open it at the very place where Macartney had been reading. That day, dining at Lord Bute's together, Macartney, in his usual way, dropped a word on the subject he wished to introduce and let the company keep up the ball; if going down, would just throw in as much as to keep it up. At last, with appearance of deep recollection: "I have read, I am not sure in what author—" and then quoted very solemnly what he had found on the subject in the *Anecdotes*, taken from some writer of eminence. Lonsdale called out, "I know where you read it: in the book of *Anecdotes* you were reading this morning." MACARTNEY. "Oh no, it was not in that." LONSDALE. "But it was, for I happened to

---

[2] In the autumn of 1758 an expeditionary force under Gen. Thomas Bligh landed on the coast of Brittany and attempted the siege of St. Malo. Finding this impracticable, the troops withdrew and were taken off in the bay of St. Cast. A strong force of the enemy followed and inflicted severe losses on the Grenadier Guards, who were covering the embarkation.

[3] Sir John Lowther (1655–1700), first Viscount Lonsdale. He was successively First Lord of the Treasury, Lord Privy Seal, and one of the "Lords Justice" (that is, Regents) under William III.

[4] Lonsdale was Bute's son-in-law. See above, 5 December 1786, p. 108, n. 4.

open it at the place and found the very passage." He coloured as red! Lord Bute burst out a-laughing. His Lordship was quite violent against him.

Who, my friend, has *reason* in his *rage*?[5]

Thundered in answer to every particular that I attempted to state. LONSDALE. "He contrived to have it reported that he lay with the Empress of Russia. Certainly not true. She sent to our Court she would not receive him any more. No merit in getting £30,000 in India. Not true that he got only that, though he swore so. We can reckon what he has expended. A poltroon; fighting when he could not help it no proof of the contrary.[6] Lady Jane best woman in world. Had she married a black or the most barbarous fellow, would from duty as a wife have wept in secret but never complained, and behaved to him constantly well."

I discovered offence had been that when L. lost his Cumberland election, he had taken a seat in Parliament from Cockermouth from Macartney rather than from Jenky. That Lord Holland had sent for Lonsdale in his dotage and said, "You are going to ruin poor Macartney among you by turning him out of Parliament." LONSDALE. "Is it not my own seat? Is it not to come in myself?[7] Is not he going to Ireland with Lord Townshend?"[8] Lord Holland said, "I'll apply to Lord North not to allow it." LONSDALE. "Good morning, my Lord"; hastened to House of Commons and made Jenky (who was very glad to do it) get Lord North to order Chiltern Hundreds to Macartney. Done in an hour. Sent it to Lady Bute, and she immediately got Macartney's acceptance. (I could see how Macartney felt hardly treated thus in his

[5] Pope, *Moral Essays*, iii. 152.
[6] Lord Macartney, who was considered by many one of the most accomplished young men of his day, formed a close connection with Lord Holland early in his career, and through Holland's influence became Envoy to St. Petersburg, 1764–67. As Governor of Madras, 1781–85, he subordinated military to civilian power, was firm with incompetent British leaders, and won the warm approval of Pitt and the Court of Directors of the East India Company. He fought a duel in 1786 with Gen. James Stuart, with whom he had quarrelled in India, and was severely wounded.
[7] The situation was somewhat more complicated than this implies. "Jenky" (Charles Jenkinson) and Macartney were returned in 1768 for Cockermouth, both at Lonsdale's bidding, for he controlled the borough. Jenkinson was also returned for Appleby, another of Lonsdale's seats, and chose to sit for the latter. Lonsdale filled the gap with a third henchman, Gov. George Johnstone. He had himself, after a bitter struggle with the Duke of Portland, been elected for the county of Cumberland, but was unseated on petition by a Committee of the House of Commons. In order to get a seat himself, he had to oust one of his Members and chose to turn out Macartney.
[8] Macartney was Chief Secretary for Ireland, 1769–72.

political career, and that Lord Bute's son-in-law should have been preferred to his secretary.)⁹ Lonsdale said Macartney, who had been always saying, "Why does not this man and that man speak in the House?" tried it, and in a few minutes was so confused, obliged to sit down.¹ "He is proud and vain, but will stoop to lick the shoes of one who can get him what he wants."

Able speech by Lonsdale on slave trade, but without any allowance for humane feelings. Read first chapter of Revelation, Foote's *Taste*, some of Lord Bacon on science, a little of Swift on Test (clear sense),² and found in steward's room Heylyn's account of France, an old book in a most lively style, of which I read some, and borrowed it for journey. Floated in the sea of existence. Dull dinner. Long in dark. Long reading of his letters and newspapers. Off abruptly.

[EDITORIAL NOTE. Boswell had been in London only a week and Lord Lonsdale's cause had not yet come on when he received letters from Euphemia and Dr. Campbell warning him that Mrs. Boswell was sinking. A letter to Temple tells the rest of the story.]

[Boswell to Temple]

Auchinleck, 3 July 1789

MY DEAR TEMPLE,—Your letter upon my late most severe loss proves that you are now the same steady and warm-hearted friend that I have ever known you. O my friend! this is affliction indeed! My two boys and I posted from London to Auchinleck night and day, in sixty-four hours and one quarter, but alas! our haste was all in vain. The fatal stroke had taken place before we set out. It was very strange that we had no intelligence whatever upon the road, not even in our own parish, nor till my second daughter came running out from our house and announced to us the dismal event in a burst of tears. O! my Temple! what distress, what tender painful regrets, what unavailing earnest wishes to have but one week, one day, in which I might again hear her admirable conversation and assure her of my fervent attachment notwithstanding all my irregularities. It was some relief to me to be told that she had after I was set out mentioned what I think I wrote

---

⁹Jenkinson was for a time private secretary to Lord Bute. Acceptance of the stewardship of the Chiltern Hundreds was tantamount to resignation from the House of Commons.
¹Macartney spoke for the first time on the petition against Sir James Lowther in November 1768 "and with very bad success, though his parts had been much cried up" (Namier and Brooke, *The House of Commons, 1754–1790*, 1964, iii. 79).
²Foote's two-act comedy, first produced in 1752; presumably Bacon's *Novum Organum*; and *A Letter Concerning the Sacramental Test*, 1708.

to you, that she had pressed me to go up and show my zeal for Lord Lonsdale. But when on my return before the cause came on, I found that by my going away at that unlucky time I had not been with her to soothe her last moments, I cried bitterly and upbraided myself for leaving her, for she would not have left me. This reflection, my dear friend, will I fear pursue me to my grave. She had suffered a great deal from her disease for some weeks before her death. But the actual scene of dying itself was not dreadful. She continued quite sensible till a few minutes before, when she began to doze calmly and expired without any struggle. When I saw her four days after, her countenance was not at all disfigured. But alas! to see my excellent wife, and the mother of my children, and that most sensible, lively woman, lying cold and pale and insensible was very shocking to me. I could not help doubting that it was a deception. I could hardly bring myself to agree that the body should be removed, for it was still a consolation to me to go and kneel by it and talk to my dear, dear Peggie. She was much respected by all who knew her, so that her funeral was remarkably well attended. There were nineteen carriages followed the hearse, and a large body of horsemen, and the tenants of all my lands. It is not customary in Scotland for a husband to attend his wife's funeral. But I resolved if I possibly could to do her the last honours myself, and I *was* able to go through with it very decently. I privately read the funeral service over her coffin in the presence of my sons and was relieved by that ceremony a good deal. On the Sunday after, Mr. Dun delivered almost verbatim a few sentences which I sent him as a character of her. I imagined that I should not be able to stay here after the sad misfortune. But I find that I cling to it with a melancholy pleasure.

Honest David is perpetually pressing my confining my family to Scotland. But alas, my dear friend, should I or could I now be satisfied with narrow provinciality, which was formerly so irksome and must now be much more so? I have agreed that my second daughter shall pass the winter at Edinburgh, as she has desired it, in order to finish her education. But were my daughters to be *Edinburgh-mannered girls*, I could have no satisfaction in their company. Veronica wishes to be boarded this winter with a lady in London. Little Betsy, who is just nine year[3] old, goes tomorrow to a quiet boarding-school at Ayr, our county town, till I settle where to place her for a year or two. I am thinking of a convent in France, or rather in Flanders, where she can be well-educated a certain length very cheap, and then I would finish her at one of the great English boarding-schools. Yet if I can find a

[3] Dialectal.

good and cheap English one I may probably not send her abroad. Can you and Mrs. Temple advise me? My eldest son I am resolved shall go to Eton this winter. I am to have only chambers in the Temple after Christmas. I may perhaps come to you in autumn if Malone goes to Ireland, so that the revising of Johnson's *Life* cannot proceed till winter. I am much obliged to you for your prayer. I *experience* that piety affords the only true comfort. My kindest love to you and yours. I am forcing myself to be as busy as I can and think of going the Northern Circuit. Ever most affectionately yours,

J.B.

Pray write often, though but a few lines.

APPENDIX

Correspondence between
Boswell and Lord Thurlow

[Boswell to Lord Thurlow]
To the Lord High Chancellor of Great Britain

General Paoli's,
Portman Square [London], 18 December 1785
MY LORD,—I find myself in a state of distressful perplexity from which your Lordship's advice may relieve me.

After much hesitation the encouraging notice with which your Lordship has pleased to honour me makes me venture to try if your Lordship *cum tot sustineas et tanta negotia*[4] will think it worth your while to employ a few minutes in considering and deciding upon my Case, of which I presume to enclose a short state in perfect confidence.[5]

Should your Lordship reckon me of consequence to merit enough such attention, you will open the seal. If not, you will be pleased to return the enclosure.

I am to remain in London till Wednesday evening and then am to go down and pass the Christmas holidays with my family at Edinburgh. I have the honour to be, with profound respect, my Lord, your Lordship's most obedient and most humble servant.

[Boswell's "Case"]

London, 18 December 1785
Mr. Boswell has practised at the bar in Scotland eighteen years, with credit. He however passed much of his vacation time in London and acquired a strong inclination to try his fortune in the wider sphere of England. His father, a respectable judge, was averse to this, from an apprehension that it would estrange the family from their ancient hereditary estate, supposing the attempt to succeed; and supposing it not to succeed, would involve it in debt by the difference of expense in living.

[4]Horace, *Epistles*, II. i. 1 (trans. H. R. Fairclough, Loeb ed.): "Seeing that you [alone] carry the weight of so many great charges."
[5]See the document following this one.

Mr. Boswell, however, still indulged an ambitious restlessness, kept occasionally his terms as a student in the Inner Temple, and at length this year quitted the Court of Session with the declared purpose of becoming an English barrister. He has only one other term to keep and may be called next month.

But upon more close consideration, the wisdom of his father presses upon his mind. He is now five-and-forty, and he fears the acquisition of new technical knowledge and new modes of practice will be more difficult to him than he imagined. He has a wife and five children, and the state of his affairs is such that he cannot maintain his family in London with a suitable decency without an addition to his income either by an office or by practice. Yet if neither can be had, how can he retreat without being exposed to ridicule and some disgrace?

It appears to him that since he has advanced so far, he should take the degree of barrister; and if he could obtain the rank of King's Counsel and be one of the benchers of the Honourable Society of the Inner Temple, all that he has done in this line might be fully justified and be closed with a good grace.

And if he could then be appointed to the office of a judge in Scotland, for which he trusts that his experience, assiduity, and principles (and, he will add, his services to the King's cause) render him not less deserving than others, he would (with some remains of fond regret that his ambition was not early enough put in a train to succeed) conscientiously endeavour to be of use to his country and take care of his family.

At present he apprehends that his embarrassment would be great were he to return to the bar in Scotland. His having thwarted Mr. Dundas in his job of diminishing the number of Lords of Session has drawn upon him the displeasure of that provincial despot, and his having had candour enough to speak without prejudice of Scotland in his *Tour* with Dr. Johnson has given very general offence to an irritable people.[6]

Could he be so fortunate as to be honoured with Lord Thurlow's attention and advice, it would animate him to pursue with resolution whatever plan his Lordship may be pleased to point out. He is miserable without stated occupation. He cannot suppose that his adding some knowledge of the practice of the law in England to that of Scotland can be any reasonable objection to his being promoted to the office of a judge in Scotland some time hence, should it be thought best for him

---

[6]In the corrected draft which is the text for this letter, Boswell has struck through everything in this sentence from "Dr. Johnson" on.

to make trial of the English bar; but should Lord Thurlow say that he ought to return to the bar in Scotland, he will do it, and give as his reason that he has received advice of such weight as he could not resist. Mr. Boswell has only to add that if Lord Thurlow generously takes the trouble to quiet the anxiety of his mind, his Lordship will lay him under the highest obligations of gratitude.

[Lord Thurlow to Boswell]

London, 5 January 1786

SIR,—If I had been so fortunate as to open your letter before you left London, I should have been glad to converse with you. In such a conversation your objects would have been more intelligible and my views of them more distinct than volumes of remote and general observations can render them.

As it is, I neither know how Dr. Johnson estimated your situation in Scotland or your prospect in England;[7] nor do I think it in general true that one who has left the practice of any bar stands on the same level of competition for advancement in his profession with those who hold a considerable footing of business and reputation there.

His confidence, however, did not forget all bounds. The limitation he prescribed seems now to decide what course you should hold. You reason right, that practice gives inferior men an ascendancy which better, unpractised talents must spend much time and attention in attaining. And Fortune, which alone can do it, opens new roads to success much too rarely for a wise man to depend on such expectations.

This needs not be insisted on. Dr. Johnson's authority and your own good sense have fixed your ideas on that head.

Your succedaneum is to be called to the bar and to the place of Kings' Counsel and to the Bench of the Inner Temple at once. This idea shows how much you are a stranger to the situation you think of. The thing is impossible, morally speaking; and if done by an act of power, it would aggravate every inconvenience of breaking through the limitation you have set yourself and place you at a still greater distance from the common chance of success.

If you think the parade of such a circumstance would forward your approach to the Scottish bench, or grace it, I am too much afraid it

[7] This sentence and the first two sentences in the next paragraph disclose that in the copy of the letter Boswell actually sent to Lord Thurlow he reported the letter from Johnson of 11 July 1784 finally consenting ("*mirabile dictu!*") to Boswell's settling in London, the conditions being that he save enough money to bring his family to London and that his expenses never exceed his annual income.

would be differently received by the world and produce a different effect. But, as I shall not be consulted on that subject, my thoughts upon the means of obtaining a judge's robe will be of little use.[8] The road of merit you are familiar with. If the rectitude of your sentiments and the sufficiency of your talents require any further advantage ground, that will be gained by taking that situation at the bar and in practice which your talents entitle you to expect. I have the honour to be, Sir, with great respect, your most obedient, humble servant,

THURLOW

[8]Thurlow means that all appointments to the Court of Session were in Dundas's control.

DOCUMENTATION AND BIBLIOGRAPHY

Unless otherwise stated, the documents described here are owned by Yale University and stored in Beinecke Rare Book and Manuscript Library. Dr. Marion S. Pottle's exhaustive official Catalogue of the Yale Boswell Collection, on which we rely, is not yet published but is available at Yale in galley proof and typescript.

A. The text of the present volume is mainly furnished by the eleven sections of Boswell's journal and other documents listed below. Documents now printed for the first time, in whole or in part, are signalized at A5, 9, 10, 12, 13, 14, and 16.

1. Journal in England and Scotland, 12 November 1785 to [13] March 1786. 28 quarto and 1 duodecimo leaves, unpaged, 57 sides written on, loose. Fully written journal (several brief periods covered by reviews).

2. Journal of the Lancaster Assizes, 28 March to 6 April 1786. 2 unpaged folio leaves, 3 sides written on, loose. Fully written journal.

3. Journal and notes for journal in London, 10 April to 2 August 1786. 26 quarto and 3 narrow octavo leaves, unpaged, 55 sides written on, loose. Mixture of rough notes, memoranda, and fully written journal.

4. "Full Trial of My Fortune at the English Bar," 20 September to 23 November 1786. 8 unpaged quarto leaves, 16 sides written on, loose. Fully written journal (periods at the beginning and end covered by reviews).

5. Journal in Carlisle, 25 November to 12 December 1786. 20 unpaged octavo leaves, 40 sides written on, loose. Partly in Italian and macaronic Italian with one word in French: silently reduced to idiomatic English in the present volume. Fully written journal (period at the beginning covered by a review). Now published for the first time.

6. Journal in London, 1 March to 16 June 1787. 16 unpaged quarto leaves, 30 sides written on, loose. Fully written journal.

7. Journal and notes for journal in London and towns on the Home Circuit (Chelmsford, Hertford), 17 June to 13 August 1787. 4 unpaged octavo leaves, 8 sides written on, plus a leaf at the end, blank save for the heading of an abandoned letter, loose. Rough notes and fully written journal.

8.   Notes for journal at Auchinleck, 20 August to 29 September 1787. 4 unpaged octavo leaves, 5 sides written on, the last leaf containing Boswell's memorandum written at Dumfries, 24 September, loose. Rough notes.

9.   Journal in London, Lowther, Whitehaven, and Carlisle, 29 September 1787 to [16] May 1788. 62 unpaged quarto leaves, 124 sides written on, loose. Fully written and condensed journal (two periods covered by reviews). Entries for 21 December 1787 to 7 January 1788 now printed for the first time.

10.   "Northern Circuit, Autumn 1788," 1 to 29 July 1788. Octavo notebook with marbled paper covers, 45 unpaged leaves, 90 sides written on, plus a blank leaf at the beginning. Partly in Italian and macaronic Italian: silently reduced to idiomatic English in the present volume. Inserted is a loose leaf of notepaper on which Boswell has written the names of counsel attending the Circuit. Fully written journal. Now printed for the first time.

11.   Journal at Auchinleck and Lowther, 18 to 24 May 1789. 3 unpaged quarto leaves, 6 sides written on, loose. In the main, fully written journal, but with some highly condensed entries.

12.   "Feigned Brief," 15 April 1786. 2 folio sheets. Endorsed by Boswell, "A circuit joke by which I was for some time deceived." Now printed for the first time.

13.   Opinion on the Right of Honorary Freemen to Vote, 7 December 1786. Pages [26–39] of "Carlisle Election, 1786," 30 November to 15 December 1786. (29 octavo leaves, 57 sides written on. Legal notes). Now printed for the first time.

14.   Veronica's Reflection, 10 May 1788. 1 leaf, both sides written on, unsigned. Now printed for the first time.

15.   Two memoranda about Mrs. Rudd. Undated scrap, 1 side written on.

16.   Twenty-eight letters. 19 letters from Boswell to Margaret Boswell, 18 May 1786 to 30 March 1789 (those of 28 January and 9 February 1789 are in the Rosenbach Library). 1 letter from Boswell to Alexander Boswell, 4 August 1786. 1 letter from Boswell to Edmond Malone, 12 July 1788 (part in the Hyde Collection). 1 letter from Robert Burns to Bruce Campbell, 13 November 1788. 1 letter from James Boswell, Jr., to Margaret Boswell, 5 December 1788. 1 letter from Veronica Boswell to Margaret Boswell, 7 December 1788. 1 letter from Margaret Boswell to Alexander Boswell, 14 December 1788. 1 letter from Boswell to W. J. Temple, 3 July 1789 (in the Pierpont Morgan Library). 1 letter from Boswell to Lord Chancellor Thurlow, 18 December 1785. 1 letter from Lord Chancellor Thurlow to Boswell, 5

January 1786. Margaret Boswell's letter to Alexander Boswell and Boswell's letters to and from Thurlow are now printed for the first time.

17. Extract from *Lord Eldon's Anecdote Book*, ed. A. L. J. Lincoln and R. L. McEwen, 1960, pp. 19–20.

18. "Extract of a Letter from Kilmarnock," 25 September 1788, *Edinburgh Advertiser*, 26–30 September 1788.

B. Many other documents have been quoted in editorial notes and in the annotation. They include Boswell's journal memoranda, the Register of Letters, the Book of Company, financial papers, legal cases, a legal notebook, verses, upwards of 40 personal letters, letters to the newspapers, the second *Letter to the People of Scotland*, *The Journal of a Tour to the Hebrides*, and the *Life of Johnson*. Boswellian material not at Yale is in the Hyde Collection, the Pierpont Morgan Library, the Crown Court, Liverpool, and in the possession of Janet Dick-Cunyingham. ne sentence from a letter is quoted from a nineteenth-century bookseller's catalogue.

Non-Boswell material quoted includes extracts from contemporary periodicals, election broadsides, poems, and other printed matter, as well as later sources.

C. A selected bibliography. Boswell's journal was edited by Geoffrey Scott and F. A. Pottle and published without annotation in the eighteen volumes of *Private Papers of James Boswell from Malahide Castle in the Collection of Lt.-Colonel Ralph H. Isham*, (1928–34), an expensive, privately printed edition limited to 570 sets. The Yale-McGraw-Hill trade edition initiated in 1950 is the first to make this matter available to the general reader. The twelve volumes of journal published so far are listed on p. [i]. Much of the journal printed in *Boswell: The English Experiment* first appeared in the sixteenth and seventeenth volumes of Isham's *Private Papers*. The final volume of the Yale-McGraw-Hill trade series is now being edited, but until it is published the *Private Papers* will provide the only printed text for the journal after 24 May 1789.

The only general collection of Boswell's letters yet printed is *Letters of James Boswell*, ed. C. B. Tinker (2 vols., 1924), but three volumes have been published in the Yale research edition of Boswell's correspondence: *The Correspondence of James Boswell and John Johnston of Grange*, ed. R. S. Walker (1966); *The Correspondence and Other Papers of James Boswell Relating to the Making of the "Life of Johnson,"* ed. Marshall Waingrow (1969); and *The Correspondence of James Boswell with Certain Members of The Club*, ed. C. N. Fifer (1976). "The Correspondence of James Boswell with David Garrick, Edmund Burke, and Edmond Malone" will appear in 1986.

The authoritative edition of Boswell's *Life of Johnson* is that edited by G. B. Hill, revised by L. F. Powell (6 vols., 1934–64); the fifth volume of this edition contains Boswell's *Journal of a Tour to the Hebrides*, as published in 1785. Boswell's original journal of this tour appears as a volume in the Yale-McGraw-Hill trade series. A one-volume edition of the *Life of Johnson*, edited by R. W. Chapman, is available in a revised edition, with an introduction by Pat Rogers (1980). The edition of the manuscript of the *Life of Johnson* is now being prepared by Marshall Waingrow.

F. A. Pottle, *Pride and Negligence: The History of the Boswell Papers* (1981) is the introduction to the three-volume "Catalogue" of the Yale Boswell Collection, to be published in the near future. Two catalogues of papers now mainly in the Yale Collection were printed fifty years ago: F. A. Pottle and M. S. Pottle, *Private Papers of James Boswell from Malahide Castle* (1931); and C. C. Abbott, *A Catalogue of Papers relating to Boswell . . . Found at Fettercairn House* (1936). The standard bibliography is F. A. Pottle, *The Literary Career of James Boswell, Esq.* (1929), supplemented by Professor Pottle's article on Boswell in the *New Cambridge Bibliography of English Literature* (1971) and A. E. Brown's useful *Boswellian Studies* (2nd ed., 1972). The standard two-volume biography is F. A. Pottle, *James Boswell: The Earlier Years, 1740–1769* (1966), and Frank Brady, *James Boswell: The Later Years, 1769–1795* (1984).

INDEX

This is in general an index of proper names with an analysis of actions, opinions, and personal relationships under the important names. Abbreviations used are D. (Duke), M. (Marquess), E. (Earl), V. (Viscount), B. (Baron), Bt. (Baronet), W.S. (Writer to the Signet), JB (James Boswell), LA (Lord Auchinleck), MM (Margaret Montgomerie Boswell), SJ (Samuel Johnson), T.D. (Thomas David Boswell).

Index

Montagu, John, *styled* V. Hinchingbrooke, *later* 5th E. of Sandwich,
230
Montgomerie, Archibald, 11th E. of
Eglinton, described, 60; and Ayrshire politics, 60, 200, 226–7, 251;
JB calls on (dines, sups with), 62,
70, 73, 131, 136, 207, 210; Eglinton's indifference towards JB, 87,
124; and Lonsdale, 87, 121; signs
presentation to Kilmaurs, 127–8;
and coldness towards MM, 180; JB
introduces T.D. Boswell, to, 219;
and JB's Address to Prince of
Wales, 280
Montgomerie, Col. Hugh, *later* 12th E.
of Eglinton, 124, 251, 256
Montgomerie, James, of Lainshaw, bro.
of MM, 180
Montgomerie, Frances (Twisden),
Countess of Eglinton, 2nd wife of
11th E., 130, 180
Montrose, 2nd D. of. *See* Graham, Wil-
liam
Moray, 9th E. of. *See* Stewart, Francis
Morning Post, 143
Morris, Capt. Charles, Whig song-
writer, 74
Mounsey, Robert, attorney, 228
Mountstuart, Lord. *See* Stuart, John
Mudge, Thomas, watch-maker, 213
Muirkirk, Ayrshire, 281
Mundell, James, schoolmaster, 30
Mungo, JB's servant, 259
Murdoch, James, Auchinleck tenant,
267
Murdoch, Robert, Auchinleck tenant,
279
Mure, James, counsellor, 125
Murphy, Arthur, author and barrister,
and JB on returning to Scots bar,
68, Murphy advises persistence at
English bar, 71; at Essex Head
Club, 97, 138, 141; dines at Brock-
lesby's, 98, 151, at Devaynes's, 145,
at JB's, 148; *Essay on Johnson*, 68,
186
Murray, Catherine (Stewart), wife of fol-
lowing, 229
Murray, James, of Broughton, 229

Murray, William, 1st E. of Mansfield,
11, 38, 72, 96, 99, 118, 247
Musgrave, Col. Thomas, *later* Bt., 157

Nairne, William, Lord Dunsinnan, *later*
Bt., Scottish judge, 23, 30, 268
Naworth Castle, Northumberland, 247
Naylor, Samuel, attorney, 136
New Cumnock, Ayrshire, 227
Newcastle-upon-Tyne, 31, 245–6
Newcastle, 1st D. of. *See* Pelham-Holles,
Thomas
Nichols, John, editor, 86, 143
Nicholson, Margaret, lunatic, 99
Nicholson, Joseph, Clerk of Peace, Ap-
pleby, 165–6
Nicol, George, bookseller to the King,
217
Noel, Thomas, 2nd V. Wentworth of
Wellesborough, 91, 157
Norfolk, 11th D. of. *See* Howard,
Charles
North, Maj. the Hon. Francis, son of
following, 122, 140, 157
North, Frederick, *styled* Lord North,
later 2nd E. of Guilford, 109, 159,
199, 211, 226, 284
Northallerton, Yorks., 238–9
Northcote, James, painter, 154
Northern Circuit, 32
Norton, Edward, M.P., 54–5, 86
Norton, Fletcher, 1st B. Grantley, 118
Nova Scotia, 156
Nuthal, Mrs., housekeeper at Lowther,
282

O'Hara, Kane, *Midas*, 144
O'Keeffe, John, *The Farmer*, 158
O'Reilly, Mr., husband of following, in
London, 268
O'Reilly, Margaret, dau. of Robert Sib-
thorpe, 268
Ogden, Samuel, D.D., *Sermons on Prayer*,
26
Oldmixon, John, *Life of Arthur Main-
waring*, 127
Orford, 1st E. of. *See* Walpole, Robert
Orme, Rev. Robert, nephew of 4th V.
Townshend, 12
Osborn, Sir George, Bt., 123, 158